Work and revolution in France

The language of labor from the old regime to 1848

WILLIAM H. SEWELL, Jr.
UNIVERSITY OF ARIZONA

CAMBRIDGE
UNIVERSITY PRESS

D1481379

PUBLISHED BY THE PRESS SYNDICATE OF THE UNIVERSITY OF CAMBRIDGE
The Pitt Building, Trumpington Street, Cambridge CB2 1RP, United Kingdom

CAMBRIDGE UNIVERSITY PRESS
The Edinburgh Building, Cambridge CB2 2RU, United Kingdom
40 West 20th Street, New York, NY 10011-4211, USA
10 Stamford Road, Oakleigh, Melbourne 3166, Australia

© Cambridge University Press 1980

First published 1980
Reprinted 1981, 1982, 1985, 1987, 1988, 1989, 1993, 1995, 1997

Printed in the United States of America

Typeset in Sabon

A catalogue record for this book is available from the British Library

Library of Congress Cataloguing-in-Publication Data is available

ISBN 0-521-23442-5 hardback
ISBN 0-521-29951-9 paperback

To Ellen

I would like to restore to men of the past, and especially the poor of the past, the gift of theory.

Eric J. Hobsbawm

Contents

vii

Contents

Preface

I BEGAN THIS BOOK with the intention of writing a brief article on the ideology of French workers during the Revolution of 1848. The article was to explore an intriguing but little-noticed paradox: that the discourse of revolutionary workers in 1848 was laced with seemingly archaic terminology dating from the guild or corporate system of the old regime. By analyzing this use of corporate terminology, I meant to show that the new socialist vision the workers were developing in 1848 was founded on a very old sense of craft community. I quickly found that the subject was both richer and much more complex than I had imagined, and by the time I had finished a draft of my article it was more than twice as long as I had planned. More alarming yet, when I showed the draft to friends and colleagues, their opinion was unanimous: It had to be either cut and simplified or expanded into a book. I tried the first alternative, but after two months of work I found the essay longer and more complex than ever. Analyzing and explaining the workers' use of corporate language in 1848 seemed to lead me in all directions at once: to corporate institutions under the old regime, to the historical relationship between corporate and revolutionary forms of language and organization, to the changing work process in artisan shops, to the means employed by workers in struggles with their employers, to changes in property relations, to the impact of the Revolutions of 1789 and 1830, and so on. I finally decided the subject was too complicated to treat in an article and too important to abandon. The result is a book that attempts to recount and explain how French workers understood and acted in their world from the corporate communities of the old regime to the socialist experiments of 1848.

But for a five-year fellowship from the School of Social Science at the Institute for Advanced Study in Princeton, New Jersey, this book would never have been written. Only the prospect of an extended liberation from the normal commitments of academic life convinced me, during my first year at the Institute, that I could afford to put aside other work for a moment to write my projected essay on workers' ideology. It was with this same sense of freedom that I began to expand it into a book. By the time I realized that it would be a very difficult book to write, I was too deeply engaged to turn back. Begun as a brief diversion from the main line of my work, this book has taken nearly all of my sojourn at the Institute to finish. I cannot imagine a more congenial place to have written it. The freedom and tranquility of the Institute have allowed me to give it my undivided attention, and the flow of stimulation from the annually renewed community of scholars has kept me in touch with the best thinking in contemporary social science. In the insistently interdisciplinary atmosphere of the School of Social Science I have had the privilege of exchanging my ideas with anthropologists, political scientists, philosphers, sociologists, and economists – not to mention fellow historians – and I believe that both my book and I have gained by these encounters. I therefore wish to express my deep gratitude to Carl Kaysen, director of the Institute when I first arrived, to Harry Woolf, his successor, and to the two permanent professors in the School of Social Science, Clifford Geertz and Albert Hirschman, whose continuing generosity and encouragement made this book possible.

I have benefited from the thoughts and suggestions of many colleagues. Portions of the argument of this book were discussed in seminars at the Institute for Advanced Study and at the Davis Center for Historical Studies at Princeton University. I have also had valuable readings of various portions of the manuscript from Ronald Aminzade, John Bossy, Natalie Davis, Sanford Ellwitt, Herbert Gintis, Stephen Gudeman, Stephen Holmes, Renato Rosaldo, Michelle Rosaldo, Quentin Skinner, Michael Stürmer, and Michel Vovelle. Cynthia Truant not only gave me criticisms of several chapters, but generously shared with me her unpublished research on *compagnonnage*. The entire manuscript has been read by Keith Baker, Robert Bezucha, Ronald Inden, William Reddy, Joan Scott, and Allan Sharlin. Their suggestions have helped me to clarify many obscure points in my argument and to avoid errors of fact and judgment. The lion's share of the typing has been done by Peggy Clarke with rare intelligence, efficiency, and good cheer.

My wife, Ellen, first convinced me to write this book, and she has lived it with me every since. She has read and commented on the entire manuscript twice and has read parts of it several times; she has been over nearly all of its arguments with me in discussions at all hours of the day and night; she has offered her insights, her enthusiasm, her learning, and her fine critical sense. For all this, I am grateful. This book is dedicated to her.

W. H. S.

I Introduction: social history and the language of labor

THE PAST TWENTY YEARS have seen an enormous proliferation of research on the history of working people. Carried out from widely varying perspectives and trained on many different aspects of working-class life, this research has inevitably generated its share of divergent findings and scholarly controversies. Yet there is almost universal agreement on one point: that skilled artisans, not workers in the new factory industries, dominated labor movements during the first decades of industrialization. Whether in France, England, Germany, or the United States; whether in strikes, political movements, or incidents of collective violence, one finds over and over again the same familiar trades: carpenters, tailors, bakers, cabinetmakers, shoemakers, stonemasons, printers, locksmiths, joiners, and the like. The nineteenth-century labor movement was born in the craft workshop, not in the dark, satanic mill.[1]

This fact has important implications for the practice of labor history. Above all, it suggests that research can no longer be confined exclusively to the period since the industrial revolution. If the labor movement *were* a specific product of the factory, ignoring the period before factories existed would be defensible. But because it was initiated by artisans, workers in trades with long and rich histories, ignoring the preindustrial period can have only pernicious effects. It is true, of course, that artisans were subjected to new pressures and challenges by the development of industrial capitalism. But their responses were inevitably shaped by values, traditions, and organizational experiences that predated the modern industrial era. The discovery that artisans created the nineteenth-century labor movement makes the problem of continuity with preindustrial forms and experiences impossible to escape.

The need to address this problem is particularly great in France, where the special discontinuities introduced by the French Revolution make the preindustrial past seem even more remote. In labor questions, as in nearly all others, the French Revolution marked a fundamental break. The guild system – or, as it is usually called in France, the corporate system – had been the dominant mode of organization of French industry since the Middle Ages. The guilds, or corporations, were dismantled during the Revolution, and the affairs of the trades were thereafter left to the free play of the market. Most French historians have assumed that trade corporations were utterly swept away in the Revolution, and that nineteenth-century labor organizations were created in response to the new industrial economy – for which the French Revolution had created the preconditions. Labor historians have therefore been sensitive to early nineteenth-century anticipations of the class-conscious workers' movements of the later nineteenth or the early twentieth century but have generally ignored what seemed to hark back to the old regime.[2] This tendency has been reinforced by the organization of the French historical profession, which has made the old regime, the Revolution, and the nineteenth century domains of different specialists. Only the occasional interloper – for example Maurice Agulhon[3] – has undertaken studies spanning the revolutionary era, and until now no one has done so in labor history.[4]

This book traces the organizations and the ideologies of French workers from the old regime to the Revolution of 1848. It seeks to demonstrate that themes and sentiments originating in the prerevolutionary corporate system remained central to workers' consciousness and experience through all the changes of this remarkably turbulent era. In spite of three major revolutions (1789, 1830, 1848), ten changes of constitution, and the onset of the industrial revolution, there were important continuities in the way French workers perceived, and acted in, the world. It would be insufficient, however, simply to note that workers retained corporate sensibilities as late as 1848. For the *meaning* of corporate phrases or institutions was inevitably altered by changes in the surrounding society. This history, consequently, pays as close attention to what divides as to what unites the subordinate journeyman of the prerevolutionary corporations, the *sans-culotte* of 1793, and the socialist worker of 1848. It seeks to encompass both the consistencies *and* the revolutionary breaks in the workers' evolving social practice.

THE PARADOX OF CORPORATE LANGUAGE

I began my research on nineteenth-century French workers with a study of the working class of Marseille. In reading public discourse by and about workers, I was repeatedly struck by the use of such unambiguously corporate terms as *corporation, corps, état, corps d'état,* and *corps de métier.* In fact, this corporate terminology was particularly prevalent among left-wing republicans and socialists during the Revolution of 1848, the last place one would expect to find sympathies with the old regime. Nothing in my training had prepared me for this seemingly paradoxical flowering of the old regime's language in the midst of a radical revolution; although historians had sometimes reproduced these terms in quotations from contemporary sources, they had never commented on their usage or significance. My initial hypothesis was that terms like "corporation" and "corps d'état" were vestigial, that they no longer carried their ancient messages and were now merely a convenient shorthand for designating the collectivity of workers employed in a given trade. But as my research progressed, I became convinced that the terms had a deeper resonance and that a continuity with the corporate notions of the old regime was much greater than had generally been allowed. There were many reasons for my growing conviction: the fact that in the first three-quarters of the nineteenth century, labor organizations were concentrated almost exclusively in the same urban crafts that were organized as corporations under the old regime; the striking similarities in purpose, form, and function between mutual-aid societies formed by trades in the nineteenth century and the religious confraternities they had formed under the old regime; the continuing vitality of the self-evidently corporate workingmen's associations called *compagnonnages*; the elaborate and seemingly archaic structure of some of the most successful nineteenth-century labor organizations; the tendency for the most powerful labor organizations – in Marseille at least – to exclude outsiders and to pass the trade on from father to son just as trades had been passed from father to son in old-regime corporations.[5] There was, it seemed to me, something distinctly corporative about the working-class world of nineteenth-century France that fit with the continued usage of corporate terms in the workers' language. But what these terms really meant in the nineteenth century, and what they implied for the experience and consciousness of mid-nineteenth-century workers, remained obscure. The obscurity, moreover, had little chance of being cleared up with the evidence at my disposal. To establish what meaning corporate terminology had for workers, I needed a much larger body of writing produced by and/or intended for workers than existed in the libraries and archives of Marseille.

Rémi Gossez's study of Parisian workers in 1848 supplied the documentation I lacked in my study of Marseille.[6] Based on a lifetime of detailed and painstaking research, Gossez's book is packed with quotations from documents written by and for workers. When I first read this book a few years after its publication in 1967, it confirmed my belief that corporate notions were central to the working-class experience of the Revolution of 1848. Yet Gossez did not solve the problem of the *meaning* of the workers' corporate idiom. His long immersion in the mental world of Parisian workers enabled him to display that world in the most vivid detail, but it also deprived him of the sense of distance so essential for formulating a critical interpretation. His book did not resolve the paradox of a radical revolution carried out in corporate terms. It did, however, supply a body of evidence sufficiently rich and abundant to make an attack on that paradox possible.

My original plan had been to juxtapose a brief description of the corporate system of the old regime with an account of workers' ideology and practice in 1848, pointing out the continuing vitality and importance of corporate themes and showing how much the socialism of 1848 owed to the long-standing collectivism and the strong sense of solidarity of the corporate trades. The problem was that there were as many differences as continuities – both immediately discernible differences in rituals, phrases, and practices, and somewhat subtler differences in their meaning. It soon became clear that the corporate content of workers' ideology in 1848 had not been delivered intact from the old regime but had been reshaped by the vast historical changes of the intervening years. Hence, what began as a demonstration that the old regime was still alive in the working class in 1848 became a history of how corporate language and practices came to mean something very different in 1848 than they had meant before 1789. To write this history, I had to consider a wide range of transformations that affected the meaning of corporate notions: changes in the legal system, in economic life, in political constitutions, in property relations, in moral and religious ideas, in conceptions of labor, and so on. This history of the corporate idiom has therefore become a general history of labor from the old regime to 1848 – although a general history of a peculiar sort. Rather than skipping directly from the old regime to the Revolution of 1848, the bulk of the book now deals with the historical transformations that took place between 1789 and the 1840s. Although the subjects treated range from contemporary metaphysical conceptions of labor to details of the organization of production in nineteenth-century workshops, the book is still centered on the problem of corporations, and the analysis is designed to lead to the Revolution of 1848. The accounts of the old regime, the French Revolution, and the social and political changes of the first half of the nineteenth century are meant to be valid in their own terms; they have been written, however, from the perspective of 1848, a perspective that has surely caused me to overlook or undervalue some things that specialists in these periods would consider more important but has also enabled me to see things other historians have missed.

This book is what the French call an *essai de synthèse* – "synthetic essay" might be an acceptable translation. It is an attempt to draw together the findings of a large number of more specialized studies into a new general interpretation. Although I have occasionally drawn on my own archival research in Marseille, the book has been written mainly from sources available in the United States. I have attempted to base my arguments on the best available scholarship, both recent and not-so-recent, but my purpose is not to summarize and evaluate this scholarship. It is, rather, to use it – often in ways quite different from the intentions of the author – to formulate a new interpretation of a broad field of historical research; to suggest connections not hitherto perceived, and to place particular findings within a larger – or at least a different – framework. As specialists will recognize, I have generally avoided the venerable controversies that so dominate the historiography of the old regime and the Revolution, preferring, instead, to develop my own line of argument.[7] Like Marc Bloch's explorer, who must make "a rapid survey of the horizon before plunging into thickets from which the wider view is no longer possible,"[8] I am attempting to sketch out a new map that will indicate relations between already explored regions and suggest useful approaches to those not yet explored. Thus, although this book does not aim to be "definitive" in the usual sense of the term, it aims precisely to be definitive in a more literal sense: to give sharp *definition* to a set of problems and processes that hitherto either were not perceived or were perceived only indistinctly; to *define* a theoretical perspective, a set of questions, and a line of interpretation that will make sense of previously disconnected findings and, by doing so, may help to shape future research.

"THE NEW SOCIAL HISTORY" AND THE PROBLEM OF IDEOLOGY

This book is written from a particular theoretical perspective, one that, in large part, I have had to construct for myself – albeit with materials borrowed shamelessly from such sources as "the new social history," intellectual history, cultural anthropology, and certain new strains of Marxism. A brief description of this perspective and of how I reached it should help the reader see why this book is written as it is.

Like most labor historians trained in the 1960s, I began as a practitioner of what was called "the new social history" or "history from the bottom up." Inspired by the populist spirit of the time, "new social historians" wished to write about the masses of ordinary workers who had been left out of traditional – that is, political and institutional – labor history. In part, this simply meant going to old archival sources with new questions in mind – inspired, perhaps, by the examples of Soboul, Rudé, Cobb, or Thompson.[9] But it frequently also meant using new sources and, above all, sources that could be analyzed quantitatively. Even the most obscure and inarticulate men and women, we began to realize, came into contact with the state apparatus at some point in their lives: when they were counted by the census taker; when they were born, married, and died; when they paid taxes; and when they got into trouble with the law. By aggregating and analyzing records of such encounters, we could reconstruct the social experiences of whole categories of the population that had hitherto escaped the historian's net. We could, at last, hope to write labor histories that said as much about the experiences of ordinary men and women as about the pronouncements of leaders and the factional struggles of socialist parties.

Utilizing these quantitative sources required major changes in the conduct of research. In America, at least, this meant borrowing methods from the social sciences and above all from sociology. Along with the new methods came a whole range of new questions and theoretical perspectives.[10] One result was an enormous expansion in the range of topics addressed by labor historians. Before 1960 our knowledge had been restricted almost exclusively to three topics: the institutional history of the labor movement, the intellectual development of socialist ideology, and the declining, stagnant, or rising real wages of the workers – this latter considered as an index of workers' suffering and exploitation. To these, the new, more sociologically aware, histories of labor added urbanization, political mobilization, demography, occupational recruitment, voting behavior, social mobility, family structure, migration, kinship, residential patterns, the fine structure of work experience, and so on.[11] Consequently, our knowledge of working people in the past is now immeasurably more complete, subtler, and more exact than it was in 1960.

But this vast expansion of our knowledge has not been achieved without cost. One of the conditions of carrying out the new style of research has been a reduction in the scale of the populations studied. As long as most research focused on working-class parties or trade-union movements, work on a national scale remained feasible. But once historians determined to reach entire working-class populations – by laboriously searching through manuscript census schedules, tax records, and the like – research had to be confined to a single town or region. Even with the aid of computers, the sheer volume of data would otherwise have been overwhelming. Adopting new techniques of research, thus, also meant redefining the object of study. Rather than the institutional history of a national or international labor movement, labor history has increasingly become the history of a series of local working-class communities. These accounts of local communities are vastly richer and more complex than the old institutional histories; at their best they approach the inspiring but ultimately unrealizable French ideal of *histoire totale*. But their greater richness and complexity could be obtained only by limiting their geographical scale.

This limitation of scale could hardly be counted a loss when it came to questions of demography and social structure, because the findings of the new social historians were filling a void left by earlier scholars. But on political and ideological questions, the superiority of the new ways was far less certain.[12] Politics and ideology were, of course, part of the total community experience we wished to describe. Indeed, it was common for the new social histories of labor to be centered on some important political struggle – a revolution, an uprising, or a strike – in which the local working class gained a new or transformed consciousness of itself. Although our methods and our locus of research were different from those of the older institutional labor historians, we continued to pursue the same larger question: the emergence and development of working-class consciousness. It was our ambition, however, to understand such transformations of consciousness as the life experiences of complex communities of workers, rather than as purely doctrinal or institutional events played out against a vague background of suffering and exploitation. Once again, the new style of history can boast of real achievements. The best local studies have succeeded in making much firmer and more complex connections between political or ideological events and social and economic processes. But it is by no means clear that they have adequately explained – or even adequately grasped – the ideological transformations that these events embodied and brought about.

This problem can be illustrated by my own study of the workers of Marseille. The Revolution of 1848 marked a fundamental turning point in the history of Marseille's workers. Once well known for their quiescence and conservatism, Marseille's workers turned revolutionary in 1848 and have remained consistently on the left ever since. I undertook my largely quantitative investigation of the working class with the intention of illuminating this great transformation of workers' consciousness. My hopes were not entirely disappointed. I was able to demonstrate that unskilled trades and those skilled trades that recruited mainly from within the native-born artisan community of Marseille remained politically apathetic or conservative, whereas those skilled trades that recruited their members from a wide geographical area – nationally, as it were – were also more receptive to national revolutionary politics. I could explain differential rates of participation in the revolutionary movement with unexpected precision; yet I found myself quite incapable of explaining why such a movement had come into existence in the first place or why it took the form it did. In Marseille, at least, the Revolution of 1848 and the ideology of democratic socialism appeared suddenly and unexpectedly from the outside. Like other local historians, I could explain the reception of a new ideology, but explaining its shape and content seemed to lie beyond my powers as a social historian.[13]

Part of the problem, clearly, is that the process of ideological development transcended local communities. To explain the content of the ideology of Marseille's workers in 1848, for example, we would have to look both at the intellectual development of socialist theory in the course of the 1840s and at the revolutionary agitation of Parisian workers in the spring of 1848, because these were the major sources of the ideas taken up by Marseille's workers. Although certain aspects of economic, demographic, and social structure can be studied most profitably at the local level, a history of workers' ideology can scarcely avoid taking a national persepctive. In France, ironically, this means that one local community – Paris – must be examined with particular care. The extreme centralization of French political life meant that events taking place in Paris were by definition national events. The actions of Parisian workers, especially in the great revolutionary upheavals of 1789–94, 1830–34, and 1848–51, are crucial to an understanding of national ideological developments. But the strictly local perspective of most social histories is only part of the problem. An inability to come to grips with workers' ideological experience is also built into the research procedures of the new social history. In borrowing methods and theories from sociology, historians have tended to pick up the sociologists' pervasive assumption that quantification yields "hard" or "scientific" knowledge, whereas other sorts of evidence are "soft" or "impressionistic." Few historians have gone so far as to adopt the common sociological practice of defining research problems so that they can be pursued exclusively by quantitative means – in part because we do not have the option of administering questionnaires to the dead. But social historians have frequently been led to emphasize those aspects of social experience that could be described quantitatively or systematically over such seemingly ineffable matters as consciousness, attitudes, currents of opinion, sentiments, and the like. Among labor historians this sociological prejudice has sometimes been reinforced by the Marxist distinction between the material "base" and the ideological "superstructure," which also assigns a greater solidity to social and economic than to "mental" phenomena, and sometimes by a populist suspicion that the study of ideas is inherently "elitist," whereas the study of economic and social conditions is inherently democratic. Hence the mental or ideational aspects of working-class social experience have generally been slighted in favor of economic and social structures, leaving social historians ill-equipped to handle ideologies when these make an appearance in their locality.

The obvious place for social historians to turn for help and inspiration would be intellectual history. There are, for example, some important and useful works on the history of socialist thought that bear on the problem of workers' ideology in nineteenth-century France.[14] But on closer inspection, they are only of limited utility. These works analyze the ideas of particular theorists or recount the transmission and transformation of ideas from one theorist to another. But they fail to engage the issue of *workers'* consciousness. Intellectual histories of ideology can tell us a great deal about the formally expressed ideas that were available to workers, but they are virtually silent about the workers' own ideas, which were often very different from those of the theorists. Nor are the methods employed by most intellectual historians very useful. Here the main problem is the analytical primacy of the author in intellectual history. Intellectual historians are trained to see thought as emanating from the minds of authors, and thus to continually refer ideas back to the authors and their biographies. This method is quite workable in dealing with complete and considered texts that can be fit into the corpus of known authors. But it breaks down when confronted with collective movements of thought of the sort that characterize transformations in workers' consciousness. In trying to make sense of the workers' agitation following the revolutions of 1830 or 1848, for example, the ideas we are pursuing were stated partially and in fragments, written down in the heat of action, often by unknown persons or by groups of persons, and are available only in the most heterogeneous forms – in manifestos, records of debates at meetings, actions of political demonstrators, newspaper articles, slogans, speeches, posters, satirical prints, statutes of associations, pamphlets, and so on. In such situations the coherence of the thought lies not in particular texts or in the "work" of particular authors, but in the entire ideological discourse constituted by a large number of individually fragmentary and incomplete statements, gestures, images, and actions. The key problem thus becomes not the delineation of the thought of a series of authors but the reconstruction of discourse out of fragmentary sources.[15] In reconstructing such discourses, the skills of the intellectual historian are, of course, indispensable. But it is notable that the most impressive studies of collective and quasi-anonymous ideological discourse have been carried out not by intellectual historians but by the Marxist social and political historians Albert Soboul, Christopher Hill, and E. P. Thompson.[16]

It is hard enough to reconstruct workers' discourse even in periods of revolutionary outbursts – such as 1793–4, the early 1830s, or 1848 – when the usual restraints on working-class political voice were broken and revolutionary struggles created endless occasions for oratory, polemic, manifestos, and demonstrations. The problems are greatly multiplied in "normal" periods of repression and political quiescence. In times of intense ideological discussion, workers' consciousness is at least accessible – even if it takes hard work to tease it out of the available documents. But what of periods when ideological discussion ceases or goes underground? Are we then thrown back on a purely economic and social analysis of the working class? Must our understanding of the workers' mental life be limited to those rare and privileged moments when workers' discourse flows into a public space that is normally denied to them?

It need not be, certainly, but it must be pursued by methods very different from those of either conventional social history or conventional intellectual history. In recent years, historians dissatisfied with the economic, social-structural, and quantitative biases of the "new social history" have increasingly turned to cultural anthropology as a source of inspiration.[17] Social historians have sensed a certain affinity between the anthropologists' concerns and their own. Ethnographic methods were originally developed in the study of nonliterate people, and the anthropological concept of "culture" as a collectively held pattern of symbols and beliefs suits the social historian's requirements much better than the concept of biographically informed "ideas" that are the stock in trade of the intellectual historian.

9

Moreover, the anthropologist's use of a wide range of materials and customs in establishing cultural patterns – not only explicit statements about people's beliefs but rituals, iconography, the spatial patterns of villages, dietary taboos, agricultural and hunting practices, myths, rules of kinship, sexual division of labor, incantations, forms of address, systems of classifications, semantic and grammatical properties of the language, and so on – suggests many new avenues for investigating the mental universe of ordinary men and women in the past.

HISTORY AND CULTURAL ANTHROPOLOGY

Most attempts to apply anthropological insights and methods to history have dealt with such typically anthropological subject matter as popular religion, magic, witchcraft, rituals, and festivals – just as the "new social history" has dealt with such classical sociological topics as social mobility, urban ecology, demography, and occupational structure. These new anthropologically inspired studies have given us access to entire ranges of experience that were previously closed to historical inquiry. But the enthusiasm for anthropological *subject matter* must not lead us to forget the deepest and most powerful message of cultural anthropology: not only that certain kinds of activities can be analyzed to reveal popular beliefs and preconceptions but that the whole of social life, from such symbolically elaborate practices as religious festivals to such seemingly matter-of-fact activities as building houses or raising crops, is culturally shaped. "Ideas" or "beliefs" are not limited to certain classes of activities or to certain classes of people. They are woven into the very fabric of the everyday life of ordinary people; "all experience," as Clifford Geertz puts it, "is construed experience."[18]

The problem, then, is to understand how people in the past construed their experiences. Here historians are at a disadvantage, because they cannot employ the ethnographers' procedure of living among the people they study, of participating in their daily activities and continually asking them to explain what they are doing and why they are doing it. If anthropologists' knowledge of cultures were, as is sometimes supposed, a matter of putting themselves into the skin of people they study, of internalizing their culture by a kind of osmotic process, then historians who wished to imitate anthropologists would be in serious trouble. But as Clifford Geertz has recently pointed out, ethnographers never actually achieve a unity of perception with their informants; rather they learn what informants "perceive 'with,' or 'by means of,' or 'through.'" The ethnographer succeeds in grasping an alien culture "by searching out and analyzing the symbolic forms – words, images, institutions, behaviors – in terms of which, in each place, people actually represent themselves to themselves and to one another."[19] Although we obviously cannot hope to experience what nineteenth-century workers experienced or to think their thoughts as they thought them, we can, with a little ingenuity, search out in the surviving records the symbolic forms through which they experienced their world. In part this means reconstructing the meanings of the words, metaphors, and rhetorical conventions that they used to talk about and think about their experiences. But because communication is not limited to speech and writing, we must also seek out the intelligible forms of many other activities, events, and institutions: of the practices of artisans' organizations, of rituals and ceremonies, of the shape of political demonstrations, of legal regulations, or of details of the organization of production. If we can discover the symbolic content and conceptual coherence of *all* kinds of working-class experiences, then the workers' adoption of explicit political ideologies will no longer appear as a sudden intrusion of "ideas" from the outside but as the introduction or elaboration of yet another symbolic framework into lives that – like all ours – were already animated by conceptual issues and problems. This approach will enable us to see class consciousness not as the imposition of the ideas of bourgeois theorists on an intellectually inert working class but as a collective conceptual achievement of thousands of workers who developed or discovered it as a more satisfactory way of construing their inevitably construed experience.

This continual search for meaning embodied in workers' action implies a certain approach to workers' economic life. Labor historians have normally seen economic developments as a material substratum more basic than, or prior to, ideological awareness. The perspective adopted here denies the ontological priority of economic events. Although economic forces and changes must retain a central role in labor history, they should be treated as continuous with all other aspects of workers' experience. Processes of production and exchange, like all other social processes, are subject to conceptual limits and symbolic definitions, and their outcomes must be evaluated according to culturally specific standards. To treat economic experiences in this way is not to deny their importance. Quite the contrary, it is to capture them as *experiences,* as being construed by those who lived through them, as having meanings that need to be recovered. Hence I have endeavored to treat from a single perspective phenomena that are usually thought to be essentially different in kind and therefore to require distinct methods of analysis; to treat a philosophical tract by Diderot, the political discourse of sans-culottes, or of members of the National Assembly, the statutes of mutual-aid societies, the corporate terminology of nineteenth-century workers, the rituals of journeymen's brotherhoods, the recruitment patterns of stonemasons, the organization of production in hatters' workshops, the piece-rate schedules that determined artisans' wages, all as meaningful statements, as a set of interrelated texts that demand close reading and careful exegesis. Only by this means, I am convinced, can we hope to understand workers as active, thinking agents who, in the words of E. P. Thompson, "contributed, by conscious efforts, to the making of history."[20] This book, in other words, is about the "language of labor" in the broadest sense – not only about workers' utterances or about theoretical discourse on labor, but about the whole range of institutional arrangements, ritual gestures, work practices, methods of struggle, customs and actions that gave the workers' world a comprehensible shape.

Cultural anthropology suggests a unified framework for analyzing the whole range of workers' experiences. It gives us much less guidance, however, for analyzing the ways in which these experiences changed over time. For reasons that have much to do with its own historical origins, ethnography has until recently been little concerned either with processes of change or with the social and political struggles that so often act as motors of change. The ethnographic method was developed as a means of recording and thereby preserving the indigenous cultures of the peoples subjected to Western domination in the nineteenth and twentieth centuries. Ethnographers wished to demonstrate the ultimate coherence of exotic ways of life and hence their value as authentic expressions of what it is to be human. But in order to describe exotic cultures as integrated and smoothly functioning wholes, the ethnographer abstracted their features from the real temporal sequence in which they were increasingly being eroded by Western influences and presented them sychronically, timelessly, as they would have been had they gone on without Western intervention. This search for the coherence of exotic cultures, together with the fact that Western political domination sharply limited the possibilities of indigenous political life, also led ethnographers to neglect problems of social and political conflict or to interpret conflict as ultimately contributing to the stability of society.[21] Abolishing conflict and change from the analysis was an essential step in developing the "holistic" approach that remains anthropology's most distinctive contribution to the human sciences.

Whatever its adequacy for relatively small-scale and homogeneous societies (a debatable point), this static approach is clearly inadequate for complex societies such as those of Europe or the "state societies" of traditional Asia, Africa, and the Americas.[22] Indeed, a "holistic" approach to such societies *demands* consideration of conflict and change.[23] French artisans cannot be treated as Trobriand Islanders, as an isolated, static, finely tuned, and fully coherent society. Artisans were part of a complex society that was rent by all sorts of conflicts and contradictions – between classes or orders, between different regions, between rival dynasties and political factions, between opposed ideologies, and so on. French society was, moreover, changed fundamentally as a result of these conflicts. The culture of artisans must be seen as part of the cultural complex of France as a whole, as being defined in relation to the culture of other groups, and as both participating in and reacting to the larger social, political, and ideological struggles that clustered around the French state. Artisans' experiences cannot be understood apart from the history of political conflicts and the relations of domination that these conflicts enacted, challenged, or reinforced. Throughout the period covered by this book, workers were a subordinate group – subject not only to the rules and pronouncements of the state but to the authority, or at least to the power, of their employers. Workers' relations with the state and with employers were rarely harmonious; even in the most peaceful times they were tense and guarded, and on occasion they could be hostile or violent. But at the same time, workers shared the political, religious, and social language of the day and could not help but be influenced by the ideals proclaimed by the current political regime. Even when they opposed their employers or the state, their opposition was necessarily expressed in terms that their opponents could understand; the bitterest of battles bear witness to the workers' engagement in a common, if contested, frame of discourse.[24] It therefore follows that a history of workers' actions and consciousness must constantly move back and forth between the particular experiences of workers and the changing patterns of the larger society – the form of the state, major political battles, the nature of relations between various classes or orders, the ideas that informed public discourse, and so on. Although the core of this book is an account of the changing ideologies and organizations of urban skilled workers, it ranges far afield when such excursions are required to set workers' actions in a proper context. Readers should, therefore, not be surprised to find discussions of the ideas of Turgot and the Abbé Sieyès or of the constitutional principles of the French Revolution alongside discussions of the practices of journeymen's associations or of the nature of industrial conflicts.

Finally, although the consciousness and the actions of workers must always be understood in the context of a changing larger society, we must also be attentive to what is particular about *their* version of the disputed world they inhabited. Their views, ideals, and judgments were never just a lower-level recapitulation of the values endorsed by the state and the dominant classes, nor were they ever a simple negation of those values. In all their successive organizations and ideologies, there were certain continuities of substance and tone – a consistent moral collectivism, an assertion of their own capacity to preserve order and pursue the common good, an insistence on the distinct value and identity of the various trades, and a pride in their work as a contribution to the public welfare. It is this elusive but consistent artisan ethos, no less than the transformations it underwent in a century of struggles, that I hope to capture in this book.

SCOPE OF THE BOOK

This book begins with two chapters on trade corporations of the old regime. Both of these chapters proceed analytically rather than chronologically and cover the long span from the middle of the sixteenth century to the eve of the French Revolution. Chapter 2 considers the place of the corporate trades in the social and political order of the old regime and then examines masters' corporations – as legal institutions, as social organizations, and as religious and moral bodies. Whereas Chapter 2 deals with the officially established, legally recognized corporations of master artisans, Chapter 3 probes the clandestine corporate brotherhoods that were maintained by journeymen. The legal corporations of the masters and the illegal corporations of the journeymen, I will argue, shared a common outlook and a common idiom in spite of all their differences.

Chapters 4, 5, and 6 treat the French Revolution, which destroyed the legally recognized corporations of the masters and transformed the social and political order of which they were an integral part. Chapter 4 investigates the Enlightenment attack on corporations and the Revolution's systematic destruction of the entire corporate order of the monarchy. Chapter 5 examines the role of artisans in the Revolution, from their attempts to adapt their corporations to the new political order to their participation in a sans-culotte movement dedicated to wiping out all vestiges of loyalty to bodies intermediate between the individual and the state. Chapter 6, finally, examines the transformation of property in the Revolution, a transformation that set the stage for the development of a very different kind of corporate organization among nineteenth-century workers.

The remaining chapters cover the period from the beginning of the nineteenth century to the Revolution of 1848. Chapter 7 treats the growth of the French economy in the first half of the nineteenth century. It shows how the French pattern of economic growth both multiplied the number of skilled artisans and threatened their status and well-being. Chapter 8 looks in detail at the nature and the activities of the corporations that workers formed to defend their standards in the nineteenth century and briefly at their corporate vocabulary. Whereas Chapters 7 and 8 treat workers' economic conditions and the labor organizations they formed in response to their conditions, Chapters 9, 10, and 11 chart the development of a distinctive working-class political voice. Chapter 9 considers the widespread workers' agitation that followed the Revolution of 1830, in which workers combined their corporate notions of trade solidarity with revolutionary notions of popular sovereignty to create a new revolutionary workers' ideology. Chapter 10 examines the explosive discourse about labor that grew up in response to the upheavals of the early 1830s, and Chapter 11 treats the Revolution of 1848, in which working-class socialists attempted to transform the entire social and political order into an egalitarian community of corporately organized laborers. Chapter 12, finally, attempts to answer two concluding questons: Was there an underlying logic by which socialism and class consciousness developed in France? And what was the form of the class conflict and class consciousness that had emerged by 1848?

2 Mechanical arts and the corporate idiom

TRADE CORPORATIONS were a ubiquitous feature of French cities of the old regime. Given the particularism of old-regime culture, corporations inevitably differed from one city to the next: Trades joined in a single corporation in one city would be rivals in another; the privileges and exemptions of corporations were never quite the same; ceremonies and rituals varied in minor or major respects; and even the legal forms according to which the corporation and its privileges were established by the state could be different in different cities. Yet across all the variations, not only from city to city but over time as well, French trade corporations from the sixteenth to the eighteenth century had certain essential characteristics in common. The purpose of this chapter is to describe these essential characteristics and to indicate their relation to the larger social and political order of the old regime.

CITIES IN AN AGRARIAN SOCIETY

The trade corporations of the old regime were a strictly urban phenomenon, and it is important to remember that they occupied a rather small and special niche in the overwhelmingly agrarian society of the old regime. According to Pierre Goubert, at least 85 percent of the population of the French kingdom lived in the countryside in the late seventeenth or early eighteenth century, and most of these lived by agriculture.[1] It is true that French cities grew substantially during the seventeenth and the eighteenth centuries; moreover, beginning around 1750 there was a sustained quickening of industrial growth. But in part because much of this growth of industry actually took place in rural areas – especially in textile production – it is far from certain that the urban population of the kingdom increased more rapidly than the rural, so that the percentage dwelling in cities was probably not very different on the eve of the French Revolution than it had been at the beginning of the seventeenth century.[2] Even in 1789, the number of truly large cities was quite restricted. Paris, in a class by itself, had a population of about a half million souls on the eve of the French Revolution. Besides Paris, only Lyons and perhaps Marseille had as many as 100,000, with Bordeaux, Rouen, Lille, Strasbourg, and Nantes rounding out the group with populations above 50,000. Another ten or so cities contained between 25,000 and 50,000 souls, and perhaps a few dozen more had between 10,000 and 25,000.[3] Some of the remaining cities were not much larger than overgrown villages, although many had their proud walls and their ancient privileges.

In such a predominantly agrarian society, the economic activity and social life of most cities was intimately linked to the surrounding countryside. Even in some of the larger towns a significant proportion of the population might be directly engaged in agriculture, and gardens and cow sheds were not infrequently found within city walls. Moreover, much of the wealth of cities was drawn from agriculture. Cities provided markets and legal and administrative services for the surrounding countryside – at a price – and city people owned and extracted profits from vast tracts of the kingdom's agricultural land. The fortunes of many urban dwellers were comprised almost exclusively of agricultural holdings, and even merchants preferred to hold part of their wealth in land, partly for reasons of status and partly because of the security it offered as an investment. Thus, in most cities, strictly commercial and industrial activities existed side by side with a deep involvement in the rural economy. Fluctuations of the agrarian economy also dominated the rhythm of urban production: As Ernest Labrousse has shown, the most serious industrial and commercial depressions during the old regime – and right down to the middle of the nineteenth century – occurred as a result of harvest failures.[4] Not only was the urban economy smaller than the agrarian economy in its proportion of national economic output and the number of persons it employed; its very rhythms of prosperity and slump were dominated by fluctuations in the size of the annual harvest.

Nor did all industrial production take place in cities. Nearly all villages had a scattering of artisans – bakers, shoemakers, harness makers, wheelwrights, blacksmiths, and the like – who serviced the needs of the local cultivators. Far more important than these village artisans was another very different type of rural industrial producer: the thousands of rural people in textile districts scattered from Flanders to Languedoc and from Alsace to the Vendée, who were employed in the production of cloth that was sold on the national and world market.[5] Unlike village blacksmiths or wheelwrights, who were often more prosperous than the general mass of cultivators, rural weavers were usually the poorest of the poor. They were typically holders of tiny agricultural plots who combined weaving with the cultivation of their inadequate morsel of land – usually supplemented by occasional wage labor on others' fields – to scratch out a meager existence. These rural weavers were utterly dependent on urban entrepreneurs, who supplied them with yarn and then transported the woven cloth back to city workshops for finishing operations before placing it on the market. Already widespread in the seventeenth century in the countryside surrounding traditional linen or woolen centers, such as Lille, Reims, Rouen, Beauvais, and Amiens, this same pattern was adopted in the newly implanted and rapidly growing cotton industry in the eighteenth. Virtually none of the rural industrial producers – neither the weaver-peasants of the textile districts nor the more independent village blacksmiths, shoemakers, or bakers found in all regions of the country – had corporate organizations of any kind. Indeed, textile entrepreneurs had originally resorted to rural production largely to avoid the detailed technical regulations, high wages, and incessant labor troubles of the urban textile corporations.

Most cities, then, were small islands in the predominantly rural and agrarian society of the old regime. Their economies were deeply dependent on agricultural production, and even many of the manufactured goods sold in urban markets had been made in the countryside. Yet juridically, cities were sharply distinct from the surrounding countryside. Although the contrast between city and countryside was no longer a contrast between free men and serfs – as it had been in the early Middle Ages and still was in Eastern Europe – city and countryside differed far more in the seventeenth or eighteenth century than in the period since the French Revolution. Cities had their origins in the Middle Ages, when kings or territorial counts granted charters containing a whole set of privileges and liberties that distinguished city dwellers from residents of the surrounding countryside: personal freedom, immunity from local seigneurial jurisdiction, the right to erect walls, exemption from certain tolls and dues, and the right to establish governments, laws, and courts. Although the autonomy of cities had been greatly reduced by the expanding power of the monarch, French cities still possessed charters and privileges to the very end of the old regime. They still had separate systems of courts and local government; they still had walls that marked them off physically from the countryside; and their customs, styles of life, and social hierarchies were still sharply distinct from those of the rural world. Despite their deep dependence on agriculture and rural society, French cities retained their own autonomous social, cultural, and juridical personalities until the French Revolution dissolved their privileges in the common status of national citizenship. It was in these autonomous, bounded, urban social communities that the corporate system of the old regime took root and flourished.

One distinctive feature of urban society during the old regime was its pronounced degree of internal diversity. Although it is true that only the most important cities had opulent nobles or great merchants and financiers, all had a remarkably complex social hierarchy and great contrasts of wealth and poverty. Every city had its share of judicial and administrative officers, wealthy commoners living on their investments (*bourgeois,* as these were termed in the eighteenth century), lawyers, notaries, doctors, merchants, apothecaries, innkeepers, grocers, and shopkeepers of all sorts. All cities had a bewildering variety of artisans: jewelers, wigmakers, and bookbinders patronized by the local rich; bakers, butchers, tailors, seamstresses, coopers, shoemakers, barbers, and wheelwrights to supply the wants of daily life; masons, carpenters, glaziers, plasterers, joiners, sawyers, and roofers to house the population; and perhaps workers in some local industry producing for the regional, national, or international market – say, weavers, stockingers, hatters, potters, cutlers, ribbon makers, or printers. In a society that contained great extremes of wealth and poverty, there were always swarms of servants to attend the rich – domestics, nannies, cooks, coachmen, footmen, grooms, butlers, and valets. There were also crowds of lifters and carriers – porters, carters, loaders, masons' laborers, dock workers, water carriers, or simple casual laborers, variously and expressively called *journaliers* (day laborers), *gagne-deniers* (penny-earners), *manoeuvres* (literally "handworkers"), *gens de bras* (literally "men of arms"), or *hommes de peine* (literally "men of pain or punishment"). Many of these were unmarried transients who found work where they could and then moved on to another job or another city or perhaps drifted into casual labor in the countryside. Finally, French cities of the old regime always contained many who did not work or who eked out a precarious living on the margins of the urban economy: beggars, vagabonds, street musicians, prostitutes, pickpockets, and a prodigal variety of hawkers and peddlers.

THE MECHANICAL ARTS

Among these diverse urban occupations, only a portion was organized into corporations. Of these, the largest group were the artisan trades. With rare exceptions, these trades were practiced in small workshops by highly skilled craftsmen who had undergone a long period of apprenticeship. Normally there was very little division of labor among the journeymen; each was expected to be able to perform all the operations required to lay a floor or to build a staircase or to make a pair of shoes, a chair, a suit of clothes, a batch of pastries, a barrel, or a cooking pot. The workers were supervised by a master, who often worked beside his employees and was expected to be a particularly skilled practitioner of his trade. But the master was also an entrepreneur and a shopkeeper. Usually assisted by his wife, he dealt with clients, took orders, kept the books, invested in tools, raw materials, and stock, and paid the workers their wages. Some of these trades required sizable capital investments in tools, vats, furnaces, ovens, forges, and the like. But with rare exceptions, these implements were operated by hand

and powered by human muscles. The typical enterprise in artisan trades was small, with perhaps two or three workers for each master, but the range was enormous – all the way from masters working alone or with a single apprentice to big-time operators like the Parisian master joiner in the Section de la Grange Batelière who had seventy-one employees in 1791 – in a trade where the majority of masters had fewer than ten.[6] In most cities nearly all of these industrial or manufacturing occupations were organized into corporations.

But the world of corporate trades was not confined to what we would call industry or manufacturing; it included most commercial occupations as well. Among commercial occupations, only financiers, bankers, brokers, and the opulent wholesale merchants of the great cities – who were termed *négociants* rather than *marchands* – fell outside of the corporate sector.[7] There were corporations of apothecaries, mercers, and hotelkeepers, of sellers of wood, wine, grain, books, spices, cloth, cattle, fish, and straw – in short, of merchants and shopkeepers of all kinds. Members of these commercial corporations usually engaged in only small-scale retail commerce, although some, such as members of the celebrated *six-corps* of Paris (the drapers, grocers, mercers, furriers, hosiers, and goldsmiths), engaged in large-scale, long-distance, and extremely lucrative mercantile activity. All of these commercial trades were grouped together with industrial occupations into a common corporate sector or stratum of urban society collectively designated as *arts et métiers* (arts and trades), whose members were known as *gens de métier* (tradesmen).[8]

These corporately organized commercial and industrial occupations occupied an intermediate place in the urban social hierarchy. Above the world of the gens de métier – besides négociants, ecclesiastics, nobles, royal or municipal officers, and great financiers – were the learned or liberal professions – physicians, lawyers, men of letters, notaries, professors – whose activities were considered to be intellectual rather than mechanical. Below the gens de métier were the inferior strata of the urban population: servants, unskilled workers, and the disreputable poor. Servants were juridically incapable of forming corporations. They were considered to be members of the family they served, under the paternal authority of its head, and they therefore had no independent juridical or social standing. Because they had no public personality, they could not legally form corporations representing them in the public sphere. The occasional corporations that occurred among lifters and carriers were almost always formed either among groups whose occupations were essential for the maintenance of public health – such as water carriers – or among dock workers, whose probity and discipline were regarded by municipal and royal authorities as essential to the maintenance of public order on the crowded and chaotic waterfronts of old-regime ports. However, the vast mass of journaliers, gagne-deniers, gens de bras, manoeuvres, or hommes de peine remained untouched by the corporate order – and by the stability of employment, the sense of community, and the legal and social standing that corporations implied.[9] And what was true of these casual laborers was all the more true of beggars, prostitutes, vagabonds, and petty criminals, who formed the lowest rank of the urban social hierarchy.[10]

In some ways this urban social hierarchy seems quite recognizable, whether from the point of view of the twentieth century or from that of the mid-nineteenth century. Then and now, the idle rich and the learned professions were at the top, unskilled laborers and criminal elements were at the bottom, and other occupations fell somewhere in between. But the way in which occupations were grouped within this roughly similar array was sometimes strikingly different. Most surprising is that under the old regime industrial crafts – shoemakers, blacksmiths, carpenters, and so on – formed a common group with commercial occupations and were sharply distinguished from unskilled laborers. In the middle of the nineteenth century – or today – industrial craftsmen would be grouped together with unskilled manual laborers and would be sharply distinguished from the world of commerce. This striking change in social classification attests in part to the enormous changes – industrialization, bureaucratization, the advance of capitalism – that both industrial and commercial activity have undergone in the two centuries since the end of the old regime. But at the same time it also represents a fundamental change in the conceptual categories through which people perceive, understand, and act in the social world.

Why were occupations so diverse as penurious shoemakers and opulent merchants bracketed together in the single social category of gens de métier? In what did their unity as a category consist? In the first place, it must be remembered that the trades engaging in industrial production also engaged in commerce – in the language of the time they were at once *mestiers et marchandises*.[11] The master shoemaker not only made shoes but sold them as well; the master carpenter was a contractor as well as a builder. The entire range of gens de métier were engaged in commercial transactions of some kind. Second, in the social vocabulary of the old regime, commercial as well as manufacturing occupations were considered to be a form of manual labor and therefore to be base. They were "mechanical arts" as opposed to the intellectual or learned "liberal arts." In principle, a noble could suffer *dérogeance* (deprivation of nobility) for becoming a merchant as well as for apprenticing himself to a shoemaker. Finally, although the occupations of the gens de métier were manual or mechanical, they were also arts – that is, they required the exercise of discipline and intelligence. It was this quality that distinguished them from the occupations of the gens de bras. Both gens de bras and gens de métier engaged in manual labor, but only the labor of the gens de métier was raised by the application of intelligence to the level of art. According to these criteria, the gens de metier made sense as a single social category. To put it rather formally, the gens de metier could be defined as the intersection of the domain of manual effort or labor with the domain of art or intelligence, an intersection neatly summarized in the expression "mechanical arts," which designates those activities simultaneously requiring bodily effort and the exercise of intelligence.

To understand the place of trade corporations in the social order of the old regime requires a close look at conceptions of labor and of art in old-regime culture. In 1848, both in the discourse of revolutionary workers and in French culture generally, the word *travail* (labor) carried strong connotations of productivity and even of creativity. But under the old regime, these creative connotations of labor were absent. Rather, labor had the traditional Christian connotations of pain, burden, and penitence. *Travail* was defined in the dictionary of the Académie française of 1694 as the "toil, pain, fatigue taken to do something," and *travailler* was defined, "to do a task, a painful work, to take some fatigue of the body or the spirit."[12] *Travail*, in short, was not the work (*oeuvre, ouvrage*) that is created but the pain required to create it. It was the curse of Adam to labor in the sweat of his brow for his daily bread and of Eve to bear children in labor. Adam's fate was thus precisely parallel to Eve's: to sustain the human species through painful, exhausting, and unreflective effort of the body, through pure animal exertion. In the Christian scheme of things, labor was a badge of vileness, the proof of and the punishment for man's original sin. It was not an ennobling activity but a mark of man's fallen nature and of his abject humility before God.[13]

Art, by contrast, was uplifting and ennobling. If the requirement of labor signified man's bondage to brutish nature, art signified the power of intelligence or spirit to raise man above nature. Animals, after all, could engage in labor, but only humans could practice arts. In old-regime France, the term "art" referred to a very broad range of human activities, and it was used much more commonly in everyday discourse than it is today – not just for poetry or architecture or painting but for the mechanical arts, the arts of government, the military arts, and so on. In the words of *Le Grand Vocabulaire françois* of 1762–4, "art is said of everything that is the effect of the skill and industry of man." This conception of art differs importantly from the romantic nineteenth-century notion of art as the expression of creative genius unbounded by the conventions of ordinary life. Quite the contrary, art was not a matter of originality, inspiration, and genius but of rules, order, and discipline. To quote *Le Grand Vocabulaire françois* again, art was defined as a "method for executing a thing well according to certain rules."[14] Even the *beaux arts*, although spoken of as "children of genius,"[15] were considered to be subject to strict rules – of proportion, measure, harmony, rhyme, meter, and so on. In this scheme of things, art was a rule-giving or legislative activity; art and its rules were the means of creating and maintaining order in human life generally, of subjecting our unruly passions to reason and directing them to orderly and useful ends of whatever kind. Thus there were rules of war, statecraft, jurisprudence, rhetoric, theology, philosophy, medicine, painting, poetry, drama, music, tapestry weaving, the buying and selling of wine, carpentry, shoemaking, joinery, silversmithing, and hundreds of other arts. It was these arts and their order-giving rules that raised man above the condition of an intelligent half brute, unreflectively scratching out a living from an ungrateful earth and covering its surface with his progeny.

These conceptions of art and labor explain not only the place of the mechanical arts in the overall hierarchy of the old regime but also the ranking of various trades within the category of mechanical arts. The privileged orders – the clergy and the nobility – were of course exempted entirely from vile manual labor, which was relegated to the Third Estate. Within the Third Estate, the liberal arts – defined as those arts "whose productions appertain more to the mind [*esprit*] than to the hand" – were ranked above the mechanical arts – defined as appertaining "more to the hand than to the mind."[16] The same principle of ranking was also employed within the category of mechanical arts. As the jurist Loyseau put it at the beginning of the seventeenth century in his *Traité des ordres et simples dignitez:*

> Trades which are crafts and commerce [mestiers et marchandises] combined . . . are honorable and those who exercise them are not numbered among the vile persons. . . . On the contrary there are trades which rest more in the effort of the body than in the traffic of commerce or in the subtlety of the mind, and those are the most vile.[17]

The same ideas are found in the *Encyclopédie,* as the following entries demonstrate.

> *Artiste.* Name given to workers who excel in those mechanical arts which suppose intelligence.

> *Artisan.* Name by which one designates workers who profess those mechanical arts supposing the least intelligence. One says of a good shoemaker, that he is a good *artisan,* and of a clever watchmaker, that he is a great *artist.*[18]

It is particularly significant that the same principle of ranking was used by Loyseau, whose treatise was one of the most famous justifications of a society of orders and privileges, and in the *Encyclopédie,* the Philosophes' most important weapon in their attack on privileges. The notion that honor came from art and not from labor was a commonplace of old-regime culture; it was shared by thinkers of all persuasions. Indeed, this assumption was shared not only by the educated upper classes but by manual workers as well. The mythical accounts by which clandestine journeymen's associations known as *compagnonnages* explained their origins – myths probably dating from the eighteenth century – stressed the superior skill or art of their founders as a factor that originally set them off from ordinary workmen. This emphasis on art as the source of honor also found expression in the exacting technical training, capped by the production of a masterpiece (*chef d'oeuvre*), that the compagnonnage required of its members. Workers who were accepted into a compagnonnage were expected to manifest their elevated rank by perfecting their art.[19] Hence, to judge from the myths and customs of compagnonnage, even manual workers who fell near the bottom of Loyseau's hierarchy based their claims not on the honor of labor but on their possession of superior art.

The significance of the art/labor, or the mind/hand, dichotomy is most clearly revealed in the way unskilled labor was thought of and written about. Once again, Loyseau stated it well: "And for all the more reason those who exercise neither crafts nor commerce, and who gain their livelihood with the labor of their arms . . . are the vilest of the *menu peuple* [little people]. For there is no occupation so bad as no occupation at all."[20] Those whose activity was considered to be labor alone, unredeemed by some admixture of art or intelligence, were at the bottom of the social hierarchy – "the vilest of the *menu peuple*" and hence the vilest of the vile. But Loyseau's statement goes further than this. The exercise of nothing but labor was less than the lowest possible occupation – it was no occupation at all. This same idea is also expressed in another common phrase: The gens de bras were customarily said to be *sans état*. *Etat*, in the old regime, had a multiplicity of meanings. It meant rank, standing, or status; it implied stability of condition and regularity; and it also meant occupation or profession.[21] Thus, to be "sans état" was to be without occupation or profession, without status or standing, and also without stability or regularity. All this implies that labor was not only intrinsically demeaning; labor alone, without art to give it rules, to inform it with reason, was a social and moral nullity. Gens de bras were incapable of internal discipline and were kept in order only by external authority and by the press of hunger and want.

Thus, the boundary dividing the corporately organized gens de métier from the noncorporate gens de bras was fundamental: It was a boundary between order and disorder. It is thus not surprising that the gens de bras were not organized into corporations. If their labor lacked all rule and regularity, how could it be governed by the detailed technical regulations of a corporation? And if such men were sans état, how could they form a corporation with officially recognized privileges, a body that, however low in the overall scheme of things, had a securely established place in the state? It was only art, with its order-giving and rule-governed qualities, that made corporations possible.[22] In this connection, it is significant that the liberal arts, although clearly superior to the mechanical arts in rank and honor, were organized in an analogous way. As François Olivier-Martin has pointed out, the universities, the academies, the legal and medical professions, and the royal officers all had organizations juridically similar to the *corps d'arts et métiers* – with their privileges, their internal regulations, and their recognized standing in the state.[23] In the Middle Ages, the similarities between universities and trade corporations were clearly signaled in language: Not only were both headed by "masters," but apprentices in the manual arts were frequently called *escolans* and journeymen, *bacheliers*. And as late as the sixteenth century a royal decree banning disorderly banquets could include in a single sentence "all banquets whether for doctorates and other degrees in any faculty, or for masterships of sciences, arts and trades."[24] Although differences between the organizations of learned professions and those of tradesmen probably increased in the seventeenth and eighteenth centuries, important juridical similarities remained to the very end of the old regime. For that matter, the analogy could be pushed much higher up the social scale. The nobility, the clergy, chivalric orders, and even orders of monks and friars were legally recognized, privileged, internally regulated, semiautonomous bodies organized in a fashion analogous to trade corporations. In a sense, then, the corps d'arts et métiers stood at the bottom of a hierarchy of corporately organized groups, groups whose functions became increasingly honorable and increasingly spiritual the higher the rank, ranging from the vile physical operations of the most manual of the mechanical arts to the monks' and friars' selfless devotion to God. The gens de métier may have been base, defiled by their manual labor, but their possession of art raised them above mere cultivators and unskilled laborers and made them capable of orderly self-government and worthy of officially recognized privileges and rights.

CORPORATIONS

Such was the place of trade corporations in the social hierarchy of the old regime. But what was the nature of these corporations as institutions – their rules, privileges, customs, rights, and obligations? How did they actually operate in practice in the cities of seventeenth- and eighteenth-century France? Given the state of the historical literature on corporations, these questions are not as easy to answer as one would like. Trade corporations were a major focus of historical studies in France between the late nineteenth century and World War II, and there are excellent general studies by Etienne Martin Saint-Léon, Henri Hauser, François Olivier-Martin, and Emile Coornaert dating from this period.[25] But since the corporative experiments of Vichy, the subject has been in bad odor in the French historical community, and there has been no important general study of corporations since the publication of Coornaert's work in 1941. This is particularly unfortunate because it means that corporations have never been subjected to the kind of rigorous and exhaustive study that the French Annales school has devoted to historical topics ranging from demography and rural social structure to attitudes about death and honor.[26] There are, however, several excellent recent studies of seventeenth- and eighteenth-century cities by historians of the Annales school, which contain valuable new information correcting or amplifying some conclusions of earlier accounts.[27] In the absence of an up-to-date synthetic study of corporations, the sketch that follows must inevitably be somewhat speculative and uncertain at times. But I trust that most of my interpretations will be acceptable – or at least not seem outrageous – to specialists in the field.

According to juridical doctrine of the seventeenth and eighteenth centuries, the act that created a trade corporation was the ratification of its statutes by *lettres patentes* of the king.[28] This made the trade into what was known as a *métier juré* (sworn trade) or *jurande*, so called because its members were required to swear *(jurer)* an oath of loyalty upon entering the mastership. The nature and importance of this act of ratification can be illustrated by examining a particular case. In 1585 Parisian wine sellers and tavernkeepers were involved in a dispute with vinegar makers, who were contesting the wine sellers' and tavernkeepers' practice of converting soured wine into vinegar, thereby competing with them in the fabrication and sale of their product. The wine sellers and tavernkeepers found themselves at a disadvantage in this dispute because the vinegar makers were organized as a métier juré and they were not. Hence, they offered King Henri III a *finance modérée*, asking him to "establish them as a body and community [*en corps et communauté*]." The king responded by ratifying their statutes in a lettre patente. By means of this act he established *"en perpétuité ledit état . . . en état juré pour y avoir corps, confrairie et communauté"* (in perpetuity the said trade . . . as a sworn trade in order to have body, confraternity and community).[29]

A number of salient characteristics of métiers jurés can be illustrated by this example. First, it is clear that the wine sellers and tavernkeepers felt they would have a firmer legal basis for pursuing their dispute with the vinegar makers if they too were organized "en corps et communauté," as a métier juré. When a trade was *erigé en corps et communauté* (instituted as a body and community), all those practicing the trade were united into a single, recognized unit with a legally secure and fixed place in the state. In the jurisprudence of the old regime, a legally constituted corps or communauté was considered to be a single person, a subject of the king, empowered to address requests or remonstrances to the sovereign, to initiate lawsuits, and to own property like any other subject. As the seventeenth-century jurist Domat put it: "Legitimately established communities stand in the place of persons . . . They are considered as a single whole. And as each particular

26

person exercises his rights, treats of his affairs and acts in justice, it is the same with communities."[30] Thus the wine sellers and tavernkeepers, locked in battle with the vinegar makers, greatly strengthened their juridical status when they became a métier juré. By making the wine sellers and tavern-keepers into a fictitious person, the king was granting them full legal powers as a recognized royal subject and thus a status equal to the vinegar makers.

According to the jurist Lebret, the king established métiers jurés in order to perfect the mechanical arts and to enhance public welfare: "Princes have particularly reserved the power to establish them as corps, to give them statutes and to grant them immunities and privileges, in order to encourage artisans to make themselves perfect in their art and to serve the public faithfully."[31] Artisans were encouraged to act virtuously by the grant of immunities and privileges. "Privilege" means "faculty accorded to a particular person or to a community, to do something, or to enjoy some advantage to the exclusion of others."[32] Literally, *privilèges* were "private laws," that is, laws that applied exclusively to a single person, either to a collective ficti-tious person or to an individual. Trade communities were but one of many types of privileged bodies in the French kingdom. Universities, academies, law courts, cities, chartered companies, provinces, the nobility, the clergy – all of the vast and heterogeneous multitude of recognized bodies and communities that constituted the French kingdom had their own particular privileges. The grant of privileges to any of these bodies automatically en-tailed the grant of immunities: To the extent that a collective or a particular person was governed by private law, the person was necessarily given im-munity from common law.

The privileges of a trade community were embodied in its statutes, as ratified by the king. These statutes varied greatly from trade to trade, from century to century, and from city to city. This was only proper, given that each community was a distinct legal person. But because they were similar *kinds* of persons, there were also recurring features in the statutes of nearly all trades. Virtually all statutes granted members of the community the ex-clusive right to engage in the exercise of their trade within a certain district, usually a city. Thus the statutes of the pewter and lead workers *(étameurs-plombiers)* of Rouen, dating from 1544, begin: "Art. I. No one, of whatever trade he may be, may open in the city or suburbs of Rouen, nor make and sell any work of the trade of pewter and lead working, if he is not a sworn master of the said trade."[33] With infinite variations in wording, a statement of this kind is to be found in the statutes of métiers jurés from one end of the kingdom to the other.

This exclusive privilege was the most important and lucrative right of the trade community, and it was defended jealously, indeed aggressively. Dis-putes between neighboring trades were ubiquitous in French cities of the old regime and were a source of interminable lawsuits. Jean-Claude Perrot's fine study of eighteenth-century Caen portrays the trades of that city in a state of virtually continuous warfare: tanners against curriers, curriers against shoemakers, saddlemakers against harness makers, tailors against old-clothes dealers, grocers against apothecaries, locksmiths against blacksmiths, blacksmiths against cutlers, and so on. The outcome of such disputes was crucial to the survival of the community, and the loser might simply be swallowed up by the winner, like the twelve different trades, ranging from cutlers to tapestryweavers, who were annexed by the mercers of Caen between 1700 and 1762.[34] Nor was this fierce intertrade warfare limited to Caen. Recent works on seventeenth-century Amiens and Beauvais and eighteenth-century Lyons have found precisely the same phenomenon, and it appears that intertrade conflicts were characteristic of cities all over France.[35] Indeed, the statutory statements of the rights of trade communities sometimes read like peace treaties concluded after open hostilities. Thus Article 38 of the statutes of the goldsmiths of Rouen, dating from 1739, states:

> No master jeweler or other masters who are not goldsmiths can sell any works of goldsmithery, nor buy any, except for their own private use, with the exception, however, of merchant-mercers, who can continue to sell dishes coming from Germany or other countries, provided that they have them marked at the bureau of the goldsmiths.[36]

Others, in view of the danger of hostile encroachments, state the extent of their monopoly in unbelievably exhaustive detail. Thus the statutes of the Rouen cutlers, engravers, and gilders on iron and steel, dating from 1734, list no fewer than 113 distinct items that they had the exclusive privilege to manufacture and sell.[37]

This ubiquitous intertrade warfare was one of the most salient characteristics of the seventeenth- and eighteenth-century social category of mechanical arts or *gens de métier*. Unlike the nineteenth-century working class, which was thought of as uniting all manual workers in bonds of solidarity, the *gens de métier* did not constitute a solidary unit. Because they all practiced mechanical arts, the *gens de métier* were a distinct and readily definable social category. But in sharp contrast to the nineteenth-century social idiom that grew up around the concept of labor, an idiom that emphasized the similarity between workers employed in different occupations, the old regime's idiom of art emphasized their differences. Each art had its own distinct qualities and its own rules that distinguished it from every other art. Thus each métier formed a particular community devoted to the perfection of a particular art, and these communities of artisans had no bonds uniting them with one another. In pursuing their own interests and guarding and extending their own privileges, these communities were inevitably drawn into conflict with neighboring communities whose range of artistic competence overlapped in practice with their own. Although the gens de métier formed a single category under the old regime, it was a category constantly riven by mutual jealousy and suspicion.

Within the privileged domain defined by its statutes, each trade community was responsible for assuring the honesty of its own members and the quality of the goods they produced. For this purpose, each community had officers chosen from among its members. These officers were called *jurés, syndics, gardes, principals, prieurs, maieurs, consuls,* or *bailles* – the titles varied widely from century to century, from region to region, and from trade to trade. In addition to being charged with a general policing of the trade, they also judged disputes between masters or between masters and workers, represented the trade in relations with local or royal authorities, initiated legal proceedings, and generally tended to the affairs of the community. The jurés were usually chosen by election but were sometimes selected by co-optation or royal appointment and in a few cases were even chosen by lot.[38] The entire body of masters usually met at least once a year in order to oversee the work of the jurés and to discuss and take action on the common affairs of the community.[39]

The most prominent duty of the jurés was to assure the quality and honesty of the work done in the trade. The jurés were required to make unannounced visits, sometimes a specified number of times per year, to the shop of every master in the trade. There they were to inspect the work being done and the objects offered for sale. If any work was defective, the master, or sometimes the journeyman who produced the defective object, was fined; it was frequently added that, as in the words of the statutes of the Rouen cutlers, "any defective works will be broken and shattered" on the spot by the jurés.[40] The specific standards to be applied by the jurés in these inspection tours varied from trade to trade, of course, but they regularly included restrictions as to the types and quality of raw materials, the kinds of tools to be used, and the design of the objects to be produced. Sometimes these standards were extremely specific. Thus the cutlers of Rouen could not put gold or silver decoration on the handles of knives if these were made of bone, and the lead workers could not use nails in the fabrication of rainspouts except under certain conditions.[41] It was nearly always required that each master stamp his work with his own particular mark, and when unmarked works were found the master was fined. But in addition to all these specific regulations, the work was to be *"bon et loyal"* – "good and loyal," or well and honestly done. In other words, the jurés were given a certain degree of discretion to judge whether the work of a given shop was of sufficiently high quality even if it met the basic standards outlined in the statutes.

In this careful surveillance of production by the jurés of the community, it can be seen precisely how the métier juré encouraged artisans "to make themselves perfect in their art and to serve the public faithfully." Because art itself was a matter of rules, it was logical that the art could best be perfected by the establishment of detailed regulations in the statutes of the trade community, regulations to be administered by jurés who were themselves experienced practitioners of the art. This same concern with perfection of the art was also embodied in another kind of regulation that appeared in all statutes: regulations for the training of apprentices. Usually each master in the community was limited to a single apprentice, who would normally serve in that capacity for a term varying from three to six or more years. The apprentice, usually a youth in his teens, lived in the house of his master and was to obey him as a *père de famille* (father of the family) for the duration of his contract. During this period of initiation by the master into all of the secrets of the art the apprentice was paid only a nominal wage. By the end of his term of service, the apprentice was expected to have learned his craft thoroughly. It was then customary to serve for at least two or three years in the intermediate grade of journeyman *(compagnon)* before becoming a master. For the large number of journeymen who lacked the capital and the connections to acquire a mastership, this period could last for many years, and some were destined to remain journeymen for life.[42]

To become a master, a candidate was required to have satisfactorily completed his apprenticeship. He was also usually required to undergo a test of his art, by producing a masterpiece that was judged acceptable by the jurés. In addition, the candidate had to have sufficient capital to open a shop and also had to pay a substantial entry fee to the community. Having satisfied these requirements, he made a solemn oath of fidelity to the community and its rules (thereby becoming a *maître juré* or "sworn master") and was henceforth admitted to the full rights and privileges of the corporation. The entry fees were generally substantially reduced for sons of masters, and on some occasions masters' sons were actually spared from the requirement of formal apprenticeship. There was a sort of hereditary presumption in corporations from the earliest times, and in the fifteenth, sixteenth, and seventeenth centuries the requirements and entry fees demanded of candidates who were not related to a master tended to become more and more exacting.[43] Most historians of the corporate system have therefore concluded that access to mastership became increasingly restricted over time and came increasingly to be based on bonds of kinship. However, the evidence from more recent and more detailed studies is mixed, particularly concerning the proportion of new masters who were sons of masters.[44] But it was always much easier for sons of masters to obtain masterships than for men who lacked such kinship ties.

It was the masters who formed the core of the corporate community. Although the statutes applied to masters, journeymen, and apprentices alike, the community was technically constituted by the masters alone, as is signaled by one of the common terms for corporations, *maîtrises*. Because journeymen and apprentices were legally considered to be incorporated in the master's family, they therefore lacked any independent juridical personality. As Emile Coornaert points out, jurists who wrote on the law of corporations simply did not treat relations between masters and workers; journeymen and apprentices were under "the domestic authority of the masters," as an edict of 1776 put it, and therefore beyond the reach of public law.[45] With rare exceptions, only the masters swore an oath of fidelity, which Coornaert correctly characterizes as "the essential act of social relations of that epoch."[46] Moreover, and again with rare exceptions, only masters had the right to participate in assemblies and other public acts of the community and usually only they had the right to receive *charités* from the trade confraternity that was almost always an annex of the corporation. These charités usually included corporate funerals, widows' pensions, and aid in sickness or disaster. As members of the master's family, journeymen and apprentices should, of course, be aided by the père de famille in times of trouble, but they had no legal claim to such aid and were subject to the goodwill of the master.[47] As might be expected, given this idiom of paternal authority, women were normally excluded from active participation in corporations, except in a few exclusively female corporations in the clothing trades. A widow could inherit the privileges of a mastership from her husband, but she was not expected to exercise these privileges on her own for long; they would normally be assumed in time by a son, a second husband, or a journeyman who had worked in the master's shop. Women very often assisted their husbands or fathers in various ways, but their sex made them incapable – in the eyes of contemporaries and of the law – of exercising the paternal authority implied in a mastership.[48]

The standing of journeymen in the corporate community was also problematic. In the case of apprentices, filial subordination to the master was clear, and it was sanctioned by a legal contract and a solemn oath. But the relationship between masters and journeymen was far more ambiguous. A journeyman or compagnon was conventionally expected to live with his master and eat at his table. (The word "compagnon" was derived from the Latin *cum* and *panis,* therefore signifying "one who shares bread.") For this reason if for no other, a journeyman was subject to his master's paternal authority. Yet even when they lived with the master, their subordination to his authority was less total than that of apprentices. They were older than apprentices; they were presumed to be fully capable workmen; and they were hired for wages without a long-term contract binding them to their master. In some cases they actually had a public role in the corporation, swearing oaths of fidelity to the statutes, having rights to participate in assemblies and to receive charités, although such cases were always rare and became increasingly so in the sixteenth and seventeenth centuries.[49] During these same centuries, as access to the mastership became more and more restricted, the grade of journeyman came frequently to be a lifetime status rather than an intermediate stage between apprenticeship and mastership. As a result, journeymen often ceased to live with their masters and not infrequently married and became pères de familles on their own.

In this situation, the relationship of masters to journeymen was not easily encompassed by an idiom of filial subordination and paternal authority. Under the conditions of the seventeenth and eighteenth centuries, journeymen did not fit comfortably into the corporate scheme. Indeed, it is revealing that statutes dating from this period invariably contain a multitude of articles defining the status and specifying the rights and duties of both apprentices and masters but rarely mention journeymen at all. No longer wards of the masters, yet not fully adult members of the corporate community, their status was shadowy and problematic. In these circumstances, it is quite understandable that journeymen began to form organizations of their own. Excluded from the confraternities of the masters, they frequently founded parallel confraternities of journeymen.[50] In some trades, these journeymen's organizations evolved into compagnonnages, elaborately structured secret organizations of itinerant young journeymen (compagnons) with complicated rituals and myths, a system of rooming houses in cities all across the kingdom, and complex regulations assuring employment, aid in times of sickness, and funerals for the dead.[51] Both compagnonnage and confraternities contested with the body of masters over wages, job placement, and working conditions, and labor disputes became an endemic problem in corporations by the eighteenth century. Thus, at least during the last two centuries of the old regime, the relationship of compagnons to the corporations was ambiguous and vexing.

MORAL COMMUNITY

As a legal and institutional entity, the métier juré appears as a rather harsh, punitive, and hierarchical organization, pervaded by a spirit of extreme and unrelenting particularism. French corporations of the old regime were unceasingly suspicious, constantly watching for encroachment on their privileges from without and maintaining a tight surveillance over members within. Moreover, the masters used their unchallenged juridical supremacy in the corporation to restrict access to the mastership and to keep journeymen in a position of strict subordination. Viewed through their statutes, métiers jurés seem to belie the epithet communauté (community) by which they were so universally called, an epithet that then, as now, implied unity, brotherhood, and a feeling of love and compassion between fellow members. But in addition to the legal and institutional existence specified in their statutes, corporations also had a moral existence that complemented

32

and attenuated their harsh particularism and their detailed statutory regulation.

The moral dimension of corporations can be illustrated by returning to the lettre patente by which Henri III created a métier juré of wine sellers and tavernkeepers in Paris in 1585. It will be recalled that in this lettre, the king proclaimed that he was establishing *"en perpétuité ledit état . . . en état juré pour y avoir corps, confrairie et communauté"* (in perpetuity the said trade . . . as a sworn trade in order to have body, confraternity and community).[52] The legal implications of the king's act have already been considered. But the moral implications of several terms in this phrase need to be elucidated further. A *confrairie* (the modern spelling is *confrérie*) or confraternity was a lay association, formed under church patronage, for the practice of some devotion. For a trade to *"avoir . . . confrairie"* therefore meant to have a common devotional association; and in practice each métier juré nearly always had its own confraternity. Thus the entire phrase *"avoir corps, confrairie et communauté"* meant to have a recognized single legal personality *(corps et communauté)* and to have a common devotional association *(confrairie)*. But the phrase implied something beyond this as well. For a trade to be a *corps,* or body, also implied that it had a common will or spirit – an *esprit de corps* – and a deep and indissoluble bond such that harm done to any one "member" is felt by all. To be a *communauté* implied a similar commonality of sentiment and commitment. And to be a *confrairie* also implied to have a bond of brotherhood or fraternity. Thus, beyond its denotative, legal meaning, the phrase *"avoir corps, confrairie et communauté"* meant to be united in bonds of solidarity.

This did not mean that relations within the trade were bathed in an aura of self-abnegation and fellow-feeling, as some nostalgic modern admirers of the corporations would have it. It has already been noted that disputes between journeymen and masters were common. There were also continual tensions and disputes within the body of masters – rich masters against poor masters, masters from one quarter of the city against those from another, and so on. The term communauté did not describe the tone of relations within a trade so much as the assumption that whatever their differences, members of a trade community belonged together and owed one another and their art a certain loyalty against other categories of the population. Institutionally, it was in the confraternity of the trade that this solidary aspect of corporations was most clearly displayed. Before the seventeenth century, it was not uncommon for a single corporate organization to be simultaneously a devotional confraternity and an institution for the regulation of industry and commerce in a trade. But after the Counter-Reformation, with its zeal for classifications, the religious confraternity almost always became organizationally distinct from the secular métier juré or jurande, with separate regulations and officers. This separation, however, was essentially a matter of legal forms; all members of one were members of the other, and the corporation as a living human group continued to be at once an economic and a devotional unit.[53] It was the confraternity of the trade that distributed charités: payments and medical attention for the sick, pensions for those too old to work, funerals, and survivors' benefits for widows and orphans. These charités were funded by dues and by fines exacted from members who failed to perform their duties, dues and fines of the métier juré as well as of the confraternity.[54] Thus, in the confraternity the corporation showed itself, at least formally, to be lovingly compassionate and concerned with the whole life of its members, both body and soul, in sickness and in health, during their lives and after their deaths.[55]

The central religious activity of the trade confraternity was devotion to the patron saint, in whose honor the confraternity maintained a chapel in a local church or monastery. The great annual event of the confraternity was the celebration of the patron's festival day. On the festival day all work ceased in the workshops, and all members of the trade, masters, journeymen, and apprentices alike, celebrated a mass in the patron's honor, which was often accompanied by processions to and from the church, the distribution of alms to the poor, and a fraternal banquet following the mass. The festival of the patron was often the occasion for installing new jurés, admitting new masters to the community, and renewing the solemn oath of fidelity sworn by all masters. The festival of the patron saint is particularly significant because it included the journeymen and apprentices as well as the masters of the trade. Although the journeymen and apprentices might or might not participate in the processions and usually did not participate in the banquet of the maîtrise, they were required to attend the mass. Because they venerated the same spiritual patron, they were united in the same spiritual community, and they were expected to share in an esprit de corps and to have a sense of unity, of belonging to a single body, and a common outlook on the world. When journeymen in the sixteenth and seventeenth centuries organized their own confraternities, they generally placed themselves under the patronage of the same saint as the masters. And the illegal conpagnonnages required their members to celebrate the festival of the patron saint of their trade. The sense of membership in a common, if often contested, moral community is thus far more evident in the religious life of the corporations than in statutes of the métier juré.[56]

The practices of trade confraternities show that corporations were "corps et communautés" in the moral as well as the legal sense, that their members were united by spiritual bonds as well as by subjection to the detailed regulations of their statutes. The nature of these bonds is disclosed in the epithet "sworn trade" – métier juré or, to return to Henri III's lettre patente of 1585, "état juré" – by which these corps et communautés were so frequently designated. The essential act that bound members of a corporation to one another was a solemn religious oath, an oath similar in form to those pronounced by priests at ordination, monks taking orders, the king at his coronation, knights entering orders of chivalry or swearing fealty, or members of universities receiving doctorates.[57] Thus it was that an artisan's trade was commonly known as his *profession,* which denoted a solemn public declaration or vow. Although the most important oaths were those sworn by the masters upon receiving their mastership, it is significant that apprentices were also frequently required to swear oaths when they began their apprenticeship.[58] To apprentice oneself in a trade, then, was not simply to acquire the skills necessary to practice an adult occupation. It was to enter a wide-ranging and deep-reaching moral community, a community made up of men who had sworn solemn oaths of loyalty, who were spiritual sons of the same patron saint, and who venerated him in company on his festival day. In short, the corporation was not only a body of men who shared in the same legal personality but also a sworn spiritual brotherhood.

Henri III's lettre patente of 1585 also signals another characteristic of the corporation as a moral community. In ratifying the statutes of the wine sellers and tavernkeepers, he was establishing *"en perpétuité ledit état . . ."* That is to say, the état juré, once created, was to exist *permanently* as a *"corps, confrairie et communauté."* A corporation was a permanent community in two senses. First, once established by royal authority, the community with its rights and privileges was recognized as a permanent body in the state, and its statutes did not have to be ratified again by succeeding monarchs. Second, those who entered the community remained members for their entire lives – at least in principle. This assumption that membership in a trade was a lifelong commitment was marked in a number of ways in the corporate idiom. First, it was implied by the term *état,* which was used, both by the king in this particular lettre patente and in the social vocabulary of the old regime more generally, to designate a tradesman's profession. According to the jurist Loyseau, one's état was "the dignity and the quality" that was "the most stable and the most inseparable from a man."[59] When an artisan entered a trade, therefore, he acquired a particular état, a stable social condition or state of being, which he shared with others practicing the same trade and which distinguished him from practitioners of other trades. An artisan's membership in his état permanently fixed his place in the social order and defined his rights, dignities, and obligations, much as did, at a higher level, a person's membership in one of the three états of the realm, the *Clergé* (clergy), the *Noblesse* (nobility), and the *Tiers État* (Third Estate). One's trade was thus thought to fix one's position in life.

This assumption of permanence was also marked in the statutes of corporations, which frequently forbade the accumulation of two professions.[60] Surely this was in part a practical matter, because a man who was a master in more than one corporation could not be trusted to have the interests of a single corporation at heart in its assemblies or when serving as a juré. But the prohibition also had a moral or spiritual side. After all, the oath of fidelity was a religious oath patterned on the oaths of priests, monks, and knights. For this reason, to resign from one's profession or to pronounce a new profession that conflicted with the old could take on something of the moral color of apostasy. This was only an analogy, of course: Men could and did change professions during their lives. But in principle, to enter a profession was to make a lifelong spiritual commitment, and to go back on one's profession was therefore a serious step.

The permanence of one's commitment to a trade community was also marked by the corporations' seemingly obsessive concern with funerals for their members. It was a rare confraternity that did not provide for funerals at the corporation's expense, and many enjoined attendance by all members of the corps.[61] This obsession with funerals is of course understandable in a society that viewed life on earth as a trial, a pilgrimage, and a preparation for life eternal. But that the passage from this life to the hereafter was a matter for corporations – rather than simply for the family or the parish – tells us something important about corporations and about their place in the lives of their members. Nothing could state more eloquently either the corporation's concern for the whole person or the permanence of the members' commitment to the trade and to one another than the centrality of funerals in the corporation's ceremonial life. To borrow from the language of another religious oath that created another permanent moral body, the corporate funeral demonstrated and reiterated to the members of the community that they were bound to one another "until death do us part." Nor was the meaning of the corporate funeral lost on those shadowy members of the corporation, the journeymen. In both their confraternities and their compagnonnages, the celebration of members' funerals was among the most solemn of obligations.[62] For journeymen, as well as for masters, both life and death were experienced within the moral and spiritual community of the trade.

Corporations were therefore units of pervasive and enduring solidarity as well as hierarchical, punitive, and jealously particularistic privileged institutions. Nor was there anything paradoxical, in the culture and society of the old regime, about this combination of hierarchy, surveillance, particularism, and solidarity. The very word "corps," or body, which was used to designate a bewildering variety of institutions in seventeenth- and eighteenth-century France, necessarily implied all of these characteristics. All bodies were composed of a variety of organs and members, which were hierarchically arranged and were placed under the command of the head. Each body was distinct from every other, with its own will, its own interests, its own internal order, and its own esprit de corps. Each body was made of a single internally differentiated but interconnected substance, and harm inflicted

36

on any member was felt by the whole. Hierarchy, surveillance, particularism, and solidarity characterized the highest and most exemplary body of the old regime, the church, or body of Christ; they characterized the orders of monks, nuns, and friars, which most perfectly realized the Christian conception of virtue; and they also characterized the state, which through the person of the Prince drew together, organized, and gave direction and purpose to the whole national community. Indeed, one might argue that the entire French kingdom was composed of a hierarchy of such units – from corporations, seigneuries, and parishes at the bottom, through cities, provinces, and the three estates of the realm at an intermediate level, to the monarchy at the top.[63] Trade corporations were recognized units of a corporate society, and as such they exhibited a jealous attachment to the particular privileges that defined them as a corps, a carefully defined system of mutually interdependent and hierarchically arranged ranks, a detailed regulation and surveillance of their members, and a pervasive solidarity that bound them together as a spiritual and moral community.

Corporations, like all the other bodies that made up the French kingdom, were assigned a public role in the functioning of the state. Trade communities were given wide public powers, powers that extended far beyond the limits of their statutory privileges. Corporations were made responsible not only for paying their own special fees to the crown but often for assessing and collecting all the other taxes paid by their members. Until the seventeenth century, service in the militia was organized by corporation. Corporations were also electoral units, a function they still exercised in the elections for the Estates General of 1789. They participated as a body with their emblems and banners in great ceremonies of state – at the coronation and at receptions and entries for the king and for other great personages.[64] In short, corporations were seen – not only by their own members but by the governing authorities and by the society at large – as constituent units of the kingdom, as indissoluble parts of the constitution of the realm.[65]

VARIETIES OF CORPORATIONS

Thus far the discussion of trade corporations has focused on what were called métiers jurés or jurandes – communities established by royal lettres patentes, possessing written and juridically recognized statutes, whose masters swore oaths of loyalty upon being admitted to the mastership. This form of corporation had been dominant in the arts et métiers of Paris ever since 1268, when Etienne Boileau, the royal provost under Saint Louis, drew up his celebrated *Livre des métiers,* a compilation of the regulations and practices of all the city's trade communities.[66] But for the next three centuries, métiers jurés were confined chiefly to cities that fell within the royal domain and were not universal even there. Through the sixteenth century, the métier juré was only one of many types of trade organizations that flourished in different French cities – and indeed in cities spread over the entire face of Europe. In some regions, for example Provence and some parts of Flanders, the only trade organizations were confraternities, although these confraternities concerned themselves with regulation of the trade as well as with charités and devotions. In others, for example, parts of the Center and the Midi, it was the municipality rather than the crown that exercised authority over trade organizations. In some cases this meant that autonomous trade communities very similar to métiers jurés were formed by the municipal authorities; in other cases it meant that regulation of the trade was undertaken more or less directly by the municipality itself. Near the end of the sixteenth century, Henri III and Henri IV adopted the policy of creating uniform métiers jurés in all cities of France, but this policy – like many of the centralizing policies of the French monarchy – was carried out only very slowly and unevenly. By the eighteenth century the métier juré was surely the dominant form of trade organization in most of the kingdom, but even then there were many exceptions. Thus the métiers jurés described in this chapter were a distinctly minority phenomenon in the arts et métiers of French cities until sometime in the seventeenth century and never became the exclusive form of organization at any time during the old regime.[67] This fact raises an obvious question: To what extent do the generalizations made about corporations apply to trades that were not organized as métiers jurés?

In answering this question, let us return to the familiar case of the Parisian wine sellers and tavernkeepers in 1585. It will be remembered that the king's lettre patente proclaimed the establishment of *"ledit état . . . en état juré"* (the said trade . . . as a sworn trade). Once again the phrase is revealing. The king's use of this particular construction implies that the winesellers and tavernkeepers already constituted an état – that is to say, a stable and recognized condition and occupation – before they were made into an état juré. The king's act, in other words, did not establish their existence as a distinct community but simply made them into a particular kind of community, an état juré. Indeed, the winesellers and tavernkeepers had already engaged, as a body, in a legal dispute with the vinegar makers. Furthermore, they were already recognized by the king – they had previously paid him taxes (*payé finance*) in the past, and they were able to address him collectively with their request to be established as a métier juré.[68] Thus, even in Paris as late as 1585, there existed trades that had never been established as métiers jurés but that were nevertheless recognized as units by the king, that collected and paid their own taxes, and that were capable of acting in justice, and thus, in effect, of defending what they regarded as traditional privileges – in this case, the right of turning their spoiled wine into vinegar. In old-regime society, all of the trades constituting the mechanical arts were assumed to be distinct communities, and even those trades that lacked the registered statutes and official juridical status of métiers jurés acted as communities and were treated as such by the authorities. In spite of their shadowy legal status, such trades were accepted by contemporaries both as moral communities and as recognized bodies in the constitution of the state.

If this was true in sixteenth-century Paris, where the métier juré had been the standard form of trade organization for three centuries, it was all the more true in cities where the traditional form of trade organization was the confraternity or some kind of municipally recognized and regulated community. In the beginning, the rules of all trade communities were customary rather than written; their privileges and practices had the force of law only as a result of immemorial possession and usage. Thus the rules of trade communities that were written down – first in Etienne Boileau's *Livre des métiers* and subsequently in statutes accompanied by royal lettres patentes or in municipal regulations – were merely the customary practices of preexisting communities, codified, regularized, and spelled out on parchment or paper. The corporate practices that can be traced out in documents of the sixteenth, seventeenth, and eighteenth centuries – election of jurés, technical regulations, requirements of masterpieces, rules about apprenticeship and access to the mastership, local monopolies and market regulations, collection of fines, devotion to patron saints, distribution of charités, corporate funerals, swearing of oaths – all of these had been in existence long before the documents were written.[69] There were, of course, infinite minor variations according to time, place, and trade. But whether organized as métiers jurés, as municipally regulated trades, as confraternities, or as simple customary communities, corporations everywhere had the same essential characteristics. They were at once hierarchically structured and privileged bodies regulating the practice of different mechanical arts; moral and spiritual bodies expressing the brotherly solidarity of the trade, and publicly recognized bodies that were part of the constitution of the realm. The métier juré was only one specific juridical form, one sub-idiom of a much broader corporate idiom that existed before the first métiers jurés had been established and continued to exist in a variety of specific forms down to the French Revolution, even in trades where métiers jurés were never established. The métier juré, as the favored form of trade organization in Paris, inevitably became the favored form throughout France as the capital extended an increasingly detailed sway over the rest of the kingdom. But essentially similar corporate trade communities, defined by a similar set of practices, spoken and written about in similar terms, and marked by similar ceremonies and rituals, existed in the arts et métiers of all French cities throughout the entire span of the old regime.

3 Journeymen's brotherhoods

T H E   F L E X I B I L I T Y of the corporate idiom is nowhere more apparent than in the clandestine brotherhoods constructed by journeymen in the sixteenth, seventeenth, and eighteenth centuries. As noted earlier, the place of journeymen in corporations was ambiguous and troubling. Juridical doctrine of the old regime cast relations between masters and journeymen in terms of paternal authority and filial obedience, but this juridical idiom fit badly with the lived experience of seventeenth- and eighteenth-century gens de métiers, particularly in trades that engaged predominantly in manufacture. In essentially commercial trades – tavernkeeping, grain selling, or shopkeeping of all kinds – the labor force was very small, and masters rarely had more than one apprentice or journeyman, who would usually lodge with the master. But in manufacturing trades – shoemaking, masonry, barrel making, baking, hat making, printing, carpentry, and the like – masters generally employed a larger labor force; indeed, there were usually considerably more journeymen in these trades than masters. Under these circumstances, the period spent as a journeyman was typically quite long; many journeymen never attained masterships; journeymen tended to move from employer to employer and from city to city as conditions in the labor market dictated; only a minority of journeymen lived with their masters; and many older journeymen married and had families of their own. In short, journeymen lived quite independent lives, and they developed a sense of their own interests as distinct from, and often in conflict with, the interests of masters. From today's vantage point, relations between masters and journeymen in the manufacturing trades of the old regime appear to be more like class relations than relations of paternal authority and filial subordination.

This perception is borne out by the fact that labor disputes between masters and journeymen were endemic during the old regime – struggles over control of job placement, boycotts of particular shops, even city-wide strikes affecting the entire trade.[1] These conflicts between journeymen and masters had the classic characteristics of class struggles. They pitted men

40

who owned and controlled the means of production, the masters, against men who were forced to sell their labor power in order to live, the journeymen. In order to wage a struggle against such odds, the journeymen banded together into tightly organized clandestine brotherhoods that gave them collectively the force they lacked as individuals. Thus, whatever moral community existed in the manufacturing trades of the old regime, it was hardly a harmonious or peaceful one. But in spite of all the struggle and antagonism, it is striking that journeymen's brotherhoods affirmed – in their rituals, their daily activities, and their institutional structures – both the ideal of the moral community of the trade and the broader corporate order that gave the masters their superior place in the scheme of things. Although journeymen's brotherhoods engaged in struggles against masters, they in no way opposed the existence of the masters' corporations. Indeed, these brotherhoods themselves – with appropriate rearrangements and changes of emphasis and elaborations – embodied the characteristic features of masters' corporations. In this sense, journeymen's brotherhoods were transformed versions of masters' corporations. Even the conflicts between journeymen and masters of the old regime were acted out entirely within the confines of the corporate idiom.

Because most journeymen's brotherhoods of the old regime were illegal, information concerning their activities is far from plentiful. According to a long succession of decrees and ordinances, all *"confréries, associations ou congrégations"* (confraternities, associations or congregations) were illegal unless they had been expressly approved by royal authorities.[2] But such permission was virtually never given to journeymen, because allowing them to form associations would both undermine the paternal discipline of individual masters and set up rivals to the masters' legally constituted corporations. Associations formed by journeymen were therefore bound to be illicit. The very fact that decrees against such illicit associations were reiterated again and again demonstrates that they did not keep journeymen from organizing themselves. But because journeymen's associations were illegal, they had no publicly registered statutes and undertook few lawsuits or other legal proceedings whose records would have found their way into state archives. As a result, information about them comes mainly from the authorities' attempts at repression. These records are very uneven in coverage, but they do allow at least a glimpse at a large number of journeymen's associations and in a few cases provide quite rich detail.

Probably the most common form of journeymen's associations, at least until the late seventeenth century, were confraternities modeled on those of the masters. Often these confraternities were accepted by local clergy and were allowed to establish chapels to their patrons in houses of religious orders or in parish churches. But they were viewed with suspicion by secular authorities and could be dissolved if they strayed beyond purely devotional matters. This was a problem, because the confraternity was usually just the most publicly visible aspect of a more ambitious journeymen's community that was concerned not only with devotions and charités, but with regulating the trade and – when necessary – resisting the masters.[3] By the middle of the seventeenth century a more complex form of journeymen's brotherhood, compagnonnage, had become increasingly prominent. Formed chiefly among itinerant young artisans moving from city to city on their *tour de France,* compagnonnage was a federation that included a number of different trades in many different cities. It developed a complex and distinct ritual life and proved remarkably hardy in the face of attacks, whether from masters, from the state, or from ecclesiastical authorities. Compagnonnage seems to have been involved in most of the extensive labor unrest of the eighteenth century. It was certainly the most widespread and powerful journeymen's organization of its day, although it never entirely supplanted confraternities and indeed was sometimes scarcely distinct from confraternities in practice.[4]

Because information on journeymen's brotherhoods is so scattered and so uneven, it is impossible to describe a representative sample of such brotherhoods for any period of the old regime, let alone to establish a definitive account of the ways they changed from the sixteenth century to the eighteenth. Instead, two particularly well-documented examples will be examined: a sixteenth-century printers' brotherhood in Lyons, which Natalie Zemon Davis has described in two remarkable articles,[5] and the much larger and more widespread compagnonnage of the seventeenth and eighteenth centuries. In both cases the symbolic and ritual features of these journeymen's brotherhoods can be described in some detail, which provides a clear picture of how journeymen took up the symbolic forms of masters' corporations and modified them to create corporations of their own – corporations that stood in opposition to those of the masters.

THE COMPAGNIE DES GRIFFARINS

The Lyons printers' brotherhood was known as the Compagnie des Griffarins. The meaning of the term *Griffarin* is somewhat obscure, although it apparently was derived from *golfarin,* Old French for "glutton."[6] Their title, hence, might be rendered as "The Company of Gluttons." The brotherhood had its origins in the second and third decades of the sixteenth century, when it was organized in part as a confraternity. But when many of the printers' journeymen joined the cause of Reformed religion, the confraternity, by definition Catholic, disappeared entirely. It was not until the very end of the sixteenth and the beginning of the seventeenth century, when the Counter-Reformation church had once again established an unchallenged supremacy in Lyons, that the printers' journeymen returned to the confraternity as an organizational form. However, throughout the sixteenth century they used two other forms of officially recognized organizations. They established their own units in the urban militia of Lyons, and they formed one of a number of Lyonnais youth festival associations that staged plays, parades, and charivaris – antic events typically presided over by the "Seigneur de la Coquille," in printers' slang the "Lord of Misprint."[7] But in addition to these legally tolerated forms of organization, the printers' journeymen also formed a secret brotherhood. It was this secret brotherhood, the Compagnie des Griffarins, that organized a fierce industry-wide strike in the Lyons printing trade in 1539 and a long succession of smaller, less spectacular actions against the master printers.[8]

Journeymen were initiated into the Compagnie des Griffarins when they finished their apprenticeshp, or if they had been apprenticed in another city, when they arrived in Lyons to begin work in its printing shops. A candidate for membership first had to be approved by the captain of the company and a committee of members. He then was assigned, or chose, four "godfathers" among the company's members, who gave him preliminary instruction on the company's regulations. The initiation proper took place at a banquet attended by the company's officers, a number of senior members of the company, the godfathers, and all the company members who worked in the candidates' shops. The candidates had to pay the bill for this banquet as well as an entry fee. When the banquet was over, everyone retired to a back room, where the godfathers baptized the initiates with wine and water and gave them new names – usually vulgar – which served as aliases. This was followed by a song, each verse of which began *"O domino,"* proceeded to profane matter, and closed with *"de spiritu sancto."* The initiates then swore a series of oaths. Some of the oaths were sworn with the initiates' hands clasped between those of an officer, the rest with their hands on the bare blade of a dagger. The initiates swore on the dagger to maintain the rules of the company to the death and were threatened with death by the dagger should they break their oaths. They were then shown the company's special greeting and password, by which they could identify fellow members. Finally, the initiate leaned over a table and was whacked three times on his buttocks with the broad of a sword. This final ritual, called the *assolia,* completed the initiation.[9]

This ceremony, as bizarre and obscure as it may seem to the modern reader, would have presented few interpretive difficulties to a sixteenth-century printers' journeyman. Some of the stages in this process of initiation were familiar from the practices of masters' corporations. It was customary, for example, for candidates for mastership in métiers jurés to have to pay both an entrance fee and the costs of a banquet for the existing masters.[10] Such banquets were also featured in the ceremonial life of many other kinds of corps, for example, learned professions and confraternities of all kinds. The swearing of oaths, as we have seen, was also ubiquitous in masters' corporations. The oaths sworn by masters on entering a métier juré, however, were usually much simpler than those of the Griffarins. Thus, the master butchers of Paris swore simply "to observe the regulations, to show honor and respect to the jurés, and to suffer their visits." Like the oath of the Griffarins, the master butchers' oath was sworn with the initiate's hands clasped between those of an officer of the corps, although it was then repeated before a royal police official.[11] The Griffarins, as a secret organization, multiplied these oaths and added the oath on a dagger – a not uncommon means of initiating a conspirator into a conspiracy. This oath on a dagger signified that it was the Griffarins themselves, not the police authorities, who would enforce the initiates' promises. It also impressed on the initiate the necessity of maintaining secrecy and the dire consequences to himself of disobeying his oath.

As the oath on a dagger indicates, the Griffarins' oaths were modeled not only on those of masters joining a métier juré but on the ubiquitous and infinitely various practices of oath taking engaged in by a wide variety of groups and bodies in old-regime France, from religious orders to officers of the crown to short-lived conspiracies. Swearing an oath with one's hands clasped in those of a superior, for example, was part of the classic ceremony by which a vassal swore fealty to his lord and was used in any number of other oath-swearing ceremonies as well. The assolia, or sword whacks, also seem to be borrowed from knightly ceremonial. On being inducted into an order of chivalry, the aspirant was knighted by blows with the flat of a sword on both shoulders. But this practice, too, was part of a wider family of symbolic gestures. For example, the initiate received a series of blows in the tonsure ceremonial that inducted a layman into the clerical estate, in the ordination ceremony for priests, and in the ceremonies granting degrees in universities.[12] According to Davis, assolia was derived from the Old French *assolir,* "to acquit or absolve."[13] The sword whacks thus punished the initiate and absolved him of his previous wrongs; it was therefore parallel to the baptism, which symbolically washed him of his sins. That the Griffarin received his blows on the buttocks while leaning over a table, rather than on his shoulders while kneeling, introduced an element of parody into the gesture. But this element of parody did not erase the significance of the act.

The initiate's baptism, of course, was modeled on Christian ceremonial. As in a "real" baptism, the initiate had godfathers, who took on a special responsibility for assuring his fidelity to his new state.[14] In the Griffarins' baptism it was the godfathers themselves who baptised the initiate, using not only water but wine as well. The Griffarins' baptism also paralleled the Christian ceremony in providing the initiate with a new name. Alternatively, the practice of giving the initiate a new name could be seen as having its model in another Christian institution: the religious order. When monks, nuns, or friars took vows, they chose the name of a saint with whom they felt a special affinity or who best exemplified a virtue they wished to cultivate. The adoption of this new name signified their passage to a new spiritual state.

It is significant that the Griffarin's new name, although it too signaled his passage to a new state, was vulgar, not saintly. This same mixture of sacred form and vulgar content is also found in the song sung by the celebrants immediately after the baptism. For that matter, the use of wine in the baptism itself might also be interpreted as suggesting revelry – although given the sacramental significance of wine, the meaning of this particular gesture remains ambiguous. But generally speaking, the Griffarins' use of religious gestures in their ritual seems to border on parody or perhaps even blasphemy. Although it must be assumed that this quality of parody was intentional, it is hardly likely that it was intended as an assault on religion – however much it might have seemed so to contemporary theologians. In fact, the Griffarins were generally very serious about their religion, whether they adhered to the Roman or the Reformed version of Christianity.[15] Perhaps the tone of parody was intended to convey precisely that these gestures were *not* to be taken as religious acts but to mark their profane or secular character. Perhaps the suggestion of blasphemy was intended to impress upon the initiate the special and secret character of the Griffarins. Whatever the reasons for this mixture of vulgarity with religious symbolism, the tone of parody was certainly consistent with the antics of the "Lord of Misprint" and his subjects, who were, of course, only Griffarins in another guise. Moreover, parody was also present in stages of the ceremony that had no apparent connection with religion, such as the assolia. Parody, revelry, and irreverence seem to have been a characteristic tone of the Griffarins in many of their doings.

The tone of parody notwithstanding, the Griffarins' initiation ceremony was serious business. It irreversibly inducted the initiate into a vital and busy organization that claimed the absolute loyalty of its members. The rules and ordinances of the Griffarins embraced not only their internal affairs but "the right order of the Printing Industry," as one of their oaths put it.[16] Like masters' corporations, the Compagnie des Griffarins attempted to regulate all aspects of their art. They had officers who, like the jurés of masters' corporations, were charged with looking after the affairs of the community. But both their regulations and their means of enforcement were necessarily different from those of a privileged and juridically recognized métier juré. The Griffarins' chief concerns included maintaining fair wages, prohibiting what they regarded as improper practices in the workshops, keeping apprentices from doing journeymen's work, and – perhaps most important – banning "Forfants," their term for journeymen who would not join the company, from the industry. If a master infringed the

Griffarins' ordinances in any of these matters, his journeymen would all walk off the job on signal. In addition to these single-shop work stoppages, the Griffarins mounted industry-wide strikes on a few occasions. The Griffarins also engaged in frequent physical assaults on Forfants, attempting to drive them out of the city or to make them join the company. Besides engaging in coercive actions, they also formed peaceful negotiating committees to try to reach agreements with the masters, and on some occasions they even took their disputes with the masters to the courts. In addition to these attempts to regulate the industry, the Griffarins also showed a concern with the whole person of their members. They maintained strict standards of probity in the workshops, and members found guilty of pilfering or other offenses were banned from the company, usually for a fixed term of several months. The Griffarins also maintained a fund to provide charités to journeymen who were sick, retired, or out of work.[17] Because the company contained both Protestants and Catholics, it included no devotion to a patron saint, but the Griffarins did have a yearly festival in honor of Minerva, "the Mother of Printing and the Goddess of Knowledge."[18]

The Griffarins, then, were in many ways simply a journeymen's version of the usual masters' corporations. Like the masters' corporations, they claimed to act for the trade as a whole, attempting to impose their ordinances on masters and Forfants as well as on actual members of the company. Furthermore, they concerned themselves with regulation of the entire art of printing and with the general moral and physical well-being of printers, not simply with questions of wages and working conditions. They even had a patron – albeit a Greek goddess rather than a Christian saint. And in spite of the disputes with Forfants and with the masters, the Griffarins accepted the principle of a single, united body of printers. In their oaths they swore to do no wrong to any master or fellow journeyman – except, of course, Forfants, who were regarded as outlaws.[19] One of their own statements best sums up their views about the proper relationship with masters: "There should be mutual and reciprocal love between us. Indeed, above all the Arts, the Masters and Journeymen [in printing] are or ought to be only one body together, like a family and a fraternity."[20] One could hardly ask for a more pregnant statement of the idea of the trade as a moral community.

If the Griffarins were at all representative, it would appear that sixteenth-century journeymen's brotherhoods were transformed corporations. Although the Compagnie des Griffarins was by no means a slavish copy of masters' corporations, it embodied the same symbolic forms and acted on a similar set of moral assumptions. Although it challenged the masters' exclusive dominance of the trade, its goal was to establish a properly ordered trade community in which the masters' authority was tempered with respect and charity for journeymen. It aimed to actualize the moral community of all printers, not to replace it with either a more restricted community of journeymen printers alone or a broader one of journeymen in all trades struggling in common against all masters. It is, of course, unlikely that most journeymen's associations of the sixteenth century were so tightly organized as the Griffarins or had such elaborate ritual practices or were able to stand up so effectively to their masters. But it is certainly suggestive that even such a sophisticated and powerful organization as the Compagnie des Griffarins did not challenge, but rather affirmed, the basic forms and assumptions of the corporate system.

COMPAGNONNAGE

The journeymen's association known as compagnonnage departed considerably further than the Griffarins from the standard form of French trade corporation, at least by the late seventeenth or early eighteenth century. Compagnons – members of compagnonnage – certainly did not regard their brotherhoods as having developed out of masters' corporations. On the contrary, they traced their origins back to the construction of the Temple of Solomon in biblical times or sometimes, more modestly, to the construction of the great cathedrals in the thirteenth century. Some historians of compagnonnage – for example, Emile Coornaert – have claimed to discern its origins as far back as the thirteenth or fourteenth century.[21] However, the earliest documented usage of terms and practices peculiar to compagnonnage dates from the late fifteenth and early sixteenth centuries in Dijon.[22] Compagnonnage as a specific form of journeymen's organization seems to have developed mainly during the course of the sixteenth and seventeenth centuries, out of confraternities and other assorted journeymen's associations – that is, out of the same general milieu that gave rise to the Griffarins. But if the sixteenth-century Compagnie des Griffarins can be recognized without difficulty as a journeymen's version of a trade corporation, seventeenth- and eighteenth-century compagnonnage was a trade corporation – or a collection of trade corporations – transformed almost beyond recognition.

Compagnonnage flourished above all in trades where journeymen practiced the tour de France – for example, hat making, shoemaking, saddlery, and cutlery in the seventeenth century, with the building trades becoming increasingly prominent in the eighteenth. A journeyman began his tour de France after completing his apprenticeship and before settling down to take a wife, rear a family, and perhaps establish himself as a master. During a period of some three to six or seven years, he would move from city to city all over France, both in order to see something of the world and to perfect his mastery of his art by learning the special skills of different localities. A journeyman in one of these trades would be inducted into compagnonnage in one city and would then find communities of compagnons in each of the cities where he worked during the course of his tour. In each city the compagnons of a given trade would have a special inn or boardinghouse, which they called the *mère*, or "mother," where they would live – or, failing that, where they would take meals, come for good fellowship, and engage in the innumerable ceremonies and activities of compagnonnage. Many of the compagnons' activities were connected with the specific problems of itineracy. In the boardinghouse community of the mère, they found a home away from home, both a community of "brothers" and an older couple – significantly called the père and the mère, or father and mother – who ran the boardinghouse and showed them parental solicitude. Among the officers of the local group of compagnons was the *rôleur* (which might be rendered as "keeper of the roll"), who was charged with finding newly arrived journeymen jobs in local workshops. There was a special ceremony to make certain that the new man was an authentic member of compagnonnage and, this once established, to welcome him into the local group. There was another ceremony to bid him farewell and send him on to his next stop on the tour. And if there was no work for the new arrival, he would be put up in the mère for a few days and provided with enough food and money to make it to the next city.[23]

In all these ways, compagnonnage served the special needs of journeymen on the tour de France. But compagnonnage also had many of the now-familiar features of more conventional corporations. Like masters' corporations, they collected both dues and fines that were used to provide charités for members. In case of sickness, the compagnons not only provided a payment, but also carefully prescribed visits to the sick, one compagnon being required to visit each day, in order of their seniority in the association – *à tour de rôle*, as they put it – until the sick compagnon was able to return to work.[24] Compagnons also provided funerals, which included a particular and rather elaborate set of rituals, punctuated by their own distinctive mournful howls. Compagnons also strictly observed the festival day of the traditional patron saint of their trade. They typically went to and from mass in procession and then gathered for a banquet at the mère and a special assembly in its meeting room. This meeting on the patron's day was often made the occasion for initiating new members and for choosing and installing new officers.

In addition to all these practices borrowed from trade confraternities, the compagnons also showed a concern with regulating the practice of the trade in a way that paralleled the masters' corporations. They usually had three officers who were charged with the day-to-day management of their affairs: the *capitaine* or *premier compagnon;* his assistant, sometimes called the *cotterie;* and the rôleur, who was charged primarily with the formalities of arrival and departure and with job placement. They also had frequent assemblies of all members. The officers and assemblies acted not only on the internal problems of the local community of compagnons but on affairs of the trade in general. If any master failed to live up to the accustomed standards of the trade or mistreated his journeymen or cut wages below the level accepted by the compagnons, he would be *mis à l'index* (put on the index) or *damné* (damned) – note the theological terminology – and the compagnons would desert his shop until he came to terms with them. On some occasions disputes with masters would even lead the compagnons to call a work stoppage for the entire trade. The key to the compagnons' ability to carry out disputes with masters successfully lay in their control of job placement: Without the cooperation of the compagnons and their rôleur, a master who had been put on the index would not be able to find qualified workers.[25] The compagnons' methods of controlling job placement were so successful that they could be adopted even by trades in which the tour de France was not practiced, and compagnonnage seems, in fact, to have embraced a number of trades with basically sedentary labor forces. During labor disputes with compagnons, the masters sometimes attempted to set up job-placement bureaus controlled by their own corporations, but these rarely succeeded in supplanting compagnonnage.[26]

Compagnonnage also had its own system of internal ranks. Lowest of the compagnons were the *aspirants,* or candidates, who were barred from the compagnons' assemblies and ceremonies, who had to show deference to the initiated or "received" compagnons (*compagnons reçus*) and had to prove themselves before they could be "received." Besides showing sufficient seriousness and strength of character, the candidate had to demonstrate his mastery of the art by producing a masterpiece, which the officers of the compagnons, like the jurès in the masters' corporations, came to inspect in the shop where it was made.[27] Only then could the candidate be presented for his initiation, or *réception*. This distinction between the aspirant and the compagnon reçu was a fundamental distinction between those who truly were and those who were not yet members of compagnonnage. But at least in some trades, there was a higher grade of *compagnon fini* ("finished" compagnon) beyond that of the simple compagnon reçu. Sometimes officers could be chosen only from among the compagnons finis. However, the main principle of rank in compagnonnage beyond the fundamental aspirant/reçu distinction was the date of reception of each compagnon, the higher rank belonging to the compagnon who had been received at the earlier date. This ranking by seniority governed most of the compagnons' formal or ceremonial activities: everything from the order of march in processions, of entry into the chamber for assemblies, of speaking once in the chamber, of filling offices, of visiting the sick, or of throwing a spadeful of dirt on the coffin at funerals.[28]

Yet for all the formal hierarchy, compagnonnage was far more egalitarian in tone than the masters' corporations. Because rank depended strictly on seniority, every compagnon who remained in the organization was assured of rising in dignity as time went by. Furthermore, the offices of compagnonnage all rotated from one compagnon to another. The premier and his assistant were replaced on anything from a quarterly to a yearly rotation, and a new man might be assigned rôleur as often as every week.[29] These offices were usually assigned by either seniority or a majority vote of the assembly. Finally, the compagnons' assemblies were held very frequently, usually every month but more often if there was special business. This is in sharp contrast to assemblies in masters' corporations, which usually met only once a year. Moreover, the compagnons' assemblies gave all members a genuine voice in the affairs of the community. Every compagnon was invited to speak his mind, and all decisions were reached by majority vote.[30]

The most important ritual event of compagnonnage was the initiation, the réception, which made a candidate a full member of the association. Available accounts of reception ceremonies, dating all the way from 1645 to the late nineteenth century, differ in a number of respects, but they all have the same essential form, a form with intriguing similarities to the initiation rite of the sixteenth-century Compagnie des Griffarins.[31] The reception usually took place in a darkened room, often the back room, basement, or attic of the mère. The candidate was first brought to the door of the room by the rôleur, where he was questioned about the sincerity of his desire to be received and warned of the rigors of the tests he would have to endure in the reception ceremony and of the gravity of the oaths he was about to pronounce. The candidate was then conducted into the room, often with his eyes blindfolded. In the room were all the compagnons of his trade, standing in order of rank, and a table covered by a white cloth on which had been placed wine, bread, salt, and water – called the four nourishments by the compagnons. The aspirant was questioned at some length by the premier compagnon and was often subjected to physical punishment and humiliation of some sort – stripped of his clothing, beaten, forced to walk around and around the room on his knees, and so on.

After submitting to these ordeals, the candidate chose one of the compagnons as his godfather, and the godfather baptized him and gave him a mixture of salt and water to drink. At this point the initiate was given a *nom de compagnon,* a new name by which he would henceforth be known to fellow compagnons. Unlike the names given to the Griffarins, the nom de compagnon was usually uplifting rather than vulgar. It was formed by adding a virtue or an attribute to the compagnon's place of birth. Thus a compagnon from Lyons might become Lyonnais de franc-coeur (Lyonnais the Frankhearted) or one from Bordeaux, Bordelais l'aimable (Bordelais the Amiable). The initiate was then administered a solemn oath, sometimes placing his hand on the Bible, sometimes swearing on bread and wine. He swore, in essence, to be loyal to compagnonnage and to reveal its secrets to no one – as one oath put it, "under pain of mortal sin or damnation of my soul." Once his oath had been taken, the initiate consumed the bread and wine, thus ending the initiation proper. He then paid an entry fee, after which the entire body of compagnons celebrated the event with a joyous feast.

This reception ceremony, with its familiar features of godfathers, baptism, the giving of new names, the swearing of oaths, the payment of entry fees, and the feast – to which the compagnons added the consumption of bread and wine, a gesture obviously borrowed from the eucharist – raised the candidate to the dignity of a compagnon reçu and inducted him into the permanent moral community of compagnonnage. The key term that designated this community was *devoir* (duty). It was the devoir of compagnonnage to which the initiate swore his loyalty, and it was also the devoir that he swore never to reveal. In swearing to keep the devoir the initiate meant in part that he would do his duty to his fellow compagnons. But devoir also signified the countless specific secret formulas, chants, rituals, and gestures that the initiate would learn and use repeatedly in his life as a compagnon. Devoir also signified the entire institution of compagnonnage, with all its mères, members, officers, rules, customs, and paraphernalia. When an initiate embraced the devoir of compagnonnage, he was embracing an entire community with its own rules, secrets, and way of life.[32] He was to remain a member throughout his life, although he left active membership when he terminated his tour de France. This departure from active membership, like all the other significant events in a journeyman's life in compagnonnage, was marked by a special ceremony called the *remerciement,* or thanksgiving.

Compagnonnage, then, was a journeymen's trade community comparable in many ways to the sixteenth-century printers' Compagnie des Griffarins. It was a sworn band of brothers, whose membership in the community was conferred by an elaborate baptismal ceremony, marked by the bearing of new names, and realized in practice through common rituals, through acts of mutual charity, and through collective efforts to regulate the trade. But it also differed from the Compagnie des Griffarins in important respects. First, there was a marked difference in tone. The Griffarins were bawdy and antic and introduced an element of parody into their most serious rituals. The compagnons, by contrast, seem to have been consistently serious and rigidly virtuous. Their rituals and assemblies had an air of awesome solemnity about them, and compagnons were assessed stiff fines for jesting, laughing, grimacing, speaking out of turn, spitting, or farting on these occasions. They could sometimes be fined for making jokes about one another even under ordinary circumstances.[33] Perhaps this tone of solemnity helps to explain the extraordinary resilience and longevity of compagnonnage, which not only defied the combined efforts of the church, the state, and the masters during the seventeenth and eighteenth centuries but survived the French Revolution, continued to be one of the leading forms of journeymen's associations up to the Revolution of 1848, and indeed continues to exist today. On another plane, this tone of virtue and solemnity also seems consistent with the overall history of French civilization of the old regime, in which the advance of the Counter-Reformation church made the seventeenth century an era of increasing discipline and moral rigor in many areas of life. In this respect the differences between Griffarins and compagnons seem to mirror a broader cultural difference between the France of the sixteenth century and of the seventeenth and eighteenth – a journeymen's version of the contrast between the century of Rabelais and the century of Pascal and Racine or of Rousseau and Robespierre.

A second contrast between compagnons and Griffarins is that the latter were essentially confined to Lyons. They do seem to have had close relations with another brotherhood of printers' journeymen in Paris, and the Griffarins even went so far as to automatically recognize members of the Parisian association when they came to work in Lyons.[34] But compagnonnage far surpassed the Griffarins in forging links between journeymen of different localities. In the first place, compagnonnage encompassed a vastly greater number of cities. But more fundamentally, where the Griffarins and the Parisian journeymen's association were two independent bodies that had found it convenient to recognize and cooperate with one another, compagnonnage constituted a single, unified body with, in principle, identical regulations and ceremonies in every city on the tour de France. When a journeymen was initiated into compagnonnage, he joined not a local society but the nationwide body of compagnonnage, a body whose constituent members were expected to circulate from city to city as a matter of course, carrying with them their brotherly amity and their common devoir. Here compagnonnage broke decisively with the masters' corporations, which were always insistently parochial in their loyalties.

An even more remarkable originality of compagnonnage was that it included more than one trade in a single organization. As noted earlier, mutual isolation, suspicion, and intense rivalry between trades was the norm for masters' corporations all over France during the old regime. But in compagnonnage, even journeymen in neighboring and therefore potentially rival trades – carpenters and joiners, cutlers and blacksmiths, saddlers and shoemakers – were members of the same organization. However, the links between trades were not nearly as strong in practice as the links between compagnons of the same trade. Each mère was normally the mère of a single trade, so compagnons in different trades were not likely to live together. Moreover, all the ordinary business of compagnonnage went on within the cells formed by single-trade communities. Assemblies, the election of officers, receptions, and other ceremonies – damnations and mises à l'index, charités, funerals, celebrations of the patron saint's day – all took place within the bounds of the trade community. As a result, the ceremonies of compagnonnage tended to vary consistently by trade; the carpenters, for example, tended to have particularly brutal initiation rituals.[35] Yet the variation in ceremonies was only within very narrow limits. All trades had the same cycle of important rituals – the reception, greeting and parting ceremonies, assemblies and saints' days, a special funeral, the thanksgiving – and certain distinctive symbolic elements, such as the "four nourishments." To judge from the written descriptions of rituals that have survived, the range of variation from trade to trade was surprisingly slight, and even variations over time seem to have developed very slowly. Relations with fellow compagnons outside the trade usually lacked the familiarity and intimacy of relations within the trade; they had something of the character of a formal brotherhood. Loyalties between compagnons of different trades were called up mainly in emergencies. Compagnons from outside the trade might provide aid during a prolonged strike, put up a compagnon from a different trade when his trade had no mère in the city, or help compagnons in another trade to set up a mère in the first place. Or, perhaps most important, fellow compagnons of different trades would join together for pitched battles against members of a rival sect of compagnonnage. For – and this is the most original feature of all in compagnonnage – there were three rival sects of compagnons.

The historical origins of the three distinct sects of compagnonnage are unknown. By the seventeenth century, however, police officials in Dijon remarked that there were rival groups of compagnons calling themselves *dévorants* or *dévoirants* (from devoir) and *gavots,* and these same terms continued to be used for rival rites for more than two centuries.[36] During the second half of the eighteenth century these rival groups developed two different myths of their origins and began to call themselves the Enfants de Maître Jacques (Children of Master Jacques) and the Enfants de Salomon (Children of Solomon). The third sect, which came to be called the Enfants de Père Soubise (Children of Father Soubise), was initially composed only of carpenters and seems to have broken off from the Enfants de Maître Jacques during the eighteenth century. The earliest written accounts of origin myths that have survived date from the late eighteenth century, after all these schisms had taken place. These myths include a great deal of symbolic and narrative detail, which Cynthia Truant has analyzed very fruitfully in her study of compagonnage; only their barest outlines will be presented here.[37] The myths of all the sects began with the construction of Solomon's Temple in ancient Jerusalem. The Enfants de Salomon claimed that their devoir was conferred on them by Hiram, the director of the building of the temple. He was subsequently murdered by unworthy workmen, but the devoir was preserved and passed on to later generations. The Enfants de

Maître Jacques claimed to have received their devoir from Maître Jacques, master of the stonecutters who worked on the temple, who, with his disciples, came to France when the temple was completed. There he was eventually killed by disciples of Père Soubise, his former companion at the temple. The Enfants de Père Soubise, who claimed their devoir was given to them by this same Père Soubise, told essentially the same story but denied that Père Soubise was the author of Maître Jacques's murder. These myths were clearly much influenced by Freemasonry, which was flourishing in eighteenth-century France. Not only did the compagnons, like the Freemasons, trace their origins to the Temple of Solomon but much of the symbolic detail in their myths was borrowed, with modifications, from Freemasonry.

These myths provided both a charter of unity for members of each sect and a charter of hatred between sects. Each sect had its own heroic and saintly founder who became the spiritual "father" of his subsequent followers. The members of a given sect of compagnonnage, whatever trade they practiced, were united to one another as children of Maître Jacques, of Solomon, or of Père Soubise. But they were also divided from members of other sects, even from journeymen who practiced the same trade. The Enfants de Maître Jacques and the Enfants de Père Soubise, according to their myths, had been locked in deadly battle for more than two and a half millennia. And whereas Enfants de Salomon and the Enfants de Maître Jacques made no reference to one another in their myths, each regarded the stories of the other as not merely false but blasphemous and heretical. The myths of the compagnons thus justified the rival sects in their already established mutual hatreds and at the same time exalted their own particular rules and customs by giving them a long and glorious history. The rivalries between sects were passionate and sometimes deadly. Compagnons made up scores of songs insulting their rivals, and these were sung at all occasions. When compagnons of different sects encountered one another, they staged ambushes, skirmishes, and occasionally pitched battles, and serious injuries and even deaths could result. Sometimes different sects came to control different cities, and sometimes single cities were effectively partitioned between different sects. But mutual hatred, suspicion, and the threat of open warfare were always present.

From today's point of view – and above all from the point of view of reformist compagnons like Agricol Perdiguier in the nineteenth century – the division of compagnonnage into rival sects seems paradoxical.[38] On the one hand, compagnonnage reached across the deep rifts that had traditionally divided trade from trade in medieval and early modern French cities and united journeymen from dozens of different cities and dozens of different trades into a common brotherhood. Yet at the same time, it created new rifts that crosscut the old, making even journeymen of the same trade and the same city into mortal enemies if they happened to belong to different sects of compagnonnage. By making the local trade community the basic cell of its practical and ceremonial life, compagnonnage recognized and expressed the notion of the trade as a moral community. Yet by splitting into mutually hostile sects, it also erected a higher moral community, one that both encompassed a multiplicity of trades in the same body and had the practical effect of severing into two the moral body of individual trades. Paradoxical or no, such was the nature of compagnonnage, and it was to prove resistant to all attempts at reform, either by the repressive efforts of the state or by the enlightened preachments of an Agricol Perdiguier in the nineteenth century. The schisms that compagnons created in the seventeenth and eighteenth centuries and reinforced in their ceremonies and myths turned out to be impossible to heal in the nineteenth century, even when the conditions seemed right for a general reconciliation of all laborers. In the end, the brotherhood of workers of all trades, which nineteenth-century reformers and socialists like Perdiguier, George Sand, and Louis Blanc thought they saw prefigured in compagnonnage, could only occur beyond its stern and unyielding bounds.[39]

JOURNEYMEN AND THE CORPORATE IDIOM

Neither compagnonnage nor the Compagnie des Griffarins can be properly understood from a nineteenth-century standpoint as somehow prefiguring the movements that eventually issued in trade unions and socialist parties. Rather, they must be seen as arising historically out of the particular social and cultural context defined by the ubiquitous corporations described in the last chapter. The journeymen who created these associations created them in opposition to masters and to the masters' corporations, and this of course meant that they differed from standard masters' corporations in many ways. But the journeymen also shared in the masters' and the ambient society's conception of the trade as an ordered moral and spiritual community engaged in the practice and perfection of a mechanical art. It should therefore not be surprising that the symbolic forms embodying this conception in the masters' corporations – detailed regulations, chefs d'oeuvres, charités, corporate funerals, oaths, patron saints – served as the journeymen's initial models in creating their own rival corporations. But working from these conventional models, journeymen modified and transformed them to create corporations that were significantly different in shape, style, and purpose, corporations that suited the purposes of journeymen rather than of masters.

These modifications and transformations were most highly developed in compagnonnage, but they were present in the Compagnie des Griffarins as well. Take, for example, the establishment of links with other cities and other trades. The Griffarins had close relations not only with the journeymen printers of Paris but with other groups of journeymen in Lyons as well. The butchers' and dyers' journeymen aided the Griffarins in their struggles against the Forfants, and the Griffarins did the same for the butchers and dyers.[40] Where the masters' legal privileges bound them to their own particular town and set them into hostility with the masters in neighboring trades, journeymen had every reason to cooperate across trade and municipal boundaries. A mastership and the privileges it conferred were valid only within the geographical limits covered by its statutes. Because a master baker or locksmith from Rouen or Amiens or Caen could not transfer his mastership to any other city, there was no reason for masters' corporations to establish links between one city and another. But among journeymen, quite the opposite was the case. It was common in most trades for journeymen to move from one city to another, if not on an organized tour de France, then following the local fluctuations of the labor market. Given the high level of itineracy, effective control of the local labor market might very well hinge on cooperation between journeymen's organizations in different cities. A similar point can be made about links between different trades within the same city. It was the privileges of masters' corporations that made them so suspicious of one another; without their statutory monopolies they would have had no distinct boundaries to defend so jealously against encroachment by other trades. Journeymen, on the other hand, had little interest in the masters' boundary disputes, but they did find it useful both to cooperate with one another in punishing those who refused to join their organizations and to offer mutual assistance during disputes with masters. Given these differences between the masters' and journeymen's situations, it is not hard to imagine how the multi-trade and multi-city structure of compagnonnage evolved over time out of initially unconnnected journeymen's organizations.

Another striking difference between masters' and journeymen's organizations was the tendency of journeymen to split into mutually hostile competing factions. The development of permanent splits like those that rent compagnonnage was impossible in masters' corporations, because there could be only one legally recognized corporation for each trade. Masters' corporations could harbor divisions and quarrels of all kinds, but fission could occur only in cases where two or more trades were included in a single corporation, as when the locksmiths and blacksmiths of Caen, who had merged into a single corporation in 1755, split into separate bodies again in 1779.[41] In journeymen's organizations there were no such legal constraints against fission, because organizations like the Compagnie des Griffarins and compagnonnage had absolutely no standing in law. It is not known how the splits in compagnonnage or the warfare between the Griffarins and the Forfants originally occurred. In nineteenth-century compagnonnage, splits sometimes developed out of the haughty or cruel treatment of candidates by established compagnons; the candidates would rebel and set up dissident associations, and in one case they actually managed to establish an entire dissident federation.[42] Whether similar events were at the origin of the earlier splits in compagnonnage is impossible to say. But whatever the source of the splits, the complex symbolism and ritual that characterized both the Griffarins and the compagnons provided a fruitful idiom for elaborating, justifying, and accentuating a dispute until it became a permanent and unbridgeable rift.

This tendency of corporate brotherhoods to develop splits and rivalries was by no means limited to journeymen. It was inherent in the corporate idiom, which the journeymen shared not only with masters' corporations but with countless other corps and orders of old-regime France – confraternities, chivalric orders, learned professions, religious orders, various bodies of officials and magistrates, and so on. All these bodies had certain common characteristics. They tended to use a common vocabulary (compagnie, communauté, corps, frère, frairie, confrérie, état, ordre, etc.) that signaled the nature of the bonds uniting fellow members, enduring bonds of love and brotherhood, not fleeting ties of interest. These bonds were spiritual in character – they were created by the exchange of solemn oaths and renewed by common devotion. This idiom of corporate solidarity created powerful ties between members of the group – what we still call esprit de corps – but it also created sharp boundaries between different groups. Disputes between rival corps – over precedence or rank, over conflicting jurisdictions, over rights and privileges – were a ubiquitous and seemingly inevitable feature of the corporate society of the old regime. The form these disputes took varied according to the specific functions, character, and situations of the different corps. But both the disputes between trades in the masters' corporations and the splits within trades in the journeymen's brotherhoods may be seen as particular manifestations of a spirit of corporate rivalry that was inherent in old-regime society.[43]

The fact that compagnonnage – and to a lesser extent the Compagnie des Griffarins – established ties of brotherhood between different trades and cities yet created rifts between trade members in a single city is not paradoxical once it is viewed in the context of the society and culture of the old regime. The outward reach of journeymen to other trades and other cities was not a nascent nineteenth-century class consciousness that was cruelly and inexplicably flawed by the division of compagnonnage into rival sects. That it could seem so in the nineteenth century even to a man who loved compagnonnage so deeply and understood it so thoroughly as Agricol Perdiguier only attests to the fact that Perdiguier was a man of the nineteenth century and not of the eighteenth or the seventeenth. The development of rival sects of compagnonnage was not an accidental and tragic denial of the principle of the universal brotherhood of labor but an outgrowth of an inherently divisive and exclusive corporate idiom when applied in the specific milieu of journeymen in the mechanical arts of the old regime. Seventeenth- and eighteenth-century journeymen, and the brotherhoods they created, were not marching – nor were they even groping – toward the new world of the nineteenth century. They participated deeply in the values, the presuppositions, and the general cultural forms of old-regime society, and compagnonnage illustrates perfectly the depth and intensity of this participation.

But if journeymen's brotherhoods of the old regime cannot be seen as prefigurations of nineteenth-century class consciousness, their relationship to the masters and the masters' corporations certainly was not always harmonious. Rather, this relationship combined elements both of harmony and of discord. Both masters and journeymen accepted the principle that the entire trade was a community, a community that encompassed masters and journeymen alike. As the Griffarins put it, masters and journeymen "are or ought to be only one body together, like a family and a fraternity." Nor was this merely a matter of abstract ideals. The Griffarins took an oath to do no wrong to masters, and they could be punished for breaking it. Compagnonnage also postulated a moral community including both masters and journeymen. After all, many of the masters in trades dominated by compagnonnage had once been active compagnons themselves and were still linked to it by a solemn and binding oath. As a result, they commonly accepted compagnonnage and cooperated with it openly. According to their rules, when the turner compagnons of Bordeaux moved from one mère to another, they were to call in masters who were old compagnons to aid them in settling accounts with the old mère and in choosing a new one.[44] Nor was this cooperation between masters and compagnons exceptional. It was common for masters to cooperate fully with the rôleur in the placement of new compagnons, and masters could not help but appreciate the good order and professional skills that the compagnons' tight discipline, technical training, and practices of mutual charity created in the labor force.[45] Moreover, masters and compagnons frequently formed either explicit or tacit agreements about the wage rates that were to obtain in their art and maintained them jointly in practice. In short, the moral community of the entire trade was not only an ideal; it was also a lived experience of daily life.

But the relationship between masters' corporations and journeymen's brotherhoods was also one of persistent opposition. Although masters and journeymen could cooperate in regulating the trade community, their interests were distinct and were often in conflict. Journeymen's brotherhoods were structured to resist the masters in times of rupture, as well as to cooperate with them in times of peace. Even when relations were amicable, both sides knew that they contained an ever-present potential for antagonism. The very form and shape of journeymen's brotherhoods – their secrecy, the links between different cities and different trades – are comprehensible only in the context of continuing tensions with masters over the control of the trade. Masters and journeymen may have agreed that the trade was a moral community, and they may frequently have cooperated in practice to maintain it, but for journeymen, cooperation with the masters was a difficult goal that could only be won from the masters at the price of intermittent struggle and unceasing vigilance.

The symbolic form of journeymen's brotherhoods mirrored this relationship of simultaneous unity and opposition. On the one hand, the brotherhoods clearly were modeled on masters' corporations, borrowing their detailed regulations, their surveillance of the practice of the art, their requirements of masterpieces, their mutual charity and corporate funerals, and their celebrations of the patron saint's day (or in the case of the Griffarins, of the patron goddess's). By borrowing all these practices, journeymen made it clear that their brotherhoods, like the masters' corporations, were formed for the purpose of properly regulating the trade community and the art it practiced. Yet equally clearly, journeymen's brotherhoods were not mere copies of the masters' corporations, for journeymen added to the masters' practices a number of practices of their own – especially new, different, and often rather exotic ceremonies, symbols, and ritual gestures that served to distinguish their brotherhoods sharply from those of the masters. The symbolic forms of journeymen's brotherhoods thus aptly summed up their situation: Unified with masters in a common concern for the well-being of the trade community, compagnons and Griffarins, as members of distinct journeymen's communities with their own rituals and purposes, were also systematically opposed to masters. In creating their brotherhoods, journeymen began with the model of the masters' corporation, but they modified it by a whole series of additions, subtractions, and symbolic elaborations, thereby forming a body that was still recognizable as a corporation, but a corporation that served and expressed the distinct personality and interests of journeymen. Compagnonnage and the Compagnie des Griffarins were corporations, but they were corporations transformed.

This malleability of the corporate idiom in the hands of journeymen reveals something important about the corporate idiom in general. The trade corporation of the old regime was not a single and unchanging institution formed in the Middle Ages that was passed down intact to the great cataclysm of the French Revolution. Rather, it was a complex and flexible set of practices, rituals, and symbols – and of sentiments and commitments created by and given form in these practices, rituals, and symbols – that could be rearranged, modified, or transformed to suit the requirements of different social groups at different times. Thus, masters' corporations, initially a heterogeneous collection of trade communities that varied in form from city to city and region to region, were increasingly transformed into a single type – the métier juré of the Parisian style – as the royal bureaucracy gradually knit the kingdom into a centralized administrative state in the course of the sixteenth, seventeenth, and eighteenth centuries.

But just as the royal bureaucracy could transform corporations, so, from a very different angle, could journeymen. In these same centuries, journeymen took up the corporate idiom and transformed it to create their own trade brotherhoods distinct from and in opposition to the masters' corporations, brotherhoods that increasingly took the form of national federations of compagnonnage. Nor was it accidental that the construction of uniform national federations of workers' brotherhoods paralleled the increasing uniformity of masters' corporations. Both were manifestations of the increasing uniformity of French national life and the growth of a national market under the centralizing efforts of the royal administration. But in spite of an increasing tendency toward uniformity, the journeymen's corporate idiom remained extremely flexible. This flexibility is perhaps most strikingly demonstrated in the sixteenth-century Compagnie des Griffarins, which could be – either at once or in succession – a secret brotherhood, a confraternity, a unit of the city militia, and a festival association. This interchangeability of forms continued right through the eighteenth century. As noted earlier, compagnonnage, though developed by journeymen who practiced the tour de France, was also adopted with some modifications by trades with essentially sedentary labor forces. Moreover, the distinction between compagnonnage and confraternities was often quite fuzzy in practice. Thus, the compagnon shoemakers of Toulouse, under attack by local ecclesiastical authorities, simply regrouped as a confraternity and had their statutes approved by the archbishop in 1651. This did not keep them from pursuing their interests as journeymen, and the same shoemakers' brotherhood managed to force a fixation of wages as late as 1702.[46] Journeymen's brotherhoods of the old regime were capable of assuming a number of different forms and of changing their forms as the demands of their situation changed.

Yet, all journeymen's brotherhoods had certain common features. In creating their brotherhoods, journeymen began with the traditional symbolism of the masters' corporations and then proceeded to reach beyond it, both borrowing from other sources and inventing symbolism of their own. But it is striking that they borrowed almost exclusively from other types of corporate bodies – the church, the Freemasons, or religious and chivalric orders – and not from such other domains as scientific discourse, legal contracts, administrative practice, or Enlightenment doctrines. In this respect, journeymen demonstrated a firm attachment to the traditional corporate culture of the old regime. Although the development of compagnonnage may be said to demonstrate a growing opposition between masters and journeymen in the mechanical arts of the old regime, it also demonstrates the journeymen's continuing commitment to the ideal of the trade as a moral community and to the broader corporate idiom of which masters' corporations and journeymen's brotherhoods were both manifestations. The last three centuries of the old regime·witnessed important transformations in trade corporations. But they were far less radical than the transformations that were destined to occur when the French Revolution swept away the corporate framework of the kingdom and replaced it with a new framework based on individualism, formal liberty, and private property.

4 The abolition of privilege

THE FRENCH REVOLUTION was not just a change in the form and personnel of government. It was a radical transformation of the entire social order, from politics to private morality, from the army to education, from taxation to the maintenance of public order, from weights and measures to calendrical reckoning, from science and philosophy to agriculture and the mechanical arts. In the eyes of its makers, the Revolution swept away a corrupt society based on privilege, despotism, and supersitition and replaced it with a society based on the invariant laws of nature and the crystalline simplicity of reason, in which equality under the law and the liberty of the individual citizen would be at once the foundation and the goal of public life. However violently they may have disagreed about its practical implementation, all the great revolutionary leaders, from Sieyès and Mirabeau to Brissot and Condorcet to Danton and Marat to Robespierre and Saint-Just, shared this vision of the Revolution as the victory of reason and nature over superstition and privilege. The French Revolution was a self-conscious attempt to dismantle the hierarchical social framework of the old regime and to shatter the metaphysical assumptions on which it depended. In carrying out what they saw as a salutary act of destruction, the revolutionaries abolished trade corporations along with all the other privileged corporate bodies that constituted the traditional monarchical state.

The abolition of corporations must be understood as part of this general destruction of the corporate social order, not as a result of processes internal to the world of mechanical arts. This is not to say that trade corporations had no internal problems in the final decades of the old regime. Many of them were seriously indebted, owing to the expense of their incessant lawsuits and to the fiscal burdens placed on them by the state. There is also evidence that some corporations found it hard to maintain effective monopolies on their products. For example, legitimate masters were sometimes bothered by competition from *chambrelans* – independent and unauthorized producers who worked in hiding in their own rooms.[1] Moreover, in cotton and woolen textiles – among the largest and fastest-growing industries in the country – most cloth was produced by quasi-independent country weavers uncontrolled by the urban corporations.[2] Finally, as noted earlier, the corporate trades were continually rent by conflicts and quarrels – between one trade and another, between masters and journeymen, and between rival groups of journeymen.

The experience of the textile industries suggests that in the long run the development of capitalism may have been incompatible with trade corporations. In industries producing on a vast scale for a national or international market, and in which large outlays of mercantile or industrial capital were necessary, the restrictions imposed by locally based corporations would have been difficult or impossible to maintain. But in the late eighteenth century the penetration of capitalism into most urban trades was still very modest. In the overwhelming majority of these trades, production took place on a limited scale and was intended mainly for the local market; and corporations remained vigorous to the very end of the old regime. That corporations remained popular among gens de métier can be seen in the *cahiers de doléances* (lists of grievances) drawn up by the masters' corporations for the Estates General on the eve of the French Revolution. Although these cahiers denounced all sorts of abuses and called for the abolition of the privileges of many corporate bodies, they were nevertheless unanimous in demanding that trade corporations be retained.[3] Opposition to trade corporations arose not in the world of arts and trades but in a very different sector of society – the literary and administrative elite constituted by the Philosophes and their disciples – and for reasons that have more to do with the logic of Enlightenment thought than with the internal problems of the corporations.

The Enlightenment was a potent force in French society in the last years of the old regime. Although the Philosophes were highly critical of French mores and political institutions, their ideas became extremely influential among the governing elite of the monarchy by the 1760s and 1770s. Many leading officials of the royal government were enthusiastic supporters of Enlightenment ideas – in part because they seemed to provide a rational administrative program for the burgeoning royal bureaucracy – and they introduced numerous reforms inspired by the Philosophes. The pinnacle of Enlightenment influence in the royal administration was reached from 1774 to 1776 when Turgot, himself a Philosophe of some note, served briefly as the *contrôleur général,* or prime minister, of the kingdom. Turgot enacted a whole program of reforms – including a short-lived abolition of trade corporations – but he soon fell from power and his reform measures were quickly reversed.[4] Yet by 1776, even Turgot's enemies spoke with an Enlightened accent; even the defense of traditional institutions was now couched in terms of appeals to nature, reason, and liberty. By the end of the old regime, Enlightenment ideas and terminology pervaded the discourse of all factions and of all political opinions. And in the Revolution, these ideas and terms provided the framework of the entire political and social order.

The essential project of the Enlightenment was to give a purely natural account of the world. Enlightenment thought was elaborated in opposition to the essentially Catholic Christian ideas that underlay the social order of the old regime. Rather than seeing the material world as a realm of disorder and sin that was tamed only by the discipline of spirit and authority, the Philosophes turned to nature as the source of all truth and to reason as the sole means of attaining knowledge. They eschewed theological speculation, which they regarded as beyond the ken of human reason, and took the new natural science as their intellectual model. In social and political speculation, as well as in natural science, the Philosophes rejected authority and sought natural and rational justifications for social institutions.

Their scientific ideal of simplicity and universality was particularly corrosive when trained on the social and political order of the old regime, composed as it was of a multitude of distinct and privileged hierarchical bodies. The traditional political thought of the old regime sought the origin of social arrangements in God's will and saw earthly hierarchy as "following the example of the celestial hierarchy," as Loyseau put it in the early seventeenth century.[5] As against this hierarchical and religiously justified picture of the social order, the Philosophes counterposed their own vision of society, in which all men – now understood as purely natural beings – were essentially equal and in which order derived from nature rather than from a divinely sanctioned hierarchy. In developing this vision, they focused particularly on man's productive activities, on the ways humans transformed their natural environment to win their subsistence and to improve their conditions of life. Agriculture, commerce, and the mechanical arts, the Philosophes tried to demonstrate, were governed by natural laws, and only such natural laws – not the arbitrary will of monarchs or the sophistries of priests and theologians – could bring harmony and order to social and political life.

MECHANICAL ARTS AND THE ENLIGHTENMENT

Enlightenment opposition to corporations arose from this belief that order must be sought in nature rather than in spirit and hierarchical discipline. The attack on corporations was part of an effort to raise the mechanical arts – and all productive labor – from the disdain in which it was held by contemporary opinion and to enhance the productivity of labor by freeing it from the archaic restrictions of a barbarous past. From the point of view of the Philosophes, corporations were an insult to human dignity and a perversion of the nature of things. The idea that labor should be exalted as an essential foundation of human happiness rather than despised as a stigma of baseness and sin was pervasive in Enlightenment thought. It was expressed, for example, in Locke's *Second Treatise of Government*, where labor was recognized as the origin of property and therefore of civil society; and in Voltaire's equation of commerce and freedom in his *Philosophical Letters* and in his famous admonition to "cultivate our garden" at the end of *Candide*. But it was nowhere more prominent than in the pages of Diderot's *Encylopédie ou dictionnaire raisonné des sciences, des arts et des métiers* (Encyclopedia or Rational Dictionary of Sciences, Arts and Crafts).[6] Diderot, who was the son of a cutler, gave the mechanical arts a central place both in the *Encyclopédie* and in his overall program of Enlightenment. Diderot himself wrote at length about the mechanical arts in his long articles "Art" and "Encyclopédie," and he composed numerous detailed and admirable articles on a number of particular trades and manufactures. He also saw to it that the *Encyclopédie* contained magnificent plates illustrating the raw materials, tools, machines, and techniques of all varieties of eighteenth-century industry.[7] Diderot's writings on the mechanical arts were the deepest and the most influential of any Enlightenment author's. Better than any other, they express the philosophical assumptions underlying Enlightenment thought about corporations and the mechanical arts.

In Diderot's view, not only artisans but the whole of society had suffered from the invidious distinction between the mechanical and the liberal arts.

> Place on one side of a scale the real advantages of the most sublime sciences and the most honored arts, and on the other side those of the mechanical arts, and you will find that the estimation given to the one and the other has not been distributed in a just relationship to these advantages, and that we have praised far more the men occupied in making us believe we were happy than the men occupied in making us happy in fact. How bizarre are our judgments! We demand that people be usefully employed and we disdain useful men.[8]

He therefore called on practitioners of the liberal arts to join him in

> pulling the mechanical arts up from the debasement where prejudice has held them for so long . . . Artisans have believed themselves worthy of scorn because we have scorned them; let us teach them to think better of themselves: it is the only way to obtain more perfect productions.[9]

Thus Diderot's concern with the mechanical arts was partly utilitarian. By praising the mechanical arts and by publicizing the soundest and most up-to-date information about techniques of production in the *Encyclopédie*, the useful work of society would be advanced. But Diderot went beyond a purely utilitarian evaluation. Mechanical arts were equal to liberal arts not only because they were useful but because they were equally subtle and complex productions of the human mind.

> In what systems of Physics or Metaphysics does one find more of intelligence, wisdom, consequence, than in machines for spinning gold, making stockings, and in the crafts of Passementerie makers, Gauzemakers, Drapers or Silk workers? What demonstration of Mathematics is more complicated than the mechanism of certain clocks . . . ? What can we imagine, in whatever genre we wish, that shows more subtlety than the mottling of velvet?[10]

In this connection, it is significant that in his famous article on "Art" in the *Encyclopédie* Diderot consistently used the mechanical arts rather than the liberal arts as his examples. In part, Diderot did this because "the liberal arts have sung about themselves enough."[11] But it was also because the mechanical arts served as better illustrations of Diderot's general conception of the conditions of human life and human creativity.

For Diderot, man belonged strictly to the natural order, and his intelligence and capacities grew out of his interactions with nature. Man's intelligence was not – as in the traditional Christian view – a property of his divine soul and therefore most perfect when directed to purely mental or spiritual things rather than to the base productions of the material world. Quite the contrary, in Diderot's view – and in that of the Philosophes in general – all knowledge, however sublime in appearance or form, could only be knowledge of nature.

> Man is but the minister or the intepreter of nature: he understands and he acts only up to the limits of his knowledge, whether experiential or reflective, of the beings that surround him.[12]

> It is the industry of man applied to the productions of nature, either for his needs, or for luxury, or for his amusement, or for his curiosity, etc., that has given birth to the Sciences and the Arts.[13]

As Locke had long since demonstrated, even the lofty reflections of the philosopher or theologian are only combinations of and reflections on sense data gathered from the natural world. In this view of knowledge, the fact that mechanical arts were concerned with the manipulation of material objects in no way made them inferior to the more abstract liberal arts. Indeed, their intimate and direct contact with the productions of nature made the mechanical arts the most telling exemplification of art in general, the paradigmatic case for any convincing philosophical account of the arts.

Throughout Diderot's article on "Art," even when he was discussing the arts in general, it was the mechanical arts that claimed the center of his attention. Take, for example, the following passage:

> [Man's] naked hand, as robust, tireless and supple as it may be, can only suffice for a small number of results: it achieves great things only with the aid of instruments and rules; the same must be said for the understanding. Instruments and rules are like muscles added to his arms, and

> springs accessory to those of his mind. The goal of all art in general . . .
> is to imprint certain determined forms on a base given by nature; and
> that base is either matter, or mind, or some production of nature.[14]

This is an account of "The Goal of the Arts in General." But in the construction of this passage, Diderot has given the mechanical arts a consistent primacy over the liberal arts. He begins with man's naked hand, not with his rational soul; the great achievements of the hand that are made possible by art precede those of the understanding – indeed, the achievements of the understanding are appended in this sentence as a kind of afterthought. The same order is followed in the next two sentences as well: Muscles are added to the arms before accessory springs are added to the mind; and in specifying the natural base on which forms are imprinted, matter is listed before mind. Hence this passage, although ostensibly dealing with the goal of art in general, prepares the reader for the next two sentences.

> In the mechanical arts, to which I am paying particular attention here,
> since authors have spoken less about them, the power of man is reduced
> to combining and separating natural bodies. Man can do everything or
> nothing, depending on whether this combination or that separation is
> possible.[15]

In this passage Diderot turned his discussion of the arts in general into a discussion of the mechanical arts alone; and in the two-thirds of the article that remained, he made only the most passing references to the liberal arts. Moreover, the mechanical arts were reduced here to their essence: the combination and separation of natural bodies. Thus a discussion of the combination and separation of natural bodies became the centerpiece of Diderot's philosophical discourse on art in general.

In order to know whether separations and combinations of natural bodies are possible, one must know the properties of different natural bodies. It therefore follows that a proper treatise on the mechanical arts must begin with the products of nature.

> Our author will begin by drawing up a plan of classification according to
> which the various branches of industry will be attached to the natural
> substances which they transform. This will always be a workable plan,
> for the history of the arts and crafts is nothing but the history of nature
> put to use.[16]

This plan will not only place the known arts into a logical order, it will also lead to the discovery of hitherto unknown ones: "An exact enumeration of these productions [of nature] will give birth to many arts now unknown. A great number of others will be born out of a detailed examination of the different aspects under which the same production can be considered."[17] Thus, an inquiry based on truly philosophical principles will lead to a proliferation and perfection of mechanical arts. But carrying out such an inquiry is no easy task. Its author must be well versed in natural history, mechanics, chemistry, and theoretical and experimental physics.

> As a naturalist, he will recognize at a glance the materials employed by craftsmen and artisans, materials which they generally claim are endowed with all sorts of mysterious qualities.
>
> As a chemist he will be fully conversant with the properties of these materials, and the reasons for a multitude of operations will be known to him . . . He will grasp the whole nature of a process, no motion of the hand will escape him, for he will easily distinguish a meaningless gesture from an essential precaution . . .
>
> Physics will make him master of an infinite number of phenomena which continue to be a source of lifelong astonishment to the simple workman.
>
> With some knowledge of mechanics and geometry he will arrive without difficulty at a true and exact calculation of forces. He will need only to acquire experiential knowledge to moderate the rigor of his mathematical hypotheses.[18]

Diderot did not believe that scientific knowledge was required to practice the mechanical arts. On the contrary, untutored workmen may have an excellent command of their art, yet endow the materials they use with mysterious qualities or be astonished by physical phenomena that are well known to the scientist. Workmen's understanding of their art is habitual and empirical, not philosophical. Thus, although Diderot wished to raise the mechanical arts from the disdain in which they were commonly held, his opinion of artisans was by no means elevated. His ambivalence about manual workers is clear even in his brief article "Métier" (trade), which was clearly intended as a defense of artisans.

> *Métier.* This name is given to all professions which require the use of the arms, and which are limited to a certain number of mechanical operations that the worker repeats incessantly. I do not know why a vile idea is attached to this word; it is trades that bring us all the things necessary for life. Anyone who will take the trouble to walk through the workshops, will see there utility joined to the greatest proofs of sagacity . . . I leave it to those who have some principle of equity, to judge whether it is reason or prejudice that makes us look at such essential men with such a disdainful eye. The poet, the philosopher, the orator, the statesman, the warrior, the hero would be entirely nude, and would lack bread, without this artisan, the object of their cruel scorn.[19]

Diderot censors his countrymen's disdain for artisans and presents the trades as the very foundation of civilization, without which the sublime arts of poetry, philosophy, government, and war would be impossible. Yet he portrays the very artisans that are to be admired as human automatons, incessantly repeating a prescribed set of mechanical operations. The artisan is admirable not because he is intelligent but because he is useful, and although the craft he pursues may be subtle and complex, the artisan's understanding of it is merely habitual. For Diderot, the wisdom of a mechanical art was embodied in its rules, not in the persons of its practitioners.

It was the philosopher who could raise the mechanical arts to a higher perfection by spelling out the truths implicit in the artisan's practice. However untutored the artisans may be, and however habitual and unsystematic the rules by which they work, if these rules are efficacious they must necessarily conform to general natural laws discoverable by science. The philosopher's task is to render the rules of the arts comprehensible to all by converting the craftmen's conventional gestures, half-verbalized rules of thumb, and traditional lore into scientifically demonstrable natural laws – and in the process discard those practices that have no scientific foundation. This procedure would disseminate to the public at large the useful knowledge that has hitherto remained private and secret. Moreover, by setting forth the real scientific basis of the mechanical arts, it would necessarily lead to their perfection – by dispelling the artisans' mistaken ideas, by pointing the way to more efficient processes and equipment, and so on. By discovering and disseminating to the public the true natural and rational basis of the mechanical arts, Diderot intended to improve the lot of man – extending and perfecting his powers and enlightening him about the true nature of things.

Diderot's discussion of the mechanical arts was a perfect expression of his overall program of Enlightenment. It began with the inherent order of nature and demonstrated that man's achievements were nothing but the use of nature in accord with its own laws. And it set out to improve human life by bringing human contrivances and institutions into a more perfect harmony with the laws of nature – by rationally establishing the natural basis from which human action must begin; by exposing erroneous ideas and superstitions that hide the truths of nature from man's mind; and by broadcasting these truths to the public at large by means of the printed word. Diderot's discourse on mechanical arts paralleled Enlightenment discourse on human life in general even in the smallest details. For example, in his discussion of the origins of the different arts, Diderot asserts that when the true historical origins of a particular art are not known, "one must have recourse to philosophical suppositions, depart from some likely hypothesis, from some prior and fortuitous event, and proceed from there to the point that the art has advanced."[20] Because nothing is known about the actual origin of the art of paper making, a philosopher charged with writing its history must suppose that a piece of linen fell into a vessel of water, and that when it was poured out, much later, it had become a fibrous sediment that eventually dried into a rough primitive piece of paper. Similarly, he may suppose that glass was first discovered when bricks were fired in too hot a furnace. This method, according to Diderot, will give better results than true history, for

> the obstacles that must have been surmounted to perfect [the art] will present themselves in an entirely natural order, and the synthetic explanation of the successive steps of the art will facilitate in their understanding the most ordinary minds, and put Artists on the path they ought to follow to approach yet closer to perfection.[21]

Here Diderot's discourse replicates the method of "philosophical supposition" employed by Enlightenment political philosophers like Locke – and later by Diderot's friend Rousseau. These philosophers, incapable of knowing the actual historical origins of political society, began with the state of nature and then deduced a hypothetical event – the social contract – from which civil society, constitutions, and governments must have had their origins. And in political philosophy, as in mechanical arts, the resulting "synthetic explanation" was clearer and more satisfactory than the recitation of actual historical detail.

Diderot, in using the method of philosophical supposition, was recurring – consciously or subconsciously – to a well-established philosophical and rhetorical device, a kind of characteristic Enlightenment trope, that gave his discussion of the origin of mechanical arts resonance with a wider Enlightenment discourse. But what is true for Diderot's remarks on the origins of the mechanical arts is true of his entire discussion. His account of mechanical arts acquired a special fascination and power, both in his mind and in the minds of his readers, because it exemplified and validated an entire way of thinking – a set of metaphysical assumptions, a philosophical method, a picture of human nature, a set of tasks for the philosopher – that applied no less to cosmology or religion or criminal law or political economy or political philosophy than to the mechanical arts. Diderot's discussion of the mechanical arts, in this sense, presented the whole of the Enlightenment in microcosm. It was, therefore, pregnant with radical implications not only for the mechanical arts but for the entire social order.

But if Diderot's discussion of the mechanical arts constituted a radical challenge to the traditional social order, it did not differ from conventional discourse on the arts in its formal definitions. Diderot accepted all of the old regime's standard formal definitions: Art was a matter of rules; the liberal arts were those appertaining more to the mind than to the hand; the mechanical arts were those appertaining more to the hand than to the mind, and so on.[22] What Diderot changed were not the formal definitions but the metaphysical assumptions within which the definitions were set. For a world composed of radically distinct realms of inherently orderly spirit and inherently disorderly matter, Diderot substituted a world composed of a single, unified, orderly realm of nature. And man, rather than a rational spiritual soul joined by an express act of God to a gross material body, became a sentient natural being, capable of combining, reflecting upon, and acting upon data presented to his senses by the natural world. Art therefore became not the imposition of order onto recalcitrant matter by the disciplined efforts of man's rational soul but the discovery and elaboration by a sentient being of an order implicit in natural substances themselves.

The traditional metaphysics of the old regime were, of course, consistent with the practice of organizing arts into hierarchical moral and spiritual bodies charged with disciplining the art and its practitioners. But the new metaphysics of the Enlightenment implied a very different form of organization. If the rules of the mechanical arts were to be discovered by the scientific investigation of natural substances, then the mechanical arts themselves should be organized in a fashion similar to science. Individual artisans should be encouraged to experiment with new techniques and processes and should therefore be kept free from arbitrary restrictions and regulations. Moreover, knowledge in the mechanical arts – about technical processes, raw materials, tools, inventions, and the like – should be made readily available to the public, rather than maintained as trade secrets of particular corporations or of particular masters. Thus, although Diderot did not take up the question of corporations in his article on "Art," his entire discussion implied that they should not be allowed to exist.

No other figure of the eighteenth century examined the mechanical arts with anything approaching the depth, the vision, the scope, or the consistency of Diderot. His specific views on the mechanical arts, although deeply influential in Enlightenment thought generally, did not directly inspire attacks on the corporations. Rather, the Philosophes' attacks on corporations came from a related but somewhat different quarter – that of the economists, whose chief interest, in France, was always in agriculture rather than in industry or the mechanical arts.[23] But the economists' views on the mechanical arts and corporations were at bottom consistent with those of Diderot. Like Diderot, they conceived of production as the manipulation of the products of nature according to nature's laws. Like Diderot, they wished to reform human institutions to bring them into greater harmony with the laws of nature. And like Diderot, they believed that this required a release of human inventiveness and enterprise from arbitrary laws and restrictions. The economists' central doctrine was that production and exchange were governed by natural laws and that the wealth of the nation would be maximized if everyone were rendered free to produce, to buy, and to sell whatever they wished at prices determined only by the free workings of the market. The most celebrated exponents of such doctrines in France were the Physiocrats. The Physiocrats believed that only agriculture was productive of wealth, and the most important economic controversy in which they were involved was over free trade in grain. But similar views were also applied to industry and to the mechanical arts, and the conclusion was always the same: Corporations restricted the free operation of the market and should therefore be abolished.[24]

CORPORATIONS ATTACKED - AND DEFENDED

It was the Physiocrats who launched the most important prerevolutionary challenge to trade corporations. Turgot, who was appointed contrôleur général by Louis XVI in 1774, was a leading exponent of Physiocratic ideas and had also written several articles for Diderot's *Encyclopédie.* That such a man could have been chosen to head the king's government shows how seriously the Philosophes' views were taken in the councils of power.[25] Turgot's policies were genuinely radical. He instituted a whole series of reforms intended to break down restrictions on the national economy, including freedom of the grain trade, assorted tax reforms, abolition of the *corvée* (compulsory labor service for the building and maintenance of roads), and suppression of the trade corporations. These reforms all met with resistance – from Turgot's enemies at court; from the Parlement of Paris, the high court of the monarchy, which remonstrated with the king rather than simply registering the reform edicts; and, in the case of the edict freeing the grain trade, from ordinary peasants and townspeople, who staged a series of grain riots when prices rose beyond the accustomed level.[26] By the summer of 1776 the king had dismissed Turgot, and all his reform schemes had been repealed. Because they attacked the privileges of corporations and the nobility, Turgot's reforms were seen as attacks on the very constitution of the French monarchy. They therefore could not be sustained, at least not in the political climate of 1776.

Turgot's edict suppressing the corporations summarizes neatly the grievances that Enlightenment opinion charged against the corporations – and in doing so it states many of the arguments that lay behind their final suppression in the French Revolution. The purpose of Turgot's edicts was to assure "to commerce and industry the entire liberty and the full competition which they ought to enjoy."[27] In the prologue to the edict, Turgot detailed the multitude of ways that trade corporations denied this liberty: by restricting the practice of a trade to those who had obtained masterships; by limiting entry into masterships by means of long apprenticeships, masterpieces, and impossibly high entrance fees for all but sons of masters; by excluding goods made outside the city; by arbitrarily limiting the techniques to be employed in fabrication; by subjecting masters to frivolous charges for ceremonies, banquets, assemblies, and lawsuits; by restricting entrepreneurs in their choice of workers. The results of these restrictions on the liberty of commerce and industry were nefarious: higher prices to consumers, indigence for those deprived of their natural right to live by their labor, and a retardation of the progress of the arts because of difficulties placed in the path of innovators.[28]

For these reasons, the edict declared:

> It will be free to all persons, of whatever quality and condition they may be . . . to embrace and to exercise throughout our kingdom . . . whatever species of commerce and whatever profession of arts and crafts they may wish. . . ; to this effect we . . . extinguish and suppress all corps et communautés of merchants and artisans, as well as maîtrises and jurandes; abrogate all privileges, statutes and regulations given to the said corps et communautés, so that none of our subjects can be troubled in the exercise of his commerce or his profession, for any cause or under any pretext whatsoever.[29]

The suppression of corporations announced in this edict was thorough and radical. Not only were all the rights, privileges, and statutes of corporations abolished, but persons exercising the same trade were henceforth forbidden to congregate or associate for any purpose.

> We forbid likewise to all masters, journeymen, workers and apprentices of the said corps et communautés, to form any association or assembly among themselves, under any pretext whatsoever; in consequence, we . . . extinguish and suppress all confraternities that may have been established, whether by masters of the corps et communautés or by journeymen and workers in the arts and crafts.[30]

Henceforth, any person wishing to exercise a given profession would be required simply to declare his intention to the local police and to sign a document indicating his name, residence, and the nature of the profession he wished to exercise.

Before this edict could become law it had to be presented to the Parlement of Paris for registration. The Parlement – the highest court of the kingdom, composed of magistrates of noble rank – objected to the edict in the strongest terms and delivered a blistering remonstrance to the king before submitting to his will and registering the edict as a valid law of the realm. The Parlement's defense is interesting on two counts. First, it was a particularly cogent statement of the traditional justification for corporations, a statement that linked corporations firmly to the entire corporate monarchical order. But second, although the Parlement contradicted Turgot on almost every point, its defense of the traditional order was itself cast to a significant extent in Enlightenment terminology. The clash between Turgot and the Parlement thus pitted a radical Philosophe who wished to destroy the corporate order – but who was acting on behalf of the king – against self-proclaimed defenders of the traditional monarchy who opposed the will of the king in language laced with Enlightenment terms. Nothing could exemplify more perfectly the complex political and intellectual crisis of the French monarchy in the last years of the old regime or serve as a better introduction to the central issues of the Revolution.[31]

One key Enlightenment term that the Parlement employed was "liberty." It agreed with Turgot that liberty is "the life and prime mover of commerce,"[32] but it immediately challenged his definition. Liberty, it protested,

> must not be understood as an unlimited liberty that knows no other law than caprice and admits no rules but those that it makes itself. This kind of liberty is nothing more than a veritable independence which would soon be transformed into license, opening the door to every abuse. Liberty, this source of wealth, would then become a source of destruction, a cause of disorders, an occasion for fraud and plunder, and the inevitable result would be the total annihilation of the arts and of artisans, of confidence and of commerce . . .[33]

> In a well-ordered State, there is no liberty, there can be no liberty other than that which exists under the authority of law. The salutary fetters which it imposes are not in the least an obstacle to the usage one can make of it; they are a provision against all the abuses that independence brings in its wake.[34]

This was a restatement of traditional old-regime conceptions that understood liberty not as an absolute and abstract right but as contingent on the maintenance of order and as subject to constraints imposed by legitimate authority.[35] Although the Parlement cast itself as the defender of public liberty, its arguments against Turgot were based on a fundamentally different conception of the nature of things. The Parlement espoused the traditional Christian view that the human world was an arena of sin and disorder. Without the discipline imposed by detailed legal regulation and continual surveillance, humans would soon fall prey to their passions and society would be thrown into criminal disarray. And if this was true of all humans in general, it was all the more true of that base class of humans who engaged in the mechanical arts, "these beings born for the trouble of societies, whose passions, less tamed by education, join to the brute energy of nature that activity which they acquire in the midst of the license of cities."[36] Abolition of the corporations and their regulations would not, as Turgot believed, liberate a natural order inherent in human society but hitherto suppressed by mistaken customs and laws; rather, it would liberate unruly passions capable of destroying all social order.

Far from improving the arts, the license set loose by Turgot's decree would bring about their degradation and thereby cause a "total subversion of all areas of commerce."[37] The "annoyances, fetters and prohibitions" denounced by Turgot were in fact the sources of "the glory, the soundness and the immensity of the commerce of France." According to the Parlement,

Our merchandise has always won out in foreign markets ... [It] is sought after all over Europe for its taste, its beauty, its finesse, its solidity, the correctness of its design, the perfection of its execution, the quality of its raw materials ... Our arts, brought to the highest degree of perfection, enrich your capital, of which the entire world has become the tributary.[38]

But the "undefined liberty" introduced by Turgot's decree "will soon cause this perfection to vanish."[39]

Without a preparatory noviciate, without a prior test, without need of a chef d'oeuvre, the artisan will only be determined in his choice by an often ill-considered interest or by a presumption that will mislead him into enterprises that are beyond his abilities ... in deceiving himself, he will deceive others.[40]

Without corporations to guide and discipline them, artisans would not only cease to be properly trained in their crafts, they would also cease to be honest.

Each manufacturer, each artist, each worker will regard himself as an isolated being, depending on himself alone and free to indulge in all the flights of an often disordered imagination. All subordination will be destroyed, there will be no more weights and measures, thirst for gain will dominate all the workshops, and since honesty is not always the surest way to fortune, the entire public, natives and foreigners alike, will be the constant dupes of artful methods secretly prepared to blind and seduce them.[41]

False gold will be mixed with true; cloth will have neither the width nor the quality required, without inspectors who verify and surveillants who examine.[42]

Liberty in the style of Turgot, in other words, would turn men into isolated beings and remove them from the ordered communities that were the only guarantees of true liberty and morality. As a result of the suppression of corporations, discipline in general, both technical and moral, would be destroyed, and the now flourishing commerce and industry of France would be reduced to a state of indigence.

But because the corporations were a part of the constitution of the kingdom, the disorders attendant on their suppression would extend far beyond matters of production and exchange. To begin with, corporations were a means of surveillance and control of the urban population; the corporation disciplined and watched its members and was therefore an important auxiliary to the royal or municipal authorities.

In vain would one wish to substitute the bonds of a new police ... One maintains surveillance fruitfully only when one commands. What will

become of the authority of masters when their workers, always independent, always free to pick up and go, will continually be able to escape from their houses? . . . Who will follow them in the details of their
domestic life, who will answer for them to the police?[43]

If masters are to be stripped of their authority, workers will be subject only
to the discipline of municipal or royal police officials. But this would be a
task far beyond the abilities of the police as presently constituted. Therefore, to replace the corporations would require an entirely new system of
police that would be at once costly, harsh, and inefficient. By contrast:

> What governance could be milder than that of the jurandes? Workers
> were inspected by their masters, the masters by jurés they had chosen; a
> correspondence of interests united them to one another, harmony
> reigned in the interior of the community.[44]

The real result of Turgot's reform would not be liberty but an increase in
despotism.

Corporations were not only the best guarantee of true liberty; they were
also in accord with nature itself.

> The existence of corporations has been sought in their origins, when it
> should be sought in nature. From the first of all, which are Empires,
> down to the last, which are families, men are everywhere united to
> protect themselves, always commanded by superiors or watched over
> by parents. These corporations correspond to the general calm by their
> interior calm. It is a chain of which all the links are joined to the first
> chain, to the authority of the Throne, and which it is dangerous to
> break.[45]

Hierarchy, in other words, was the natural condition of human life, and only
by recognizing this natural, hierarchical order could calm and harmony be
maintained. Moreover, the maintenance of order among the gens de métier
could not be separated from the maintenance of order in the state as a
whole. The entire kingdom was constituted of corporations, and kingdoms
– that is, empires – were themselves the highest type of corporation. An
assault on the principle that informed jurandes and maîtrises was therefore
an attack on the very principle of the monarchy, and the metaphor of the
chain implies that it could be broken at its weakest link.

> Your subjects, Sire, are divided into as many different bodies as there
> are different estates in the Kingdom. The Clergy, the Nobility, the sov-
> ereign courts, the lower tribunals, the officers attached to these tribu-
> nals, the universities, the academies, the financial companies, the com-
> mercial companies; in every part of the state there exist bodies which
> can be regarded as links in a great chain, the first link of which is in the
> hands of Your Majesty as head and sovereign administrator of all that
> constitutes the body of the nation.

76

The very idea of destroying this precious chain should be appalling. The communities of merchants and artisans form a part of this insepara-ble whole which contributes to the good order of the entire realm.[46]

What was at issue between Turgot and the Parlement was, then, not simply the question of how best to organize the mechanical arts. The question of trade corporations was but one aspect of the fundamental issue that divided them: the proper constitution of the state. For the Parlement, the state was composed of a hierarchy of privileged corporate bodies, and the good order of the state required that corporations and their privileges be maintained. For Turgot, the state was composed of free and independent individual citizens, and corporate privileges of any kind were fetters on their natural right to liberty. The gap between them was unbridgeable.

In 1776 the issue was decided in favor of traditional views. Although the Parlement had no choice but to register the king's edicts, its opposition, together with the machinations of Turgot's enemies at court, soon suc-ceeded in bringing him down. His successor quickly withdrew Turgot's re-form schemes, and the corporations were restored to life. The restored corporations, however, were not the same as those that had been abolished by Turgot's edict. New legislation, which was issued between 1776 and 1780, reduced entrance fees, reduced the number of corporations by grouping similar professions together, allowed masters to cumulate more than one profession if they obtained permission from the authorities, simpli-fied corporate administration, and limited lawsuits between corporations.[47] It was, thus, a reformed set of corporations that drew up cahiers de doléances and participated as constituent bodies in the elections to the Es-tates General in 1789. But the elections to the Estates General were to be the last public act undertaken by corporations. Like all the other privileged bodies of the monarchy, they were annihilated in the ensuing revolution.

1789: THE ASSAULT ON PRIVILEGE

In 1786 the French public learned that the state was in danger of imminent bankruptcy. This fiscal crisis touched off a constitutional crisis of the first order and immediately brought the issue of privilege to the fore.[48] Bank-ruptcy could not be avoided without drastic financial reforms, and any meaningful reform would necessarily entail a revocation of the privileges of the Clergy and the Nobility – the First and Second Estates, as they were called – who were traditionally exempt from taxation. Blocked in its efforts to unilaterally impose taxes equally on all three estates, the royal govern-ment finally had to call the Estates General, which alone, according to ven-erable constitutional doctrine, had the power to consent to new taxation. The Estates also had the right to demand redress of grievances before vot-ing any new taxes. This resort to the traditional constitution marked a radical departure from the recent practices of the French monarchy. The Estates had not been called since 1614, and the crown had in the interim imposed all sorts of new taxes by royal fiat – on pretexts of all kinds. The calling of the Estates implied that royal absolutism had reached its limit and that the crown would henceforth have to share power in some way with representatives of the nation.

The relationship of the Estates General to the people and to the crown was uncertain and hotly contested in 1788 and 1789. Representative government held an important place in the political theory of the Enlightenment, and the calling of the Estates was widely interpreted as a recognition of the people's natural right to participate in the formation of laws. Yet the Estates General originated in a purely corporate conception of representation; it was composed of three assemblies, each representing one of the estates or orders of the realm, and according to traditional procedures each order had an equal number of representatives who deliberated and voted as three separate bodies. These contrasting interpretations came to a head in a debate over the composition and procedures of the Estates. The conservative party insisted on a strict adherence to precedent, whereas the "patriots" demanded a "doubling of the Third" – that is, giving the Third Estate twice as many representatives as each of the privileged orders – and voting by head rather than by order, so that the enlarged Third Estate would not be automatically outvoted by the First and Second Estates. The patriots, in other words, wished to turn the Estates General into a single assembly representing all the people of the kingdom – and to give the Third Estate the preponderance of representation.

The calling of the Estates General gave rise to feverish political discussions and to a deluge of pamphlets on all sides. By far the most influential pamphlet was *What Is the Third Estate?* by the Abbé Sieyès.[49] Sieyès was a canon of the Cathedral of Chartres and therefore a member of the First Estate. His pamphlet, however, was an unequivocal attack on privilege. Its effect was at once electric and formative. It focused public attention on the problem of privilege, and at the same time it provided the deputies of the Third Estate with a concrete revolutionary program, which they followed almost to the letter during the summer of 1789. *What Is the Third Estate?* is the best statement not only of the political position of the patriot party in the first months of the Revolution but of the philosophical assumptions that underlay its political actions. And while it said nothing about the problem of corporations, both its exaltation of useful labor and its unflinching assault on privilege presaged the National Assembly's later actions against the corporations.

Sieyès's pamphlet began with three questions and answers that summarized its argument.

The abolition of privilege

1. What is the Third Estate? *Everything.*
2. What has it been until now in the political order? *Nothing.*
3. What does it ask? *To be Something.*[50]

The Third Estate was everything in the sense that it was "a complete nation," without the need of the first two estates. "What does a nation need to survive and prosper?" Sieyès asks. *"Private* labors [*travaux*] and *public* services." And both of these are – or should be – performed by the Third Estate.

Private labors can all be comprised within four classes:

1. Since land and water provide the basic materials for human needs, the first class, in logical order, includes all the families connected with work on the land.

2. Between the initial sale of materials and their consumption or use, a new labor-force [*main d'oeuvre*], more or less numerous, adds to these materials a second more or less compound value. In this way human industry manages to improve the gifts of nature and the value of the raw material may be multiplied twice, or ten-fold or a hundred-fold. Such are the labors of the second class.

3. Between production and consumption, as also between the various stages of production, a variety of intermediary agents intervene, as useful to producers as to consumers; these are the merchants and the shopkeepers . . . This type of utility characterizes the third class.

4. Besides these three classes of useful and industrious citizens who deal with objects fit to be consumed or used, society also requires a vast number of particular labors and services *directly* useful or pleasant to the *person.* This fourth class extends from the most distinguished liberal and scientific professions to the least esteemed of domestic services.[51]

Such, argues Sieyès, "are the labors that support society." And all of them were performed by the Third Estate.

As to public service, which Sieyès divided into the army, the law, the church, and the administration, "nineteen-twentieths" of it was also performed by the Third Estate. But in public services "the lucrative and honorific posts are filled by members of the privileged order."[52] This was not because they were more able but because they had succeeded in excluding members of the Third Estate – "a social crime . . . a veritable act of war against the Third Estate."[53] The results of this were doubly harmful. Not only was it unjust to the Third Estate, but it resulted in badly performed public services.

Do we not understand the consequences of monopoly? While discouraging those it excludes, does it not destroy the skill of those it favors? Are we unaware that any work from which free competition is excluded will be performed less well and more expensively?[54]

Thus, he concludes, were it not for the privileged orders,

the higher posts would be infinitely better filled . . . They ought to be the natural prize and reward of recognized ability and service . . . If the privileged have succeeded in usurping all well-paid and honorific posts, this is both a hateful inequity towards the generality of citizens and an act of treason to the commonwealth.[55]

To summarize, all of the private activities that uphold society were already being performed by the Third Estate, and those few public services that they did not perform would be performed infinitely better if they did. Thus it follows that the Third Estate is "everything," "a complete nation."

> Who would then dare to say that the Third Estate does not include everything necessary to the formation of a complete nation? It is like a strong and robust man with one arm still chained. If the privileged class were dispensed with, the nation would not be anything less than it is, but rather something more. Thus, what is the Third Estate? Everything, but a hobbled and oppressed everything. What would it be without the privileged classes? Everything – but a free and flourishing everything. Nothing can function without the Third Estate; everything would work infinitely better without the others.[56]

Thus, in the very first section of his pamphlet, Sieyès reached an extremely radical conclusion. But no less interesting than this radical conclusion are the implicit premises upon which it was based. In these opening paragraphs of *What Is the Third Estate?* Sieyès erected an entire alternative definition of the political order in which privileges had no part. Sieyès's discussion of the various categories of private activity and public service made it clear, without saying so explicitly, that a nation was not to be thought of as a hierarchical community bound by common reverence for and subjection to the king nor to the king's laws nor to the ancient constitution of the realm. Rather, the nation was constituted by useful work – either private or public – and by the citizens who performed that work. And in this conception of the nation as a collection of busy producers, Sieyès began – like Diderot in his discussion of the arts – with nature. For Sieyès, the essential activity of the nation was the transformation of natural substances into useful goods. If the nobility was harmful to the nation, it was because it took no part in this cooperative work on nature. As Sieyès put it, the nobility "is foreign to the nation because of its *idleness*."[57]

Sieyès conveyed this implicit definition of the nation by elaborating his four categories of private activities. By presenting this division of citizens at the very beginning of his pamphlet, Sieyès simultaneously established production as the central activity of the nation and replaced the traditional division of the nation into three hierarchically arranged orders by a new division into four functionally distinct but equal classes. Sieyès used the term "classes" rather than "orders" or "estates" precisely to avoid any connotation of hierarchy. "Class," in Sieyès's time, was an utterly neutral term, with overtones of disinterested scientific precision rather than of nobility and baseness or domination and subordination; it meant simply "category." However, Sieyès's categorization of citizens, like the traditional schema of the three estates, began with the ultimate source of order and proceeded outward to activities more distant from this source. Spirit was the source of order in the traditional schema: Therefore the Clergy, who were devoted to purely spiritual affairs, were the First Estate; the Nobility, who magnanimously defended the realm and served the king with their counsel and as magistrates, were the Second Estate; and the commoners, who worked with their hands for material gain, were the Third Estate. Descending down the orders, one passed from the most spiritual to the most material of concerns. In Sieyès's schema, the source of order was not spirit but nature, and the categories of citizens proceeded outward from the productions of nature to personal services. As one moves from agriculture – the first class – to industry, to commerce, and finally to services, one moves progressively farther from nature: from the direct cultivation of the products of nature, to the transformation of these products by human labor, to the exchange of the goods produced by labor, and finally to the services, which do not entail physical products at all. But Sieyès's classes, though increasingly remote from the ultimate source of order, did not differ in dignity. This he made clear in the last sentence of the paragraph: The fourth and last class "extends from the most distinguished liberal and scientific professions to the least esteemed domestic services." There were indeed differences in the dignity of different occupations, but these differences were unrelated to the division of the population into functional classes. Moreover, Sieyès made it clear that all useful work, whether menial or distinguished, was a contribution to the well-being of the nation. Only *idleness* was to be despised.

Thus, at the very outset of his pamphlet, Sieyès undermined both the traditional concept of the nation and the traditional division of the nation into three estates. By presenting his own division of the nation into four functionally distinct classes, based on the type of productive work they performed and ordered scientifically by their distance from the raw products of nature, Sieyès demonstrated the falsity of the standard division of the nation into three estates and shifted the definition of the nation from a hierarchically ordered spiritual community united in the person of the king to a collection of producers united by their common work on nature.

Sieyès consolidated this radical shift in the terms of political discourse in his discussion of public service, the area of national life in which the privileged orders had always claimed to perform their distinctive services to the nation. According to traditional ideas, the upper levels of public service were properly the sphere of the nobility, whose special function in life was to serve the king and protect the people and whose disdain of base material interests suited them particularly for the direction of public affairs. Sieyès attacked this traditional notion but, once again, not by a direct frontal assault. Rather, he cast his entire discussion of public service in terms that contradicted the traditional conception of public service and replaced it with a new one. Sieyès implicitly denied that public service was different in kind from private productive activity by applying to it terms normally applied to private production. Reserving the higher posts in public service to nobles, Sieyès tells us, is a case of monopoly, no different in kind from a monopoly in the production of shoes or the sale of grain. Because the result is always the same – bad work and high prices – public service will not be done well unless it is open to free competition. By thus arguing that public service must be governed by the same natural laws that govern all other forms of productive activity, Sieyès, in effect, reduced public service from the status of a special and extraordinary category to a subtype of his fourth class of productive activity, the services. And by doing so he removed the nobles' last claim of utility to the nation. In Sieyès's discourse, their pursuit of high office became not a magnanimous service but a social crime.

The nobility, then, was "a burden for the nation" and could "only weaken and injure it." But Sieyès went beyond this in his condemnation of the nobility and declared that "the nobility is not part of our society at all."[58] This was true in part because the nobility made no contribution to society's useful work. But it was also true in a political sense.

> What is a nation? A body of associates living under *common* laws and represented by the same legislature, etc.
>
> Is it not obvious that the nobility possesses privileges and exemptions which it dares to call its rights and which are separate from the rights of the great body of citizens? Because of this, it does not belong to the common order, nor is it subjected to the common laws. Thus its private rights make it a people apart in the great nation.[59]

Here Sieyès supplemented his original implicit definition of the nation as a body of producers working together on nature by an explicit political definition of the nation as "a body of associates living under common laws." Because the Third Estate was at once the productive community and the community subject to common laws, the two definitions corresponded perfectly. And by both of these definitions the nobility was foreign to the nation. It lived under private rights or laws (privilèges) rather than under the common laws, and it was precisely these private rights or privileges that exempted the nobility from labor and thereby kept it from working beside ordinary citizens for the common good. Thus the nobility's foreignness in the economic sense was inseparable from its foreignness in the political sense. Only if they renounced their privileges and accepted the law common to all Frenchmen could they become true and useful citizens of the nation. But because they had long preferred their "odious privileges"[60] to liberty, such a renunciation would be difficult to effect. "How easy it would be to get along without the privileged classes! How difficult it will be to convert them into citizens!"[61] And until they were willing to renounce their privileges, the Third Estate would have no choice but to regard the privileged orders as foreigners and enemies: By insisting on the maintenance of their privileges, the privileged orders made themselves "no less enemies of the common order than are the English or the French in times of war."[62]

Having thus redefined the privileged orders as outlaws and enemies of the nation, Sieyès proceeded to some practical conclusions. Judged by the true principles he had set forth, the Third Estate had been extremely modest in its demands. Rather than demanding to be recognized as the entire nation, it had only asked for parity – that is, a doubling of the Third and the counting of votes by head rather than by order. Although he chided the Third Estate for the "timid insufficiency"[63] of these demands, he nevertheless argued for them as preliminary steps in the right direction. Although he supported the current demands of the Third Estate, he also went on to point out, in two concluding chapters, "What Ought to Have Been Done" and "What Remains to Be Done." What ought to have been done was not calling the Estates General but convoking an "extraordinary representative assembly . . . formed without regard to the distinction of social orders,"[64] which could then legislate changes in the constitution of the nation, an assembly that, because it would have been based on true principles, would have been capable of rendering binding constitutional decisions. But because the Estates General had now been called, the Third Estate was faced with a different problem. It had to consider how to make use of the Estates General without recognizing it as competent to decide on constitutional questions – a recognition that would make the distinctions between orders appear legitimate. This was "what remains to be done," and here Sieyès suggested two possible courses of action. One would be for the Third Estate to refuse to constitute itself as the Third Estate of an illegitimate assembly and simply use its meetings as a forum to appeal to the nation for the convocation of an extraordinary constitutional assembly formed without division of orders. The other course, which Sieyès characterized as more "abrupt,"[65] would be for the deputies of the Third Estate to meet separately from the First and Second Estates, to declare itself the National Assembly, and to proceed to deliberate and vote on the affairs of the entire nation. It was this latter course that the deputies of the Third Estate actually adopted in the summer of 1789.

It is hardly an exaggeration to say that *What Is the Third Estate?* set forth and justified the program of the Revolution that was carried out by the patriot party during the summer of 1789. This was due in part to the direct influence of the pamphlet and in part to Sieyès's personal influence in the meeting of the Third Estate as a deputy elected from Paris. At the same time, it could also be argued that events followed the scenario laid down in Sieyès's pamphlet because he had understood the inherent logic of the situation with unusual clarity. But the pamphlet, whether viewed as a causal agent or as merely a register of the logic of events, charted the direction of the first phase of the Revolution with uncanny accuracy. It presented a vision of the nation as a body of citizens living together under common laws and working together to transform the productions of nature into useful goods. It dissolved the idea of the three estates as the constituent units of the nation. And it defined the privileged orders as enemies to be either transformed into common citizens or expelled from the national soil. Thus it propelled the Revolution – or perhaps recorded the propulsion of the Revolution – in the direction of an all-out attack on privilege. In the first instance, this meant an attack on the political privileges of the Nobility and the Clergy, on their right to constitute separate orders in the representative assembly of the nation. But the logic of the attack implied the destruction of all privileges, not only those of the Nobility and the Clergy, but those of cities, provinces, bodies of magistrates, chartered companies, and trade corporations as well. For only if all privileges were annihilated could the nation become a body of associates living together under common laws and working together in productive harmony for the common good. Thus Sieyès's pamphlet, in denying the political privileges of the Nobility and the Clergy, also set forth the logic that led to the abolition of corporations.

It was on the night of August 4, 1789, that Sieyès's program of annihilating privilege was finally carried out. By then the representatives of the Third Estate had solemnly proclaimed themselves the National Assembly and, joined by some of the more advanced representatives of the First and Second Estates, had begun to draw up a new constitution for the country. The king's resistance to the National Assembly had been broken by the Parisian insurrection of July 14 – the taking of the Bastille – and the sympathetic uprisings it touched off all over France. By August the Assembly's greatest problem was to restore order, especially in the countryside, where the peasants were in open revolt against their seigneurs – attacking the local châteaux, burning the manor rolls that contained records of their feudal dues and obligations, and refusing to pay rent and taxes.[66] The events of the night of August 4, which rang down the final curtain on the old regime, began as a proposal – by an important noble – that feudal dues and services be made redeemable by purchase, thereby validating, but also limiting, what the peasants had already achieved by violent means.

This proposal, however, was soon surpassed by the Assembly as a whole, as renunciations of privilege were proposed from all quarters. From the nobles' privilege of maintaining exclusive dovecotes and game warrens, to

84

property in office, to tithes, to manorial courts, to the privileges of cities and provinces, to plurality of benefices, to the First and Second Estates' exemption from taxation, one after another the varied and motley privileges of the old regime were abolished by vote of the Assembly. The Assembly also decreed that "All citizens, without distinction of birth, are to be admitted to all ecclesiastical, civil, and military positions and honors, and no useful profession shall imply a loss of honor."[67] Swept by a torrent of magnanimous emotion, the Assembly annihilated the privileges of the old regime amid raptures of enthusiasm and tears of joy. The achievement of the night of August 4 was put most aptly in the article abolishing the privileges of provinces and cities:

> A national constitution and public liberty being more advantageous to the provinces than the privileges which some of them enjoy, the sacrifice of which is necessary for the close union of all parts of the country, it is decreed that all special privileges . . . are abolished without reversion, and will be absorbed into the law common to all Frenchmen.[68]

The constitution of France was no longer to be composed of assorted and infinitely various corporate bodies – estates, orders, communities, cities, provinces – each with its own distinct "special privileges." On the night of August 4 these bodies and their privileges were sacrificed to the "close union" of the nation, which became, at last, the nation as defined by Sieyès: a body of equal, individual citizens living together under "the law common to all Frenchmen."

Having demolished the constitutional structure of the old regime on the night of August 4, the National Assembly began the long process of writing a new constitution based on natural rights of individual citizens and equality under the law. The first step was to issue a solemn Declaration of the Rights of Man and Citizen, which was passed by the Assembly on August 26 after long debates. It began by declaring that all men "are born and remain free and equal in rights" and went on to list the "natural, inalienable and sacred rights of man," which it specified as liberty – including liberty of opinion, speech, and the press – property, security, and resistance to oppression. Declaring the "aim of all political association" to be the preservation of these rights, it went on to sketch out the principles of the new constitution. Sovereignty was placed firmly in the nation, and law was to be the expression of the nation's general will. The law must be the same for all, and all citizens had the right to participate in its formation, "personally or by their representatives." Citizens must be free to do anything not forbidden by law, and law may prohibit only those actions that are injurious to society.[69] The night of August 4 and the Declaration of the Rights of Man and Citizen terminated the old regime and inaugurated the new. By taking these epochmaking steps, the National Assembly consolidated its grip on the political destinies of the nation. Of course, there were still major problems confronting the Assembly and the king. But the next year and a half was a period of relative social and political peace, and this gave the Assembly time to elaborate a new constitution for the nation. It was during the fashioning of the new constitution that corporations were finally and definitively abolished.

THE ABOLITION OF CORPORATIONS

The question of corporations had been taken up briefly on the night of August 4. A deputy from the Beaujolais proposed and obtained passage of a motion stipulating "reform of the laws relative to corporations of arts and trades" that would result in their "reduction to the terms of justice and the common interest."[70] This motion was somewhat anomalous, in that it merely called for "reform" of corporations, whereas all other privileged bodies were entirely abolished, and the reform of corporations was left out of the definitive decree that was issued, after several days of debates, on August 11. Why corporations did not figure more prominently in the actions of the fourth to the eleventh of August is something of a mystery, although it is easy to see why the Assembly may have hesitated to abolish institutions whose maintenance was almost universally requested in the cahiers de doléances of the cities. In any case, the Assembly decided, in August 1789, to defer the question. It was nevertheless clear that survival of the corporations could only be temporary: The general destruction of privilege on August 4 and the proclamation of liberty as a natural right in the Declaration of the Rights of Man and Citizen doomed the privileges of corporations no less than those of nobles, clerics, or provinces.

During the period spent in drafting the constitution, the question of corporations was placed before the committee on public contributions, which was charged with finding a new means of assessing taxes heretofore paid by corporations. The result of the committee's deliberations was the d'Allarde law, presented to the Assembly and passed after brief discussion in March 1791. D'Allarde, the rapporteur of the committee, was a disciple of the Physiocrats and an admirer of Turgot. In his presentation to the Assembly, the establishment of the new tax took precedence over the aboliton of corporations. The "patent," as the new tax was called, was to be paid annually by all small businessmen and was to be assessed according to the rental value of the businessman's premises. After establishing the need for this new tax somewhat apologetically, d'Allarde changed his tone and announced a supplementary measure, which he felt would prove more attractive to the Assembly. Because the patent would impose a burden on industry and commerce, "your committee believed that it should link the existence of this tax to a great good for industry and commerce, to the suppression of jurandes and maîtrises that your wisdom should lead you to abolish if only for the reason that they are exclusive privileges."[71] The abolition of corporations would introduce freedom of commerce, which would more than compensate for the burden imposed by the patent and bring great benefits to producers and consumers alike. D'Allarde rapidly surveyed the grievances charged against jurandes and maîtrises, essentially summarizing the prologue to Turgot's decree of 1776, and he explicitly invoked Turgot as the author of their first abolition: "He enlightened the king for a moment, and for a moment these abuses ceased to be." But because in 1776 "the times were not yet ripe for these ideas," the task of finally liberating commerce and industry from corporations had been left for the National Assembly to accomplish.[72] Hence the law establishing the patent included as Article 8: "Beginning on the coming April first, it shall be free to every citizen to engage in whatever commerce, or to exercise whatever profession, art or trade he may wish, after having provided himself with a patent and paid its price, according to the rates hereafter determined."[73] Thus, on April 1, 1791, corporations ceased to exist.

The way in which the corporations were abolished in March 1791 indicates how far things had come from the passionate summer of 1789. There was no dramatic renunciation of the corporations' privileges nor was there any dramatic attack. Rather, the abolition of corporations had become so uncontested that it was added to the d'Allarde law as a kind of legislative sweetener to counteract the bitter draft of new taxation. Nor was a word said in defense of corporations in the ensuing debates. One legislator denounced the attempt to impose the new tax, proposing that "if there are patents to be re-established, it is on those who do not work, on those who are idlers."[74] Others questioned or proposed amendments to articles dealing with the particulars of administering the new tax. But d'Allarde judged rightly; the suppression of corporations was unanimously desired. In the end the patent was accepted with minor changes, and the abolition of corporations was enacted without dissent.

There seem to have been no public protests from masters' corporations against the passage of the d'Allarde law. Whether this was because the masters themselves now opposed the retention of privileges, or simply because they could see the handwriting on the wall, is impossible to say. In any case, they disbanded quietly. But journeymen's corporations showed no such readiness to disband. Of course, the d'Allarde law could only abolish those corporations that had an existence in law; it had no effect on corporations whose existence was purely extralegal. Journeymen's brotherhoods – particularly the Parisian compagnonnage – had remained very active in 1790 and 1791. Indeed, as the masters' corporations were weakened and finally disbanded and as the police authorities became less repressive of popular effervescence, compagnonnage found itself in a very favorable position. As a result, there were several attempts to obtain wage guarantees or other concessions from the masters.[75] In May 1791 the carpenter compagnons presented the master carpenters with a request that they join in drafting regulations to govern their trade. When the masters refused – and by May their corporation had in any case ceased to exist – the workers wrote a regulation of their own and attempted to impose it on the masters. This led the master carpenters to petition the National Assembly in June, warning it of a "general coalition of 80,000 workers in the capital."[76] The result of this petition was the Le Chapelier law, which forbade workers to form "coalitions" under penalty of fines and imprisonment and completed the abolition of corporations that was begun in the d'Allarde law.

If the abolition of corporations in the d'Allarde law was a foregone conclusion and was therefore treated routinely by the Assembly, the Le Chapelier law raised the liveliest emotions. It is a mark of the Assembly's concern that the law was drawn up not by the relatively obscure d'Allarde but by Le Chapelier, one of the most important men in the National Assembly. A member of the committee on the constitution, he had presided over the Assembly on the night of August 4 and had coauthored the famous tennis-court oath of June 20, 1789. Le Chapelier presented the "coalition" of carpenters as "a contravention of the constitutional principles that suppress the corporations, a contravention which gives birth to great danger to public order."[77] The workers' actions, in Le Chapelier's eyes and in those of the Assembly, were attempts to "re-create the abolished corporations."[78] Even associations formed for the ostensible purpose of "procuring aid to workers of the same profession who are sick or out of work" must not be allowed, because they

> tend to bring about the rebirth of corporations; they require frequent meetings of individuals of the same profession, the naming of syndics and other officers, the formation of regulations, the exclusion of those who do not submit themselves to these regulations. It is thus that privileges, masterships, etc. will be reborn.[79]

In spite of the seeming good intentions that animated such associations, they posed the most serious threat to public order because they challenged the fundamental principles of the constitution.

> It must without doubt be permitted to all citizens to assemble; but it must not be permitted to citizens of certain professions to assemble for their supposed common interests. There are no longer corporations in the State; there is no longer anything but the particular interest of each individual, and the general interest. It is permitted to no one to inspire an intermediary interest in citizens, to separate them from the public interest [*la chose publique*] by a spirit of corporation.[80]

The abolition of privileges, as this passage makes clear, implied more than the destruction of the many and vexatious particular rights and exemptions previously held by corporations – or by any of the other bodies that had constituted the nation under the old regime. It implied not only the reduction of all citizens to an equal submission to the law common to all Frenchmen but the annihilation of any sense of common interest intermediate between the individual and the nation. Loyalties to provinces, estates, orders, communities, corporations, all were to vanish before the interests of individual citizens and the supreme loyalty of every citizen to the nation. Thus, to prevent the rebirth of a counterrevolutionary "spirit of corporation," even the liberty of assembly had to be denied to those who claimed to be assembling "for their supposed common interests." In a nation of free individuals, wages and working conditions must be individually contracted: "We must then return to the principle, that daily wages [*la journée*] must be fixed for each worker by freely contracted agreements [*conventions libres*] between individual and individual; thereafter each worker must maintain the agreement he has made with the person who employs him."[81] Wages in a free nation ought indeed to be higher than they are at present, "so that those who receive them may be placed out of that absolute dependence which produces deprivation of goods of the first necessity, and is nearly a condition of slavery."[82] But increases in wages must not be sought by coalitions that revive the spirit of corporation.

The Le Chapelier law was passed enthusiastically after only the most cursory discussion. It began: "The annihilation of all sorts of corporations of citizens of the same trade or profession, being one of the fundamental bases of the French constitution, it is forbidden to re-establish them in fact, under any pretext or under any form whatsoever."[83] Citizens of the same trade or profession were therefore forbidden

> when they find themselves together, to name for themselves a president or a secretary-syndic, to maintain registers, to form regulations on their supposed common interests . . . If, against the principles of liberty and of the constitution, citizens attached to the same professions, arts and trades, should make deliberations, should make agreements among themselves tending to refuse in concert, or to accord only at a determined price the aid of their industry or of their labors, the said deliberations and agreements . . . are declared unconstitutional and an assault against liberty and against the declaration of the rights of man, and of null effect.[84]

Citizens found guilty of these offenses would have their rights as citizens suspended for one year and would have to pay stiff fines. Thus the National Assembly had found that its suppression of the privileges of corporations in the d'Allarde law was an insufficient guarantee of the liberty of industry so necessary to its conception of a free nation and was forced explicitly to forbid citizens of the same profession to act together on the common interests of their profession. Citizens, in the view of the Assembly, not only had to be liberated from the legal shackles of corporate privilege. They also had to be constrained to shun "the spirit of corporation," to be forced to act as free individual citizens.

The Le Chapelier law has acquired a very bad reputation among supporters of the labor movement in nineteenth- and twentieth-century France. For although its formal prohibitions and penalties applied equally to employers and workers, in practice it was used almost exclusively against workers. In the nineteenth century it became one of the key weapons in an extensive legal arsenal directed against workers and their "coalitions." This nineteenth-century practice has deeply colored historians' interpretations of the law. Thus Philippe-Joseph Buchez, a socialist theorist and the coauthor of the massive and meticulous *Histoire parlementaire de la Révolution française*, commented on the law as follows in 1834:

> In the session of the 14th [June 1791], the question of coalitions was carried almost without discussion. We shall see according to what singular doctrines a law still in vigor was decreed. What proves, finally, how much the true foundations of revolution were hidden at that time from the eyes of the most sincere patriots, is that not one of them spoke up on this occasion.[85]

More recent historians, although no more favorable to the law, have seen its passage as a result not of blindness but of the purposeful cunning of the revolutionary bourgeoisie. Thus Lefebvre comments:

> The proletariat was given little attention except for the Le Chapelier law ..., which confirmed proscription of journeymen's associations and strikes. The Constituent thereby denied workers the means to protect their wages at the same time that it refused to control commodity prices ... Wage earners ... drew no benefit from the Revolution.[86]

And Michel Vovelle concludes: "In the conflict of two liberties, the liberty of association against the liberty of labor, the arbitration of the Constituent Assembly caused that which was more favorable to the bourgeoisie to prevail ... In the end, 'laissez-faire, laissez-passer' triumphed."[87]

Lefebvre's and Vovelle's assessments are certainly correct. The Le Chapelier law did indeed proscribe strikes and it was an important triumph of the principles of "laissez-faire, laissez-passez." In the long run, these were probably its most important effects. But such assessments, although they do justice to the long-run effects of the law, do not capture the dominant motives for its passage. There is no doubt that the intent of the law was repressive. By June 1791, Le Chapelier had become something of a specialist in legislation to enforce "the respect due to the law,"[88] and the law of June 14 was very much in this mold. But to judge from Le Chapelier's own speech and from the short discussion that followed, the Assembly's intention was not to repress labor but to repress the counterrevolutionary "spirit of corporation" wherever it showed itself. Le Chapelier reproached the workers not for demanding higher wages – indeed he argued against some opposition that they deserved higher wages – but for willfully and perversely denying their dignity as citizens by attempting to reconstitute corporations, for voluntarily contravening natural law and the rights of man and citizen. Had the Le Chapelier law been seen as a way of protecting the rich against the poor or the propertied against the propertyless, it would have met with strenuous, if not necessarily successful, opposition by one of the Assembly's self-appointed defenders of the poor – as when Robespierre's interventions succeeded in loosening the harshness of the Assembly's decree on "respect due to the law" in February 1791, or when Robespierre and Pétion intervened to protect the right of poor citizens to present petitions to the Assembly on May 9, 1791.[89] The Le Chapelier law was passed without opposition because it seemed evident to the entire National Assembly that the reconstitution of corporations in any form was a fundamental threat to the nation and its free constitution. Whatever the long-run effects of the Le Chapelier law, the Assembly's purpose in passing it was not to protect the rights of property against the claims of labor but to protect the Revolution against the counterrevolutionary "spirit of corporation."

It was, thus, only in the Le Chapelier law that the significance of the abolition of corporations was finally and fully spelled out. Skipped over on the night of August 4, made illegitimate in principle by the Declaration of the Rights of Man and Citizen, dismantled legally as an adjunct to establishing a new tax in the d'Allarde law, corporations were finally attacked head-on and unambiguously in the Le Chapelier law. The Le Chapelier law made it clear that the existence of corporations in any form, with or without legal privileges, was in profound contradiction to the fundamental principles of the new, regenerated state. No intermediary body could stand between the individual – now armed with his natural rights – and the nation – now the repository and guarantor of natural rights and the sole arena for the exercise of public will. Corporations, by inspiring an intermediary interest, by giving rise to a corporate spirit that stood between and perverted relations between the individual and the nation, were inherently counterrevolutionary. Thus, when the final draft of the French constitution was approved in 1791, it began by explicitly abolishing "irrevocably the institutions that have injured liberty and the equality of rights." And in the honor roll of iniquity that followed, corporations were listed side by side with nobility, peerage, hereditary distinctions, orders of chivalry, the sale and inheritance of public office, religious vows, and the privileges of provinces and cities as unconstitutional and "contrary to natural rights." Corporations had been an integral part of the old regime. As such, they were incompatible with the new.

5 From gens de métier to sans-culottes

THE GENS DE METIER OF PARIS, both masters and journeymen, were active in the Revolution from the start. They constituted the numerical majority of the Parisian *menu peuple* (little people or populace), and they participated in large numbers in all of the great popular movements of the Revolution. According to George Rudé's figures, for example, workers and masters in the arts and trades of Paris made up some 75 to 80 percent of those who took part in capturing the Bastille.[1] They continued to play a central role in the Parisian revolution, participating prominently in the insurrections that toppled the monarchy in 1792 and purged moderates from the Legislative Convention in 1793. Moreover, it was workers and masters in the Parisian trades – shoemakers and tailors, locksmiths and stonecutters, hatters and typographers, jewelers and wheelwrights, brewers and pastrycooks – who made up the mass of the sans-culotte movement of 1792 to 1794 and gave the Committee of Public Safety the popular backing it needed to carry through its resolute and merciless policies when the Revolution was most in danger.[2] The victory of the Revolution over the leagued monarchs of Europe and over the internal rebellions of the Federalists and the Vendée was in no small part due to the limitless energy and the fanatical patriotism of the Parisian sans-culottes.

The patriotism of the gens de métier did not mean that they had abandoned their corporations – at least not in the beginning. During the first two years of the Revolution, many eminently revolutionary workers and masters felt that corporate loyalties of one sort or another were perfectly compatible with the new revolutionary ideology and state. It was only with the passage of the d'Allarde and Le Chapelier laws and the rise of the sans-culotte movement in 1791 and 1792 that masters and journeymen abandoned corporate loyalties and embraced the ideal of a "one and indivisible Republic" – an ideal that precluded loyalty to any body intermediate between the individual and the republic. Yet even when they adopted an ideology that opposed all forms of corporation, Parisian masters and journeymen could not entirely escape the influence of their corporate past. The moral world of the sans-culottes still contained, although in revolutionized forms, some characteristic features of the corporate ethos.

REVOLUTIONARY CORPORATIONS

The combination of revolutionary sentiment and support for corporations can be seen in many of the cahiers de doléances of the corporations. As already noted, the cahiers were virtually unanimous in requesting that corporations be maintained. Occasionally support for corporations was joined to support for the entire hierarchical structure of the state, as in the cahier of the porcelain makers, bottle makers, glassblowers, and stained-glass makers of Rouen, which concluded:

> Finally, let the people . . . respect the privileges attached to rank and to dignities, which are the ornament and the security of the throne; let them not attempt to limit the munificence of the throne . . . ; above all, let His Majesty be immediately and unanimously begged not to suffer even the slightest infringement of his sovereignty.[3]

But words of this sort were extremely rare. Far more representative was the cahier of the restaurant keepers and pastrycooks of Bourges, whose demands for improvements in their statutes were combined with the standard set of radical political demands of the spring of 1789: doubling of the Third Estate and voting by head; suppression of the privileges of the Clergy and the Nobility in matters of taxation; commuting of feudal dues; abolition of the salt tax and other oppressive taxation.[4] Like most gens de métier in 1789, they favored the retention of corporations, but they also favored a sweeping reform of the state.

Even the most radical of the cahiers, those that demanded the suppression of all kinds of privileges, did not favor the abolition of corporations. The stocking merchants and manufacturers of Rouen, for example, wrote an unusually long and sophisticated cahier, including not only the typical demands of the patriot party but proposals for reform of criminal justice, liberty of the press, the "natural right" to bear arms, equal access to all public offices, the abolition of internal customs barriers, the unification of weights and measures, and so on.[5] The first article of their cahier demonstrated their revolutionary sentiments and their hostility to the privileges of the Clergy and the Nobility:

> The assembled nation, in order to set the government on an unshakable base, will determine the form of the Estates General which . . . must meet without distinction of *order* and vote by head, because where it is a question of votes, it is wisdom and opinion, not the brilliance of rank, which should shine, and because it is not good for corps, always divided from each other in interests, to meet together separately.[6]

This statement, with its hostility to the particular interests of corps, would seem to imply that trade corporations also ought not to meet and deliberate separately. This implication would seem to be strengthened by Article 28 of the cahier, which demanded that "all exclusive privileges will be annihilated everywhere in France."[7] Yet the stocking merchants and manufacturers elsewhere asked that the "prerogatives" of masters' corporations be maintained and passed on to the widows and children of masters.[8] Clearly, they did not regard these "prerogatives" as constituting "exclusive privileges," nor did they feel that their remarks about the corps of the Nobility and the Clergy applied to trade corporations.

The place of corporations in their view of the state can be seen best in the prologue to their cahier.

> In the French monarchy, every corporation is an individual part of a free and generous people which adores its laws, but which does not conceive of any power above the constitutional law of the land, sanctioned in the general assembly of the nation. The wish of each community must therefore have equally as its object that which tends to render the prince happy and to make his supreme authority respected, and that which can establish the nation in its rights, which cannot be legally superseded, either by feudal anarchy, or by ministerial despotism, or by the barbarism of centuries of ignorance.[9]

This prologue is pervaded by revolutionary political ideas. The people, which must sanction the constitutional law of the land by means of a "general assembly of the nation," is the ultimate authority in the state. Its rights must be guaranteed by the constitution, and neither king nor ministers nor feudal lords are above the power of the law. But the people, as conceived by the stocking merchants and manufacturers, is not composed of isolated individual persons. The "individual parts" of the people are *corporations,* and it is as *communities* that they must desire the public good. The gens de métier, this example suggests, could adopt a political stance scarcely distinguishable from that of the Abbé Sieyès and still assume that corporations, rather than single persons, were the individuals who composed the nation. Revolutionary language and revolutionary sentiments were perfectly compatible, from their point of view, with a corporate definition of their own political action.

Masters seem generally to have stayed loyal to their corporations until they were dissolved, although the doubtful legal status of corporations between August 1789 and March 1791 must have limited their activities and forced them to rethink their political ideas. But if the masters' corporations were reduced to a kind of semiparalytic lethargy in this period, the Revolution seems to have acted as a stimulus to at least some journeymen's associations. The Revolution, by dismantling the repressive machinery of the old regime, by weakening the hold of the masters' corporations, and by forging an alliance between the people and the National Assembly, opened up new possibilities for journeymen. The people, as the popular orators put it, had annihilated privilege and conquered liberty, and the new government itself was based on the people's sovereignty. Although the precise consequences of all this were far from clear, it certainly was clear that ordinary people could now undertake all kinds of actions that were unthinkable under the old regime. In these circumstances, journeymen in a number of trades experimented with new ways of organizing themselves. How widespread these experiments were is very hard to determine. In fact, the very lack of repression that made such experiments possible also means that judicial and police archives – normally our best source of information – are virtually silent. But in spite of the paucity of documentation, there is positive evidence of new attempts at organization among Parisian tailors, wigmakers, shoemakers, blacksmiths, carpenters, and typographers in the period between the taking of the Bastille and the passage of the Le Chapelier law.[10] That similar efforts may have taken place in other trades seems likely, but is, for the moment, impossible to determine. In any case, some of these associations have left documentation that provides revealing glimpses of the state of mind of at least an active minority of journeymen in these years.

A particularly curious document – and a difficult one to interpret – is a petition presented to the National Assembly by journeymen carpenters in May 1790. The petitioners were *renards* (foxes) – that is to say compagnons of the sect of Solomon – and the purpose of the petition was to obtain the suppression of their rivals, the compagnons du devoir, or Enfants de Père Soubise. In this petition, which was never acted on by the Assembly, they employed a good deal of distinctly revolutionary language.

> Your glorious labors, our lords [*nosseigneurs*], have assured liberty to all the individuals who have the happiness to compose France; however not all are free. The suppliants, who are in great number in this vast empire, are perhaps the only ones who do not enjoy this title so dear to all Frenchmen; the carpenter compagnons who call themselves du devoir, commit atrocious brigandage against the suppliants, who cannot work either in Paris or in the great cities of the kingdom . . . The suppliants request a decree that abolishes the absurd privileges that the compagnons called du devoir . . . arrogate to themselves, forbidding them in the future to trouble or to stop the suppliants either on the roads or at their labors . . . so that it will be free to the one or to the other to labor anywhere that he may find work.[11]

The renards spoke of France as composed of "individuals" and praised the National Assembly for assuring liberty to all Frenchmen. They denounced the compagnons du devoir for robbing them of their liberty to work where they pleased and asked that their "privileges" be abolished. The use of this language indicates that they had understood something of the intentions of the National Assembly and of its legislative program.

But if the renards had assimilated and correctly employed the National Assembly's language of individualism, liberty, and hostility to privilege, the petition as a whole is deeply ambiguous. To begin with, the renards' choice of words elsewhere in the petition indicates a very incomplete mastery of the new revolutionary lexicon. Their use of the term "our lords" to address their representatives and of "suppliants" rather than "petitioners" to refer to themselves was redolent of the hierarchical notions of the old regime and was therefore quite maladroit. Similarly, their apparent espousal of individualism and liberty of labor is open to considerable doubt. One plausible interpretation of the petition is that the renards' use of the language of liberty and individualism is purely cynical, a somewhat naïve attempt to trick the National Assembly into abolishing the compagnons du devoir while leaving the renards intact. But it also seems possible that the renards were groping toward some sort of redefinition of compagnonnage that would leave the sects intact as solidary brotherhoods but accept open hiring in the workshops. They were the weaker of the two sects of carpenter compagnons, and this may have made them willing to sacrifice the principles of exclusive workshops in order to be free of harassment and to increase their access to jobs. In this respect, it is worth noting that they did not ask the National Assembly to abolish the compagnons du devoir as an organization but only to abolish their "absurd privileges." Perhaps the renards saw the destruction of exclusive workshops as just one step in a wider reform of compagnonnage that would put it more in harmony with the new revolutionary social and political order.

It is clear in retrospect that even modified versions of compagnonnage could never have been tolerated; compagnonnage in any form would have been an intermediary body between the nation and the individual and would have reeked of the "spirit of corporation." But what is clear in retrospect was surely not clear to journeymen in the spring of 1790. In 1790 a government basing its claims on the sovereignty of the people was still an astonishing novelty, and no one knew what the new social and political order would finally look like. The renards, like everyone else, were exploring an unknown terrain, trying to interpret and to take advantage of the emerging, but still hazy, revolutionary order of things. It will never be known precisely why the renards wrote this petition, or what they expected from the National Assembly, or how they envisaged the future of their own sect. But the very maladroitness of their action testifies eloquently to the shape – and the shapelessness – of their world. In the two years that followed the taking of the Bastille, journeymen faced a world full of immense but inchoate potential. In these circumstances, the renards seem to have been trying, as much as anything else, to define for themselves the practical consequences of the Revolution, to have been searching, uncertain but confident in the aftermath of popular victory, for new forms of action and association that would be appropriate to the new order of things.

Another group that took up this search for new forms of association were the journeyman printers of Paris. By June 1790 they had formed an association that went variously under the name of La Société typographique (The Typographical Society) and Le Club typographique et philanthropique (The Typographical and Philanthropic Club). A good deal is known about this society because a copy of its regulations somehow found its way into the British Museum. In some respects this society appears to have been a secularized verison of a confraternity. It collected dues from all members, which it distributed to sick, aged, and infirm members of the society, and it included "visitors of the sick" among its officers. Like most journeymen's brotherhoods, its functions extended to what it termed *la police des imprimeries* ("the maintenance of good order in print shops" would perhaps be the best translation). It was to watch over the conduct of journeymen and to regulate apprenticeship in the trade. Finally, any "difficulty that would have a direct connection with the good of our art" was to be taken up in the weekly assembly of the society. The sanctions envisaged by the society clearly included strikes, because its regulations forbade workers "to cease their work all at the same time for any reason without having been authorized by the assembly." The clear implication is that such work stoppages were occasionally to be authorized. The society's rules were, then, precisely what they were entitled: a "General Regulation for the Corps of Typographers."[12]

Clearly, this society differed little in its aims from any number of journeymen's brotherhoods of the old regime, although these aims were stated openly and explicitly in the new revolutionary idiom. This society can be recognized as a refurbished journeymen's brotherhood, still very much in the corporate mold. But in the eyes of the journeymen typographers, the Typographical Society could not have existed without the Revolution. As they put it in their "preliminary discourse":

> Freed from the chains of despotism and the tyranny of the privileged, you have finally cast the foundations of this fraternal society which will always do honor to your fraternity and your knowledge and which while assuring the free exercise of your art, will procure aid for you in your infirmities and your old age . . .
> Twenty times you have attempted to form this generous establishment and twenty times ministerial tyranny, guided by those who had the greatest interest in preventing you from uniting, afraid that your

coming together would enlighten you about your rights, has forbidden you to do so and has treated you as disturbers of the public peace. But today your rights are no longer doubted, nothing can prevent your acts of benevolence and your association.[13]

The typographers saw their society as totally in harmony with the new revolutionary order. It was, moreover, revolutionary in its internal structure. Like the French nation, the Typographical Society had a representative form of government, with a legislative assembly made up of two delegates from each printshop, and officers chosen by majority vote of the assembly. Finally, the very titles of the printers' association were revolutionary in tone. "Société" and "Club" both denoted voluntary associations, which independent individuals joined by choice – as, at a higher level, the citizens contracted with one another to form a state – rather than indissoluble spiritual bodies in which membership was compulsory.

The regulations of the Typographical Society contained none of the inadvertent recurrences of the political language of the old regime that was found in the carpenters' petition. Having printed hundreds of revolutionary tracts and treatises, it is hardly surprising that the typographers had gained a full command of the new revolutionary idiom. But given this perfect fluency in the new idiom, it is interesting that the typographers consistently referred to their society as the *"corps typographique"* (typographical body), *"notre corps"* (our body), and the *"corps des ouvriers"* (the body of workers) and to one another as "confrères," a term translatable only as "brothers," but which, unlike the simple "frères," implied a "confrérie" or constituted body of brothers of which the "confrères" were members.[14] In other words, these frankly and openly revolutionary workers, who confidently founded their society on the rights assured to them by the Revolution, thought of their association not only as a "society" – that is, as an association voluntarily constructed by individual citizens – but as a corps, a solidary body of which all were members and which could act for all with a single and binding will. For the Parisian typographers – and one suspects for most other workers as well – the new revolutionary scheme of things was fully compatible with, and perhaps even implied, solidary associations of workers bound together by trade to assure collectively "the good of our art." That the National Assembly could have seen things so differently must have come as a terrible shock.

The actions of such journeymen's associations eventually provoked the National Assembly to pass the Le Chapelier law. The spring of 1791 saw a widespread agitation for higher wages among Parisian journeymen in a number of trades – carpenters, blacksmiths, hatters, typographers, joiners, locksmiths, cobblers, and perhaps others[15] – but the carpenters took the lead. At the end of April 1791 they formed a Union fraternelle des ouvriers en l'art de charpente (Fraternal Union of Workers in the Art of Carpentry), which purported to represent all the carpentry journeymen of Paris. This Fraternal Union held its meetings in the same hall as the radical Cordeliers Club, and it affiliated with the Central Committee set up by the club in May 1791.[16] The journeymen carpenters seem to have felt an affinity between their association and the explicitly political popular societies affiliated with the Cordeliers Club. Unfortunately, nothing is known about the internal structure of the Fraternal Union. It is not known, for example, whether the renards and the compagnons du devoir were both included in the union, although it seems very likely that they were. The two sects of compagnons had long been the two largest and most powerful journeymen's associations in the Parisian carpentry trade, and no city-wide association of carpenter journeymen would have amounted to much without them. Moreover, the title Fraternal Union strongly implies the uniting of previously separate associations. In any case, the Fraternal Union felt confident enough of its powers to request the master carpenters to join them in working out a single set of rules that would govern the entire Parisian carpentry trade. When the masters refused, the journeymen issued such a regulation on their own and seem, in the ensuing conflict, to have won a reduction in hours an an increase in wages.[17]

When the masters denounced the Fraternal Union to the Parisian municipal government, the journeymen responded with the argument that their association was an attempt to "soften the fate of their fellows."

> We have formed a mutual aid fund for the infirmities so frequent in our trade . . . We make ourselves useful in this establishment, and it would not be complete unless we made it capable of sustaining the members who are attached to it. To succeed in this we have formed a fraternal school where everything necessary to this art so useful to the fatherland [*la patrie*] and to private citizens is demonstrated.[18]

The Fraternal Union, then, contained features carried over from journeymen's associations of the old regime. There were the ubiquitous charités – now appropriately rebaptized as "mutual aid" – and a "fraternal school" that was undoubtedly an updated version of the technical training traditionally carried on in compagnonnage. Yet in the eyes of the carpenter journeymen, this association was a proper and entirely legal institution, a legitimate unit of the new society created by the Revolution. The carpenter journeymen had been slandered by their masters, but they were confident of the legality of their association.

> Tranquil and sheltered from tyrannical accusations, we expect from the laws the sweet satisfaction of being recognized as friends of the truth, and, persuaded of their protection, we will watch with all the exactitude demanded by the wisdom of their ordinance never to stray from the path of virtue.[19]

Nor were the carpenter journeymen alone in this confidence that their associations were in perfect harmony with the new revolutionary legal system. The blacksmith journeymen of Paris, also denounced by their masters to the municipality, responded indignantly that they were "animated by the purest civic virtue [*civisme*]" and that they "knew nothing but legal and constitutional paths."[20]

These protestations of revolutionary legality are all the more poignant because it was these same denunciations by the master carpenters and the master blacksmiths that moved the National Assembly to pass the Le Chapelier law. To judge from the cases of the carpenters and the blacksmiths, the Le Chapelier law must have marked a sharp discontinuity in the Revolution as experienced by journeymen. Up to June 1791, they understood the new revolutionary order as allowing, even sanctioning, associations that recast the journeymen's long-standing concerns for mutual aid, wages, working conditions, and general regulation of the trade into new revolutionary forms. But with the passage of the Le Chapelier law, the consequences of the Revolution for journeymen took a sudden and wrenching turn. Associations that journeymen felt should be protected by the law were instead to be repressed with the utmost vigor. From the point of view of the carpenter and blacksmith journeymen, the passage of the Le Chapelier law closed off a part of the revolutionary horizon. It gave the new regime a sharper and more constricted outline.

The sources are silent on the reaction of journeymen to the Le Chapelier law. As far as can be discovered, there were no overt protests or disruptions of public order. That such journeymen as the typographers, the carpenters, and the blacksmiths must have been stung by the National Assembly's repudiation of their associations seems certain. But because it is not known how many Parisian trades had organized themselves in this way, it is difficult even to guess how widespread such feelings may have been. It certainly cannot be assumed that journeymen's associations were simply disbanded; it seems at least as likely that they retreated into their familiar prerevolutionary ways, to live once again in the half-light of clandestinity. But the silence of the sources almost certainly corresponds to a real decline in the importance and number of journeymen's associations. In part this was a result of the repressive sternness of the new law. But at the same time, journeymen's attention was also wrenched away from the daily life of their trades by a sudden turn of revolutionary politics.

THE RISE OF THE SANS-CULOTTES

On June 20, less than a week after the passage of the Le Chapelier law, the king and his family fled from Paris. Caught at Varennes, only a few kilometers from the frontier, the king was dragged back to Paris and suspended from office. The flight of the king provoked a major political crisis. Popular agitation increased greatly and turned sharply in the direction of republicanism. But the National Assembly, maintaining the fiction that Louis had been carried off against his will, determined to reinstate him as a constitutional monarch if he would accept the constitution they had written. Meanwhile, the king's flight greatly increased the possibility of armed intervention by the hostile monarchies of Europe. From the summer of 1791 to the summer of 1794, Paris was in a state of almost permanent political crisis. The Assembly's declaration of war in April 1792 definitively launched the radical phase of the Revolution. The war quickly turned against the French, and the factionalism of Paris and the Assembly was intensified by accusations of treason and fears of the invading armies. The Parisian populace not unreasonably considered the king guilty of treason to the Revolution. On August 10, 1792, as Prussian and Austrian troops advanced on Paris, they carried out a second Revolution, deposing the king, establishing a new municipal government, and forcing the Assembly to call a new constituent assembly, known as the Convention. On September 21, 1792, the Convention met and declared France a republic. By the end of 1792, French armies had driven the invaders from French soil, and early the next year Louis XVI was executed. But the crisis of the Revolution was far from over. During the next year and a half the war continued without pause; huge counterrevolutionary revolts took place in the Vendée and in Marseille, Lyons, and Bordeaux; and the Parisian populace, in alliance with Robespierre and the Jacobins, repeatedly intervened in the affairs of the Convention to push the Revolution to ever more extreme and energetic measures. This was the period of the "reign of terror," when the Parisian sections and the Committee of Public Safety horrified Europe by their intrepid cruelty and miraculously saved the Revolution from what seemed certain defeat.[21]

During this entire period, journeymen and masters alike were swept up in the sans-culotte movement. The sans-culottes were literally those "without breeches," that is, citizens who wore the trousers of the common people rather than the breeches of the aristocracy and the rich. The sans-culottes were those who supported radical democracy and political terror; their revolutionary activities in the Parisian sections and in the streets brought down the monarchy and swept Robespierre and the Committee of Public Safety to power. Thanks to the classic studies of Albert Soboul and George Rudé, it is known that the sans-culotte movement was composed principally of wage workers and petty proprietors, with masters and journeymen in the small-scale skilled trades of Paris at its core.[22] During the period of their ascendancy, the sans-culottes elaborated their own specific ideology and vision of life, attempting to create a more democratic and more vital revolution than the legalistic revolution of 1789–91. In this goal they were largely in agreement with Robespierre, with the Jacobin society, and with the

"Mountain" – the left wing of the Convention. But the ideas and aspirations of the sans-culottes were by no means identical to those of Robespierre or the Mountain. Although they shared so much of the Mountain's vocabulary and rhetoric, they shaped it to their own specific ends, with their own tonalities, dominant themes, key phrases, recurrent metaphors, and characteristic judgments. The result was a specifically sans-culotte version of the Revolution that countered the individualism of 1789 with a powerful drive for fraternal union in the "one and indivisible Republic," and that drew both its practical power and its theoretical justification from the direct action and the undying vigilance of the people. The views of the sans-culottes were rarely set down in abstract or systematic form. Rather, they were expressed in a frenetic flow of action – in debates in the sections and in popular societies; in petitions, speeches, and proclamations; and in the rituals of insurrection and revolutionary celebration.[23] It was not until the 1950s that the fragmentary records of these utterances and actions were brought together and analyzed in the pathbreaking work of Albert Soboul. It was Soboul's books – the magisterial *Les Sans-culottes parisiens en l'an II,* first published in 1958, and the collection of documents published by Soboul and Walter Markov in 1957[24] – that made the world of the sans-culottes accessible in clarity and detail.

The sans-culottes did not envision the republic as a state governed by elected representatives and embodied in laws that the representatives made – the conception of, say, a Condorcet.[25] Rather, they believed in the continuous, direct exercise of popular sovereignty, with legislators cast as *mandataires* (mandatories or delegates) sent to the legislative assembly with specific mandates and subject to immediate recall or dismissal by popular action should they betray the people's will. The sans-culottes acted out this continuous sovereignty of the people in the Parisian sections. Initially intended as primary electoral assemblies, the forty-eight sections of Paris were declared to be in permanent session for the duration of the national emergency in July 1792, when the Prussians were advancing on Paris. It was the sections that organized and carried out the revolution of August 10, 1792. Thereafter, during the long crisis that followed, they gradually became almost independent governments of their respective quarters of Paris.

Assemblies of the sections met several evenings a week in open session to decide on the affairs of the quarter and the republic. Minutes of these assemblies, many of which are reproduced in the Markov and Soboul collection, reveal a turbulent and almost obsessive direct democracy in action. All adult males who inhabited the section were authorized to participate in assemblies, and at times of crisis the number present – which could also include women and fraternal visitors from neighboring sections – could be very large. The sections concerned themselves with all matters that might affect the section or the republic. They maintained surveillance over citizens of the section, discussed the prosecution of the war and saw to it that citizens of the section made the necessary contributions to the national effort, kept track of their "mandatories" in the Convention, made sure that neighboring sections did not stray from the path of virtue, and generally did everything in their power to maintain the energy and the ardor of the Revolution. Discussions in the sections frequently overflowed into action: petitions to the Convention, street demonstrations, "fraternal" visits to other sections in need of encouragement or guidance in the ways of revolutionary virtue, and, in the last resort, insurrection.[26]

The republic as envisaged by the sans-culottes entailed not only the direct exercise of popular sovereignty but a single, unified popular will. In the Convention's famous phrase, the republic was "one and indivisible." It was this obsession with unity that made corporations in any form unthinkable. The notion that men who exercised the same trade should have a special sense of community among themselves and should be concerned with the well-being of their own particular trade – whether this notion be expressed in the corporate idiom of the old regime or in the new postrevolutionary idiom of philanthropic aid and association – was directly contrary to the sans-culottes' ideal of the perfect unity of all citizens. For citizens to organize themselves on the basis of particular trades would be to form partial wills that could only conflict with the general will and hence would be counterrevolutionary. Both employers and workers, therefore, abandoned their loyalty to particular trades and directed their ardor toward the republic alone. They were no longer *gens de métier*, divided into autonomous and solidary trades; they were sans-culottes, united in the one and indivisible republic. But it is characteristic of the *gens de métier* that even in abandoning corporate loyalties, they by no means abandoned their collectivist morality. As sans-culottes, their collective loyalty went to a moral community much vaster than that of their trade. But the Revolution did not succeed in making them individualists.

The sans-culottes' quest for unanimity took several forms. One was an insistence that all political actions be made in public. Counterrevolution acted by conspiracy, but true republicans spoke and acted in constant view of their fellow citizens. Thus the sans-culottes insisted that votes in their sections and in the Convention itself be taken aloud so that the people might know their friends from their enemies. In the sections themselves, the sans-culottes eventually settled on the procedure of voting "by acclamation" – by cheering or applauding when the names of proposed candidates were announced. This procedure made the majority will immediately apparent to all and turned elections into a manifestation and a celebration of popular unity – and at the same time intimidated potential opponents.[27] The other side of publicity was denunciation. Those who opposed the will of the people had to be unmasked as traitors. As one sans-culotte militant put it, "political denunciation, far from being a moral crime, has become a virtue and a duty . . . Denunciation is the safeguard of liberty in a popular republic."[28] Encouraged to act unanimously by the voting procedure of the sections and intimidated by the fear of denunciation, the sans-culottes pursued the goal of unity with fervent single-mindedness.

Unity of the people, in the eyes of the sans-culottes, implied equality. One of the most important acts in forging a powerful sans-culotte movement was the admission of "passive citizens" to the assemblies of the sections toward the end of July 1792. Under the constitution of 1791, citizens who were so poor that they paid less than the equivalent of three days' wages in taxes were designated as "passive citizens"; they were given the full protection of the law but deprived of the right to vote or to serve in the National Guard. The admission of passive citizens into the assemblies of the sections therefore erased distinctions between citizens on the basis of wealth, creating full political equality. But the erasing of distinctions between active and passive citizens was only the first manifestation of the sans-culottes' passionate pursuit of equality. It was not enough that no formal distinctions exist between citizens; what was required was a uniformity of action, wealth, dress, and demeanor. One of the most consistent themes of the sans-culottes was hostility to the rich. A true republican was selfless in his devotion to the republic and to his fellow citizens. Those who had riches while fellow citizens remained in misery were consequently regarded with suspicion, and the possession of riches often figured prominently in the sans-culottes' denunciations.[29] But the sans-culottes were as hostile to outward signs of inequality as they were to inequality of means. Thus, during their ascendancy, citizens who put on any airs of superiority were suspected of counterrevolutionary sentiments and could be denounced for speaking "ironically" or for having a "haughty and proud" disposition.[30] The extreme to which this will to conformity could go among the sans-culottes may be seen in the "definition of the moderate" made by a self-styled "guardian angel of liberty and equality of the one and indivisible Republic" in May 1793. His definition of the moderate included the following: "One who out of ill-will does not wear a *Cocarde* [a *tricouleur* rosette] of three inches in circumference. One who has bought other than national clothing, and above all those who do not glory in the title and the hairstyle of the sans-culottes."[31] Even seemingly trivial outward signs – a cocarde of less than three inches in circumference or hair not cut sufficiently short – were taken as indicating reactionary political beliefs and sentiments. Inward unity of will was thought to be manifest in outward unity of comportment.

Another telling example of the sans-culottes' quest for unity was the practice of "fraternization" between sections. Upon hearing that "moderates" were threatening to take over in a neighboring section, a section would suspend its session and march off to restore unity in the threatened section.

The arrival of the visitors often led to the expulsion of the "moderates," occasionally, but by no means always, by force. Once quiet had been restored, citizens of the two sections would embrace and exchange fraternal kisses. The two sections would then deliberate as one. Often they ended by swearing an oath of unity and agreeing to "fraternize" with one another in this fashion twice weekly. By means of fraternizing, good sans-culottes could come to one another's aid in section after section to keep down the moderates.[32] But "fraternizing" was more than just a political device; it was also an enactment of the sans-culottes' somewhat mystical notion of the "one and indivisible republic." According to the sans-culottes, the people was single and undivided and could have only one will. A section, therefore, was not a distinct political unit with its own particular interests or opinions; on the contrary, each section of the people was identical with every other, and each could therefore act for the people as a whole. When moderates or other enemies of the people attempted to usurp power in any section, it was the duty of the citizens of other sections to intervene to bring the section back into conformity with the popular will. This was done less by threats or by acts of violence than by the exchange of embraces, kisses, accolades, and oaths of fraternity, by ritually restoring the citizens of a perturbed section to peace and harmony with the national will and reabsorbing them into the people as a whole. If the two sections then proceeded to deliberate as one, it was because, by means of this ritual, they had actually become one.

This same notion of the section as a microcosm of the one and indivisible republic also underlay the sans-culottes' idea and practice of insurrection. The delegates of the people who sat in the Convention were not, according to the sans-culottes, representatives of a particular district or constituency. They were mandatories of the single, undivided popular will. It was therefore the duty of the people to maintain surveillance of all its mandatories, from whatever district they happened to have been elected, and to revoke the mandates of those who contradicted the people's will. And because each section was identical with the republic as a whole, the sections of Paris, the only ones capable of monitoring the Convention closely, had no choice but to act for the whole. The sans-culottes of Paris, when they demanded and obtained a purging of the Convention in the spring of 1793, were acting not as residents of the capital but as indivisible sections of the people as a whole. The insurrection was, by the metonymic logic of the sans-culottes, a rising of the unified people of the entire country against traitors to its single will.

The sans-culottes were, in other words, profoundly collectivist. Like the revolutionaries of 1789, they abhorred any partial interests or intermediary bodies that stood between the citizen and the nation. But where the revolutionaries of 1789 recognized the legitimacy of both the general interest and the interests of individual citizens, the sans-culottes considered individual interests no less reprehensible than the interests of corporate bodies. As the wills of individual masters or journeymen were to be harmonized with the single will of the trade community under the old regime, so the wills of individual sans-culottes were to be harmonized with the general will under the one and indivisible republic. The good of the collectivity superseded and encompassed the good of all the persons of which it was composed. This collectivism of the sans-culottes did not mean that practical questions about wages, working conditions, and relations between workers and employers were simply forgotten in a selfless wave of patriotic feeling. There was a good deal of discussion about such matters in the sections, and there was a general agreement that wages should be sufficient to maintain the wage earner in modest comfort. Thus, the same "guardian angel of the republic" quoted above listed as one of his definitions of the moderate "one who has not furnished work to laborers and journeymen when he had the chance, at a price which is progressive relative to costs of food."[33] Questions of wages and other questions of commerce and industry fell within the most limitless competence of the sections, and the sections, like the trade corporations of the old regime, attempted to regulate production and exchange in the public interest. But these questions were now a concern of the sovereign people as a whole, not just of a single trade, and they were to be determined by public action, not by the action of a closed corporation of workers or masters.

The sans-culottes were passionately concerned with assuring all citizens a decent and equal livelihood. However, their efforts centered not on controlling wages but on controlling prices, and above all prices of food. The key elements of their policy of price control were the "maximum" – legislation setting ceilings on the prices of various goods – and punitive action against hoarders. The importance the sans-culottes attached to price controls is implied clearly in a petition drawn up by the *enragé* priest Jacques Roux in June 1793: "Liberty is but a vain phantom when one class of men can starve another with impunity. Liberty is but a vain phantom when the rich by means of monopoly exercise the power of life and death over their fellow men."[34] Here Roux was recurring to one of the sans-culottes' favorite themes: the perfidy of the rich. The poor were naturally patriotic and virtuous, whereas the rich, who had too long been in the habit of considering only their own interests, were incapable of republican selflessness. This drama of virtuous poverty and self-seeking riches was acted out in all realms of life. But nowhere was it so stark and so clear as in the question of the supply of foodstuffs – the question of "subsistence," as the sans-culottes put it.

Food, which was supplied by nature, was the very condition of human life. As Hébert put it in August 1793, "the earth was made for living things, and each one, from the ant to the proud insect who is called man, must find his subsistence in the productions of this common mother."[35] Naturally plentiful, and therefore cheap, food could be made scarce by speculators who hoarded the product of the harvest in order to drive up prices and then sell at immense profits. Speculation in foodstuffs was therefore a perversion of nature, and wealth gained from such speculation was at the expense of the very existence, the subsistence, of the people. The phrases used by sans-culottes to designate speculators are full of endless variations on this theme: "speculations in human existence," "men who speculate in public misery . . . enriched . . . with the substance of the poor," "vampires of the fatherland," and so on.[36] Such speculation was the ultimate in counterrevolutionary immorality, a supreme expression of the corrupt conjunction of private egoism and public villainy. Speculators therefore deserved the ultimate penalty. The guillotine must "cut off the fortunes and the heads of those who wish to take away from the nation its elements of life."[37] Or as a sans-culotte in the section de l'Unité put it, guillotines should be constructed "on all the street-corners of Paris, and at the doors of all merchants, so that goods may be bought cheaply."[38]

The problem of food prices, then, appealed to the sans-culottes as a paradigmatic representation of the drama of revolution as they understood it. But the problem of prices also had its practical side. All sans-culottes were of course consumers, and most of them – whether wage earners or petty proprietors – were far from rich. Food prices, and particularly the price of bread, had an enormous impact on their health and happiness. Although any attempt to control wages would be bound to lead to dissensions between employers and wage earners, maintaining a low price for bread would benefit wage earners and employers alike. The appeal of price controls to the sans-culottes therefore fit with the heterogeneous composition of the sans-culotte movement. Setting a maximum on food prices would help all the poor and honest patriots; it would harm only the rich and the counterrevolutionaries. Agitation for strict enforcement of the maximum, therefore, was at once an attack on the rich and a defense of the poor, and as such it served to weld together a diverse collection of wage earners and petty proprietors who shared a common dependence on cheap and plentiful bread.

Soboul makes much of the material basis for the sans-culottes' obsession with the problem of prices. That the sans-culottes were concerned with the question of food supplies rather than the question of wages, he writes, was because "a rise or fall in price of the principal products of popular consumption, of grain, above all of bread, which represented at least half of the family's expenses, constituted the decisive factor that tightened or loosened the wage earner's budget."[39] Moreover, the wage earners' acute sensitivity to food prices was shared by the rest of the sans-culotterie.

Hunger, an essential factor in all popular movements, was the cement which held together the artisan, the shopkeeper and the worker, just as a common interest united them against the wealthy merchant, the contractor, the noble or bourgeois monopolist. The term "sans-culotterie" may appear vague from the standpoint of our current sociological vocabulary, but from the standpoint of social conditions of the time it corresponded to a reality.[40]

That variations in bread prices affected wage earners as much as variations in wages was certainly true. Yet in 1848, when bread assumed virtually the same importance in the budget of Parisian workers as it had in 1793,[41] workers ignored the problem of prices and concentrated instead on problems of wages and labor. That wage earners in 1793 were obsessed with the problem of prices rather than with the problem of wages cannot be accounted for simply by the place of bread in the popular budget. Similarly, the fact that wage earners and petty proprietors both had grievances against the very rich and that both were subject to hunger in times of rising prices made a common ideology of price controls possible, but it could not generate such an ideology automatically. Indeed, it is probably no less true that the existence of an ideology of price controls caused wage earners and petty proprietors to form a political alliance as sans-culottes than that their common dependence on cheap bread caused them to develop an ideology of price controls. The ideology shaped the pattern of social cleavages as much as the social cleavages shaped the ideology.

At the same time that Soboul attributes important features of the sans-culottes' ideology to the material conditions of the time, he also argues that the social diversity of the sans-culotte movement doomed their ideology to contradictions and incoherence.

> A coalition of socially disparate elements, the sans-culotterie was undermined by internal contradictions which explain its incapacity to establish a coherent program, and, in the last analysis, its political defeat.[42]

> The sans-culotterie could have neither class-consciousness nor a coherent social program. Its aspirations remained nebulous and contradictory.[43]

Yet on reading Soboul's own account of the sans-culottes' words and deeds, one is impressed not by incoherence and contradictions but by an almost unfailing, if occasionally chilling and uncanny, consistency. Judged as a system of thought and action, the ideology of the sans-culottes may have been brutal or unrealistic or incapable of long-term success; but whatever else it may have been, it was coherent. Its coherence was not that of a class ideology, but it is not clear why a coherence of that particular kind should be expected. Indeed, the expectation that "social disparateness" from the standpoint of Marxist or other nineteenth- or twentieth-century schemes of classification should result in internal contradictions in thought and actions may be quite misplaced when applied to the sans-culottes. After all, these "scientific" schemes of social classification that are so confidently applied to the sans-culottes would have seemed *to them* not only outlandish but treasonable. In the ways that matter *to them,* the sans-culottes were not disparate but united. And their own sans-culotte form of unity both reinforced and was reinforced by their own peculiarly coherent ideology.

LABOR AND PROPERTY IN SANS-CULOTTE IDEOLOGY

One of Soboul's reasons for calling the sans-culottes' ideology incoherent is that they seem to him to have had no clear idea of labor.

> Finding it difficult to define their place in society as laborers, the sans-culottes had no clear and distinct notion of labor itself. They did not think that it could constitute a social function in itself; they could only conceive of it in relation to property.[44]

Their fixation on property and their vagueness about labor, according to Soboul, resulted from their social composition. For although the sans-culottes included both wage earners and petty proprietors, the wage earners were dominated by the proprietors and the sans-culotterie as a whole had a petty bourgeois mentality.

> The journeymen of the small trades, formed in the school of the masters, often living under their roof and eating at their table, had the same conceptions of the great problems of the time: the artisanal petty bourgeoisie fashioned the workers' mentality.[45]

> The world of labor was strongly marked in its ensemble by the mentality of the artisanal petty bourgeoisie and, like it, participated in the ideology of the bourgeoisie.[46]

For Soboul, the ideology of the sans-culottes, in spite of its violence and radicalism, remained a subtype of the dominant bourgeois ideology of the French Revolution.

The sans-culottes did not define their social position in the same way as nineteenth- or twentieth-century socialists, but they did have a clear and consistent conception of labor and its place in society. As Soboul himself remarks, the sans-culottes continually defined themselves as men who worked with their hands. A favorite theme of the Père Duchesne was the contrast between the virtuous sans-culottes, "these laborious artisans who exhaust themselves with labor," and the idle rich, "leeches of the sans-culotterie."[47] The importance of labor in defining a man as a sans-culotte is particularly evident in a document dating from the spring of 1793, which Markov and Soboul chose to print at the very beginning of their collection. Titled "Answer to the Impertinent Question: But What Is a Sans-Culotte?" it is worth quoting at some length.

> A *sans-culotte,* you rascals? He is a being who always goes on foot, who has no millions, as all you wish to have, no castle, no valets to serve him, and who lives simply with his wife and children, if he has any, on the fourth or fifth floor.
>
> He is useful, because he knows how to plow a field, to forge, to saw, to file, to roof a building, to make shoes and to spill out the last drop of his blood for the salvation of the Republic.
>
> And because he works, you will not meet him at the Café de Chartres, nor at the gambling dens where men conspire over a game of dice, nor at the theatre of the Nation . . . nor at the theatre of Vaudeville . . . nor in the reading rooms where for two sous, which are so precious, one is offered the garbage of Gorsas [a Girondin journalist] with the *Chronique* and the *Patriote française* [leading Girondin newspapers].
>
> In the evening, he attends his Section, not powdered, perfumed and booted in the hope of catching the attention of female citizens at the tribune, but to support good motions with all his force and to pulverize those which come from the abominable faction of the men of estate.
>
> For the rest, a sans-culotte always has his sabre with its sharp edge: in order to split the ears of all the evil-doers. Sometimes he goes about armed with his pike; but at the first sound of the drum, one sees him depart for the Vendée, for the army of the Alps or for the army of the North.[48]

The fact that the sans-culotte works with his hands is absolutely central in this definition. Labor is an integral element in a whole network of moral and political identities that define the sans-culotte and distinguish him from the counterrevolutionary moderate. Those who labor are poor – have no carriages or valets and live in fourth- or fifth-story walk-up flats. Their labor makes them useful to the republic; and it is precisely those who make themselves useful through their labor – plowing fields, forging, sawing, roofing buildings, making shoes – who will also make the ultimate sacrifice for the republic – spilling out the last drop of their blood. In this passage our sans-culotte author sets up an identity between labor and political virtue; those who serve the republic in their daily activities will also defend it in its peril. The next two paragraphs contrast the hardworking sans-culotte with the rich and idle moderate. It is because the sans-culotte works that he will not be found in the haunts of the idle. And where labor is identified with virtue – living simply, usefulness, patriotism; idleness is identified with both political and moral vice – conspiracy over a game of dice, wasting money that is precious to the poor on counterrevolutionary Girondin newspapers. A similar contrast carries over to the assemblies of the section. The rich and idle attend for frivolous purposes – to cut a good figure before the ladies – whereas the hardworking sans-culottes attend in order to support political virtue and pulverize the moderates. In short, the distinction between those who labor and those who do not is fundamental; manual labor is an inseparable element in the cluster of characteristics that defines the sans-culotte, and all these elements – poverty, labor, moral virtue, good political opinions, patriotism – necessarily imply one another.

The opposite of the sans-culotte – the moderate or counterrevolutionary – was most often dubbed an "aristocrat." In the vocabulary of the sans-culottes, this word underwent a revealing deformation. As used by the sans-culottes, "aristocrat" referred not only to the former nobility but to all those who opposed the sans-culottes: to the rich and idle, to large landowners and capitalists, to speculators, to Girondins, to those who paid insufficient wages to workers, to those who wore their hair long and powdered, to those who frequented priests who had not sworn loyalty to the republic, to those with moderate political opinions of any description, even to those who were merely indifferent to politics.[49] But above all, the aristocrat came to be identified with the rich. As an orator in the Mail Section put it in May 1793, "Aristocrats are all the rich, all the wealthy merchants, all the monopolists, the middlemen [*saute-ruisseaux*], the bankers, the brokers, quibbling lawyers and all those who own anything."[50]

This usage of the term "aristocrat" to designate the rich is closely linked to the sans-culottes' notion of the place of labor in society. The Abbé Sieyès, after all, had defined the nobility as enemies of the nation because they were idlers who did not participate in the "labors that support society."[51] The sans-culottes, by designating all the rich as aristocrats, were in fact making a relatively minor alteration in Sieyès's definition of labor. For Sieyès, all the Third Estate was engaged in useful labors. But for the sans-culottes, useful labor was more restricted; it was performed only by those who worked with their hands. The rest, the idlers, were – like Sieyès's idlers – enemies of the nation and thus "aristocrats." A parallel change in meaning can be traced in the term "privilege." Instead of referring to private laws distinct from the "law common to all Frenchmen," privilege came to mean the advantages of wealth – a meaning it has maintained in present-day usage. A petition to the Convention in September 1793 declared: "It is an evident verity that the Nation is sans-culottes and that the small number of those who have all the wealth in their hands are not the nation; that they are nothing but Privileged Persons, who are reaching the end of their privilege."[52] The terms are those of Sieyès: Aristocrats are idlers who hold privileges, and the unprivileged people who engage in useful labor are the true nation. But because the sans-culottes' definition of labor was more restricted than Sieyès's, the political consequences of this common revolutionary language were radically different.

The sans-culottes, then, had a perfectly clear and distinct notion of labor. Labor was a foundation of society and of the moral and political order. Those who did not labor were outcasts and enemies, privileged aristocrats who must be purged from the nation. Soboul concluded from his analysis of the sans-culottes' ideology that they lacked a clear idea of labor and subordinated labor to the idea of property. It would be more nearly correct to say the opposite: that they lacked a clear idea of property and subordinated it to the idea of labor.

As Soboul points out, the sans-culottes accepted small-scale property of the kind owned by master craftsmen and shopkeepers.[53] Indeed, they believed that a regime of greater equality would increase the number of proprietors. But unlike the National Assembly of 1789 to 1791, they did not conceive of property as an unlimited and inalienable natural right. Rather, they wished to limit the range of property rights severely – by, for example, establishing a ceiling on fortunes and limiting each citizen to ownership of a restricted amount of land or to a single workshop or store.[54] Moreover, even within the confines of a limited property of this kind, the rights of the proprietor were far from absolute. Indeed, the sans-culottes did not think of property as a strictly private affair at all; they considered an owner of property to be a trustee *(dépositaire)* of goods that in the final analysis belonged to the people as a whole. Soboul quotes numerous statements to this effect.

> Properties belong to everyone in general when they produce existence.
>   The productions of French territory belong to France, subject to an indemnity due to the cultivator; the people therefore have an assured right to the goods the cultivator has caused to be produced.
>   The rich man is less the proprietor than the happy trustee of an excess of fortune intended for the happiness of his co-citizens.
>   What is a merchant? He is the trustee and not, as has been foolishly believed up to now, the proprietor of objects necessary for life. He is the trustee of these objects, just as other citizens [i.e., public officials] are of some part of authority; he is therefore a public official and the most important of all, because he holds in his hands the existence of the people.[55]

The rights of the republic or of the people as a whole were prior to property rights, and although property was possessed by individual citizens, they possessed it only on the condition that they produce for the common good. Property, for the sans-culottes, was individual in form but collective in principle. Moreover, the fact that some hardworking sans-culottes were trustees of property, whereas others were not, did not place them in different classes. The important thing was whether or not one worked with one's hands for the common good, not whether one was, for the time being, a trustee of property. Those who labored with their hands for the common good were sans-culottes whether or not they owned property; those who did not were aristocrats and enemies of the people. Labor, in the world of the sans-culottes, was a more fundamental principle than property.

That the sans-culottes could have had a conception of property so thoroughly at odds with that of the National Assembly, or the Convention, or even the Jacobins, is surprising only if they are thought of as petty bourgeois in the nineteenth-century sense – as men whose place in society and whose sense of self were all wrapped up in their status as owners of property. But considering who the sans-culottes had been before the Revolution, their ideas about property should not seem so puzzling. Predominantly masters and journeymen in the skilled trades of Paris, the sans-culottes had been, only a few years earlier, the core of the Parisian corporate world. If they had a conception of property as intended for the public good in 1793, their prerevolutionary corporations had been established for the public good as well. If they wished to prohibit the owning of more than one workshop or store, their corporations had prohibited members from doing so up to 1789. If they wished to restrict the rights of proprietors to dispose of their property as they saw fit, their corporations had done the same before the Revolution. On the question of property as on all other questions, the sans-culottes carried over the moral collectivism of the prerevolutionary corporate mentality. The moral community of the one and indivisible republic superseded the rights of any individual proprietor just as the moral community of the trade had superseded the interests of the individual master or journeymen under the old regime. To be sure, these sentiments and ideas were utterly transformed in the ideology of the sans-culottes. It was now the sovereign people and not the king who determined the public good; it was the sections of the republic as a whole rather than trade corporations that should limit the excesses of the proprietor; and all of these notions were now bound up in the language and the practice of revolutionary politics. But for all the differences, one can still hear certain distinctive accents of the prerevolutionary gens de métier in the new political language of the sans-culottes.

6 A revolution in property

THE SANS-CULOTTES' unique and surprising ideas about property – distinct at once from the conceptions of the old regime, of the National Assembly, of the Jacobins, and of later socialist thinkers – emphasize the fact that conceptions of property were transformed during the French Revolution. The character and significance of property in the social order was far from clear in the early 1790s. Historians have long recognized that property was a crucial issue in the Revolution: After all, the Declaration of the Rights of Man and Citizen raised property to the dignity of a "natural and imprescriptible right of man." For both liberal and Marxist historians, one of the Revolution's great accomplishments was to free citizens from the entanglements, vexations, and constraints that had limited their free enjoyment of property under the old regime. Liberals and Marxists have disagreed, of course, as to how this freeing of property should be interpreted: as a triumph of liberty or as the crucial act of a bourgeois revolution that would itself be transcended in a proletarian revolution. But most historians have been content with the notion – which was that of the National Assembly itself – that the Revolution unfettered property from sundry archaic or "feudal" constraints. Few have recognized to what extent this "liberation" was actually a radical redefinition of the very nature of property, nor have they recognized how long it took for the outlines and consequences of this new system of property to become clear in practice.

In fact, "bourgeois" property was not so much unfettered by the French Revolution as it was created. Its creation entailed the destruction of whole categories of property recognized as legitimate by the old regime and the transformation or redefinition of the rest. The end result was absolute individual property as defined in the Civil Code of 1804: "the right to enjoy and to dispose of goods in the most absolute manner."[1] Property of this kind was the fundamental basis of the bourgeois social order that emerged in France in the nineteenth century and was also the main target of the socialist movement that grew up in the 1830s and 1840s and erupted with particular forced in the Revolution of 1848. Whatever else it may have been, social-

114

ism was a response to the regime of absolute private property that was established in the French Revolution. But the path that led from the creation of absolute private property to its challenge by masses of socialist workers in 1848 was far from direct. Contention over property rights in the nineteenth century occurred mainly in urban industry and above all in the urban skilled trades that had been organized as corporations under the old regime. Yet urban industrial property was quite marginal to Enlightenment discourse about property and was hardly central in the acts and thoughts of the leading revolutionaries. Enlightenment thinkers and revolutionary actors alike were concerned almost exclusively with property in land. Their efforts were an attempt – a largely successful one, as it turned out – to resolve certain problems of landed property that they saw in eighteenth-century French society. But whereas the Revolution's actions on the property question were undertaken with landed property in mind, they also had important – if slowly evolving and generally unanticipated – effects on urban and industrial property. It was the transformation of property relations in urban industry – and especially in the skilled crafts – that gave rise to the great class struggles of the nineteenth century. The transformations of property in the French Revolution were, thus, both complicated and paradoxical. But they are worth tracing in some detail, for they were crucial to the subsequent history of the French working class.

PROPERTY UNDER THE OLD REGIME

The word property (*propriété*) is derived from *"propre,"* an adjective meaning "belonging to someone to the exclusion of all others." As defined by the Académie française in the dictionary of 1694, property was "the right, the title by which a thing belongs *en propre* ["as his own" would be the nearest English equivalent] to someone." Property, then, was that which was one's own and to which one had clear legal title. Sometimes having property in a thing under the old regime meant that one had free and absolute dominion over it – as came to be the case in principle for all property after the Revolution. But this was by no means always true. For the sake of clarity, three quite different types of property that existed under the old regime can be distinguished.

1. The first type was absolute private property: something, to quote one seventeenth-century definition, over which "one is absolute master, that one may sell, pledge or dispose of at one's pleasure."[2] Most personal property and a significant amount of real estate and commercial property in old-regime France were of this type. But there were also many other legitimate properties, held by all classes and orders of the population, that did not fit this description.

2. A second type of old-regime property belonged unquestionably to its owner but by no means lay under his absolute dominion. Rather, it was held by the owner under the supposition of detailed regulation by the community for the public good. This second type of property was very common and included a vast amount of the productive property employed in agriculture, in commerce, and in industry in old-regime France. For example, in the regions of France where open-field agriculture was practiced, a piece of land was subjected by the local village community to a compulsory rotation of crops and to the practice of *vaine pâture* – letting the cattle loose to graze on the stubble after the harvest. A proprietor in these areas did not have the right to determine what crops he would plant in his own fields or when he would plant them, and if he tried to plant another crop on his field after the harvest, it would be devoured – quite legally – by his neighbor's beasts.[3] Much of the property of masters in the corporate trades was also of this type: The master, although the unchallenged proprietor of his stock, tools, and raw materials, could use these only in the restricted ways specified by the statutes of his corporation.

3. A third very important category of old-regime property not only was regulated for the public good but was derived from and had no existence apart from public authority. This was property in public functions. The most obvious and notable example was venal office. Officials ranging all the way from members of the Parlement of Paris to municipal magistrates in third-rate provincial towns possessed offices they had bought from the king, offices that carried the power to perform certain public functions and that also brought their possessors an annual income. The offices were, like other forms of property, passed on from generation to generation; legally, they even came to be assimilated to the forms governing inheritance of landed property.[4] Another example of property in public function was the *seigneurie*. The seigneur was, literally, the lord; and the seigneurie was his right of lordship over the peasants of a given jurisdiction. The origins of the seigneurial regime go back to the early Middle Ages when the local lord was the de facto ruler of his peasants; by the seventeenth or eighteenth century the seigneurie had become an extremely diverse bundle of specific and legally enforcable dues and obligations that the peasants of the jurisdiction owed to the seigneur: quitrents, fees paid at the inheritance or transfer of land, assorted personal services, *banalités* – the obligation to press one's grapes at the lord's winepress or bake one's bread in the lord's oven – and the like. Derived from the lord's quasi-public power of dispensing justice, these dues and obligations were regarded as the property of the lord; as such they could be inherited, farmed out to collectors, and occasionally – under certain circumstances – sold outright.[5]

Besides these three types of property, it is useful to consider a fourth type of rights that were considered to be a kind of quasi property or at least analogous to property: privileges, prerogatives, and hereditary distinctions of various kinds. The similarity between privilege and property was invoked, for example, by the Parlement of Paris in its remonstrance against Turgot's suppression of the *corvée* (compulsory labor services for the building and maintenance of roads) in 1776: "The first rule of justice is to preserve for every man what belongs to him . . . , a rule that consists not only in maintaining the rights of property, but also in preserving rights attached to the person and those which derive from the prerogatives of birth and estate."[6] This parallel between property and privileges or prerogatives was far from spurious; although the privileges and prerogatives usually could not be sold, they belonged to a person no less securely than his land or buildings. Moreover, many of them were also of material value, because they carried exemption from taxation, access to lucrative offices, and the like. In the case that brought forth the Parlement's statement, for example, Turgot had attempted to replace the corvée with a tax assessed equally on all proprietors of land regardless of their status; this, the Parlement complained, was to deprive the nobility of their rightful exemption from the corvée. In the legal system of the old regime, property of the absolute and individual sort was but one member of a wider family of rights, some designated as property, others as privilege or prerogative, that belonged legitimately to persons. Property and privilege, far from being opposed or antithetical categories, were similar in kind; they flowed into one another and were often difficult to distinguish in practice.

Property in the arts et métiers was in fact a perfect example of the general system of property of the old regime. A master in a corporate trade was the possessor of all three types of property enumerated above, and one of his properties was at the same time a privilege. A master's personal property, his cash holdings, his credits, and perhaps his house – should he be fortunate enough to own one – were all properties of type one: individual properties, which he was free to use and to dispose of as he saw fit. His productive capital, on the other hand, was property of type two. His tools and equipment, raw materials, stocks of finished goods, and so on: These too were his individual property, but he could by no means dispose of them however he saw fit. Rather, their use was subject to detailed regulation and discipline by the statutes and the jurés of his corporation. A master also owned property of type three: his mastership. A mastership was a share in the public authority granted to the corporation by the king; like a seigneurie or a venal office, it belonged to him by legitimate title and it empowered him to carry out certain publicly authorized functions. Finally, as noted in Chapter 2, a mastership was also a privilege.

That the privilege entailed in a mastership was also a property was a major argument of the Parlement of Paris against Turgot's decree abolishing corporations in 1776. To deprive masters of their masterships, the Parlement contended, was to despoil them of their property.

> Who will indemnify . . . the possessors of these privileges, which they have acquired only by their labor, which they bought with the first funds that their industry had amassed? They formed a portion of the patrimony of their family; they passed them on to their children, left them to their widows, who exercised them to their profit, or had them exercised by others, or who lived from the rent they produced.[7]

The privileges that constituted a mastership, this passage pointed out, were properties in the strictest sense. Like other properties, a mastership had to be bought by its possessor, and the entry fee required by a corporation generally represented a substantial investment. In Paris before 1776, for example, the cost of a mastership ranged from 175 livres for seamstresses to 3,240 livres for the opulent drapers, with most corporations charging between 500 and 1,500. These fees usually amounted to considerably more than a Parisian journeyman's wages for an entire year.[8] Unless he inherited money or could draw on a sizable dowry from his wife, it was extremely difficult for a journeyman to accumulate such a sum. The entry fee was thus a major cost of setting oneself up in business.

In return for his entry fee, a master gained rights of genuine value. As a certified possessor of a mastership he could make and/or sell certain goods that strangers to the corporation could not; he was assured a protected place in the market, which, in normal times, would afford him a decent living. And even if he fell on hard times, he usually could draw on the charités of the trade's confraternity. Possession of a mastership also, as the Parlement pointed out, meant security for a man's family. As noted earlier, his sons could usually enter his trade for half the going fee. But far more important, they were assured of having a place as masters, whereas outsiders were often denied admittance even if they had the requisite skills and money. A master, therefore, could be sure of being able to set his son up in business. And even if a master died before his time, his mastership and all the attendant privileges were inherited by his widow, who could exercise them until such time as she remarried or turned the business over to her son.

In terms of its costs, a mastership was probably worth less, in most cases, than the rest of a master's property: money, stocks of goods, commercial credits, tools, equipment, and the like. But under the old regime his mastership was actually much more significant than these other kinds of property in defining both his place in society and his place in the process of production and exchange. It was his possession of a mastership – not his possession of capital – that made a man a master, investing him with a semipublic authority and enabling him to put his capital to use in a particular art. At the same time, the terms of his mastership – the particular privileges and statutes of his corporation – specified in detail the ways in which his capital could and could not be employed. A master's capital was subordinated to and given form by his mastership. A master's authority over his workers also derived from his mastership, and once again the nature of this authority was specified by the statutes and customs of his corporation. The authority of the master, as the Parlement of Paris pointed out, was an extension of the police power of the state. Part of the public function of a master was to "follow [workers] in the details of their domestic life" and to "answer for them to the police."[9] The master commanded the worker not because of his rights as owner of the means of production but because of the authority inherent in his possession of a mastership.

Thus, the privileges that constituted a mastership were not only a property themselves but gave form and social significance to the rest of the master's property. They were the capstone of his possessions and marked his place in the social order. Nor were masterships the only sort of possession that had this dual character of privilege and property. In fact, all property in public functions – offices and seigneuries as well as masterships – conferred some sort of privilege on its owner. Even the lower venal offices made one a member of a privileged body of magistrates; seigneuries carried a presumption of nobility and the highest venal offices explicitly conferred hereditary nobility on their purchasers. Moreover, privileges everywhere stood in a relationship of superiority to other forms of property. It was, after all, privilege that gave persons their particular rank, dignity, and position in the social order of the old regime; material property or wealth could give one comfort or security, but it did not in itself confer dignity or public standing. Hence, there was a marked tendency at all levels of society for material property to be converted into privilege – or into forms of property that gave access to privilege. All the familiar tales of social ascension in the seventeenth or eighteenth centuries fit this pattern: the industrious journeyman who economizes his meager wages so as to buy a mastership; the engrossing peasant who eventually buys the country house and seigneurie of an impoverished nobleman; or the wealthy merchant, lawyer, or banker who buys land and a country house where he can live in the style of a nobleman (*"vivre noblement,"* as the expression went), perhaps also purchasing an ennobling office for himself or his son or providing a huge dowry to his daughter so that she might marry into the nobility.

Privilege and property were overlapping and mutually supporting categories in the social order of the old regime. Because they were so intertwined, the maintenance and defense of property was inseparable from the maintenance and defense of privilege. The "first rule of justice," to "preserve for every man what belongs to him," implied a preservation of privileges, of individually controlled property, of collectively regulated property, and of property in public function indiscriminately. It was only when the French Revolution drastically simplified and narrowed the definition of property that privilege and property became antithetical categories – the one a "natural and imprescriptible right of man," the other an odious usurpation. This the French Revolution did by either abolishing or transforming all property that was not under the absolute dominion of the proprietor. Both privileges and property in public function – property of type three – were abolished outright: seigneuries, venal offices, and the assorted privileges of nobles and clerics were annihilated on the night of August 4, 1789, and masterships disappeared in 1791. Meanwhile, all property of type two was freed of community regulation and thereby assimilated to property of type one. Only absolute individual property survived the Revolution, and this pared-down and purified form of property was placed in a new and much more central place in the social order. The remainder of this chapter will try to discern why the revolutionaries redefined property in this way, what they meant when they did so, and what some of the consequences of this redefinition were.

PROPERTY IN THE ENLIGHTENMENT

The revolutionaries' concept of property derived from Enlightenment discourse. Like other aspects of Enlightenment thought, the new ideas of property were quickly adopted by many powerful figures – particularly in the royal administration – well in advance of the French Revolution. Both Turgot's attempt to abolish corporations and the attacks led by the royal administrators Bertin, Trudaine, and d'Ormesson on collective obligations in the countryside were – among other things – attempts to impose the Enlightened ideal of individual, private property.[10] But until 1789, these efforts met with only minor success. Not until the Revolution was the Enlightened conception of absolute private property finally put into practice.

Enlightenment discourse about property was part of the broader Enlightenment effort to give a purely naturalistic account of the world. Property, for the Enlightenment, had its origins in man's labor on nature and was a sphere of strictly private activity that was prior to the state. The decisive statement of the Enlightenment concept – no less influential in France than in its native England – was made by John Locke in his *Second Treatise of Government.*

> Though the earth and all inferior creatures be common to all men, yet every man has a property in his own person; this nobody has any right to but himself. The labour of his body and the work of his hands, we may say, are properly his. Whatsoever he removes out of the state that nature hath provided and left it in, he hath mixed his labor with, and

joined it to something that is his own, and thereby makes it his property
. . . For this labour being the unquestionable property of the labourer,
no man but he can have a right to what that is once joined to.[11]

This property included not only the things that man appropriated from their
natural state for his own consumption – "the acorns he picked up under an
oak, or the apples he gathered from the trees in the wood"[12] – but land that
he brought under cultivation.

> As much land as a man tills, plants, improves, cultivates, and can use the
> product of, so much is his property. God, when He gave the world in
> common to all mankind, commanded man also to labour, and the pen-
> ury of his condition required it of him. God and His reason commanded
> him to subdue the earth, i.e., improve it for the benefit of life, and
> therein lay out something upon it that was his own, his labour. He that
> in obedience to this command of God subdued, tilled, and sowed any
> part of it, thereby annexed to it something that was his property, which
> another had no title to, nor could without injury take from him.[13]

Hence, man, by his labor, came to acquire property in "the earth itself, as
that which takes in and carries with it all the rest."[14]

In Locke's account, man's property in things derives from his property in
his own person. Man is a natural being, placed in a natural world by God's
ordinance. By expending the labor of his person upon certain parts of nature he transforms them into objects of value and annexes these objects to
his own person as his property. Property, in this conception, is an extension
of the person. By laboring on nature, the person expands the sphere of his
personhood by annexing to it a multitude of useful objects that increase his
comfort and his powers. Indeed, property and personhood were so nearly
synonymous for Locke that he used "property" as a term that encompassed
personhood. Thus he spoke of men's "lives, liberties and estates, which I
call by the general name 'property.'"[15] Within this sphere of his personhood
or his property, man was free and all-powerful: He was the "absolute lord of
his own person and possessions, equal to the greatest, and subject to no-
body."[16] When Locke spoke of men first entering into political society, he
was thinking not of isolated, naked, shivering creatures scarcely distinguishable from beasts but of diligent and self-sufficient cultivators surrounded by
their land and by the other material objects they had brought out of the
state of nature by their labor.

When men entered into civil society, they retained this identity with their
property. After all, "the great and chief end . . . of men's uniting into com-
monwealths and putting themselves under government is the preservation
of their property."[17] For this reason, men's property – including their life
and liberty – remained inviolable in civil society: "The power of the society,
or legislative constituted by them, can never be supposed to extend farther

than the common good, but is obliged to secure every one's property by providing against those ... defects ... that made the state of nature so unsafe and uneasy."[18] In Locke's scheme of things, property was not a set of rights held conditionally under the discipline and regulation of public authority. On the contrary, property was *prior* to public authority; it was an inseparable part of the independent persons who voluntarily came together to form the commonwealth. In the state of society, as in the state of nature, property remained a sphere of the strictest individual freedom and autonomy.

Locke had two intentions in giving this account of property. In the first place, he wished to make a purely naturalistic account of the origins and nature of government. Writing in late seventeenth-century England, at the end of a period of intense religious warfare, he wished to place the origins of government entirely outside the framework of any religious doctrines, to make government a purely secular affair safe from the excesses of religious enthusiasm. Locke treated man as a purely natural being placed in a purely natural environment and showed how his labor on nature gave rise first to property capable of sustaining him in independence and then to an ordered commonwealth complete with laws, an executive, a legislature, and a judiciary – all without direct intervention of God. God, of course, appears in Locke's account. But He is a strictly nondenominational God, who created the world, placed man in it, commanded him to labor, and then sat back and let nature take its course. By couching his theory in this naturalistic idiom, Locke effectively separated religion from the affairs of the commonwealth, making it a matter of private belief rather than of public concern and regulation. If property, for Locke, consisted of natural substances transformed by labor, this was because his concept of property was part of a wider account that derived government and social order from nature rather than from operations of divine will.

A naturalistic account of the origins of government, however, need not have been centered on property. In fact, Locke's adversary in his *Two Treatises,* Sir Robert Filmer, gave a naturalistic account of the origins of government in *Patriarcha, or the Natural Power of Kings*. Filmer derived the origin of government and the power of kings from the original fatherhood of Adam, which gave him a "natural and private domain" over the earth, and endeavored to demonstrate that the kings of his own day had inherited these powers by natural, direct descent from Adam.[19] Filmer's naturalistic account of the origins of government supported the claims of absolute monarchy. It was to counteract these claims that Locke founded his social contract on the preexisting property of free individuals. Because they already owned property, Locke's pre-social men were independent and self-sufficient, quite capable of living a full life without kings and royal decrees to guide them. They established governments only in order to enjoy their property in greater security. And because men already possessed property before government existed, the kings they chose to govern them could not claim any power over their property unless the citizens themselves gave their express consent. Royal power, thus, was strictly limited by the property rights of citizens, and taxation could not be imposed without the consent of the taxpayers or their representatives. Property, in Locke's scheme, was therefore a bulwark of liberty, a guarantee against the tyrannical pretensions of would-be absolute kings.

Locke's account of the origins and nature of property was deeply political in intent. By basing property on man's labor on nature, and by basing government on men's preexisting, naturally acquired property rights, Locke constructed a theory of government that at once separated the state from matters of religious doctrine and obliged the king to respect the liberties of the citizens. Against both the traditional Catholic and radical Protestant theories of the state as an instrument of divine providence, Locke's theory made the state a secular institution that arose unmediated out of men's interactions with nature. And against naturalistic theorists of absolute monarchy like Filmer, Locke made the king a chosen agent of the commonwealth whose duty it was to honor and preserve the lives, liberties, and estates – in short, the property – of his subjects.

Discourse on property in the French Enlightenment followed Locke both in his formal definitions and in his political intentions. Like Locke, the Philosophes wished to free government from the entanglements and the passions of religious fanaticism. And like Locke, they posed property as a bulwark of liberty against the tyranny of kings. For the French, as for Locke, discourse about property was deeply political. This is nowhere clearer than in the article on property in the *Encyclopédie*.

> *Property* is the right that each one of the individuals comprising a society has to enjoy the wealth that he has legitimately acquired.
>
> One of the principal views of men in forming societies was to secure the undisturbed possession of the advantages they had acquired or were able to acquire . . . It is for this reason that each one consented to sacrifice a portion of [their wealth] which they called *taxes* for the preservation and maintenance of the entire society. They wanted to furnish the chosen heads of state with the means of making every private individual secure in the enjoyment of the portion of wealth he had reserved for himself.
>
> However strong the affections and enthusiasm of men might have been for the sovereigns to whom they submitted, they never intended to give them absolute and unlimited power over their wealth . . . The flattery of courtiers . . . tried to convince some princes that they had an absolute right over the wealth of their subjects. Only despots and tyrants have adopted these preposterous maxims . . . In states where the rules of reason are followed, *properties* of private individuals are under

the protection of the laws; the head of the family [père de famille] is assured of enjoying for himself and of transmitting to his posterity, the wealth he has amassed by his labor. Good kings have always respected the possessions of their subjects. They have regarded the public funds that have been committed to them only as a trust that may not be misappropriated to satisfy their frivolous passions, the greed of their favorites, or the rapacity of their courtiers.[20]

However different the tone and the emphasis, this article's conception of property is fundamentally the same as Locke's. Property is unproblematically assumed to be created by labor on nature: Property is the wealth that the head of the family "has amassed by his labor." And it was to secure the undisturbed possession of their property that men formed societies in the first place. Finally, the government that resulted from this social contract was a purely secular state in which the king was obliged to respect the liberties and property of his subjects. In all of this, the *Encyclopédie* and Locke were in perfect agreement. Nevertheless, the article had a political thrust of its own; it was above all a protest against unjust taxation. Taxes, it points out, are granted "to furnish the chosen heads of state with the means of making every private individual secure in the enjoyment of the portion of wealth he had reserved for himself." The power of kings to tax their subjects does not extend beyond the limited and legitimate needs of government; to claim more makes the king a tyrant or despot. The clear implication is that French kings, who had imposed taxes by fiat without consulting their people, and who – from the point of view of the Philosophes – squandered their money on the frivolous pursuits of their courtiers at Versailles, had thereby committed unjust assaults on the liberty and property of their subjects.

This article from the *Encyclopédie* illustrates nicely how Locke's ideas came to have quite different consequences and emphases when they were borrowed by the Philosophes and elaborated in a French context. Locke and the Philosophes were in perfect agreement about the limits on the king's powers of taxation, and Locke himself had some strong things to say on the subject. But because the burden of taxation was less equitably distributed in France, and because the crown had repeatedly imposed new taxation without consulting the Estates General, the French were far more sensitive to the issue. In France, therefore, a Lockean conception of property led directly to the problem of taxation, for taxes were seen as a serious threat to the integrity of property and to the liberty that only property could ensure. Conversely, the salience of taxation as an issue in France was one reason why Locke's conception of property was especially attractive to the Philosophes, who were campaigning for a diminution and redistribution of the tax burden.

This special emphasis on taxation was by no means the only novel consequence of applying a Lockean conception of property to the French situation. More fundamentally, Locke's conception of property implied a sharp restriction on the range of things that could be considered as legitimate property. The Lockean scheme gave men a firm and undeniable title to absolute property in the assorted natural substances that they had transformed by their labor or had traded for the substances they had so transformed. But at the same time, it seemed to dissolve property rights in anything other than transformed natural substances and particularly in semipublic functions such as seigneuries, venal offices, and masterships. If property was defined as natural substance transformed by human labor, how could public functions or powers qualify as property? Moreover, if property is prior to society and government, an inseparable part of the persons who formed society in the first place, then how could men claim property rights in functions or powers that by definition could only have been established after the founding of the state? In late seventeenth-century England, these implications of Locke's theory posed no significant problem: There seigneuries had long since disappeared, the system of property in office had never been established, and trade corporations were relatively few, feeble, and on the wane. But when his theories were adopted in France, where property in public functions was ubiquitous, valuable, and central to the very constitution of public life, the result was bound to be corrosive. The adoption of a Lockean conception of property contributed much to the Philosophes' deep sense that these perfectly legal forms of property were nonetheless to be viewed as usurpations and odious privileges that ought not to exist in a truly rational and Enlightened nation.

A second consequence of the naturalistic Lockean view of property was that it gave discourse on property a subtly rural and agrarian emphasis. The idea that agriculture is more natural than other pursuits is very old; it is perhaps inherent in the Western conception of nature. It can be found both in classical antiquity and in the Old Testament and was still very much alive among Catholic theorists of the corporate order under the old regime. Thus, when Loyseau attempted to rank the various occupations within the Third Estate in 1610, he placed plowmen not only above gens de métier but also above the lowest levels of municipal officials – constables, appraisers, auctioneers, town criers, and the like – because "there is no life more innocent, nor employment more in accord with nature, than that of tilling the soil."[21] The idea that agriculture was the most natural of human occupations was manifested in Enlightenment thought in various ways: for example, in the Physiocrats' doctrine that only agriculture could actually increase the wealth of the nation or in the listing of agriculturalists by Sieyès as his first class of citizens because they had the most direct contact with the productions of nature.

This pervasive sense that agriculture and nature were intimately connected gave land a special salience in the Lockean, naturalistic theory of property. Locke's exposition of the origins of property drew its examples chiefly from agriculture, and he spoke of landed property as "that which takes in and carries with it all the rest." The image of the cultivator transforming tangled forests and barren heaths into squared-off fields, of human labor etching the ordered forms of civilization onto the very surface of the earth, also had a deep appeal to the French Philosophes. Landed property, after all, had a special permanence and substantiality about it. In agriculture the wealth amassed by a lifetime of labor was physically embodied in land, improvements, and buildings; in transformed natural substances that could be seen, touched, and passed on intact to one's heirs. By comparison, commercial or industrial wealth – stocks of goods acquired only to be sold, raw materials to be processed and placed on the market, commercial credits and bank deposits, diversified portfolios of investments – was constantly in circulation, volatile, evanescent, and insecure. Thus, when Enlightenment authors spoke of property in general, they tended to envisage it as landed property.

This tendency to identify property with land was enhanced by another feature of Lockean and Enlightenment discourse: the intimate link that it posited between property and representation. Government was originally formed by independent proprietors wishing to protect their property. It was therefore the proprietors who granted taxes for maintenance of the government, and these taxes could legitimately be levied only with their express consent. Unless property was represented in the state, it was vulnerable to royal tyranny.[22] In eighteenth-century France, much of the property that was subject to taxation had no representation in the state whatsoever. Representation through the Estates General had ceased entirely since 1617, and for the remainder of the seventeenth and eighteenth centuries, only those groups recognized by the crown as enduring corporate orders or bodies could be said to have representation in any sense. Such groups as the clergy, the nobility, the magistrates, the liberal professions, the gens de métier, the universities, cities, or provinces could represent their interests to municipal and royal authorities and could often resist potentially harmful actions – including attempts to impose new taxes. But cultivators entirely lacked such corporate representation, and they were defenseless against the rising fiscal demands of the state. As a result they had to bear by far the largest part of the increasing tax burden that was imposed by the crown during the seventeenth and eighteenth centuries. The problem of representation as it appeared to eighteenth-century French Philosophes was above all a rural problem, and their efforts to solve it in Lockean terms were therefore focused particularly on landed property. This served to enhance the rural bias already built into the naturalistic conception of property and to fix the attention of the Philosophes on property in land.

Perhaps the most thoroughgoing exponent of representation on the basis of landed property was Turgot. When he was elevated to contrôleur général in 1774, he instructed his disciple Du Pont de Nemours to draw up a *Mémoire sur les municipalités* (Memorandum on Municipalities), which proposed a reform of local representation and administration to the king. Although Turgot fell from office before he could present the *Mémoire* to Louis XVI, he nevertheless intended it as a practical proposal for immediate reforms.[23] In the *Mémoire,* Turgot proposed to base the representation of citizens in the state on their ownership of property and to ignore their personal status as nobles or commoners. By implication, this would place property ownership at the very center of the social and political order and would transform a nation composed of distinct orders or estates into a nation composed of individual proprietors. In this sense, Turgot's proposal seems a perfect example of the Enlightenment's well-known penchant for espousing the interests of the bourgeoisie. But, in fact, Turgot's conception of property was entirely rustic; he characterized citizens' property as "the indelible place they occupy on the soil,"[24] and throughout the *Mémoire* he applied this notion of property and landownership with the most rigorous consistency. Even in the cities, where land represented a tiny fraction of the overall wealth of the inhabitants, only owners of urban land were to have the right to vote. So complete was Turgot's identification of property in land with property in general that by far the largest part of urban property would have escaped both taxation and representation in his scheme. Had Turgot's system of representation been enacted, it would have given the most mediocre of peasant proprietors a greater weight in the state than a prosperous bourgeois whose wealth was entirely commercial or industrial in character.

In the *Mémoire,* Turgot proposed a hierarchy of parish, regional, provincial, and national assemblies that would be charged with administering and apportioning taxes, planning public works, and organizing relief for the poor. Participation in the parish assemblies would be based exclusively on ownership of land. According to Turgot, those who owned no land were not sufficiently attached to their parishes to be citizens: "These people have one habitation today, and another tomorrow. They are in the service of the nation in general; they must everywhere enjoy the succor of the laws, the protection of [royal] authority and the security which it procures; but they belong to no place."[25] Landowners, by contrast, were "really part of a parish or a village . . . They are attached to the land by their property; they cannot cease to take an interest in the district where it is placed." For this reason, they alone should be considered true citizens: "It is the possession of land . . . which, linking the possessor to the State, constitutes true citizenship [*droit de cité*] . . . One can only legitimately accord the usage of this right or a voice in parish assemblies to those who possess landed properties."[26]

Turgot's identification of land with citizenship was complete. Not only were those without landed property to be denied votes in the parish assembly, but votes of property owners were to be allocated in strict proportion to the value of their land. Turgot defined a full citizen as one who owned enough land to support a family, for such a man was at once fully independent and a settled member of the community. The possessor of such a property therefore would have a full vote in the assembly. Those whose property was smaller would be "fractional citizens." They would join together with other fractional citizens until their total holdings reached the level deemed sufficient to support a family and elect one of their number to represent them all.[27] By the same reasoning, those whose revenues were sufficient "to support several families of citizens and who, as a consequence, would occupy their place on the territory" should have as many votes "as they unite in their possession of complete portions of citizens."[28] According to Turgot, "this arrangement appears to be founded on justice, since one who has four times the landed revenue in a parish has four times as much to lose if the affairs of that parish go badly, and four times as much to gain if all is prosperous."[29] Moreover, multiple voting would have the advantage of assuring the rationality of the assemblies' deliberations: "By placing the plurality of voices, most often, on the side of those who have received the most education, it would render the assemblies much more reasonable than if badly instructed and uneducated people predominated."[30]

This system of apportioning votes to the value of landed property, then, would ensure that parish assemblies accurately represented both the legitimate interests and the rational judgment of the village. At the same time, it would vastly simplify local administration by providing an effortless means of apportioning taxes.

> Voices being attributed to a certain sum of revenue, the claim for a voice or for some fraction of a voice or for so many voices, will be the avowal and the declaration of such and such a revenue; so that the proportions of fortunes being known, the division of tax payments will be made with the division of voices, by the inhabitants themselves, without the slightest difficulty.[31]

The apportioning and collection of taxes, one of the most difficult, onerous, and unpopular duties of the royal administration, would be decentralized and made almost automatic by the institution of Turgot's parish assemblies. By this means, according to the *Mémoire,* the king would be freed from the necessity of making thousands of separate decisions, of issuing decrees on every particular dispute; instead he would now "govern like God by general laws."[32]

For Turgot, then, the possession of land was synonymous with citizenship. In a sense this was a simple extension of the Lockean theory; if the state was formed for the protection of landed property, then membership in the state should depend upon landownership. Under Turgot's scheme, the constituents of the state were not persons but lands that contained persons or persons who were surrounded by their lands. The aggregation of these occupied territories made up the territory of the nation. And the weight of these constituent units was proportional to the value of the land and therefore to the number of persons the land could support. Dependents of landowning heads of families – whether wives and children or other relatives, or tenants, servants, or footloose laborers – were encompassed in the parcels of land that made up the nation and were represented by the titular owners of the land. In this way, citizenship was affixed to the surface of the earth and made to correspond perfectly with parcels of transformed nature. The state, as a result, would work with the regularity of nature itself, the king – like the watchmaker God – setting up the social mechanism and ruling by general laws. In this way the duties and privileges of citizenship – the payment of taxes as well as participation in public administration – would be performed automatically, in harmony with the distribution of property, and therefore of legitimate interests and rationality, on the surface of the national territory.

Turgot's scheme applied neatly – indeed with a kind of manic precision – to rural society, where land was the main source of wealth. But what about cities, where most wealth was mobile and commercial rather than immobile and agrarian? Again Turgot's logic was relentless. Mobile wealth – like that employed in commerce and manufacture – had no permanence.

> Mobile wealth is as fugitive as talent; and unfortunately those who possess no land have a country only through their hearts, through their opinions, through the happy prejudices of childhood. Necessity gives them none. They escape from constraint; they elude taxation . . . If it happens that, in order to make them contribute their gains, taxes are raised enough to deprive them of their faculty to make a profit . . . they abandon their enterprises and their country.[33]

Mobile wealth, then, could not be an adequate basis for citizenship, and any attempt to tax it could only have the unfortunate effect of driving commerce and industry out of the country. Only the immobile wealth of city dwellers – land and buildings – gave them a real interest in their city.

> The only things that cannot be carried away are houses and the land on which they are built. If the city is prosperous and populous, houses rent dearly; if commerce does not flourish . . . men and mobile capital go eslewhere; rents fall . . . so that it is the proprietors, the only ones in the city who cannot transport their riches, who find themselves ruined.

Hence, it is "the proprietors of houses and land" who have a real stake in a city, and it is they who should constitute urban municipalities.[34]

It would therefore seem to follow that votes in urban assemblies should be apportioned according to the value of the proprietors' land and buildings. But closer examination reveals that this would be improper. In fact, votes should be apportioned only according to the value of the land on which houses are built; for even houses do not meet Turgot's standards of permanence.

> A house is a sort of property without security. Repairs carry away every year, and more and more each year, a part of the value; and after about a century, more or less, the house has to be entirely rebuilt. The capital employed in the first construction and that which has been added for maintenance are annihilated . . . A field, which does not require the same maintenance and which is not subject to the same accidents, retains its value in perpetuity . . . Its master is a citizen as long as the country endures . . . The proprietor of a field . . . can . . . in the greatest of calamities which make him lose his cultivators, become a cultivator himself, on his own domain, and there win subsistence for his citizen family by his own labor. The proprietor of houses, reduced to having no renters, to living in his own house, would die there with his family, unless he had revenue from elsewhere. A house is not a productive property, it is an expensive commodity.[35]

For this reason, Turgot concluded that a family owning only a house "is not a family *founded* in the state. It only has a *post*. It can only endure the hundred years that its house endures." It is therefore only the land on which houses are built that constitutes "the true and solid link between the proprietor of houses and the fatherland, his true means of providing subsistence for his children, his true citizenship [droit de cité]."[36]

In proposing that the allocation of urban votes be based exclusively on the value of urban land, Turgot was seeking to establish a "real parity," an "impartial equality that Your Majesty wishes to observe between his subjects in cities and in the countryside."[37] From today's vantage point, applying this common standard in the cities and the countryside would result in the most glaring inequities. Although any village in France would be bound to have a number of full and multiple citizens, very few owners of urban land possessed enough to give them even a single vote: "One would find hardly forty of them in Paris. It results from this that nearly all urban proprietors will only be fractional citizens, and that fractions of citizens will be much smaller in the cities than in the countryside."[38] Turgot's scheme seems far from equitable, because it would place greater power in the state in the hands of rural than of urban proprietors – and would also tax rural wealth far more heavily than urban. But for Turgot, this plan accurately reflected the distribution of true, permanent, legitimate interests of the state; membership in the state was to be inseparable from, indeed identical to, property in land. Other forms of property, however substantial or "bourgeois" they may seem to us, seemed to him too evanescent to be represented in the state. Turgot's inability to see commercial and industrial property as similar in kind to landed property is also evident in his decree abolishing corporations. Today – or for that matter in the middle of the nineteenth century – the obvious industrial or commercial parallel to the agriculturalist's property in land would seem to be the businessman's property in his capital. But Turgot did not see it that way. He spoke of the gens de métier as "that class of men . . . having no property except their labor and their industry."[39] Had Turgot been speaking exclusively of wage-earning employees, his words would seem perfectly comprehensible. But, in fact, he was speaking of both workers and their employers, of gens de métier in general. His conception of labor as property was strictly Lockean: "God, in giving man needs, in making labor his necessary resource, made of the right to labor the property of every man; and this property is the first, the most sacred and the most imprescriptible of all."[40] When this conception of men's labor as their property was applied in the countryside, it generated landed property. In agriculture, labor was fixed in the land, and the land remained as its solid, immovable, and sustaining embodiment. But in the arts et métiers, the products of labor were constantly circulating. The sundry objects that the master's labor created out of natural substances and then sold to others; or the tools, equipment, and commercial credits that he accumulated out of the profits of his sales, these were property in the sense that they belonged legitimately to the artisan master. But they certainly were nothing like landed property; they had no permanence and no power to fix a man's place in the state. When Turgot contemplated the mechanical arts, he failed to think of capital or stocks as a significant form of property at all. In his eyes the only thing a master could definitively and unquestionably call his own was his labor. It was, therefore, on "the right to labor," rather than on ownership of material property, that Turgot based the masters' claims to freedom from corporate fetters.

The purpose of Turgot's decree abolishing corporations was to "free our subjects from all infringements of this inalienable right of humanity,"[41] and the "right to labor" was to apply equally to workers and masters. But Turgot believed that the distinction between workers and masters was natural and inevitable.

> Those who know the workings of commerce also know that any important enterprise in trade or industry requires the cooperation of two kinds of men; of entrepreneurs who make the advance of raw materials, of implements necessary to each commerce; and of simple workers who labor for the first, receiving an agreed-upon salary. Such is the true origin of the distinction between the entrepreneurs or masters, and the workers or journeymen, which is founded on the nature of things.[42]

The distinction, then, was not between those who owned the means of production and those who did not; it was between two different types of labor. The very term Turgot used for the masters, "entrepreneurs," disclosed his conception of their role. An entrepreneur is someone who undertakes a project, who brings together the finances, materials, implements, and labor necessary to carry out a task and see it through to its completion. An entrepreneur may also be a proprietor of the means of production – and Turgot at one point speaks of entrepreneurs as "those who employ their capital in a commerce."[43] But to Turgot, it was the entrepreneur's labor that was salient, not his capital. Turgot wished to give entrepreneurs the authority to hire whatever workers they wished at whatever wages they could agree on and to employ these workers in whatever way seemed most advantageous to the entrepreneur. But even in making this most "bourgeois" of reforms, he based the masters' authority on their right to labor freely, not on their ownership of property.

For Turgot, the possession of landed property was the source of a fundamental distinction between persons – the distinction between citizens and noncitizens. Land, because it fixed a man's place in the state, entitled him to the rights and obligations of citizenship. All other forms of property – whether labor, capital, houses, or investments – were impermanent and insubstantial; all were "as fugitive as talent." From today's point of view, differences between these various forms of nonlanded property – and particularly the difference between capital and labor – seem fundamental. A present-day observer would see the world of eighteenth-century urban trades as divided into two distinct and antagonistic classes: those who owned the means of production and those who possessed nothing but their labor. But for Turgot, both masters and workers could be described as a class of men "having no property except their labor and their industry." If Turgot could be cross-examined, he would doubtless admit that the masters' capital was also a form of property and, therefore, that the masters, strictly speaking, had some property beyond their labor. But because capital lacked the permanence and solidity of land, the distinction between capital and labor – which seems fundamental to us – seemed trivial to him. Although it might be technically incorrect to say that masters had no property except their labor, it would make no difference to Turgot's argument. For him, all the differences between various forms of nonlanded property faded into insignificance before the great and fundamental distinction between the permanence of land and the impermanence of all the rest.

Not everyone saw property in precisely the same terms as Turgot, even among supporters of the Enlightenment. Some were less inclined than he to favor the power of great landowners; and some were more interested than he in the problems of mobile property. Nevertheless, in focusing his discourse on property exclusively on property in land, Turgot merely extended a general tendency of Enlightenment thought to its logical conclusion. For the Philosophes in general and for the revolutionaries who attempted to put their notions into practice, property was quintessentially property in land; when they thought of property it was land that they envisaged. This was as true for those who wished to redistribute property as for those who wished to make it inviolable. When Saint-Just – a member of the Committee of Public Safety and the most eloquent advocate of the terror – wrote down his "Fragments on Republican Institutions" at the height of the terror in 1794, he concluded that a more equitable division of property was a necessary precondition for establishing the public good. But, characteristically, he formulated this in terms of division of land. "To reform morals [*moeurs*], we must begin by satisfying need and interest; we must give some land to everyone."[44] For Turgot, for Saint-Just, and for the Enlightenment cast of mind in general, property was inseparable from land. It was only in the nineteenth century, after the transformations in property imposed by the Revolution, that problems of urban and industrial property came to occupy a significant place in public discourse.

PROPERTY IN REVOLUTIONARY LEGISLATION

The National Assembly authoritatively redefined the nature of property rights in France on the night of August 4. It is appropriate that the Assembly had been goaded into action by a crisis in rural property. The main targets of the peasants' revolts in the summer of 1789 were the dues and obligations they owed to seigneurs. Seigneuries, of course, were valid properties under the old regime, so the peasant uprisings constituted an assault on property. Yet the particular form of property that the peasants were attacking was one that Enlightened opinion had for years regarded as contrary to natural rights. The goal of the organizers of the night of August 4 had been to abolish property in seigneurial rights but to require peasants to indemnify the seigneurs. As stated by the Duc d'Aiguillon, who moved their abolition: "These rights are their property. They are the sole support of some individuals; and equity forbids that we demand the abandonment of any property without according a just indemnity to the proprietor, who cedes the enjoyment of his own convenience to the public advantage."[45] This formula, it was hoped, would at once bring the law into accord with nature and reason and establish the principle that no legitimately held property could be taken from its owner without compensation. In fact, the Assembly, in the enthusiasm of the occasion, determined that rights and dues pertaining to serfdom were to be abolished outright without compensation; however, all other rights and dues were to be redeemed by purchase. One kind of property – property in persons – was considered so repugnant to natural law that its owners deserved no compensation even though these rights had been recognized as legal in the past. The Assembly also went beyond d'Aiguillon's recommendations by extending its abolitions to other forms of property as well: It formally suppressed the sale of municipal and judicial offices. Moreover, it abolished all pecuniary privileges and declared that distinctions of birth could no longer bar a person from any ecclesiastical, civil, or military position or honor. Hence, the hereditary titles, privileges, and distinctions that the Parlement of Paris had likened to property were stripped of all material value and were reduced to a purely honorific status.

The night of August 4, then, was the holocaust of property of the old style. Some remnants of course survived the flames: The privileges of trade corporations were still intact until 1791, venal offices were to remain in their functions until the Assembly could complete a reform of the administrative and judicial system, and seigneurial dues were to be collected until redeemed by purchase – although they were finally suppressed without compensation in 1793. But the night of August 4 definitively set the Revolution's course on the question of property. With the destruction of seigneuries and venal offices, the way was opened for a redefinition that confined property strictly to pieces of transformed nature or to tokens – such as money or stock shares – that by convention represented claims on physical property. Not only were certain types of possessions – the right to perform public functions or seigneurial obligations derived from such rights – removed from the compass of legitimate property but those properties that remained intact took on new characteristics. For example, land that had been subject to diverse tenures with varying and intermingled claims by both peasant occupiers and seigneurs became the absolute property of one or the other; serfs became the absolute proprietors of their lands, and sharecroppers were judged to be free tenants renting land from its proprietor. The complex tangle of interlocking rights over land were resolved into individual freehold properties.[46] And what was true in the countryside was true generally: After the night of August 4, property in France came to be limited to the possession of things by individuals.

All of this was formalized in the following weeks in the Declaration of the Rights of Man and Citizen. In Article 2, individual private property was established as a natural right and a foundation of civil society: "The aim of every political association is the preservation of the natural and imprescriptible rights of man. These rights are liberty, property, security, and resistance to oppression." This bracketing of property with liberty, security, and resistance to oppression is an unmistakable sign of the intention of the declaration. Property here is conceived in a classically Lockean sense: as the means accumulated by labor that enable a free person to maintain his independence and liberty in the face of actual or potential oppression. Property, hence, is an extension of personhood, and it must be guaranteed the same liberty as all other aspects of the person. The nature of this liberty is specified in Articles 4 and 5.

> Article 4. Liberty consists in the ability to do whatever does not harm another. Hence the exercise of the natural rights of each man has no limits except those which assure to other members of society the enjoyment of the same rights. These limits can only be determined by law.
>
> Article 5. The law has the right to forbid only such actions as are injurious to society. Nothing may be hindered that is not forbidden by law, and no one may be constrained to do what it does not require.

A citizen was to be free from public or private interference in the enjoyment or disposition of his property except where a law had declared that his action was injurious to the rights of others. Property was no longer, as under the old regime, to be subject to manifold public regulations bringing its use into harmony with a preestablished public order. Rather, public well-being was to be maximized by increasing the liberty and the private well-being of all citizens, by setting citizens free to develop and maintain their private persons and properties as their individual sovereign reason judged best. There were, of course, some public constraints on property rights in cases where the unrestrained use of property might endanger the liberty of others. But these constraints were minimal and marginal by comparison with the old regime.

A more important limitation on individual property rights was that property was subject to taxes. But the imposition of taxes was to be far from the arbitrary affair it had been under the old regime. This was made clear in Articles 13 and 14.

> Article 13. For the maintenance of public forces and for expenses of administration, a common contribution is indispensable; it must be equally apportioned among all citizens according to their means.
>
> Article 14. Citizens have the right to determine, by themselves or by their representatives, the necessity of the public contribution, to follow the use made of the proceeds, and to determine the shares to be paid, the means of assessment and collection, and the duration.

Taxes were no longer an arbitrary exaction but a "public contribution" determined by the citizens themselves. This contribution was, furthermore, to be distributed equitably; there were to be no privileged exemptions for any class of citizens and payments were to be apportioned according to the citizens' means. Under these circumstances, taxes ceased to be a threat to the property, and therefore to the liberty, of citizens and became one of the conditions of the maintenance of a civil society founded for the protection of liberty and property.

Finally, property, as a natural right, could be taken from citizens only under the most special of circumstances.

Article 17. Property being an inviolable and sacred right, no one may be deprived of it except when a legally stated public necessity obviously requires it, and under the condition of a just and prior indemnity.

This article was probably included to justify the Assembly's decision that seigneurs were to be indemnified by the peasants for the loss of their dues. But it also stated a general principle. There were bound to be circumstances where the common good would require citizens to be deprived of their property – such as when a new road or fortifications were to be built on formerly private terrain. In such cases, the common good had to prevail over the rights of the citizen. But deprivation of property had to be carried out for an expressly stated public need, and the proprietor had to be compensated adequately in advance. Thus he was not so much being deprived of his property as having his property in land or buildings transformed into property in money of equivalent value so as to allow the common good of all citizens to be attained. Even in its deprivation, then, property was recognized as a natural right.

In the question of property, as in the question of privilege, the night of August 4 and the codification of its principles in the Declaration of the Rights of Man and Citizen were the great turning point of the Revolution. The National Assembly, by abolishing privileges, changed the French nation from a hierarchical community composed of corporate bodies united by a common reverence for and subjection to the will of the king into an association of free individual citizens living together under the law common to all Frenchmen. At the same time it transformed property from a publicly defined and regulated right that marked its possessor as a member of a particular community into a set of physically palpable possessions that a person had annexed to himself by his labor and was free to use in any way that did not infringe on the liberty of other citizens. The abolition of privilege created free and equal citizens; the transformation of property empowered them to act as genuinely independent individuals.

Property and citizenship were intimately linked in the new social order constructed by the Revolution. It is therefore hardly surprising that some form of property qualification for suffrage or for eligibility to hold office was a recurrent feature of postrevolutionary constitutions. In the constitution of 1791 there were two sets of requirements: one for "active" citizenship, the other for serving as an elector. "Active" citizens, who had the right to vote and to serve in the National Guard, were defined as those adult male citizens who paid a direct tax at least equal to the value of three days' labor; adult males whose annual tax payment was less were designated "passive" citizens and were denied suffrage and membership in the National Guard. This distinction was bitterly opposed by Robespierre in the Assembly, and it was denounced by the Parisian radicals and sans-culottes as discriminating against the poor.[47] The requirements for active citizenship, however, were not precisely property requirements. In the first place, the taxes on which this requirement was based were levied on usufructuaries or renters as well as possessors of land or buildings. Second, even those who had no mobile or landed property were required to pay a tax amounting to three days of labor if their earnings were above the standard set by the local authorities as the average wage of an unskilled laborer.[48] In practice, few people paid less than the required amount of tax. Although this requirement led to the exclusion of some unskilled laborers and textile workers in the cities, it is probable that most of the adult males denied active citizenship were excluded either by the one-year residence requirement or because they were domestic servants.[49] Women were excluded on the same grounds as domestic servants: They were considered dependents of the male head of household and therefore were believed to lack a will of their own. It was, in fact, not individual citizens but independent households, embodied in the husband and father – the père de famille – that were the political units of the French nation.[50]

All in all, about two-thirds of the adult male population had the right to vote in 1791 – a smaller proportion than in the elections to the Estates General in 1789.[51] The active citizens met in "primary assemblies" where they chose electors; the electors in turn met and chose deputies to the Legislative Assembly. But if the requirements for active citizenship were relatively slight, the requirements for electors were very restrictive: No one could serve who was not the owner, renter, or usufructuary of a very substantial property. In the whole of France, there were probably no more than fifty thousand men qualified to serve as electors.[52]

The electoral system established by the constitution of 1791 was tied to property, but not so tightly as in Turgot's *Mémoire sur les municipalités*. Unlike Turgot, the National Assembly did not insist on actual ownership of property; anyone entrusted with the governance or management of a property, whether as owner, usufructuary, or renter, was assumed to have a sufficient stake in society to act as a citizen. Nor were property requirements restricted to property in land: The ownership or rental of buildings was as good as ownership or rental of land. Moreover, a man could become an active citizen even if he managed no property whatsoever so long as his earnings were above a bare minimum. But if propertyless men could vote, the Assembly shared Turgot's concern that citizens be permanently established in their city or village; for this reason, persons who had lived in their domicile for less than a year were excluded from active citizenship. In addition, the full exercise of citizenship was sharply restricted by property requirements, because no one could serve as an elector unless he owned or managed a valuable property. Property and citizenship were not identical, as they had been in Turgot's scheme, but the constitution of 1791 made it manifest that full powers of citizenship depended on property. The constitution of 1791 remained in effect only until September 1792, when the monarchy was abolished, and was replaced by a new constitution in 1793. From then to the Revolution of 1848, the succession was rapid and frequent: There were new constitutions in 1795, 1799, 1802, 1804, 1814, 1815, and 1830. Of all these, only the *montagnard* constitution of 1793 and the first Napoleonic constitution of 1799 entirely omitted property qualifications.[53] The constitutions of 1795, 1802, 1804, and 1815 imposed high property qualifications for electors; the constitutional charters of 1814 and 1830 restricted all suffrage to owners of very substantial property in land or buildings and set even higher qualifications for deputies. Thus, holders of property had greater political rights than their propertyless fellow citizens in all but five of the fifty-seven years between 1791 and 1848. In this way, property rather than privilege became the symbolic and practical hinge of the new political order.

PROPERTY AND THE MECHANICAL ARTS

These transformations in the nature and meaning of property had little immediate effect on the urban trades. The abolition of the masters' property in privilege must have caused some initial apprehension and disarray, but on the whole, daily life in the workshop continued more or less as before. The ringing declarations of the National Assembly may have officially changed the definition of property and its place in public life, but the practical consequences of these legal and symbolic changes were worked out only gradually and over a period of decades. As noted earlier, both journeymen and masters continued to act within a framework of corporate institutions and assumptions until the passage of the d'Allarde and Le Chapelier laws in 1791, and the sans-culottes of 1792 to 1794 had views of property utterly at variance with the conceptions embodied in revolutionary legislation. Despite the revolutionary implications of the sans-culottes' views on property, their notion that merchants, shopkeepers, and farmers were only trustees of their lands and goods, rather than absolute proprietors, had a greater affinity with the quasi-collective and publicly regulated property of the old regime than with the private, individual, absolute property defined in the Declaration of the Rights of Man and Citizen. The sans-culottes, like the gens de métier of the old regime, assumed without question that property should be subject to multiple controls for the common good; and this assumption seems to have been shared by employers and wage workers alike. It was only after the sans-culotte movement had failed, and only after workers and masters had lived and worked under the new legal, social, and political system for a number of years, that they came to think and act in terms of the new conceptions of property. And it was only then that property rights became a major point of contention between them.

It should not be surprising that property relations in the urban trades were transformed only slowly into the new individualistic pattern. After all, the revolutionary redefinitions of property were undertaken above all to solve problems that were either exclusively rural or far more acute in the countryside than in cities: seigneurial oppression, inequitable and burdensome taxation, the absence of adequate representation. It was, therefore, in the countryside that revolutionary legislation had the most immediate impact. Seigneurial dues were eliminated; interlocking claims of landlords and peasants were sorted out and simplified into either rental contracts or freehold properties; vast tracts of land belonging to the church and to émigré nobles were seized by the state, divided, and sold. By 1792 or 1793 the rural regime of property was already palpably different from that of 1788. Moreover, the revolutionary settlement of the rural property question was remarkably successful and permanent. After the agrarian troubles of 1793 that led to the abolition of seigneurial obligations without indemnity, the peasants generally became staunch supporters of the regime.[54] And although there continued to be occasional struggles about property thereafter, the basic settlement was never challenged and left its indelible mark on rural France right down to World War II. The transformation of rural property was a purposeful change successfully imposed by revolutionary action. But if the French Revolution resolved the problems of property in rural France, it eventually created new and different property problems in the cities.

For the urban trades, the most important effect of the French Revolution's redefinition of property was the disaggregation of the collective body of the corporation – theoretically into individuals but often in practice into antagonistic classes of property owners and the propertyless or, as they came to be dubbed, "bourgeois" and "proletarians." As noted earlier, property in the arts et métiers of the old regime was collective in important respects. A master's productive capital, although individually owned, was not his to use as he saw fit but was subject to detailed discipline and constraint by the corporation. In addition to this, his mastership was not, strictly speaking, an individual property at all but a share in the privileges that were the collective property of the entire corporation – a fictitious person that embraced masters, journeymen, and apprentices alike. The Revolution, by abolishing corporations and redefining property, dissolved this hierarchically ordered fictitious person into a collection of free and equal individual citizens, having no links with one another – except as fellow citizens of the French nation – beyond those dictated by their individual interests. These citizens, like all citizens of France, were now empowered with the "natural, inalienable and sacred right" to dispose of their property as they wished. This was as true of those who had no property beyond their labor and a few personal effects as of those who possessed land, buildings, money, or capital. And all were free, if they wished, to contract with one another to make use of their various properties and talents to their mutual advantage.

With the destruction of corporations, relations between employers and employees were put on a new footing. Under the old regime, the authority of the employer was derived from his mastership, from his sharing in the quasi-public privileged authority of the corporation. His journeymen owed him obedience not because he owned the means of production but because he was a master and hence their superior. As a master, the employer's authority extended beyond the workplace to the personal, domestic life of the journeyman. At the same time, masters were restricted in their choice of journeymen to those who had completed legitimate apprenticeships and were therefore genuine members of the corporation, albeit at an inferior rank. After the Revolution, relations between employers and employees became – in the words of Le Chapelier – "free conventions between individual and individual,"[55] and neither of the parties were restricted, either in their choice of collaborators or in the terms of the resulting contract, by the regulations of any supra-individual corporate body. Furthermore, the authority of the employer was restricted to the items specified in the convention between himself and the employee and did not extend to the latter's conduct off the job. For this reason, revolutionaries were hesitant to denominate employers by the term "master" – Le Chapelier, for example, called them "entrepreneurs of works, the former masters" (*"entrepreneurs de travaux, les ci-devant maîtres),* just as former nobles were called *ci-devant nobles.*[56] The disparities between employers and employees were no longer founded upon their juridical status in the corporation but upon the different faculties – skills, properties, talents – that they brought to their collaboration. Those whose faculties were more valuable or more in demand could negotiate contracts very favorable to themselves, whereas those who had less to offer would obtain less favorable terms.

It turned out, of course, that possession of capital was usually far more important than any other faculty in determining the shape of industrial contracts. Those who had nothing to offer but their labor found themselves at a serious disadvantage by comparison with owners of capital – unless they possessed skills that were in very short supply. The theoretically equal individuals who came together in the market quickly sorted out into two groups: possessors of capital who offered work to others and those whose lack of capital obliged them to be wage workers. These two groups corresponded, essentially, to the masters and journeymen of the old regime. But this is not to say that nothing had changed. There were now no legal barriers keeping a journeyman from becoming a master; he could go into business for himself as soon as his savings enabled him to do so, rather than having to obtain an expensive and jealously guarded maîtrise from the corporation. By the same token, an entrepreneur whose business fared badly now faced a greater risk of falling into the ranks of wage workers, because there was no privileged corporation to assure him a niche in the market or to alleviate his misfortunes by means of charités. In this sense, the equality of employers and employees before the law was genuine. The distinction between them was now based only on their private faculties and resources, rather than on an enduring juridical privilege; if a wage earner accumulated enough private property to become an employer, he became an employer with the same rights as any other. Employers were no longer a permanent body of privileged masters but simply the most successful competitors in a free and open market at any particular point in time.

The logic of the new social order, then, made property, rather than privilege, the defining feature of a person's status in the urban trades. The older symbols and forms of the masters' authority and distinctiveness either vanished outright – as with the masters' annual assembly or religious procession – or ceased to have a basis in law even if they were sometimes still observed in practice, as with the notion that the master should exercise paternal power and solicitude over his workers. Property, which had been only one subordinate element of an entire complex of distinctions between journeymen and masters under the old regime, came to be the essential difference under the new. Here the political structure of the new regime complemented and reiterated the message of the legal structure: In a long succession of constitutions, the full powers of citizenship were granted only to those who had property. In short, the significance of the line dividing property holders from the propertyless became far greater under the new regime than under the old. And it was particularly great in the artisan trades, where it tended to sunder in two a body whose members had previously participated – although in differing degrees – in a collective privilege. Employers and wage workers were no longer superior and subordinate members of a common moral body; they were either individual proprietors or propertyless proletarians, whose only legally recognized link was through the free market.

If the revolutionary redefinition of property brought definite practical advantages to proprietors, it also contained a theoretical ambiguity that made possible a new kind of attack on property. By placing the origin of property in human labor on nature, the revolutionary legislators intended to give it a permanent and unshakable foundation. But there was a striking disparity in daily life between the exercise of labor and the possession of property: Some labored a whole lifetime without accumulating property, whereas others possessed vast amounts of property without performing any significant labor. As long as the Enlightenment discussion of property had been a discourse of political opposition, a way of demonstrating the inequity, the oppressiveness, or the irrationality of the institutions of the old regime, this ambiguity was not noticed. It became visible only after the French Revolution, when Enlightenment discourse became the dominant language of social order. Even then, the conception of property imposed by the French Revolution was not necessarily self-contradictory; whether it was or not depended on precisely what was meant by labor and by property and how the links between them were conceived. But by building a concept of property based on labor into the foundation of the society and the state, the French Revolution ensured that the nature, the functions, the significance, and the relationships of property and labor would be hotly contested – both by speculative intellectuals and by more practically minded workers. Although the Revolution armed property owners with a new battery of legal advantages, it also eventually armed propertyless workers with a new and persuasive way of justifying assaults on these very advantages.

The Revolution's redefinition of property had profound and multiple effects on relations between employers and workers in the urban trades, effects that were worked out only slowly over the following decades. Workers were generally hostile to the competitive individualism that was embodied in the new legal system of the Revolution and tended to form associations that would give them collectively the strength and standing they lacked as individuals. In constructing these collective associations, workers drew above all on corporate idioms and organizational forms – significantly altered, of course, in the new cultural and political setting – that affirmed the continued existence of the trade as a moral community. In time, they combined these corporate notions of solidarity with revolutionary claims for the sovereignty of labor over the tyranny of property. Employers in the urban trades were by no means uniformly hostile to corporate notions. They had, after all, been members of corporations before the Revolution, and even in the nineteenth century many of them passed part of their youth as members of journeymen's corporate organizations. But employers were encouraged by the political symbolism and the legal system of the postrevolutionary state to regard themselves as individual proprietors, and in the inevitable conflicts that arose between employers and workers, the masters had little choice but to stand on their property rights. An opposition between propertyless wage earners and property-owning employers came increasingly to dominate the life of the urban trades; and at times it dominated the public life of the nation as a whole. The remainder of this book will trace out the story of this opposition: the effects of economic growth and industrial development; the changing idioms of the wage earners, the employers, and the state; the twists and lurches of economic and political struggles; and finally the momentous – if ultimately unsuccessful – attempt to do away with private property altogether in the Revolution of 1848.

142

7 Industrial society

To speak of France in the first half of the nineteenth century as an industrial society may seem an exaggeration. After all, the majority of the population still lived in the countryside in 1850, and even in the cities only a minority of the labor force was employed in factories. Although factory industry and the steam engine made significant advances, the developments of these years were only the first stirrings of industrialization. But from the standpoint of the late eighteenth century, the epithet "industrial society" is much more appropriate. What now appears as the hesitant beginnings of a long and slow development seemed to be a major departure to contemporaries: Even a very few steam engines or blast furnaces or spinning mills could make a powerful impression on people who had never seen them before. From their point of view, modern industry was a distinctive feature of their age; theirs was an industrial society as no previous society had ever seen.

Moreover, when the late eighteenth century is taken as the reference point, the term "industrial society" turns out to be appropriate in quite another sense, for the term had a very different meaning at the end of the eighteenth century than it has today. "Industry" in the eighteenth century meant diligence or assiduousness; it referred to a quality of human effort. This meaning still exists, of course, but industry now refers primarily to a set of institutions and operations whose function is the production of goods and, above all, to manufacturing. (It is possible to speak of agriculture as an industry, or of "service industries," but when it stands unmodified, "industry" denotes manufacturing.) The noun "industry" and the adjective "industrial" have been reified in common usage since the eighteenth century. They no longer refer to qualities of persons but to supra-personal institutions or "structures" within which persons are constrained to live and act. Indeed, it was precisely in the early years of the nineteenth century that this reified meaning of the term came into widespread use.

A similar shift has taken place in the meaning of the term "society." In Enlightenment usage, the terms "social" and "society" implied a conscious, voluntary act of association by independent individuals. This meaning was obvious, of course, in the term "social contract" and in the discourse of contract theorists in general. Outside the bounds of political philosophy, the chief meaning of "society" was "social intercourse," which was also a voluntary coming together of persons for some purpose – in this case the pleasures of company and conversation. The term "society," then, might signify a number of things: social intercourse, or the political community created by a social contract, or what we might call a "voluntary association." But it did not mean an interrelated set of institutions bound together by its own somewhat mysterious but ultimately discoverable laws and impelled by "social forces" that were beyond the voluntary control of the persons who composed it. It was only toward the very end of the eighteenth century and above all in the first decades of the nineteenth that "society" and "social" came to take on this reified, supra-voluntary connotation. "Society," from being a voluntary *relation* between persons, became a *thing* that transcended persons, a kind of natural object that could be studied by the methods of natural science. It was only in the early nineteenth century that the term "social science" became a standard locution in intellectual discourse.[1] Likewise, the terms "social structure," "social forces," and "social laws" – which are standard in nineteenth- and twentieth-century discourse – would have been either meaningless or deeply paradoxical to eighteenth-century readers.

The eighteenth-century meaning of "industrial society," then, might be rendered as "voluntary relations formed between people on the basis of their diligence in carrying out the tasks of daily life." From this point of view it is by no means absurd to speak of nineteenth-century France as an industrial society; after all, one of the major goals and accomplishments of the French Revolution had been to create an "industrial society" in this sense. Under the old regime, the French nation was constructed as a hierarchy of bodies and communities united in common subjection to and reverence for the will of the king. The French Revolution had destroyed all these diverse bodies and communities and recast the nation as a society (in the eighteenth-century sense) formed by the combined wills (or "general will") of its citizens. Under the old regime, order derived from spirit, and sovereignty resided in the will of a quasi-sacerdotal king – a minister of God, anointed with holy chrism at his coronation, who ruled, as the cliché put it, "by divine right." In the new regime established by the French Revolution, order came from nature. Sovereignty resided in the citizens whose labor on nature – their "industry" – gave rise to property, and who formed a social contract to preserve their natural rights, including their property rights. This social contract was actually written down in the Revolution in the Declaration of the Rights of Man and Citizen. In this scheme of things, labor or "industry" was no longer a lowly activity relegated only to those groups of the population deemed incapable of higher service; rather, it was the very stuff of human life and stood at the foundation of all social order. The preservation of private property – which was the material embodiment of industry – became a central duty of the state, and the possession of property became a criterion for the full exercise of citizenship. The Revolution transformed France from a hierarchical spiritual body with the king at its head into a voluntary association of productive citizens. As such, it became in the most precise sense an "industrial society."

This revaluation of human industry meant that the production and the distribution of wealth became a central activity of the nation and that maintaining good economic performance became a central task of government. Of course, the state had been concerned about the economy under the old regime as well – one need think only of Colbert. But the concerns of old-regime and postrevolutionary governments were different in one crucial respect. Under the old regime – and here Colbert is a perfect example – fiscal questions were always foremost. The state fostered economic growth, but it did so in order to increase the yield of taxes, for it was tax revenues that enabled the king to pursue glory – above all through warfare but also through magnificence at court.[2] Fiscal motives were, of course, present in postrevolutionary regimes as well, but economic growth was now pursued for its own sake; it was no longer merely a means in the pursuit of glory. Economic questions were more central in some postrevolutionary regimes than in others. Defending property and fostering economic growth and private enrichment was a dominant concern of the "Thermidorians" – that is to say of the governments between the fall of Robespierre in 1794 and Napoleon's coup d'état in 1799 – and during the July Monarchy of 1830 to 1848 – where Marx's judgment that the July Monarchy "was nothing other than a joint stock company for the exploitation of French national wealth" was only a slight exaggeration of common opinion.[3] Under other governments economic questions were subordinated to other concerns: to the execution of the war and the pursuit of public virtue under Robespierre; to the conquest of Europe and the establishment of an orderly administration under Napoleon; to the repression of revolutionary sentiments and the fostering of deference and religious piety under the Restoration. But even these regimes recognized the centrality of private property in the social order, and they all saw encouragement of agriculture, industry, and commerce as one of their essential duties. They may have envisioned the nation as a theater of virtue, as an administrative machine, or as a pious congregation gathered around the monarch, but they also saw it as an association of productive citizens.

Nineteenth-century France, then, was an industrial society in two distinct but related senses. It was a society in which industrial production expanded rapidly and techniques of production underwent major changes. And it was also a society in which the exercise of human industry was valued as a foundation of the social order and in which economic prosperity was a major goal of public life. This chapter will be concerned mainly with "industrial society" in the first sense: with patterns of economic growth and their consequences for the urban working class. But it is worth remarking at the outset that neither aspect of "industrial society" can be neatly separated from the other. The sustained growth of the French economy in the nineteenth century was both a consequence and a confirmation of the new higher valuation placed on human industry; and the results of economic growth for social and political action depended as much on the evaluative, conceptual, and legal framework established by the French Revolution as on the sheer force of material circumstances. The production and exchange of goods and services – in nineteenth-century France and in all other societies – both partake of and influence the conceptual patterns, the values, the institutional structures, and the legal relations of the society in which they occur. Sometimes, as in this chapter, it is useful for analytical purposes to separate out economic factors for special scrutiny. But the ultimate point of such exercises should be to illuminate the whole of life – the social and cultural and political as well as the economic – not to make the economy into a self-enclosed and autonomous mechanism or to reduce the rest of life to a reflex of economic forces.

FRENCH INDUSTRIAL GROWTH

France, like England and most other European nations, experienced wide-ranging changes in its economy during the nineteenth century. Whether these changes amounted to an "industrial revolution" is a matter of some scholarly controversy. J. H. Clapham, in his classic *Economic Development of France and Germany, 1815–1914,* was the first to raise the question. "It might be said," Clapham wrote, "that France never went through an industrial revolution . . . The transformation accomplished in a century was in many ways less complete than that which Germany experienced in the forty years after 1871."[4] The contrast with England – the homeland of the industrial revolution – was perhaps even more striking. Between about 1780 and 1830, the face of England was transformed by the application of new industrial techniques. By the end of the 1820s, great areas in the North and Midlands of England had become bustling industrial districts with vast factories turning out cotton and woolen cloth or iron and steam engines.[5] France experienced no great spurt of industrial growth comparable to either that of Germany after 1871 or of England in the late eighteenth and early nineteenth centuries. As a result, economic historians have tended to speak of its economy as "retarded" or "stagnant" in the nineteenth century. Indeed, accounting for "stagnation" or "retardation" has become a dominant problem in French economic history, especially in the writings of English and American scholars.[6]

In recent years, however, economic historians have begun to look at the notion of "retardation" more critically, and the result has been a drastic shift in the perception of the nineteenth-century French economy. Detailed quantitative studies, above all those carried out by the Institut de science economique appliquée, have revealed that the French economy grew steadily and quite impressively in the nineteenth century – physical product per capita, for example, more than tripled from 1803–12 to 1905–13 – and that nineteenth-century growth was a continuation of sustained economic expansion dating back at least to the middle of the eighteenth century.[7] Although it is true that the French economy never experienced a "spurt" of industrial growth and that no area of France underwent the kind of dramatic and visible transformation from peaceful countryside to smoky and sprawling industrial district that occurred in the Midlands and Lancashire in Britain or in the Ruhr valley in Germany, the overall rate of increase in real output per capita during the nineteenth century was hardly distinguishable from that of Britain. It now appears that the French experience must be seen as one of the earliest and most successful cases of sustained modern industrial and economic growth and not as the anemic and imitative efforts of a late-starting "follower" of Britain.[8]

One of the reasons for this shift in evaluation of the nineteenth-century French economy is a more careful specification of the meaning of "economic growth." Clapham and his successors were concerned chiefly with palpable signs of economic transformation – the rise of factories, the rapid growth of cities, the adoption of new techniques in agriculture, and so on. Their critics have defined economic growth more precisely – and more technically – as a sustained increase in real output per capita. Introducing the factory system was, of course, one important means of raising output per capita: It increased the productivity of labor by using new sources of power and new large-scale mechanical technology. But there were also many other ways in which output could be increased: by other, less spectacular improvements in technology; by better utilization of existing technology; by lowering transportation costs; by improving the scope and efficiency of markets; by utilizing given factors of production more efficiently through increased specialization, an increased division of labor, or improvements in the organization of firms, and so on. Finally, because income per capita is a fraction, with the national product as its numerator and the national population as its denominator, the rate of increase of population also has a direct effect on the rate of economic growth. In both England and France the introduction of factory production, particularly in textiles and metallurgy, was an important source of economic growth. But factories figured much less prominently in the French pattern of growth than in the British.

One important feature of the French economy that allowed a sustained increase in output per capita without a massive growth of factory industry was a relatively slow rate of population growth. The population of Europe as a whole more than doubled in the nineteenth century, whereas British population rose 350 percent over the century as a whole and German population rose 250 percent from 1816 to 1900. French population, by contrast, rose by less than 45 percent in the entire nineteenth century.[9] (For a comparison of French population growth with that of other European countries, see Figure 1.) This slow growth of population – which resulted from a voluntary reduction in birthrates, not from high death rates – meant that the pressure of population on resources was less severe in France during the nineteenth century than in most other European countries.

One result of this low level of population pressure was that a sizable proportion of French population growth could be absorbed by rural areas. Between 1801 and 1851, the absolute number of people living in rural settlements probably increased by as much as the number in urban settlements, although the rate of growth of urban settlements was certainly higher.[10] This increase in rural population took place without resulting in severe overcrowding of the sort that could jeopardize agricultural productivity. On the contrary, the product of French agriculture rose by about 29 percent in per capita terms from 1806 to 1851, and the product per person employed in agriculture rose by about 38 percent.[11] In part, this combination of rising rural population and increasing agricultural productivity was made possible by a rise in the proportion of rural residents engaged in nonagricultural pursuits.[12] Some of these rural nonagriculturalists worked in nearby cities, whereas others made their livings – or supplemented them – by domestic industry or by the provision of goods or of transportation and other services to rural populations.

With the total population growing slowly and rural population continuing to increase, it should not be surprising that French cities grew only moderately in the first half of the nineteenth century. Estimates of the population living in urban settlements before the middle of the nineteenth century are far from exact, but there is general agreement that the urban population (usually defined by French statisticians as persons living in settlements of more than 2,000 inhabitants) grew more rapidly than the rural population, at least after 1831.[13] A comparison of Marcel Reinhard's relatively good figures for the population of cities in 1806 with the census figures for 1851 indicates that the number of people living in settlements with more than 10,000 inhabitants increased from about 2.6 million in 1806 to about 5 million in 1851.[14] But this still accounted for only 14 percent of the entire

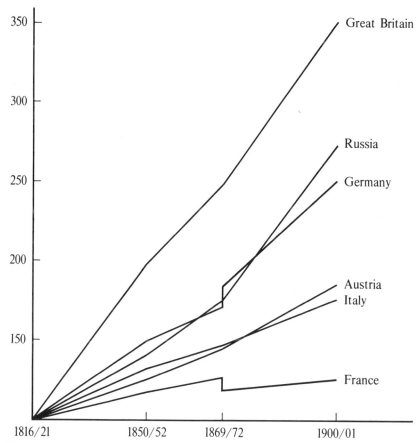

Figure 1. Increase in population in major European countries. 1816/21=100. From Mitchell, pp. 19–26.

population in 1851, and even using the census definition of 2,000 or more inhabitants as an urban settlement, the urban population accounted for just over a quarter of the total, as opposed to perhaps a fifth in 1801.[15]

As can be seen from Table 1, most of the larger French cities grew quite substantially in the first half of the century. With the sole exception of Rouen, all the cities that ranked among the top twenty-five in France in 1851 had grown more rapidly than the population as a whole since 1801 – that is, by more than 26 percent.[16] Paris, of course, grew most spectacularly. Already one of the largest cities in the world with more than 500,000 inhabitants in 1801, it had nearly doubled, just surpassing the 1 million mark by 1851. Marseille and Lyons, the largest of the provincial cities, also grew quite rapidly and were approaching 200,000 by mid-century. There

TABLE 1.
Growth of the twenty-five largest cities in France, 1801–51

	Population in 1801	Population in 1851	Percent increase
Paris	547,736	1,053,262	92
Marseille	111,130	195,292	76
Lyons	109,500	177,190	62
Bordeaux	90,992	130,927	44
Rouen	87,000	101,265	16
Nantes	73,879	96,262	30
Toulouse	50,171	93,379	86
Lille	54,756	75,795	38
Strasbourg	49,056	75,565	54
Toulon	20,500	69,404	238
Brest	27,000	61,160	126
Metz	32,099	57,713	80
St.-Etienne	16,259	56,001	224
Nîmes	38,800	53,619	38
Amiens	40,289	52,149	29
Orléans	36,165	47,393	31
Angers	33,000	46,779	42
Montpellier	33,913	45,811	35
Reims	20,295	45,754	129
Caen	30,900	45,290	52
Nancy	29,740	45,129	52
Limoges	20,550	41,630	102
Besançon	30,000	41,295	38
Rennes	25,904	39,505	53
Avignon	19,889	35,890	80

Source: Based on Pouthas, *Population française,* p. 98.

were, moreover, several smaller cities – Toulon, Brest, Saint-Etienne, Reims, Limoges – that more than doubled in this period. But there were also a large number of cities whose growth was quite slow. Eleven of the top twenty-five, for example, grew by less than 50 percent in fifty years. France was a more urban country in 1851 than at the beginning of the century, but city dwellers still comprised only a minority of the population and were far outnumbered by peasants.

Here the contrast with Britain is striking. Where only one of the ten largest French cities had so much as doubled in population in the first half of the nineteenth century, *none* of the ten largest British cities had *less* than doubled. Leeds and Birmingham, in fact, had more than tripled; Manchester, Liverpool, and Glasgow had more than quadrupled; and Bradford had multiplied eightfold. In 1801 London had been the only British city with more than 100,000 inhabitants, whereas Marseille and Lyons – in addition to Paris – had more than 100,000 inhabitants; in 1851, only Bordeaux and Rouen had been added to the French list, whereas ten cities in Britain had surpassed 100,000. And although neither Marseille nor Lyons had yet attained 200,000 by 1851, Glasgow, Liverpool, and Manchester had all topped 300,000, and Birmingham had passed 200,000.[17] Finally, only 14 percent of the French population lived in cities with more than 10,000 inhabitants in 1851; the comparable figure for Britain was 39 percent.[18] The same contrast can be seen in the proportion of the population making its living from agriculture: just over half in France but only a little more than a quarter in Britain.[19] By comparison with Britain, the pace of urbanization in nineteenth-century France was hardly impressive.

France's slow rate of population growth and leisurely pace of urbanization are of fundamental importance for understanding the French pattern of economic growth in the nineteenth century. This can be seen most clearly by contrast with Britain, where the development of large-scale, mechanized industry was intimately connected to rapid population growth. Factories, for all their advantages over handicraft methods of production, also had certain limitations, especially in the early decades of factory technology. They were superior at producing vast quantities of standardized goods of modest quality, but in order to be profitable, they also required a very large market for their goods. Otherwise, demand would be insufficient to justify the large and inflexible capital investment that a factory represented. The French market for mass-produced cotton and woolen cloth was far from insignificant, and French entrepreneurs in fact responded to this demand by constructing a large number of textile factories, particularly in such northern cities as Rouen, Elbeuf, Lille, Roubaix, Tourcoing, Mulhouse, Reims, and Saint-Quentin. But the expansion of demand in France was much slower than in England, and this limited the development of the French factory sector. Part of the British advantage in this respect was their domination of overseas markets and particularly of tropical markets, a domination that was secured by their naval victories in the wars of the French Revolution. However, the British home market also expanded much more rapidly than the French.[20] In part this was simply a function of the higher overall rate of population growth. But the market for the kind of goods that could be produced profitably by factories increased even more rapidly than the population as a whole.

Rapid urbanization was one reason for this. Whereas many of the wants of peasants were satisfied outside the market – they typically grew much of the food they ate and produced many of their own manufactured goods during the winter "dead season" – urban people's wants were satisfied almost exclusively through the market. Urbanization, therefore, implied that a rising proportion of all goods consumed would be purchased in the market. Moreover, urban residents tended to be much more alert to new fashions and receptive to new goods – to light cotton cloths rather than to the traditional linens and wools or to metal buttons and buckles of the sort that became a specialty of Birmingham.[21] Urban dwellers not only spent a higher proportion of their income in the market but were especially likely to spend it on factory-produced objects. A rise in the proportion of the population living in cities, therefore, led to a *disproportionate* expansion in the market for mass-produced goods.

At the same time, a rapidly increasing population – and in particular a rapidly increasing urban population – led to a massive commercialization of English farming. Rising urban demand for food provided a powerful incentive for English farmers to adopt new methods of husbandry in order to maximize their output and their profits. It was from about 1760 to 1830 – that is, the classic period of the industrial revolution – that a final wave of enclosures swept over the English countryside, engulfing the last areas of small-scale and inefficient agricultural production.[22] Toward the end of the eighteenth and the beginning of the nineteenth century, the dynamics of urban growth pulled even the agricultural population definitively into the sphere of the market. Independent peasants, already rare in the eighteenth century, virtually disappeared in the early nineteenth, and the land came to be tilled almost exclusively by wage-earning laborers, who, like town laborers, bought most of what they consumed in the market. This inexorable advance of a unified national market was important not only from the point of view of demand for factory products but from the point of view of labor supply as well. The development of large-scale commercial farming, with labor performed by landless wage earners, eliminated all possibility of an "Irish" solution to the population problem – that is, fragmentation of peasant tenures into tiny, marginally self-sufficient and unproductive mini-holdings – and assured that population growth would result in an abundant supply of labor for urban manufactures.[23]

All of this is not to say that rapid population growth or any other single factor by itself can "explain" British economic growth in the industrial revolution. The British economy grew as a result of mutually supporting interactions among a large number of factors: population growth, agricultural organization, foreign trade, favorable resource endowment, technological innovation, urbanization, unification of the market, and many others besides. But it is certainly true that the British economy would not have assumed its *particular* shape – with its massive development of factory production in vast industrial districts – had it not been for the rapid growth and rapid urbanization of the British population. And, by the same token, the very different shape of French economic growth was made possible by the slow growth of the French population. In Britain, the rapid increase in population and massive urbanization unified the market, wiped out peasant agriculture, and spurred demand for mass-produced goods. In France, the slow increase in population and gradual urbanization left many regional and local markets intact, allowed peasant agriculture to make piecemeal adjustments to slowly rising demand, and set limits on the market for mass-produced goods. The result was a much less revolutionary pattern of economic growth – but in the long run a no less successful one. Or to put the same point in terms more favorable to the French: Only a revolutionary transformation of the means of production enabled Britain to sustain a rising output per capita in the face of runaway population growth, whereas the French, with their slow population growth, could afford to be much more gradual.

The French pattern of economic growth, which combined substantial industrialization with the continued expansion of handicrafts and of peasant agriculture, should therefore not be seen as a failed effort to imitate British achievements but as an entirely appropriate response to the French situation. With population increasing only slowly, with much of the agricultural population only partially engaged in the cash nexus, and with the national territory divided into only partially integrated regional markets – both for commodities and for labor – there were inherent limits to the possibilities of factory production. In these circumstances, it was economically rational for a large part of the nation's capital to be invested in small-scale artisanal production.[24] This was particularly true because of the marked competitive advantage that France already enjoyed over other nations in many highly skilled, high-quality industries in the eighteenth century. Here the opinion of the Parlement of Paris, which was quoted in a different context in Chapter 4, can stand for that of most contemporaries:

> Our merchandise has always won out in foreign markets . . . [It] is sought after all over Europe for its taste, its beauty, its finesse, its solidity, the correctness of its design, the perfection of its execution, the quality of its raw materials . . . Our arts, brought to the highest degree of perfection, enrich your capital, of which the entire world has become the tributary.[25]

For all its hyperbole, this was basically an accurate assessment, and it remained accurate through the nineteenth century as well. The fine furniture, jewelry, tapestries, and countless other luxury productions of Paris; the silk cloth of Lyons and the silk ribbons and trimmings of Saint-Etienne; the porcelains of Limoges; all of these continued to be admired and sought after throughout the world, and all were major nodes of growth in the nineteenth-century French economy. The success of French industrial growth in the nineteenth century was largely a matter of maintaining and developing France's superiority in highly skilled, high-quality handicrafts. Indeed, even factory industry in France tended to be most successful in the finer and more skill-intensive branches of the trade. Both the cotton industry of Mulhouse and the woolen industry of Roubaix-Tourcoing – the fastest growing centers of factory textile production in France in the first two-thirds of the nineteenth century – specialized in the finest grades of cloth.[26]

One of the important consequences of this pattern of economic growth was that the typical French worker of the nineteenth century lived in an old city with long-standing artisan traditions, not in a new factory town. Of the twenty-five largest cities in France in 1851, all but Saint-Etienne had been chartered cities and major centers of commerce, administration, and handicrafts for centuries. Moreover, Saint-Etienne was the exception that proved the rule. Although it was a new city that had grown from a mere industrial village in the eighteenth and early nineteenth centuries to become a major metallurgical and mining center, a far larger proportion of Saint-Etienne's labor force was actually employed in the small-scale and highly skilled silk ribbon and trimmings industry than in mining and metallurgy. Even the new industrial city of Saint-Etienne was dominated by highly skilled artisans rather than by factory workers. Once again the contrast with Britain is striking. Of the ten largest cities in Britain in 1851, six – Manchester, Birmingham, Glasgow, Leeds, Sheffield, and Bradford – were essentially factory towns, and the traffic at the port of Liverpool was dominated by the Lancashire cotton trade. Only three of the top ten British cities – London, Edinburgh, and Bristol – had been important urban centers before the eighteenth century, and in legal terms, both Manchester and Birmingham were actually still unincorporated villages until the 1830s.

THE DECLINING ARTISAN?

Given the nature of French cities and French manufactures, it is quite understandable that small-scale artisan industry retained a clear numerical predominance far past the middle of the nineteenth century. Markovitch estimates that the industrial population employed in artisan industry in France was twice the population employed in large-scale industry even as late as 1876.[27] And the numerical predominance of artisans over factory workers was even greater in the first half of the century. A substantial portion of these craftsmen, of course, worked in industries producing for the national and international market. But by far the largest number of French artisans made products that were consumed locally – food, buildings, clothing, shoes, furniture, tools and utensils of all sorts, and so on. And these trades grew in virtually all cities, in factory towns as well as in centers of commerce, administration, or luxury production.

The fact that handicrafts were eventually supplanted by factories in nearly all branches of manufacture has led historians to think of factory industry nd artisan industry as directly antagonistic. Thus, the "declining artisan" as become a stock character of nineteenth-century labor history, with the ritish handloom weavers, reduced from proud opulence to pathetic misery y the competition of the power loom, as the standard example. But the andloom weaver was actually a very unusual case; generally, the growth of ictories tended not to reduce but to multiply the number of artisans, at ast in the first two-thirds of the nineteenth century. Until the last decades f the century, textiles were virtually the only industry in which factories ompeted directly with artisan producers.[28] Otherwise, factory production ither developed in industries already manned by unskilled labor – for exmple, heavy metallurgy or such food-processing industries as sugar refinig, flour milling, or oil pressing – or created entirely new industries that ad not existed before the industrial revolution, such as heavy chemicals or ie construction of steam engines or textile machinery. Thus, the advent of ictories increased the number of unskilled or semiskilled workers in the bor force, but it did not supplant artisans. And in the case of machine onstruction, the result of industrialization was to create a new demand for illed metalworkers, who, although they worked in factories, were among ie most highly skilled and best-paid workers in the economy. These proud aftsmen bore virtually no resemblance to the ill-paid and unorganized ctory hands in the textile, chemical, or food-processing factories. In the iys before assembly lines and interchangeable parts, machine construction quired great intelligence, judgment, dexterity, and finesse – what in the ghteenth century would have been called "art" – on the part of the orkers. Moreover, at least in France, many workers in mechanical conruction continued to serve their apprenticeships in the traditional metal afts and continued to call themselves by such titles as *serrurier* (locksmith) : *chaudronnier* (coppersmith), rather than the newer *mécanicien* (machint). They also tended to form the same kind of labor organizations as metalorkers who were employed in small shops; many, for example, were mem- :rs of compagnonnage. The development of machine-construction ctories, in short, did not supplant artisans but rather created a large new .tegory of particularly prosperous artisans who worked in factories.[29]

Meanwhile, the development of factories of any kind necessarily multiied the demand for artisan-produced goods. Factories had to be built, and e labor force of the factories – together with the workers who transported w materials and finished goods to and from the factories and the businessen who bought and sold them – had to be housed, clothed, and supplied ith goods of all sorts. Given the technology of the first half of the nineenth century, virtually all of these needs could be met only by artisans: by onemasons, carpenters, and joiners; by butchers, bakers, and confecners; by makers of furniture, cooking pots, carts, coaches, cutlery, and a st of other products. Factories also contributed to the multiplication of certain categories of artisans by reducing the cost of their raw materials and thereby increasing demand for their products. This was most notably true in the clothing trades, where the new lower-priced output of cotton and woolen mills made it possible for people to afford a greater quantity and variety of clothing, and in the metalworking trades, where cheaper iron meant a wider demand for assorted ironwares. In nineteenth-century conditions, then, the expansion of factory industry and the expansion of artisan industry went hand in hand.

The only major exception to this mutually supporting relationship between factory and artisan industry was in textiles, where the new factories supplanted hand spinning and handloom weaving. The main effect of spinning mills was to deprive thousands of rural women of a profitable by-employment, but the loss of employment in spinning was probably counteracted by a large increase in the domestic weaving industry, in which women could either weave themselves or assist their husbands in stringing looms, winding shuttles, and other auxiliary tasks. Later, when power looms were introduced, they displaced many full-time handloom weavers, of whom the majority were probably men. Although no detailed study of French handloom weavers exists, it seems clear that their decline was much less traumatic than in Britain. Of course, the growth of the French cotton industry bore no comparison with the British cotton boom of the late eighteenth century, and having risen less precipitously, French handloom weaving had less far to fall.[30] The fall was also slower because the moderate growth rate of the French textile industry allowed only a gradual introduction of power looms and because power looms were much more difficult to adapt to the production of the fine cloths in which the French specialized. In the silk industry of Lyons, for example, power looms were only introduced in the last quarter of the nineteenth century.[31] It also appears that many French handloom weavers made a successful transition to employment in textile factories and that the familial organization of work that characterized domestic textile production also followed them into the factory.[32] But in spite of all these attenuating circumstances, the rise of textile factories did pose a direct threat to hand production. The impact was later and more gradual than in Britain, but eventually handloom weavers were eliminated in all branches of the industry.

It is worth noting, however, that the skilled textile workers who were displaced by machines were mainly rural domestic weavers. This, of course, did not make their displacement any less painful, but it does mean that the one category of skilled workers who experienced a direct conflict with factory technology in the first half of the nineteenth century were isolated, both physically and culturally, from urban artisans. Country weavers lived in a different world, one they shared more with peasants than with urban craftsmen. And they continued to be sharply distinct from the artisans when they came to work in the new spinning and weaving factories. They lacked any corporate tradition, and, unlike the urban artisans, they rarely formed structured labor organizations, even in the city. Even their strikes in the first half of the nineteenth century often bore more resemblance to rural grain riots or festival processions than to the disciplined work stoppages of the urban artisan trades.[33] And as late as 1848, workers in textile factories generally remained quite separate from the working-class political movements that attracted masses of artisans. The textile workers' hopes, anxieties, resentments, and sufferings – both in the countryside and in the urban factories – remained distant from most artisans' experiences.

In short, the development of factory industry in France in the first half of the nineteenth century did not send urban artisans into general decline. Although the power loom slowly eliminated rural weavers, the urban trades that had been organized as corporations under the old regime generally experienced a vigorous expansion during the first half of the nineteenth century. In numerical terms, at least, this was an era of rise, rather than of decline, for urban artisans. For the better part of the nineteenth century, artisans remained the dominant sector of the urban working class, numerically, politically, and culturally.

The fact that artisans could coexist with the factory system does not mean that life within the artisan trades went on unaltered; on the contrary, these were years of widespread changes, tensions, and conflicts. Expansion of numbers could itself be a source of tension. In particular, a rapid increase in the number of journeymen working in a trade made it difficult for workers to maintain control of the labor market – to assure that only properly apprenticed men were hired, to maintain surveillance of working conditions in hundreds of workshops, to maintain adequate and uniform wages, and so on. Thus, a rapid increase in numbers could have a major impact on relations between workers and masters. There were also some changes in technology – quite apart from the rise of factories – that had important effects on artisan trades. For example, mechanical saws were introduced in the production of lumber, mechanical presses were introduced in printing, and nails and rivets began to be substituted for stitching in shoemaking. But probably more far-reaching than these technical changes were innovations in the organization of production and of marketing that occurred quite independently of any change in technology. As cities grew and markets expanded, some entrepreneurs in the urban trades responded to rising demand by turning away from the older practice of making items to order for their clients and instead came to specialize in lower-quality, standardized, ready-to-wear or ready-to-use items that could be produced more efficiently and sold at a lower price. This system was known as *confection*. Entrepreneurs who adopted the system of confection were, in the language of economists, exploiting "economies of scale" made possible by rising demand.

Labor in workshops engaged in confection could be organized quite differently from that in traditional workshops. Above all, the division of labor was greatly increased. A pair of shoes made to the specifications of a particular client could probably be produced as efficiently by a single workman as by more than one, because each part had to be made to order. But when a workshop turned out dozens of pairs of shoes made in the same style and in standardized sizes, it was much more profitable to assign a different worker to each step of the manufacturing process. The possibility of more finely divided labor meant that the optimum number of employees per entrepreneur was higher and that workers needed a narrower range of skill – a relatively unskilled man or woman could be taught to cut leather to a preset size and shape, but only a thoroughly trained worker could be trusted to make a pair of shoes to order. Indeed, if the process of manufacture was broken down into sufficiently simple and standardized steps, it did not even require the supervision of the entrepreneur and could be carried out by men, women, and children working in their own rooms or garrets. All of these phenomena – skill dilution, an increase in scale and in the division of labor, domestic production on a putting-out basis – are well attested both in Paris and in the larger provincial cities by the 1840s and probably date back to the twenties and thirties as well. Although research on confection is far too sketchy to determine the precise extent of these practices, they seem to have been particularly common in the shoemaking, tailoring, dressmaking, and furniture industries.[34]

A related set of organizational changes took place in the building industry, particularly in Paris. There a big contractor would undertake to build a number of houses and then would subcontract the actual work to *marchandeurs* (bargainers or hagglers), who in turn would engage their own workers at the lowest rate they could negotiate. This system of marchandage tended to squeeze down wages and made the maintenance of uniform standards of pay and working conditions virtually impossible. It certainly was generally regarded as exploitative by the workers. The abolition of marchandage was one of the first concessions that workers wrung from the Provisional Government after the Revolution of 1848, on the grounds that it was "unjust, vexatory, and contrary to the principle of fraternity."[35] Like confection, marchandage seems to have been connected to an increase in the scale of the undertaking. But in the case of marchandage, the economies appear to have arisen less from an increased division of labor than from intensified exploitation, both of laborers and of the marchandeurs, by the capitalist contractors.[36]

Given the present state of research, it is impossible to say how wide spread marchandage and confection were. It would be surprising, however, if these or analogous changes in the organization of production were not taking place in most of the larger French cities in the first half of the nineteenth century. After all, such changes in the organization of firms are precisely what one would expect under the stimulus of broadening markets and rising demand. Indeed, as already noted, chambrelans – that is, domestic producers who fabricated inferior goods and evaded the regulations of the corporations – were already a serious problem in some trades in the eighteenth century. From the economic point of view, the widespread development of confection and marchandage can be seen as an extension of processes already under way during the economic growth of the later eighteenth century.

Although there are certainly continuities between such developments under the old regime and in the nineteenth century, the legal transformations imposed by the Revolution both encouraged changes in the organization of production and altered their meaning. Under the old regime, attempts to employ subcontractors, or to put work out to domestic workers, or to produce low-quality standardized goods, or to multiply the division of labor, or to introduce untrained workers into the trade were contrary to the statutes of the corporations and therefore illegal. This did not mean that these practices never occurred, but it did mean that they tended to occur either on a small scale, out of sight of the jurés of the corporations, or outside the corporations' jurisdiction. It was, as noted earlier, because entrepreneurs wanted to evade the strict regulations and high labor costs of the urban corporations that weaving became predominantly a rural industry in the seventeenth and eighteenth centuries. But in the nineteenth century, thanks to the Revolution's abolition of corporations and redefinition of property rights, all these practices became exercises of the legitimate rights of individual proprietors. If an entrepreneur wished to hire untrained workers to cut out standardized uppers for mass-produced shoes, there was no legal constraint to keep him from hiring them at whatever wage rate he could negotiate. Or if a furniture maker wished to sell cheap and standardized imitations of high-style furniture, he was free to produce and to sell whatever quantity the market would bear. If such practices were to be limited at all, they could be limited only by the concerted action of workers, who might, of course, be supported in various ways by small masters fearful of the competition of more innovative rivals. But such concerted action was illegal and therefore difficult to organize and hard to sustain. In short, the tables were turned in the nineteenth century: What had been fraudulent practices became the legitimate exercise of individual industry, and what had been legitimate restrictions on the cupidity and fraud of dishonest masters became illegal conspiracies against the rights of property. The development of confection, marchandage, and other changes in the organization of production in artisan trades derived from changes in the legal framework of industry during the French Revolution, as well as from a growth of the market.

French artisans in the first half of the nineteenth century found their status, their incomes, and their working conditions under continual threat from unfavorable changes in the organization of production. This was also, for most artisans, a period of stagnant or even declining real wages. Although much less research has been done on this problem for France than for nineteenth-century England, most of it seems to point to the same conclusions. Whether one considers the aggregate calculations of Kuczynski or Lhomme, or Jacques Rougerie's observations on Paris, or my own work on wages, prices, and consumption in Marseille, it appears that real wages and per capita consumption rose somewhat from 1810 to a peak in the early 1820s, fell steadily but gradually to a little below their initial level by the 1840s, and did not attain the level of the early 1820s again until some time in the 1870s.[37] The decline between the 1820s and the 1840s was not very steep – it was on the order of perhaps 10 to 15 percent – and there was a good deal of variation from trade to trade and city to city. But overall, the performance of real wages was hardly impressive, particularly for a period of steadily rising income per capita. In an era of manifest prosperity, when commerce and industry were visibly expanding, the purchasing power of most artisans – as well as of less skilled workers – was actually declining until the middle of the century and rose only slowly thereafter. This experience of continued privation in the midst of plenty certainly must have compounded the sense of deterioration that was impressed on artisans by the advance of such practices as confection and marchandage.

Low and falling wages, of course, are bound to result in material distress in whatever historical period they occur. But when industry and material prosperity were seen as a foundation and a goal of public life – as they were in France after the French Revolution had transformed the nation into an "industrial society" – low wages were also keenly felt as a public injustice, as a kind of nagging reproach to the good order of the state. The question of inadequate wages came to be a major topic of public discussion, particularly during the July Monarchy, when the low and declining wages of workers formed a stark contrast with the government's pious espousal of economic expansion and private enrichment. At least in the 1830s and 1840s, the age-old material discomforts of low wages were compounded by a very nineteenth-century moral discomfort – a sense that artisans were being denied their rightful reward and recognition in the new industrial society and that something was therefore seriously wrong with the current social and economic system.

Thus, in spite of the continued vigor of artisan industry and in spite of an expansion in their numbers, French artisans were also beset with constant struggles, crises, and insecurities. Their skills were not wiped out by advancing industrialism, but they were often diluted by declining standards of quality and an increasing division of labor. Artisans were not ground down from respectable craftsmen to an oppressed factory proletariat, but their material standards of living often suffered serious erosion. The moderate pace of French urbanization and the continued predominance of the traditional urban centers allowed a measure of continuity in artisan traditions and customs, but the legal reforms of the French Revolution meant that the corporate organizations that carried such customs and traditions were now illegal. Industry was no longer scorned as the badge of vileness – indeed, it was now exalted as the foundation of the social order. Yet it was property that was praised and protected by the ruling powers, whereas labor, the unquestioned source of property, was subjected to the unmitigated rigors of the market. Artisans, in short, were still proud, numerous, and essential to the functioning of the economy; but they were also financially squeezed, threatened with a loss of skill and status, and provided with virtually no legal form of collective defense against the disordering forces of the free market. In these circumstances they struggled to form illicit collective organizations to promote and maintain what they saw as the good order and the legitimate interests of their trades. And in doing so they drew freely from the flexible and venerable idiom of the now defunct corporate regime. The artisans' response to their condition in the new industrial society was to construct *corporations ouvrières*.

8 Workers' corporations

W H E N   W O R K E R S   A D O P T E D   a corporate vocabulary and corporate forms of organization in the early nineteenth century, they were not attempting to restore the corporate system as it existed under the old regime. They were attracted to the corporate idiom because of its inherent opposition to competitive individualism, not because they wanted hierarchical corporations governed by masters. Under the old regime, corporations were legally sanctioned bodies, and their language and institutions recapitulated the hierarchical premises of the traditional monarchy. But after the Revolution, proprietary individualism became the dominant idiom of the state, and the corporate idiom became a language of opposition. Nineteenth-century workers' corporations were organized on the margins of the law and could not exist without the continued voluntary effort of their members. The great problem they faced was maintaining a solidary and ordered trade community against the powerful individualistic tendencies of contemporary society. The result was corporations that, in spite of the apparent continuities of language and form, were very different from those of the old regime, corporations that, given the dynamics of nineteenth-century society and politics, eventually developed into the cells of a revolutionary democratic and socialist movement in 1848.

The history of workers' organization in the first half of the nineteenth century is not well known, and the question of corporate themes in these organizations has not been addressed in the existing literature. A good deal of pertinent evidence can be culled from existing works, and such evidence has been used here extensively. But this chapter differs from all the others in this book in that it also draws extensively from my archival research in Marseille. The local detail from Marseille allows the construction of a much fuller account of nineteenth-century workers' corporations than could have been gained from published sources alone. Both the detailed evidence from Marseille and the more fragmentary evidence from elsewhere in France make it clear that workers' corporations were ubiquitous in the urban skilled trades in the first half of the nineteenth century. But they also indicate that workers' corporations differed significantly from both masters' corporations and journeymen's corporations of the old regime.

INSTITUTIONAL FORMS

The two most important institutional forms assumed by nineteenth-century workers' corporations were compagnonnage and mutual-aid societies. The development of these two institutions was closely related to the political history of France in the Napoleonic and Restoration eras. Napoleon, who came to power in 1799, dedicated his government to effecting a compromise between the Revolution and the old regime. He consolidated the legal reforms of the Revolution in the famous Napoleonic code, but he also reinstated modified versions of several old-regime institutions: a new imperial monarchy, an imperial nobility, and – much chastened after the Concordat of 1802 – an established Catholic state church. The fall of Napoleon and the restoration of the Bourbon monarchy in 1815 meant the establishment of a state openly sympathetic to the old regime. Although the restored monarchy could not turn back the legal reforms of the revolutionary and Napoleonic periods, it did everything in its power to promote deference to hierarchy and loyalty to the throne and the Catholic church. The Empire and the Restoration were both attempts to marry principles of the Revolution with principles of the old regime, and the inevitable result was a hybrid political culture beset with contradictory tensions. The ambivalence of the political authorities of the imperial and Restoration period – that is, from 1800 to 1830 – helped to establish mutual-aid societies and compagnonnage as institutional forms that workers could use to construct corporations capable of resisting the masters and the state.

Mutual-aid societies *(sociétés de secours mutuel),* alternatively known as provident societies *(sociétés de prévoyance)* or benevolent societies *(sociétés de bienfaisance),* were voluntary associations formed to provide mutual insurance benefits. Members paid regular monthly dues to the society's treasury, and benefits were paid out when members fell sick, retired, or died. To gain legal standing, these societies had to submit their statutes to public authorities, who imposed conditions of an administrative and financial nature.[1] During the Napoleonic era, the authorities regarded mutual-aid societies as eminently useful institutions, which would both relieve the poor of suffering and teach them the virtues of providence. However, they generally set very strict conditions for authorization, making certain that proposed societies would be financially sound and that they were being formed for legitimate purposes of mutual aid, rather than for ulterior ends of some sort. The authorities were particularly suspicious of societies that drew all their members from a single trade, because these could all to easily foment "coalitions" to restrict freedom of industry. This did not keep some single-trade societies from being formed under the Empire. Sometimes local officials gave such societies their authorization in spite of the danger of coalitions; sometimes essentially single-trade societies obtained authorization by including a small number of men with other occupations; and sometimes they simply constituted themselves informally and ignored the requirement of formal authorization altogether.[2] But under the Empire, and under subsequent regimes as well, many societies drew their members from a wide variety of different working-class trades, sometimes including a sprinkling of master artisans, shopkeepers, and clerks as well.

Legally, mutual-aid societies were voluntary insurance associations formed under the supervision of the state. But looking beyond the legal formalities, it is clear that they were also postrevolutionary versions of old-regime confraternities – with appropriate changes in nomenclature. The benefits they provided were precisely the same as the charités of old-regime confraternities, but they were now rebaptized with the more secular title of "mutual aid." Like confraternities, they provided funerals for the departed, which all members were typically enjoined to attend. Moreover, mutual-aid societies formed during the Empire and the Restoration were nearly always named for patron saints, whose festivals were celebrated by the *sociétaires* much as they had been by the confrères under the old regime.[3] Like confraternities of the old regime, nineteenth-century mutual-aid societies varied widely in character and could serve a number of different purposes.[4] Some were essentially trade organizations, some were merely insurance associations, some were basically devotional groups, and still others were social clubs with a great diversity of activities. One society active in Marseille in the 1820s, which was composed of workers from a variety of trades, included not only mutual aid, common devotions, and corporate funerals but frequent Sunday outings for workers and their families and guests, featuring dancing, drinking, dramatic performances, and general merriment; the consumption of wine on these occasions was "fabulous," according to one participant.[5] The mutual-aid society, like the confraternity before it, was the mark of a human association that wished to regularize and enhance its solidarity. When workers made an association into a mutual-aid society they were formally and symbolically extending such solidarity to the whole person, both body and soul, by provisions for care in time of sickness, by shared devotions, by common spiritual patronage, and by funeral corteges to send the departed comrade to his heavenly reward. A trade community was one basis for such a solidary association, but it was by no means the only one.[6]

Like officials of the Empire, Restoration officials regarded mutual-aid societies as useful institutions. But under the Restoration, mutual-aid societies also became an important instrument in the campaign to win the popular classes back to the true faith. They were actively patronized by state and church alike, and officials were now far more willing to authorize societies whose members were all from a single trade. Mutual-aid societies therefore became a particularly congenial institutional framework for workers' corporations. By registering as a mutual-aid society, a workers' corporation could operate legally and openly, with a staff of officers, a treasury, and an office. It could also express the moral community of the trade through acts of mutual charity and through common veneration of the trade's traditional patron saint. But the society could also serve as the center of a more comprehensive association that watched over working conditions, set wage levels, called strikes and boycotts, disciplined disloyal workers, and otherwise maintained good order in the trade. These latter activities, of course, had to be carried on in secret and are therefore usually as hidden from historians as they were from nineteenth-century officials. But the available evidence indicates that officially recognized mutual-aid societies were commonly only the public face of much more comprehensive workers' corporations that struggled to impose detailed regulations on their trades.

In their officially constituted, publicly visible form, mutual-aid societies were rarely large enough to encompass all the workers in a trade. In mid-nineteenth-century Marseille, for example, few had more than one hundred officially reported members. Often this was just another element of deception, and the nominally restricted society actually embraced virtually all the workers in a trade.[7] But even when a mutual-aid society included only a minority of the workers, it could still serve as the moral and organizational center of the trade, acting on behalf of all the workers, representing them in negotiations, and leading them in struggles against the masters. It could embody and manifest the moral and practical community of the trade even if it did not formally include the entire work force.[8]

When the Restoration authorities patronized mutual-aid societies, they obviously did not intend to encourage workers to subvert the competitive structure of the contemporary economic and legal system. They encouraged mutual-aid societies because they desired to foster Catholic piety and because they sympathized with the social forms and the values of the old regime. Their patronage may sometimes have had the desired effect of increasing workers' loyalty to the monarchy and to the Catholic church, but even the most pious and royalist workers could not be prevented from using mutual-aid societies for purposes of their own. By supporting mutual-aid societies, the authorities unintentionally made it possible for workers to construct much more far-reaching corporations – corporations that imposed illegal regulations and constraints on their trades in cities all over the nation. Relatively rare under the Empire, the number of mutual-aid societies grew steadily during the Restoration and continued to increase up to and beyond the middle of the century. Less common than compagnonnages in 1815 or 1820, mutual-aid societies became the dominant form of workers' corporation by the 1840s.

Compagnonnage was the most important form of workers' corporation during the Restoration, and although it was eventually surpassed by mutual-aid societies, it retained much of its vigor right down to 1848. The Restoration government's policy toward compagnonnage was marked by the same kinds of contradictions as its policy toward mutual-aid societies. Although compagnonnage had initially been weakened by the upheavals of the French Revolution and by the drain of young workers into the revolutionary and imperial armies, it had regained much of its strength by the end of the Napoleonic period and was ready to absorb the thousands of young men who were returning from military service. The early years of the Restoration saw a remarkable efflorescence of compagnonnage, during which it probably surpassed the numbers and power it had achieved in the eighteenth century. Officials of the Restoration government witnessed this renaissance with mixed feelings. Compagnonnage was still illegal, and officials were disturbed by the frequent bloody *rixes,* or battles between rival sects. After one such battle, in Bordeaux in 1820, the local prefect wrote a typical indictment of compagnonnage to the minister of the interior.

> I have often had occasion to discuss with you the compagnons and the excesses to which they abandon themselves. I believe that these men deserve the attention of the government. United in corporations to which they cling with sentiments of absurd fanaticism, they could become terrible instruments in the hands of the factious [i.e., revolutionaries]. Their audacity increases daily, because their numbers are growing rapidly, as they are no longer harvested by conscription . . . and if they commit crimes, the union that reigns among them deprives the court of their testimony, just as the fear that they inspire drives away the testimony of others.[9]

Compagnons, in short, not only engaged in violent actions; they openly disregarded the authority of the state and the courts. But in spite of this, the prefect did not feel that compagnonnage should be exterminated. Instead he concluded: "There is reason to examine seriously the measures to be taken, not to dissolve an association that resisted the Revolution, but to regulate it and to contain those who form it."[10] Like most officials of the Restoration government, he was troubled by the violence and lawlessness of compagnonnage, and he shuddered to think of the consequences should it be captured by "the factious." But for all the dangers it presented to public order, there was one irrefutable argument for tolerating compagnonnage in spite of its formal illegality: It had survived the Revolution and seemed to have resisted the taint of revolutionary ideas. Compagnonnage in the end seemed to guarantee against the spread of revolutionary sentiments in the working class.

Hence, rather than systematically repressing it, the Restoration government simply punished its excesses – occasionally sending men to prison for assaults committed during battles or for illegal coalition committed during strikes or boycotts – and allowed compagnons to carry on their day-to-day activities unhindered. The authorities' ambivalence gave workers the space they needed to create – or to re-create – autonomous and resilient corporations that were capable of resisting both the masters and the state.

The most notable feature of compagnonnage in the nineteenth century was its remarkable continuity with the past. The account of eighteenth-century compagnonnage, which was presented in Chapter 3, will stand with few amendments for the first half of the nineteenth century as well. The tour de France, the mère, the rôleur, and premier compagnon, the initiations, the assemblies, the processions and banquets, the special funerals, the ceremonies of greeting and parting, the "damnations" of workshops, the *noms compagnonniques,* the origin myths, the division into rival sects and the bloody battles between them, all of these features persisted down to and beyond the Revolution of 1848. In compagnonnage, continuity with corporate forms of the old regime was palpable. And as compagnonnage flourished in the Restoration, thousands of journeymen – above all in such building trades as the carpenters, joiners, roofers, locksmiths, and stonecutters, but also the cutlers, nailers, forgers, blacksmiths, hatters, turners, coopers, curriers, wheelwrights, harness makers, bakers, shoemakers, and others – were initiated into its special and deeply corporate world.[11]

This is not to say that compagnonnage came through the revolutionary era entirely unchanged. But most of the changes were in the opposite direction from those taking place in the rest of French society. Instead of becoming more open and egalitarian, compagnonnage became tighter and more hierarchical. Although it had been illegal under the old regime, compagnonnage had been in harmony with the principles of the surrounding society. But when the Revolution destroyed the corporate order of the traditional monarchy and replaced it with a society based on individual citizens, contracts, and private property, compagnonnage found itself profoundly at odds with its surroundings. It survived by clinging more firmly than ever to its traditional ways – indeed, by elaborating the very features that marked it off from the society at large. This succeeded in preserving and reinvigorating compagnonnage during the Empire and Restoration. Only when the Revolution of 1830 brought to power a liberal political regime and spurred the growth of a popular republican and democratic movement did the archaism of compagnonnage become a liability.

During the first three decades of the nineteenth century, compagnonnage was marked by exclusiveness, by an intense concern for hierarchy, and by strict observance of rules and ritual practices. For example, in the eighteenth century, the various trades within a devoir of compagnonnage seem to have dealt with each other on a more or less equal footing. But from the beginning of the nineteenth century there were a series of disputes about precedence between trades, disputes that frequently led to violent rixes. The compagnons also made it much more difficult for new trades to join their brotherhoods. Neither the Enfants de Salomon nor the Enfants de Père Soubise had ever shown much willingness to accept new trades, but the Enfants de Maître Jacques had admitted no fewer than eleven in the course of the eighteenth century – to judge from a list they drew up at an assembly in 1807.[12] In the first half of the nineteenth century, however, they accepted none. Workers in two large and important trades, the bakers and the shoemakers, organized themselves as compagnonnages in these years and made every effort to win official acceptance. But it was not until after the middle of the century, when compagnonnage was in rapid decline, that they were accepted by the other trades. This taste for punctilio and insistence on hierarchy was also manifested in the internal affairs of the trades composing compagnonnage. The authority of the premier compagnon was augmented, there was an increased emphasis on more exact record keeping, new internal ranks were introduced, and units of compagnonnage in different cities monitored each other much more carefully than in the past to assure that rituals were being performed properly and that the devoir was being observed down to the last detail. It was also in the early nineteenth century that the origin myths of the compagnons were set down in a definitive form.[13]

The compagnons' tenacious insistence on maintaining and increasing distinctions was a continuous source of violent battles. Not only were there battles between the rival sects, which continued undiminished in the nineteenth century, but between trades within a sect that had quarreled over precedence and between trades that had been officially recognized by a sect and those that had not. A direct comparison between the eighteenth century and the early nineteenth is impossible, given the paucity of eighteenth-century evidence, but it seems likely that battles were actually more common under the Restoration than they had been under the old regime. But in spite of all these rivalries, compagnonnage remained an effective means of defending the interests of workers against the tyranny of the masters and the legal individualism of the state – thanks to the intensity of its loyalties, its tight organization, and the links it maintained between journeymen in different trades and different cities. Of course, active members of compagnonnage were often outnumbered by older, sedentary, married workers. But because many of the older workers had passed through compagnonnage in their youth and had maintained loyalties and contacts, compagnonnage could still serve as the center of collective action for the trade as a whole.

Rivalry between sects could occasionally be a serious impediment to concerted action against the masters, because masters could sometimes play off one sect against another to keep wages depressed. But these cases were actually rather rare. There were only four trades that had members in more than one sect of compagnonnage: the stonecutters, joiners, and locksmiths, who were divided between the Enfants de Maître Jacques and the Enfants de Salomon; and the carpenters, who were divided between the Enfants de Salomon and the Enfants de Père Soubise. The stonecutters, joiners, locksmiths, and carpenters were the only trades in the Enfants de Salomon. But the remaining Enfants de Père Soubise (the roofers and the plasterers) and the remaining Enfants de Maître Jacques (some twenty trades, including coopers, forgers, cutlers, hatters, blacksmiths, saddlers, turners, glaziers, etc.) faced no rival groups of compagnons who might break their control of the trade by forming a prejudicial agreement with the masters. Men in these trades might well get into battles with rival sects, but the enmity between sects did not undermine their power in relation to masters.

Even among the stonecutters, joiners, locksmiths, and carpenters, rivalry between sects did not always weaken efforts to deal with the masters. In the first place, it was common for some towns to belong unequivocally to one sect and others to its rival; in these cases, compagnons of a given sect would seek work only in the towns they controlled. Second, compagnons sometimes arranged a partition of a city's workshops, and the two sects would then live in an uneasy truce. This was true of the carpentry trade in Paris, where the Enfants de Père Soubise, the more powerful group, worked only on the right bank of the Seine and the Enfants de Salomon only on the left.[14] Finally, the sects often cooperated in organizing strikes in spite of their rivalries. Agricol Perdiguier described one such strike in Nîmes in 1827. According to Perdiguier, these were far from rare: When it came to disputes with the masters, "gavots [Enfants de Salomon] and dévoirants [Enfants de Maître Jacques] are one." The heads of the rival sects often shared responsibility for drawing up and presenting the demands of the workers, and "if the masters will not listen or are intransigent, the compagnons say the word, and gavots and dévoirants both stop work at once."[15] Rivalries between sects usually did not seriously impair the effectiveness of compagnonnages as workers' corporations.

Moreover, compagnons were not necessarily limited in their actions to a strict and canonical set of practices laid down by the venerable traditions of compagnonnage. Although historians of the French working class have generally thought of compagnonnage and mutual-aid societies as quite distinct, the boundaries between them were often blurred in practice, and workers' corporations sometimes used the two forms of organization more or less interchangeably.[16] This fluidity of forms can be illustrated by the bakers of Marseille. They formed a mutual-aid society in 1823 and went on strike shortly thereafter; as a consequence, their society was dissolved by the authorities. Two years later they reconstituted their corporation, but this time in the form of a compagnonnage, including only unmarried, itinerant workers. A few months later, however, the compagnonnage began to admit married and sedentary workers as well. This unorthodox compagnonnage seems to have absorbed virtually all the workers in the industry and went on to organize strikes in both 1826 and 1835. In 1845, however, it was once again transformed into a mutual-aid society.[17] Thus, the surface form of the bakers' organization changed from mutual-aid society to compagnonnage and back to mutual-aid society again in the course of twenty-five years; yet there clearly was a continuity of organization and purpose beneath the changing forms. For the bakers of Marseille, compagnonnage and the mutual-aid society were by no means mutually exclusive forms of organization. Their corporation could assume either form or both simultaneously, as the circumstances required.

The bakers were relative newcomers to compagnonnage, as yet unrecognized by the established compagnons; perhaps one should expect them to be particularly flexible. But they were not an isolated case. There were three officially registered mutual-aid societies in Marseille in the 1840s whose regulations make it clear that they also functioned as compagnonnages: one of locksmiths, one of hatters, and one of joiners and cabinetmakers.[18] All of these were old compagnonnage trades. For the hatters, at least, this combination of mutual-aid society and compagnonnage was not limited to Marseille. Jean Vial, in his detailed study of hatters' labor organizations in the nineteenth century, demonstrates that their mutual-aid societies retained many features from compagnonnage – mères, travel payments for men unable to find work, job placement by a rôleur, and the use of assorted terms from compagnonnage.[19] He also cites an example of a hatters' compagnonnage that transformed itself into a mutual-aid society in Lyons in 1811 and quotes an official in Lyons in 1821 who complained that the hatters' mutual-aid societies "have degenerated into associations of compagnonnage."[20] As with the bakers of Marseille, the hatters' corporation in Lyons seems to have oscillated between compagnonnage and mutual-aid societies – or, more likely, to have been both a compagnonnage and mutual-aid society at once.

Compagnonnage, then, was a flexible form of organization, one that could occasionally be combined with mutual-aid societies or, as in the case of Marseille's bakers, adapted to the needs of a predominantly settled labor force. And if compagnonnage was flexible, the mutual-aid society was more flexible still: It was, in fact, only an outward and public form that could cover a wide variety of quite differently organized workers' corporations. Thus, to say that a workers' corporation was a compagnonnage or a mutual-aid society does not necessarily reveal very much about how it was organized, about the goals it pursued, or about how it pursued them. This is not to say that the outward institutional form of corporations was of no importance; as has been argued throughout this book, institutional forms embody fundamental principles of social organization and social action. But in order to understand what nineteenth-century workers' corporations meant and how they worked in practice, it is necessary to go beyond a purely institutional approach and examine a few representative corporations in greater detail.

VARIETIES OF WORKERS' CORPORATIONS

The tanners of Marseille are an example of how much could be accomplished by a well-organized workers' corporation. Tanning was generally regarded as a dirty, smelly trade that required little skill. Rémi Gossez, for example, remarks that the tanners of Paris were "ignorant workers . . . whose brutalizing labor arrested all development," and points out that unlike most Parisian trades, they remained completely unorganized until 1848.[21] In Marseille, however, the tanners formed a corporation that gained an impressive degree of control over their trade. The first evidence of organization in the trade was a legally registered mutual-aid society formed in 1821, about which virtually nothing is known. It was in 1833, when this society was absorbed by a new and more aggressive organization called the Société de Saint-Claude, that the tanning workers began to gain significant power. In 1834 the new society called a strike against all the city's tanneries. The strike, which lasted for three months, was nearly 100 percent effective and resulted in a clear victory for the workers. Not only were wages raised from 2.75 to 3 francs a day, but, more important, the manufacturers agreed not to hire any workers who were not members of the society.[22] Although such an agreement had no legally binding force, it was strictly observed in practice, and from 1834 to the middle of the 1860s, no one could work in Marseille's tanning industry without joining the workers' society.

The legally registered statutes of the tanners' society are in no way distinguishable from those of other mutual-aid societies, regulating only such matters as conditions of membership, dues, election of officers, celebration of the patron saint's festival, administration of benefits, and the like.[23] Moreover, even though all accounts agree that no tanner could be employed in the industry without joining the society, it had only a hundred official members in 1854[24] at a time when there were almost certainly more than six hundred tanners working in Marseille.[25] In this case, the officially registered society was the public face of a much more ambitious clandestine association, one with more specific regulations and a much larger membership. During a labor conflict in 1855, a police officer managed to lay his hands on the secret statutes of the association, which forbade the employment of nonmembers, limited the hours of work, restricted the number of apprentices, and provided payments in case of strikes. The society, he concluded, merely "hid behind a veil of mutual aid"; in reality it constituted a "permanent coalition."[26]

The tanners' society also oversaw standards of quality in the industry. In the early 1850s, at least, it maintained a tribunal of eight members, which was "invested with the mission of making a sovereign judgment about the merit of the work done, in cases of disagreement with the owner of a tannery."[27] Here the workers' society managed to establish a commission exercising many of the functions of the jurés or syndics of old-regime corporations. Another achievement was the society's ability to assure apprenticeships to sons of its members. In the early 1820s, before the founding of the Société de Saint-Claude, only 9 percent of the young tanners who got married in Marseille were tanners' sons. By the middle of the century this figure had risen to 45 percent, whereas the city-wide occupational inheritance rate *fell* from 34 percent to 23 percent. There were, in fact, only four occupations in Marseille, whether working class or bourgeois, that had higher rates of occupational inheritance than the tanners in 1846–51.[28] Here again the Société de Saint-Claude had succeeded in exercising a function that was typical of old-regime corporations, a very difficult achievement in the nineteenth century.

There were not many nineteenth-century workers' corporations that exercised as much power over their trades as Marseille's tanners, but there were others as well organized. One extremely well-organized corporation whose internal workings can be known in some detail is the hatters' corporation of Paris and Lyons. Their secret papers have been preserved in the archive of the twentieth-century hatters' *syndicat,* or trade union, and Jean Vial has used these papers to give us an unusually vivid picture of their organization.[29] Although they were an ancient compagnonnage trade, the hatters also formed mutual-aid societies with the usual death and sickness benefits – in Lyons in 1804 and 1811 and in Paris in 1808. In Paris, at least, the regular society was supplemented in 1820 by a second auxiliary mutual-aid society, also legally registered, that would provide aid in case of unemployment.[30] In addition to the statutes of these two legally registered societies, the Parisian hatters also drew up an "interior regulation" that dealt with, in the words of an old hatter writing in 1870, "questions of solidarity and resistance."[31] Under this interior regulation, a commission of hatters could draw up wage schedules *(tarifs)* to be enforced on the masters and could direct the workers to go on strike against *(faire sauter,* or "blow up") any workshop where these wage rates were not observed.[32] It also granted unemployment benefits to workers who went on strike or were fired for legitimately resisting their masters.[33] Moreover, as already noted, the hatters' societies maintained many activities of compagnonnage. As in the case of Marseille's tanners, the hatters' mutual-aid societies were just the public face of a much more complex and multifaceted organization, one that concerned itself not only with job placement and mutual insurance benefits but with the good order and welfare of the trade in general.

One of the hatters' concerns was the enforcement of strict standards of workmanship. Members were required to pass tests of their skill before they could be placed in a workshop[34] and could be punished for professional malfeasance. A certain *"sieur* Rivol," who had been fired from his workshop for having split open a hat and thrown it into the furnace, not only was denied employment aid but was banished from Paris for six months and required to repeat his "novitiate" before being accepted again as a full member of the society.[35] The corporation required good behavior in other respects as well, fining its members for drunkenness and denying unemployment aid to workers who were fired for "grave faults" of whatever kind or who engaged in begging.[36] It also required the workers to participate in common rituals of solidarity: banquets, funerals for members, masses and processions in honor of the patron saint.[37] The patron's festival was a joyous occasion. According to a police report on the hatters' festival in Paris in 1819, they first gathered at church, where they heard mass. "Afterwards they marched through several quarters of the city accompanied by a band of musicians. The parade was rather noisy, but it did not result in any disorders."[38] These ritual enactments of brotherhood were supplemented by measures to equalize the workers' incomes. In Paris in 1828, workers who earned more than forty francs a week were required to put the excess in a common fund to be distributed to less fortunate workers.[39] Beyond good wages and mutual aid, then, the hatters' corporation seems to have encompassed nearly all aspects of life in the hatters' trade.

But in spite of the sophisticated organization and the vast ambitions of the hatters' corporation, its struggles to maintain good order in the trade were seldom fully successful. The hatters faced one of the problems discussed in Chapter 7: competition from lower-quality producers. This problem is documented better for Lyons than for Paris, although it seems to have been common to both cities. According to detailed reports written by local authorities in 1817 and 1819, there were two classes of hatmaking establishments in Lyons, which the workers designated as "regulated" and "unregulated" workshops (*fabriques en règle* and *fabriques non en règle*). The regulated workshops were owned by the richest manufacturers, had larger work forces, and produced the highest-quality hats. In these workshops, where skills were at a premium, the workers' corporation had succeeded in establishing detailed control over production. It was the workers, not the masters, who determined the règles. According to police reports, the workers' society

> places the journeyman, fixes the number of hats each worker can make per day; workers who are strangers to the city cannot be admitted without paying a fee; the apprentice is obliged to pay what they call the *"béjaune"* [a term in workers' slang derived from *jaune*, or yellow; the nearest English equivalent would be "greenhorn"] . . . the workers impose fines of which they themselves are the arbiters, and until a worker has paid the fine inflicted upon him, he is excluded from work.[40]

The "unregulated" workshops were smaller, made hats of lower quality, and were often located in rooms in the upper stories of buildings rather than on street level. It was there that "unfaithful workers find it easy to sell raw materials they have pilfered" and that workers banned from the "regulated" workshops could find work – at a lower wage.[41] In addition to these two types of urban workshops, some manufacturers had "carried their industry outside the city," establishing workshops in the suburbs and in neighboring small towns and villages, beyond the reach of the urban workers' corporation. There, according to the police report, they could manufacture hats "at an average savings of more than a third."[42]

In this situation, conflicts between the manufacturers and the workers were endemic. In 1817 the mayor of Lyons, concerned about the constant tension between workers and manufacturers and also about the flight of industry from the city, attempted to put a stop to the "culpable abuses" of the workers. To this end he issued a municipal ordinance with a new compulsory tarif of piece rates that reduced the payments for all types of hats. The ordinance also forbade workers to limit the number of hats a man could produce in a day, to exact fees from workers or apprentices, to assess fines, to pronounce "damnations" or "interdictions" on workshops, or to have workers placed in a workshop by a rôleur – "each worker must present himself alone . . . to the master manufacturer."[43] In spite of warnings that infractions of the mayor's ordinance would be punished "in conformity with the articles of the penal code,"[44] the response of the workers was immediate – they deserted the workshops en masse. Three weeks later the mayor issued a revised tarif with higher rates, and within a few days the strike ended.[45] But if the mayor's modified tarif was accepted, the workers continued their "culpable abuses" unabated, as police reports written two years later make clear.

By 1819 the mayor's tarif was once again a source of conflict. Competition from rural and small-town manufacturers had decreased the price of one type of hat, and when urban manufacturers attempted to compensate by lowering their piece rates on this item, the workers went on strike, demanding a return to the tarif of 1817, a demand they won when the mayor officially reaffirmed his earlier ordinance.[46] But the legal status of the tarif was soon challenged by the minister of the interior on the ground that it was "in accord neither with true principles of political economy nor with those of our legislation."[47] The mayor's ordinance, however, was not officially revoked and presumably remained more or less in force, although the outbreak of a brief strike two months later indicates that some issues remained unsettled.[48] The situation of the Lyons hatmaking industry, then, was tangled and paradoxical. The mayor's ordinance had originally been proclaimed in order to cut wages and destroy the workers' corporation; yet two years later the tarif had become an aid to the corporation in its struggle to prevent further wage cuts by the manufacturers. At the same time, the mayor, who had introduced the tarif in order to restore competition in the hatmaking industry, found himself rebuked by his superior for ignoring "the true principles of political economy," according to which wages could only be set by competition in the free market. The mayor's tarif, rather than resolving problems, merely became a weapon in the endemic and inconclusive battles that beset Lyons's hatmaking industry.

The Lyons hatters' corporation had to fight on several fronts at once: against renegade workers, against the masters in the "regulated" shops, against cut-rate shops in the city and beyond, and against hostile local and national authorities. The Parisian hatters seem to have faced a similarly complex struggle: Like their brothers in Lyons, they had to contend with cut-rate producers and renegade workers as well as with the masters and the state. Thus, in 1830, crowds of Parisian hatters attempted to enter workshops where low-priced hats were being made, in order to halt production by destroying tools and equipment.[49] The control that the hatters' corporations exercised over their trade was never as complete as that attained by Marseille's tanners. The admirably organized and highly disciplined societies of the Parisian and Lyonnais hatters were formed for combat, and they were taxed to the limit by their multifaceted struggles. Moreover, there was always a low-cost, low-quality sector of the industry that escaped their control. But as long as the demand for high-quality hats held up and as long as the hatters' corporations could maintain discipline over the most highly skilled workers, they could maintain a significant degree of control over at least this superior branch of the trade.

There were some trades where even that amount of control was very hard to achieve. The classic cases were shoemaking and tailoring, where, as mentioned in Chapter 7, skill dilution, subcontracting, the division of labor, and the production of ready-to-wear items threatened the labor force with seriously deteriorating living standards. As the division of labor increased and skill requirements fell, these trades were flooded with poor and relatively untrained men – and a large number of women as well. The high levels of seasonal unemployment that had always plagued the apparel trades were thus compounded in the 1830s and 1840s by a good deal of chronic underemployment and sometimes by falling wages as well. According to the estimates of Marseille's Chamber of Commerce, shoemakers worked only about 200 days a year in the late 1840s and tailors only about 150, as against 300 for most trades. This reduced their yearly earnings to pitiful levels, in spite of the respectable wages they made when fully employed.[50] Both in Marseille and elsewhere, the tailors and shoemakers did their best to sustain their corporations and to defend themselves against deteriorating standards. But even when they won strikes against the masters, their position was usually soon undermined by the changes that were inexorably transforming their trades.

Marseille's shoemakers had been organized since the beginning of the nineteenth century – initially as a compagnonnage and from 1816 as a mutual-aid society as well.[51] In 1833 the shoemakers won a strike for higher wages; whether they were organized by the compagnonnage or by the mutual-aid society is not known.[52] The gains they won in this strike were soon eroded, however, and in 1845 the shoemakers organized another, particularly effective, strike. In this case the shoemakers' bad fortune was the historians' good fortune: The police broke the strike by arresting the leaders of the shoemakers' society for illegal coalition, and the records of their trial contain valuable information both on the organization of their corporation and on conditions in the trade.[53]

It is clear from these records that Marseille's shoemakers worked under widely varying regimes of production. Testimony at the trial referred at one point to "workshops where up to eighty workers were employed," but also says that during the strike certain workers "without danger to themselves could not, except in hiding, receive and fabricate the *ouvrage* that was given to them by their masters." The trial record also refers to both *directeurs d'ateliers* (directors of workshops) and *entrepreneurs d'ouvrage,* a term that implies work on a putting-out basis. It appears that some shoes were made in small workshops, others in very large shops where the division of labor was probably very advanced, and still others in the workers' own rooms or garrets – a diversity of working conditions typical of the shoemaking trade in the 1840s. The trial record also refers to production for local consumption and to "the fabrication of *pacotilles* [shoddy goods] for export abroad or to the colonies." One suspects that the very large workshops and the domestic putting-out branch of the trade corresponded chiefly to the pacotille branch, but the records are unfortunately silent on this question.

The shoemakers' strike of 1845 was extremely well organized. Although compagnons and members of the shoemakers mutual-aid society were surely involved in the strike, it was organized by a new and much more inclusive society that contained virtually all the shoemakers in the city. It was composed of thirty-six sections and had an executive bureau of twelve members. It maintained a meeting room and an office and had a permanent president, secretary, and treasurer. This society drew up a single wage scale to be applied to all branches of the trade and presented it to the masters. In addition, it demanded power over placement of workers into jobs, which would, in effect, have made membership in the society compulsory. Most of the employers refused these demands, and the offending employers were struck, with nearly 100 percent effectiveness. The society also set up a producers' cooperative to provide work for themselves and to take business away from the masters for the duration of the strike. The workers' society, in short, organized the strike with unusual care and thoroughness and managed to enforce adherence on workers in all branches of this extremely heterogeneous trade. The strikers were attempting to create a powerful and unified workers' corporation, more or less comparable to those of Marseille's tanners or the hatters of Lyons and Paris, and had the strike succeeded, they might have been able to do so. But it ended in failure when the authorities arrested the leaders of the shoemakers' society and sentenced them to prison terms ranging from one to three months. The unified corporation did not survive this defeat, but the shoemakers' compagnonnage and mutual-aid society remained intact, and struggles against the masters continued. In 1855 the compagnonnage and the mutual-aid society once again attempted to form a single, unified society, which was denied authorization by the government; whether the fusion took place in spite of this refusal is uncertain.[54] And when trade unions were legalized in 1869, shoemakers were among the first to establish a *chambre syndicale*.[55] Thus, in spite of the poverty, overcrowding, and deterioration of their trade, Marseille's shoemakers continued to keep some sort of workers' corporation alive.

These examples of workers' corporations have been chosen in part because documentation about them is unusually full. It would therefore be misleading to claim that they were representative of nineteenth-century workers' corporations in general. After all, well-organized and aggressive corporations probably tended to leave more evidence behind them than frail and ephemeral ones. Some doubtless had only the most rudimentary organization, and some probably had to content themselves with little more than the mutual insurance functions specified in their legally registered statutes, although here it is worth listening to the opinion of Marseille's police commissioner. It was, as he put it in 1855, "of public notoriety that nearly all the so-called benevolent societies are nothing but trade associations, in each of which regulations are created that are often contrary to the general interest."[56] Yet in the present state of research very little evidence exists for most trades in most cities, and often the information available only indicates whether or not some sort of organization existed – and even that is sometimes uncertain. In spite of the thinness of the documentation, the available evidence points to some kind of corporations in most skilled trades in the cities. My own research in Marseille, for example, has uncovered positive evidence of organization for no fewer than forty-three trades in the 1840s, comprising all but four of the skilled trades in Marseille that had one hundred or more employees and several of the smaller trades as well.[57] Although some cities may have had fewer organized trades than this, there is no reason to believe that Marseille was in any way unique. These corporations, in Marseille and elsewhere, were not always powerful or unified or effective. But workers' corporations of some kind were a ubiquitous feature of nineteenth-century French cities.

The few examples provided here can only begin to indicate the wide variety of workers' corporations in nineteenth-century France. These variations sometimes, but not always, followed definite patterns – by trade, by region, or by economic circumstances. Thus the building trades were especially likely to be organized in compagnonnages; tailors were particularly influenced by secular and republican organizational forms; compagnonnage was strong in most of the country but not in the extreme north; religious celebrations and processions played a more prominent part in the workers' corporations in Provence than in the rest of the country; workers' corporations were less likely to gain a dominant position in deteriorating trades such as tailoring and shoemaking than in more stable and prosperous trades such as printing, baking, or even hat making. But there were also variations that defy attempts at generalization.

A particularly baffling example was the contrast between masons in Marseille and in Paris. In Paris the masons were known as the most migratory trade in the city. Every spring thousands of rustic masons migrated from farms in distant Limousin and Auvergne to work in the booming building industry of the capital, returning to their homes only with the onset of the winter dead season.[58] But in Marseille, no farther than Paris from Auvergne and Limousin, and with as rapid an increase in population and therefore in its building industry, masons were recruited overwhelmingly from natives of the city and virtually none came from Auvergne or Limousin. When Marseille's building trades expanded very rapidly between 1820 and the middle of the century, the masons increased their numbers largely by recruiting farmers' sons from the rural areas within the boundaries of Marseille, rather than opening the trade to migrants.[59] In spite of the similarity in economic circumstances, masons' corporations in Paris and Marseille were utterly different from one another. Differences of this sort, which were extremely common in nineteenth-century France, indicate that in spite of general patterns and in spite of the constraints imposed by economic conditions, local trade communities also had their own autonomous personalities.

PERSISTENT THEMES – ALTERED RELATIONS

Nineteenth-century workers' corporations, then, were subject to a wide range of variations – resulting from long-standing differences between trades or between regions, varying economic conditions, and innumerable particular traditions, idiosyncracies, and conscious policies of local trade communities. Yet there were also continually recurring themes, themes that marked the entire range of workers' organizations as inheritors of a corporate tradition. One of these was mutual aid. Virtually all workers' organizations – whether officially registered mutual-aid societies or compagnonnages or other types of associations – included some kind of provision for sick members and funerals for the dead. Many also had provisions for small retirement benefits or widows' pensions, and some included unemployment benefits as well. These provisions were all continuations of the ubiquitous charités of the old regime's corporations and confraternities; in the nineteenth century, as in the eighteenth or seventeenth or sixteenth, these practices both manifested and reinforced the mutual solidarity of the corporation.

Under the Restoration, at least, virtually all workers' corporations also venerated the traditional patron saint of the trade and celebrated the saint's festival with more or less pomp and rejoicing. In Marseille, and probably elsewhere in the Midi, the practice of naming societies for patron saints continued well past the middle of the century; in the north it apparently declined in the 1830s and 1840s. But if this link with the devotional practices of the old regime's corporations declined over time, another remained entirely intact: corporate funerals. Even the secular and revolutionary trade associations formed in 1848 included the standard provisions for funerals.[60] Thus, the moral community of the trade, expressed in funerals and in other practices of mutual aid, was not effaced by the fading of an explicitly religious idiom.

Nineteenth-century workers' organizations also maintained the traditional corporate goal of detailed practical regulation of their trades, although it is harder here than in the case of mutual aid to demonstrate the universality of these concerns. Although the various political regimes of the first half of the nineteenth century condoned and even encouraged practices of mutual aid, they all forbade collective regulations limiting the entrepreneur's freedom to dispose of his property and to employ his workers as he saw fit. Because collectively imposed regulations were illegal, knowledge of them depends largely on conflicts between workers and masters that brought workers' claims to the attention of authorities. The documentation created by such conflicts makes it clear that nineteenth-century workers attempted to gain control over many aspects of their trades: job placement, the pace and processes of work, the arbitration of disputes, the quality of goods produced, recruitment into the trade, the level of wages or piece rates paid to workers, and so on. Examples of most of these types of claims have been described earlier in the discussion of the tanners, hatters, and shoemakers, and these examples could be multiplied indefinitely from available accounts of nineteenth-century labor conflicts.[61] Although the documentation is neither systematic nor complete, and although it is impossible to say precisely how common the different types of claims made by workers were, it is clear that workers' corporations all over France were constantly struggling to impose detailed regulations on their trades.

Conflicts between workers and masters could, of course, break out over all sorts of issues. But disputes over wages were by far the most common. Although workers in some trades and cities were paid by the day, the majority, in the first half of the nineteenth century, were paid by the task – by piece rates.[62] Payments to workers were graduated according to the particular item being produced, with articles of higher quality, greater difficulty, or higher price paid at a higher rate than low-price, low-quality, easy-to-make articles. Conflicts between workers and masters usually took the form of disputes about the tarif that specified these piece rates.[63] Agricol Perdiguier, describing strikes in the joiners' trade, set forth a typical scenario that – except for the references to compagnons, gavots, and dévoirants – could stand with few modifications for strikes in nearly all urban crafts in this era.

> The most intelligent of the workers, the most active, the most devoted, the most courageous, often the heads of the different Societies of the corporation . . . draw up a tarif, assess the value of each type of work in the trade, and meet with the masters.
>
> If these will listen to their complaints, their claims, the two parties negotiate, discuss their respective interests, fix in common the price either of a day's work, or of piece work, and everything is settled amicably as in a family. If the masters will not listen or are too intransigent, the compagnons say a word, and gavots and dévoirants stop work at once. The workshops are emptied. The patrons have no more workers. All labor is suspended.
>
> It sometimes happens that, for the sake of peace and quiet, the masters accept the claims of the workers, sign the new tarif, and then good order returns immediately. On other occasions, they call the magistrature to their aid, set traps for the directors of the strike, cause them to fall into the hands of the law, to be convicted and imprisoned as leaders of a coalition.[64]

Certain features of Perdiguier's scenario deserve special emphasis. First, the tarif is a formal document, carefully drawn up by the leaders of the strike, formally presented to the masters for their approval, and if accepted, formally signed by them. Although the particular customs and idioms might vary from place to place and trade to trade, this desire to base collective agreements with masters on written documents, as well as to surround these dealings with a certain solemnity, was quite general. For example, in 1843 the roofers of Rennes presented their masters with a document that they styled "The Decree of the Roofer Workers" ("L'Arrêté des ouvriers couvreurs"), demanding a raise in wages; it was soon signed by two of the largest employers in the city.[65] It is also notable that Perdiguier's scenario refers to "the new tarif" in a fashion that seems to imply the existence of an old tarif. To judge from this, it was normal for some sort of tarif – whether formally or informally, whether as the result of a compromise or of dictation by one party or the other – to be in force for the trade as a whole. The tradition of a unified tarif that applied to all workshops in a city was very well established. Such tarifs were standard features of trade corporations of the old regime, where they were part of the system of regulations that governed all aspects of the trade. After the Revolution, of course, tarifs lost all legally binding force. Nevertheless, it was common for a customary or even a formal and written tarif to be in existence in nineteenth-century trades and for it to be honored throughout the trade despite its lack of legal standing. But in the nineteenth century tarifs were fragile. As under the old regime, the masters could always decide in concert to lower the rates. But there was now the added danger that one or a few masters, for whatever reason, would simply refuse to honor the tarif. Under the old regime such a master not only would have been opposed by the workers but would have been condemned by the authorities of the masters' corporation. In the nineteenth century, however, an undercutting master could be stopped only by illegal collective action on the part of the workers. One reason, then, for the formality about drawing up, presenting, and signing the tarif was to give as much moral force as possible to an agreement that lacked all legal standing.

Disputes about tarifs could take a number of different forms. One of the most common types was a strike to raise rates that had been lowered by masters in a previous period of weak demand and low prices. It was this situation, where workers acted "in order to restore depressed wages," that Perdiguier presented as the typical source of strikes.[66] Sometimes the workers would demand a return to an earlier tarif; on other occasions, they would take the opportunity to make a general revision. Disputes could also arise when workers attempted to raise rates to compensate for rising consumer-goods prices or when workers felt that rising demand and profits entitled them to higher real earnings than they had enjoyed previously – although in the first half of the nineteenth century aggressive strikes of this sort seem to have been less prevalent than those intended to restore customary conditions. There were also many cases where workers' corporations acted to enforce existing tarifs on particular masters or groups of masters by forbidding workers to take jobs in shops that failed to honor the tarif. These partial strikes were still often called "damnations" or "interdictions," as they had been by the compagnons under the old regime. There were also cases, as in the Marseille shoemakers' strike of 1845, where some masters accepted the workers' demands and others refused. Then only the shops of intransigent masters would be struck, and cooperative masters were rewarded with business that would otherwise have gone to their strike-bound competitors. Finally, there were some cases – once again the Marseille shoemakers' strike of 1845 is an example – where previously existing tarifs had fallen into disuse as a result of overcrowding, destructive competition, or changes in the organization of production, and workers attempted to impose a new unified tarif in order to arrest the disintegration of their trade.

In many of these cases, a significant proportion of the masters in a trade, at times even the majority, found themselves making common cause with the workers. Small masters who continued to practice their trades in traditional ways had few means of combating the more innovative or more unscrupulous entrepreneurs who introduced new cost-cutting machinery or techniques, who reorganized production and marketing, who employed cheap domestic labor, and who otherwise engaged in "unfair" competition. Deprived of their own corporations by the reforms of the French Revolution, these masters frequently sympathized with the illicit corporations established by their workers and sometimes supported their attempts to enforce uniform tarifs and uniform working conditions in the trade. They, of course, combated workers' corporations when these tried to usurp the masters' powers in the workshop or to raise wage rates so high as to jeopardize their profits. But they would also sign tarifs that seemed to them justified and would sometimes support workers' strikes when these were directed against dangerous cost-cutting competitors. Although it is true that the nineteenth-century corporate idiom was above all a workers' idiom, it does not follow that masters were implacably hostile to workers' corporations. Here it is worth remarking that when workers' corporations attempted to establish publicly ratified, unified tarifs in the weeks following the Revolution of 1848, many masters cooperated willingly in their schemes. Although the actions of workers' corporations were normally directed against the masters, lines of cleavage and patterns of struggle were much more complicated than any simple formula can convey.

In many respects, then, workers' corporations of the nineteenth century carried on the themes, the organizational forms, the values, and the practices of corporations of the old regime. But these familiar elements of old regime corporations now stood in a different relation to each other and to the outside world. One fundamental transformation was in the relation of the corporate idiom to the state. Under the old regime, trade corporations were officially recognized, privileged bodies that exercised public authority, and their language, ceremonies, customs, and values were in harmony with a hierarchical, Catholic, corporately organized social order. The idiom of trade corporations participated in and recapitulated the pervasive social and political idiom of the French kingdom. After the Revolution, corporations were illegal and derived their existence solely from the voluntary adherence and sense of solidarity of their members; moreover, the corporate idiom was now isolated, localized, and alienated from the constituent idiom of state and society. A second and related transformation was a shift of the active center of the corporation from masters to workers. Under the old regime, the privileged corporation of the masters was the main locus of power and initiative, whereas the confraternities or compagnonnages formed by workers were secondary, oppositional, and reactive. In the nineteenth century, the now illicit and voluntary corporation centered on the workers, and the masters either resisted the workers' corporations or cooperated with them selectively against certain of their competitors.

The problems facing nineteenth-century workers' corporations were also different from those of both the masters' corporations and the workers' corporations of the old regime. Under the old regime, the main problem facing the workers' corporations was to assert some degree of workers' control over the regulations of an already existing trade community, to keep journeymen and their interests from being swallowed up by the powerful and selfish community of the masters. It was compagnonnage that solved this problem most fully. By establishing effective control over job placement, compagnonnages were able to stand up to the masters' corporations and to assure that the trade community's regulations took journeymen's interests into account. At the same time, compagnonnage focused journeymen's loyalties on a brotherhood much loftier and broader than the narrow corporations of the masters – a vast brotherhood as ancient as Solomon that embraced journeymen in different trades and different cities all over France. Of course, nineteenth-century workers' corporations also had to sustain workers' loyalty and to exert pressures on the masters. But now that the privileged and regulated masters' corporations had been abolished, the paramount problem workers faced was quite different. The tendency of the new legal and economic system created by the French Revolution was to fracture the trade into a series of unconnected workshops, each organized according to the preferences of its individual proprietor who employed workers on whatever terms he could induce them to accept. Workers' corporations attempted to impose order on a potentially anarchic industry, to create trade communities by concerted action where they would otherwise have no existence, and to maintain them in spite of the hostility of the legal system and the state.

As noted earlier, the corporations that workers constructed in the first half of the nineteenth century varied considerably in shape and in purpose. For a long time, in fact, the most common form of workers' corporations was the same as under the old regime: compagnonnage. But in spite of the continued strength of compagnonnage, the main trend during the first half of the nineteenth century was toward other forms of corporation, above all toward corporations that took the outward form of mutual-aid societies. Clearly outnumbered by compagnonnages in 1810, or even 1820, mutual-aid societies had probably reached a rough parity by about 1830 and were unquestionably the predominant form of workers' corporation by 1848. Both mutual-aid societies and compagnonnages were flexible forms of organization and were sometimes interchangeable in practice. But mutual-aid societies also had certain advantages that made a difference over the long run.

First, they were more locally based and more comprehensive, in that they included married and/or sedentary workers as well as young itinerants. It is almost certain that the average size of artisan firms increased with the growth of cities and the expansion of markets in the first half of the nineteenth century, although the present state of research does not authorize any firm conclusion about the scale or the timing of such a trend. If so, this would mean that a growing proportion of journeymen were destined to be wage earners for life. This, in turn, would imply that the young itinerant workers who made up the core of compagnonnage were a dwindling proportion of the labor force and that mutual-aid societies, which were based primarily on sedentary workers, would become increasingly attractive as a form of workers' corporation. Compagnonnages themselves seem to have responded somewhat to this problem by involving the *anciens* – compagnons who had settled down and resigned from active membership after completing their tour de France – more fully in their affairs. Another advantage of mutual-aid societies in the eyes of settled workers was their strongly local orientation. Under the old regime, workers could always count on the extremely parochial masters' corporations to maintain a local perspective, whereas their own organizations kept in touch with workers in other cities. But with the disappearance of masters' corporations, the definition of the trade as a local community depended entirely on the workers' corporations. Here, too, mutual-aid societies were a more appropriate institutional form than compagnonnages.

But the main advantage of mutual-aid societies was that they were more in tune with the surrounding society. They had no arcane mysteries, they could be joined without a long novitiate, their rituals were few and simple, they lacked internal grades and ranks, they required no blood-curdling oaths, they entailed no sectarian hatreds. Where the compagnons systematically marked themselves off from the surrounding society – by living and eating in their own lodging house, by wearing special insignia, by using distinct language, names, and gestures – mutual-aid societies demanded no special mark of distinction; one had only to pay one's dues, celebrate the festival of the patron saint, and obey the regulations that the society imposed on the trade. In the corporate society of the old regime, the special features of compagnonnage had merely marked it as another of the countless distinct corporate bodies that composed the French monarchy; but in the secular, individualistic, contractual society of the nineteenth century, these same features made compagnonnage seem superstitious, extravagant, and fanatical. This obviously was not entirely a liability for compagnonnage; its separateness was also a source of the special loyalty that enabled it to survive through many trials right down to the present (albeit greatly diminished in numbers). But especially after the Revolution of 1830, workers began to prefer mutual-aid societies, with their simpler structure, their greater openness, and their idiom of voluntary association, over the hierarchical and arcane brotherhood of compagnonnage.

This drift from compagnonnage to mutual-aid societies was paralleled by a shift in the relative importance of two devices used by workers' corporations to impose their will on the masters: control of job placement and the imposition of uniform tarifs. The most striking thing about disputes between workers and masters in the eighteenth century was the prominence of conflicts concerning job placement.[67] This was in part an economic matter; if journeymen could effectively deny skilled workers to an employer, they could thereby keep him from cutting wages. But it was also a question of loyalty: Compagnonnage, by maintaining a monopoly over job placement, assured itself of hegemony over the journeymen's loyalties; and if the masters' corporation itself could obtain a monopoly over placement, it could also challenge the moral grip of compagnonnage on the labor force. Disputes about placement continued into the nineteenth century, but they were gradually pushed to the margins by a rising obsession with tarifs. By the time of the great national strike wave of 1833, the establishment of uniform tarifs had become the dominant issue between masters and workers in the urban skilled trades.[68]

One reason for the rising importance of tarifs was the increasing diversity of the organization of production. Under the old regime, when workshops were relatively small and uniform in scale, all shops in a trade required workers with approximately the same kinds and levels of skills. A workers' corporation could therefore exercise significant control over pay rates and working conditions by threatening to cut off a master's supply of appropriately skilled workers. But as the organization of production became more and more diverse, denying highly skilled labor to a master was not always effective. Masters now could often circumvent a "damnation" or "interdict" by resorting to domestic production or to increased division of labor and simplification of tasks that allowed them to use cheaper and less-skilled workers. In these circumstances, the imposition of tarifs by a comprehensive mutual-aid society was more effective than control over placement by more elitist and restricted compagnonnages. Thus workers' corporations tended to shift their emphasis from controlling labor at the point of supply to controlling it at the point of utilization and to reducing the chaotic diversity of production and modes of payment by imposing a binding tarif.[69] The uniform tarif was in fact a kind of miniature statute. It named and set the relative cost of all the different operations or products of a trade, thereby not only regulating the wages of labor but specifying the range of operations and products allowable to the masters. The tarif, in much abbreviated form, and without legally binding force, served much the same purpose as the officially ratified statutes of the trade corporations of the old regime. Now that the masters could no longer be counted on to maintain an ordered and unified trade community, workers' corporations had to focus their efforts on the organization of production itself. Tarifs thus became crucial instruments in their attempt to control the anarchy that threatened to engulf their trades in the nineteenth century.

The fact that legally sanctioned masters' corporations no longer existed meant that workers' corporations of the nineteenth century were significantly different from the corporations maintained by journeymen under the old regime. The workers were no longer concerned with keeping journeymen from being swallowed up by the masters' community but with maintaining the existence of some kind of trade community against the competitive structure of the legal and economic system and the pervasive individualism of nineteenth-century culture. Forms, customs, language, and techniques carried over from the old regime provided a framework for the corporations workers constructed in the nineteenth century. But in the nineteenth-century setting, workers' corporations inevitably developed in new directions. Mutual-aid societies gradually displaced compagnonnage – in part because their organizational idiom was more in tune with the surrounding society and in part because their greater openness and more local orientation made them more capable of forming communities that could act for the entire trade. At the same time, workers' efforts increasingly centered on the establishment of uniform tarifs that would assure a practical unity of conditions in all the workshops that constituted a trade.

Finally, workers' corporations of the nineteenth century were notable for their openness to innovation. This openness arose largely from their precarious situation. Operating outside the law, with their officers constantly subject to arrest for "coalition" and their tarifs enforceable only by the most constant vigilance, corporations had to be resourceful in order to survive. One response, and in the short run a successful one, was that of compagnonnage: to tighten the organization, to elaborate the very characteristics that set them off from the rest of society, to seek in the arcane tradition of compagnonnage the strength to face a hostile world. But this was never the only response, even within compagnonnage. Both the hatters of Lyons and Paris and the bakers of Marseille blithely combined features of compagnonnage with features of mutual-aid societies, showing more concern for finding effective ways of organizing their trades than for the strict observance of tradition. The shoemakers of Marseille maintained both a compagnonnage and a mutual-aid society and formed a third, yet more comprehensive, corporation to organize the strike of 1845. This continuous experimentation with new organizational forms was perhaps inevitable in the hostile environment of the nineteenth century, where all forms of workers' corporations were unstable and at odds with the surrounding legal order. In the years following the Revolution of 1830, which will be discussed in the next chapter, this experimentation began to include more ambitious attempts to make workers' corporations compatible with the political assumptions of the surrounding society – and, at the same time, attempts to make the surrounding society more compatible with the collectivist moral assumptions of workers' corporations.

CORPORATE LANGUAGE

If the institutional history of nineteenth-century workers' corporations can be described as a combination of continuities and transformations that both linked them to and distinguished them from corporations of the old regime, an analogous set of continuities and transformations can be seen in nineteenth-century corporate language. Some terms common in the corporate discourse of the seventeenth and eighteenth centuries disappeared altogether in the usage of nineteenth-century workers; new terms were added; virtually all underwent greater or lesser shifts in meaning. Yet, in spite of all the changes, the language that workers used to discuss their trades and their work retained a palpable continuity with the corporate discourse of the old regime.

Tracing changes in corporate language through the entire first half of the century would be an extremely difficult task. That such terms as "corps," "état," "corps d'état," "corporation," and "corps de métier" were in daily usage is evident from the fragments of documentation available for working-class life in the period. But given the scarcity of materials written by workers, assembling enough examples to pin down the meaning and usage of these terms would be very difficult. Abundant documentation is not available until the spring of 1848, when the euphoria of a new revolution, the abolition of controls on the press, the Provisional Government's apparent sympathy for the workers, and an explosion of associations of all kinds produced an outpouring of materials written by and for workers. It is above all in these works – speeches, statutes of associations, petitions, manifestos, letters to newspapers, and so on – that the employment of corporate terminology can be observed in detail.

Certain common terms from the corporate vocabulary of the old regime had entirely or virtually disappeared from the language of mid-nineteenth-century artisans. Among these were two terms for the privileged masters' corporations of the old regime: "maîtrise" and "jurande." The departure of "maîtrise" is hardly surprising: It specifically designated the corporation as a body of masters and was, therefore, hardly applicable in the nineteenth century. "Jurande" presented no such etymological problems, as it laid stress on the sworn (juré) character of the corporation; but under the old regime it had been used particularly to designate the body of "jurés" who were the corporation's executive officers, and this usage probably made it distasteful to workers. "Juré" as a term for an officer of the corporation also virtually disappeared after the Revolution, although "prieur" and especially "syndic" were still used occasionally. The disappearance of these terms associated specifically with the power of the masters is hardly surprising in corporations formed exclusively by workers. Harder to explain was the virtual disappearance of the terms "communauté" (community) and "corps et communauté" (body and community) to designate or to describe the corporation. These terms were especially common in the juridicial language of the old regime; perhaps they had never been part of the discourse of ordinary artisans, or perhaps their association with legal discourse made them seem inappropriate for extralegal nineteenth-century workers' corporations. In any case, they virtually disappeared from the corporate lexicon in the nineteenth century.

Other terms that had been used only rarely, if at all, in the discourse of seventeenth- or eighteenth-century trade corporations became commonplace in the nineteenth. Among the most prominent of these was "société," which was used to designate nineteenth-century workers' corporations of all descriptions – not only mutual-aid societies and analogous organizations but compagnonnages as well. This usage of "société" to designate a group of persons joined in a common venture was not unknown under the old regime – witness, for example, the well-known abolitionist organization called the Société des Amis des Noirs (Society of Friends of the Blacks). Until the Revolution, however, this usage seems to have been restricted to the educated classes. But when the French nation itself was recast as a "société," formed by voluntary adherence to a social contract, all kinds of other organizations, formed for various purposes by people from all classes of society, came to be termed "sociétés" as well. Hence, when workers' corporations called themselves "sociétés," they were simply conforming to general post-revolutionary French usage. The analogous term "association" was much rarer than "société" until the July Revolution, after which, as will be discussed in the next chapter, it became very common. "Association" was from the beginning freighted with political overtones; unlike the commonplace "société," "association" was a word to conjure with. Along with "société" and "association" came "sociétaire" and "associé" as terms for the persons who made up a society or association. These terms tended to displace "membre" (member), which was tainted by strong connotations of subordination to a head. Similarly, the terms "président" and "secrétaire" tended to replace "juré," "prieur," "syndic," and "capitaine." Alongside these additions and deletions were a set of corporate terms – "état," "corps," "corps d'état," "corporation," "corps de métier" – that continued to be used under the new regime as under the old. Most of these terms were used with approximately the same meanings as in the seventeenth and eighteenth centuries, although the decline of corporate language in the society at large tended to reduce their resonance. "Corporation," however, underwent much more fundamental changes. "Corporation" was a relative newcomer to the corporate vocabulary of the old regime. An early example of *franglais,* it was borrowed from English in the early eighteenth century as a general term for bodies endowed with a single legal personality. It was not listed in such dictionaries as the *Grand Vocabulaire françois* of 1762–74, and the entry under "corporation" in the *Encyclopédie* reads as follows:

> Political body [*corps politique*] that one calls such in England, because the members of which it is composed form a single body . . . because they are qualified to take, acquire, accord, attack or be attacked in justice in the name of all. We have no term which corresponds directly; communauté comes close, but is not the same: it does not have so extended a signification.[70]

This English term, however, was rapidly adopted into French usage. "Corporation" was at first employed chiefly by enemies of the corporate regime, such as the encyclopedists, but it was soon adopted by its defenders as well. Both Turgot and the Parlement of Paris, in their arguments over the former's attempt to abolish the maîtrises and jurandes in 1776, used the term "corporation" to designate both privileged trade communities and other analogous privileged bodies. But under the old regime, "corporation" remained above all a term of philosophical and juristic discourse.

It was only during the Revolution that "corporation" entered into ordinary discourse and came to refer particularly to trade communities. Indeed, it was mainly as a result of the revolutionary efforts to abolish trade communities – such as the Le Chapelier law – that "corporation" entered common parlance with this signification. Thus, the term that workers used constantly to refer to their cherished trade organizations in the nineteenth century entered their lexicon not from the ordinary speech of old-regime artisans but from the political discourse of the Revolution – and from a concerted attempt to annihilate trade communities, not from an attempt to preserve or defend them. That nineteenth-century workers called their organizations "corporations," rather than, say, "communautés," indicates to what extent these organizations were formed in response to the new order created by the French Revolution. The transformation of the term "corporation" from the eighteenth century to the nineteenth is thus emblematic of the overall transformation in corporate vocabulary and institutions from the eighteenth century to the nineteenth. The use of "corporation" in the nineteenth century marks both a continuity with the old regime and a new beginning since the French Revolution.

The corporate terminology of the middle of the nineteenth century, then, was not identical to that of the old regime. But the workers' usage of this terminology indicates that they still lived in a recognizably corporate world. This can be seen, for example, in their usage of the word "état," a key term in the social vocabulary of the old regime. "Etat" had of course lost many of its political and social referents during the French Revolution. Although "état" was still used to refer to the state, there were no longer three états of the realm, and the provincial états and the Etats Généraux had all been dissolved. Moreover, the use of "état" to signify ranks, orders, honors, pomp, and position faded with the passing of a hierarchical corporate social order. Now lacking these larger resonances, "état" had remained in use as a synonym for "profession" or "métier." In the nineteenth century, it designated occupations of all sorts, either within or outside the urban skilled trades. The main usage of "état" by urban workers, then, was simply to designate their occupations. Yet the term had not been entirely leached of its old contents. Witness the following threatening letter in the general correspondence of the Constituent Assembly from the late spring of 1848: "Let all workers make at least three francs a day; principally the hommes de peine; and those who have the happiness of having états should be given more. Otherwise gunshots."[71] If the man who wrote this letter were asked his état, he would doubtless have answered, "homme de peine." Yet in this quotation he characterizes hommes de peine as having no état. What did he mean?

The author of this letter was recurring to a common usage of "état" under the old regime. "Etat," as noted earlier, meant a stable or fixed condition that determined one's place in the social order. As such, it applied to the état de l'Eglise (the estate of the Church), the état de la Noblesse (the estate of the Nobility), and the Tiers Etat (Third Estate), and also to the various professions or métiers that composed the Tiers Etat. But it was not applied to journaliers, manoeuvres, or hommes de peine, who shifted from one employment to another, whose labor was not disciplined by art, and who were not encompassed in any corporation. These workers lacked the fixed place in the social order that "état" implied and were, therefore, commonly termed "sans état."[72] Their lack of any distinct place in the occupational world was also marked by the very vagueness of their appellations: "journalier" signified "one who works by the day," "manoeuvre," "one who works with his hands," and "homme de peine," "one whose work is difficult or painful." By contrast, the terms for workers who had états designated a specific skill: *tailleur de pierre* (stonecutter), *menuisier* (joiner), *boulanger* (baker), and so on. The work performed by journaliers or hommes de peine was thus literally nameless; it was unmarked and undifferentiated labor in a world where work was verbally characterized and practically organized by specific occupation.

The homme de peine who wrote to the Constituent Assembly in 1848 apparently still saw the world in these same terms; he felt a gulf between men like himself and those happier workers who had états. This suggests that as late as 1848 there was a fundamental cultural distinction between workers who had états – skilled workers with long-standing corporate traditions and some kind of trade organizations – and workers who were sans état – unskilled, unorganized, and without corporate traditions. This is also the conclusion reached by Rémi Gossez, who remarks of journaliers, hommes de peine, and manoeuvres that they were "men without état [*gens sans état*], thus in principle without corporations, without membership in a professional community, without an organization to protect them."[73] The principal meaning of "état" in the middle of the nineteenth century, then, was simply "occupation." But it could also be used to designate a specific set of occupations: those which presupposed skills and a certain discipline and commitment, and whose workers were organized into corporations – the same trades that would have been designated as "arts mécaniques" under the old regime.

"Corps," another key term in the social vocabulary of the old regime, also remained in use in the nineteenth-century working class. As with "état," the resonance of "corps" was greatly diminished when the Revolution destroyed the corporate social order of the old regime, but the meaning of the word remained essentially the same. As under the old regime, "corps" emphasized the unity of the diverse persons joined together in a single organization. If "état" signified the men whose occupations gave them a single and enduring common condition, "corps" signified the body formed when their wills were joined into a single, unified, active trade community. This notion of the corps as formed by the unified actions of those who made it up was typical in expressions utilizing the term in 1848, for example, "the joiner workers of the City of Paris having recognized the necessity of uniting in one single *corps* in order to enlighten ourselves and to instruct ourselves about our rights."[74] "Etat" and "corps," in the nineteenth century as under the old regime, designated two distinct but complementary aspects of trade communities.

The most common term for the collectivity of men exercising a trade actually combined "état" and "corps" to form the expression "corps d'état." By joining these two key terms of the social vocabulary of the old regime, "corps d'état" said a great deal. "Corps" implied unity, organization, activity, and solidarity, and "état" implied stability and distinctness. A corps d'état, therefore, was a solidary body, organized and capable of acting as a unit, composed of permanent members of a distinct trade. "Corps d'état" could be used in at least three different ways. First, it could simply designate a passive category, the trade in which men worked, as in "Let us form a society of laborers for all the workers of the corps d'état."[75] Second, it could designate the active collectivity made up of all the workers in the trade. In this usage it was usually the subject of an active verbal construction: "It is necessary for each corps d'état to organize itself on its own," or "that the state encourage the corps d'état to organize themselves as enterprises."[76] These usages, however, are ambiguous, in that they cast the corps d'état as agents, but also stress their need to organize themselves. Thus, a certain sense of unstructured passivity, which comes from the état side of this coupled term, characterized even many of its formally active usages. Exceptionally, however, corps d'état could also designate an unambiguously active agent. For example: "Let each corps d'état then be a sort of truly fraternal disciplinary tribunal."[77] But most commonly, "corps d'état" retained a sense of passive category even in its active uses. It was above all a body *in which* committees were to be formed or *from which* delegates were to be chosen; it was, to use an analogy appropriate for 1848, an active force parallel to the sovereign people, which elects legislatures or presidents and ratifies or overturns constitutions, rather than to the highly organized, busy, and frenetic government, which the people constitutes. All of these remarks about "corps d'état" apply equally to "corps de métier," which was less frequently employed in 1848 but was essentially a synonym of "corps d'état."[78]

The structured, active, organized aspect of the corps d'état was usually designated by the term "corporation." Perhaps the most common construction employing "corporation" in the discourse of Parisian revolutionaries in the Revolution of 1848 was "to constitute corporations" *(constituer les corporations)*. As a commission of painter workers put it in 1848, "the workers must establish a distributive justice . . . by first constituting corporations in every profession."[79] These corporations, once constituted, were bodies that met, marched, adopted resolutions, and took other kinds of action. A typical usage is, "each corporation, banner at its head, will march with order."[80] "Corporation," like "corps d'état," could on occasion refer simply to the collectivity of workers employed in a trade. But it normally implied a constituted body acting in concert toward some common end. Both the organization of these corporations and the ends they sought to attain were broader and more ambitious in 1848 than they had been under the more repressive regimes that preceded the February Revolution. But the implications of activity and organization that adhered to the term in 1848 were far from novel.

The world that emerges from this brief examination of workers' vocabulary in 1848 has a recognizable continuity with the world of corporate trades under the old regime. It was composed of workers who had stable and disciplined états, who were joined together into corps usually known as corps d'état or corps de métier. And these corps d'états were organized into structured, constituted bodies called corporations that acted as solidary units in the society. Yet nineteenth-century workers' corporations were part of a new moral and social world. These corporations were no longer hierarchically organized jurandes or maîtrises controlled by masters but were sociétés or associations composed exclusively of workers. And where the corporations of the old regime had existed to impose spiritual discipline on the inherently disorderly world of manual labor, corporations in 1848 were to become constituent units of a state based upon labor as the preeminent source of social order. This chapter has described how nineteenth-century corporations were constructed by workers to defend their collective interests and to impose order on their trades. How such corporations came to be seen as appropriate vehicles for a revolutionary transformation of the entire society is the subject of the chapters that follow.

9 The July Revolution and the emergence of class consciousness

By 1830 WORKERS' CORPORATIONS were well entrenched in cities all over France with a distinctive set of conventions, customs, rituals, and formulas to shape the day-to-day conduct of their affairs – what I have called a "corporate idiom." Derived from the usages of corporations of the old regime and worked out in opposition both to the claims of the masters and to the proprietary individualism imposed by the state, this corporate idiom expressed and informed the workers' aspirations for a moral community of the trade. Moreover, whereas masters often rejected corporate claims and stood on their rights as individual proprietors, most of them certainly understood the workers' idiom and could themselves operate within its assumptions when necessary. As previously noted, they quite frequently negotiated agreements with workers that set collective controls over their trades. Within the urban skilled trades, then, the corporate idiom framed not only conflicts but also the accords that resolved them.

But if the corporate idiom could unify workers in a trade and could sometimes move the masters as well, it was powerless beyond the domain of the urban skilled trades, the former "mechanical arts." It was by developing a corporate vocabulary that workers found their own voice in the early years of the nineteenth century, and although the workers' language served admirably for the internal affairs of their trades, it denied them all access to the larger realm of public discourse. What was a regulation for the good of the trade to workers was a violation of the liberty of industry in the eyes of the legal code; what workers regarded as a brotherhood for mutual assistance was an illegal coalition in the eyes of the state. In the new system established by the French Revolution, public avowal of corporate goals was an invitation to state repression. Thus, it is quite understandable that up to 1830 workers' corporations were content to exist in a half-light of clandestinity, either as illicit compagnonnages or as mutual-aid societies whose real shape and purposes were reflected only dimly in their official statutes. It was not until the weeks following the Revolution of 1830, when workers attempted to formulate their demands publicly, that they became clearly aware of the limitations of their idiom. When these demands were presented to the government, workers were dismissed summarily as speaking nonsense. As the workers quickly discovered, the corporate idiom as it existed in 1830 was without moral or even cognitive force in the public sphere; if workers were to make public demands, they would have to do so in a new vocabulary.

THE JULY REVOLUTION

The workers' efforts to speak out in public arose from their widespread involvement in the insurrection of July 1830. The crowds that filled the streets of Paris, built the barricades, and fought off royal troops to cries of *"Vive la Liberté!"* were composed primarily of workers, above all from the skilled trades.[1] The success of the insurrection forced the Bourbon king, Charles X, to flee to England; he was replaced by Louis Philippe, head of the rival Orleanist dynasty, who promptly initiated various liberal reforms – limiting the arbitrary powers of the monarch, setting a somewhat lower property requirement for suffrage, increasing the powers of the elected legislature, and guaranteeing personal liberties and freedom of the press.[2] In the days following the insurrection, the press and political leaders of the new regime were full of praise for the bravery and the patriotism of the Parisian workers. Encouraged by this public recognition of their pivotal role in the revolution, Parisian workers now felt they could legitimately and publicly put forward the demands they had hitherto pursued quietly within the bounds of their particular trades. In August and September 1830 a large number of trades held street demonstrations or sent delegates to the government, requesting it to outlaw machines, to raise wages, to establish uniform tarifs, to shorten the workday, and so on.[3] Although Parisian workers had joined in the cries of *"Vive la Liberté!"* during the insurrection, it soon became clear that their conception of liberty was at odds with that of the government.

The response of the new liberal government to these requests was a mixture of shock, incomprehension, and stern parental reproaches. When, for example, the Parisian stonemasons appealed to the prefect of the Seine (the administrative *département* that included Paris), asking him to forbid piecework and to limit hours in their industry, he responded with a proclamation chiding them for this "rash" (*irréfléchie*) proposal, which he characterized as unworthy "of their past conduct and their habitual loyalty." They had, he continued, "forgotten for a moment all the principles for which they had fought and which several of them had sealed with their blood . . . They had lost sight of the fact that the liberty of labor [*liberté du travail*] is no less sacred than all our other liberties."[4] Another proclamation, this one issued by the prefect of police (the well-known liberal Girod de l'Ain), warned workers that their demonstrations would henceforth be viewed as offenses against public order and that workers risked prosecution under the penal code for illegal coalition.

> If, faithful to the sentiments that animate the heroic population of Paris, they commit no act of violence, their meetings, more or less tumultuous, are themselves a grave disorder . . . If the workers of Paris have well-founded claims to raise, these should be presented individually and in a regular form to the competent authorities . . . Any demand addressed to us requesting that we intervene between master and worker on the subject of fixing wages, or the duration of the working day, or the choice of workers, cannot be admitted, since these are in opposition to the laws that have consecrated the principle of the liberty of industry.[5]

These two official proclamations stated unequivocally the government's interpretation of liberty. Liberty was an attribute of individuals, and mass meetings or demonstrations, even if peaceful, were a "grave disorder." These demonstrations made claims on behalf of the aggregate of workers employed in a trade, when the state recognized only individual citizens. Only if claims were presented *individually* to competent authorities could they be considered at all. And even then, the kinds of requests actually being made were utterly unacceptable, because the imposition of collective regulations would deny individuals their sacred liberty to exercise their industry as they saw fit. "Liberty of labor" or "liberty of industry" was inseparable from all the other liberties consecrated by the July Revolution; to infringe it would be to betray the very principles the workers of Paris had so recently "sealed with their blood."

To the liberal officials of the new regime, the actions and demands of the workers were not only unacceptable but utterly irrational and inconsistent. This helps to explain the patronizing tone of these proclamations. If the workers' "sentiments" were "heroic" and their "loyalty" was "habitual," their actions were *"irréflechie"* – rash, unthinking, literally taken "without reflection." More like children than rational adults, they "forgot" or "lost sight of" their principles and perpetrated "grave disorders" in spite of their good intentions. Hence, they had to be reminded of their duties by their more rational superiors. And if fatherly lectures proved insufficient, workers would be subjected to the rod – prosecution under the penal code. Thus, when printing workers smashed mechanical presses that displaced their labor while shouting *"Vive la Liberté!"* or when they argued that mechanical presses serve "only the interests of a few individuals and are contrary to true liberty," these demonstrations of patent irrationality could be answered only by force; the printers' leaders were therefore arrested and brought to trial for illegal coalition.[6]

The authorities' unyielding response to the workers soon achieved its desired result. The flood of demonstrations in August and September dropped to a trickle by October and November and ceased altogether by December. In part this was because unemployment, already high before the July Revolution, had risen yet higher as a result of political uncertainty. In a period of high unemployment and slack orders, the workers' only hope lay in government intervention; once this possibility faded, strikes against the masters had little chance of success. Although the working-class agitation following the July Revolution was intense, it was also very brief.[7] But the repressiveness and incomprehension of the officials of the new regime also had another outcome they had not foreseen: an attempt by a few militant and articulate workers to reformulate and state more forcefully the workers' point of view. This can be seen most clearly in the foundation of three newspapers written and edited exclusively by workers, all of which appeared near the end of September 1830: *L'Artisan, journal de la classe ouvrière* (The Artisan, Journal of the Working Class); *Le Journal des ouvriers* (The Workers' Journal); and *Le Peuple, journal général des ouvriers, rédigé par eux-mêmes* (The People, General Workers' Journal, Edited by Themselves).[8]

As the printing workers who founded *L'Artisan* made clear in their prospectus, events since the July Revolution had demonstrated the need for an independent working-class voice.

> Without a tribune where they can expose their grievances and their complaints, how can workers make themselves understood by the government? And let it not be said that this is a frivolous reason, experience comes to its support. One would never have seen the sixth chamber of the police court, assembled on September 14th to judge what was pompously called the *coalition* of workers [this is a reference to the trial of the printers], if publicity had been real, impartial; and it is the fault of journalism if the public ministry was mistaken in this affair, if eighteen workers were momentarily deprived of their liberty.
>
> Who can erect this tribune for the working class, if not men taken from its own midst? We have had journals for the use of workers; but they have spoken to us in a foreign language, because they were made by men who know nothing of our needs.[9]

Workers and the bourgeois journalists, these last lines imply, had been speaking different languages and living in different worlds. It was only by establishing a journal written and edited by workers that an authentic working-class point of view could be placed before the government and the public.

But *L'Artisan* did not proceed to state and explicate the demands and needs of the Parisian workers – in fact, it actually argued against the printers' demand that no mechanical presses be allowed on the ground that it was wrong "to impede any industry whatsoever."[10] It was concerned, rather, with a prior problem: how to establish workers as legitimate actors and speakers in the public arena. The language they used to accomplish this purpose tells us a great deal about the practical and theoretical problems facing workers in the wake of the July Revolution.

> The most numerous and the most useful class of society is, without contradiction, the class of workers. Without it capital has no value; without it no machines, no industry, no commerce . . . Certain journalists shut inside their petty bourgeois aristocracy insist on seeing in the working class nothing but machines producing for their needs alone . . . But we are no longer in a time where the workers were serfs that a master could sell or kill at his ease; we are no longer in that not too distant epoch where our class counted in society only as the arm of the social body. Three days have sufficed to change our function in the economy of society, and we are now the principal part of that society, the stomach, which spreads life into the superior classes, now returned to their true functions as servants.
>
> Cease then, oh noble bourgeois, to repulse us from your breast, for we too are men and not machines. Our industry, which you have exploited for so long, belongs to us as our own, and the enlightenment of instruction, the blood that we have spilled for liberty have given us the means and the right to free ourselves forever from the servitude in which you hold us.[11]

This is a passionate, complex, and occasionally puzzling text. It is on the one hand a poignant plea to the bourgeoisie for recognition of workers as "men and not machines." But this plea is tinged with seething anger and resentment and overlaid by an implicit threat of violence. The bourgeoisie, the prospectus implies, would prefer to think of workers as serfs whom they could sell or kill at their ease or as mere machines "producing for their needs alone." And although pleading for recognition, the authors remind the reader that workers have already spilled their blood for liberty and warn that "three days" – a reference to the three-day insurrection of July – "have sufficed to change our function in the economy of society." If the bourgeoisie should fail to recognize this new function, would workers not be justified in taking to the streets again "to free ourselves forever from the servitude in which you hold us"? *L'Artisan* seems torn between a deferential respect for the bourgeoisie as the workers' natural leaders and a hatred for them as implacable class enemies, between an appeal to their sense of justice and a threat of civil war. This tension is present in nearly every line; even the plea "cease then . . . to repulse us from your breast" is punctuated by the dripping sarcasm of "oh noble bourgeois."

A similar sense of tension and unstable equipoise is conveyed by *L'Artisan*'s ambiguous and rather maladroit use of the body metaphor.

Body metaphors normally imply hierarchy, and the editors of *L'Artisan* clearly mean to call forth that implication when they speak of workers as "the principal part" of the social body. But this claim is immediately cast into doubt when workers are identified as the stomach, because the head, rather than the stomach, is conventionally considered the principal part of the body. And when those fed by the stomach are referred to as "the superior classes," it is hard to resist thinking of them in their usual role as the head. By now the reader is thoroughly confused, and the next phrase, stating that the superior classes have returned to their true functions as servants, only compounds the confusion – and mixes the metaphor. The final impression is that the authors are unable to articulate a fully coherent vision of the proper relationship between workers and the (formerly) "superior classes." Here, the ambivalence of the text accurately reflects the position in which the authors found themselves in September 1830. Thrust suddenly and without preparation onto the public stage, inexplicably betrayed by the liberals who had seemed to be their allies during the July Revolution, even the most articulate and sophisticated workers initially found it hard to get their bearings.

But a recognition of these tensions and confusions should not be allowed to obscure the most powerful and in the end the most significant feature of this text: its creative adaptation of the rhetoric of the French Revolution. Even the body metaphor is introduced only as an accessory to the main argument, which is cast in a familiar revolutionary form. Just as the Abbé Sieyès began *What Is the Third Estate?* by demonstrating that the Third Estate performed all the useful labors of society, *L'Artisan* begins by establishing the primacy of the working class: Workers are "the most useful class of society," the source of all industry and commerce – in short, of all wealth. The implication is that workers, as the producers of all wealth, are in fact the sovereign people, whereas the bourgeoisie is a new aristocracy separated from the nation by its privileges. In fact, this conclusion is not explicitly drawn in the prospectus, although the claim that workers are being held in servitude and the ironic imputations of aristocracy to the bourgeoisie – "petty bourgeois aristocracy," "oh noble bourgeois" – indicate that it is not far from the authors' minds. And in the very next issue, *L'Artisan* declared "we believe that the people is nothing but the working class."[12] This heavy reliance on revolutionary rhetoric was by no means peculiar to *L'Artisan*. The argument that labor was the source of all wealth and that laborers were therefore "the people"; the incessant attributions of "aristocracy" and "tyranny" to the bourgeoisie and to the government; the ever-present claim that workers were held in a position of servitude, with the implication of a future emancipation, all these revolutionary politico-literary devices became commonplaces of workers' discourse in the 1830s.[13]

The affinity of workers for revolutionary language is in one respect paradoxical. After all, they had been driven to develop their distinctive public voice by their unhappy encounters with the authorities of the new regime. In these encounters, the authorities' unwillingness and inability to listen to workers had been based above all on steadfast adherence to a central principle of the Revolution, one which they believed the workers were ignoring: individual liberty. Yet instead of attempting to construct some alternative corporate or collectivist rhetoric, the workers chose to ground their claims in the rhetoric of the Revolution. They did so even though this rhetoric, as it existed in 1830, made it virtually impossible for them to voice their cherished claims for the collective regulation of their trades. For revolutionary rhetoric offered workers something far more important: It validated them as legitimate actors on the public stage and endowed them with the power of comprehensible speech. It was only as the sovereign people, whose supreme utility as the producers of all wealth underlay the supreme patriotism they had demonstrated in the July insurrection, that they could command the attention of the government and the governing classes. The editors of *L'Artisan,* and legions of workers after them, understood this perfectly.

Workers' employment of revolutionary language was not, moreover, simply a matter of repeating stock phrases from a familiar repertoire. Utilized in a new context, revolutionary rhetoric was subtly but significantly transformed in meaning. A telling example was the application, both by *L'Artisan* and by countless other workers, of the language of servitude and aristocracy to relations between workers and the bourgeoisie. Here a venerable revolutionary rhetorical opposition was used to place worker-bourgeois relations in a new moral frame and to cast as privileged tyrants precisely that class which had been exalted as citizen-proprietors by the legal and political reforms of the Revolution. Another example of such a transformation was *L'Artisan's* claim that "our industry, which you have exploited for so long, belongs to us alone." By claiming ownership of their labor, workers were recurring to a familiar revolutionary theme: In revolutionary discourse, men's property in their own labor was the source of all property. But *L'Artisan* turns revolutionary discourse back on itself, invoking men's ownership of labor as an argument *against* the claims of property owners, who are pictured as unjustly "exploiting" labor.

This pejorative usage of "exploit," which was still novel in 1830, reinforces *L'Artisan's* transformations of revolutionary rhetoric. The normal usage of "exploit" in the early nineteenth century was entirely morally neutral; it signified the productive utilization of some resource, as in exploiting a mine or a piece of land. To speak of the "exploitation" of labor, therefore, was to speak ironically, to imply that the labor of a human was being treated as if it were a nonhuman resource. Instead of the rather general moral opprobrium the term now connotes – that of selfishness, unfairness, or callousness – "exploitation" in 1830 had a very specific meaning: treating laborers as dehumanized "factors of production." As *L'Artisan* put it in a later issue, the worker's labor "becomes in the hands of the master a land that he cultivates, a machine that he exploits."[14] Thus, accusing the "noble bourgeois" of exploiting labor is of a piece with the outraged declaration that "we too are men and not machines." Both reproach the bourgeoisie for failing to recognize the workers' humanity. Just as the Third Estate had to wrest its "rights as men and citizens" from the aristocracy, the workers must win their humanity from a new bourgeois aristocracy, which holds them in a new nineteenth-century form of servitude. To do this, workers must claim their labor as their own property. Otherwise, they will be reduced to mere factors of production, becoming, in effect, the property of their masters. By combining the notion of exploitation with claims of property in labor and with accusations of aristocratic behavior on the part of the bourgeoisie, *L'Artisan* succeeded in casting the rhetoric of the Revolution into a specifically working-class form. Revolutionary language and rhetoric not only endowed workers with the power of public speech. It also provided the power to redefine the moral and social world.

THE IDIOM OF ASSOCIATION

Revolutionary rhetoric of the sort represented in *L'Artisan* was echoed over and over in workers' writings of the early 1830s and was eventually worked out at greater length and much more explicitly. But the most important development of the revolutionary idiom in these years centered around the term "association." If the charm of the revolutionary idiom for workers was its forthright validation of labor as the foundation of society, its great flaw was an insistent individualism that fit badly with the collective and corporate moral universe of the urban skilled trades. Society, according to the revolutionary scheme, was composed of free individual citizens, not of supra-personal corporate bodies, and attempts to impose collective obligations on a trade therefore became an infringement of the liberty of individual citizens. It was the idea of association that offered workers a way out of this bind. The freedom to associate with others was a classic component of liberty, along with freedom of conscience, of speech, of industry, of religious belief, of the press, and so on. Freedom of association had never been stressed in the French Revolution – not surprisingly, as the great effort of the Revolution was to suppress the countless bodies that stood between the individual and the nation under the old regime. But the principle of liberty of association was nevertheless an inseparable part of the *liberté* proclaimed in 1789 and revived so conspicuously in the Revolution of 1830. It was by developing the idea of association – that is, the voluntary aggregation of individuals into a constituted "society" of some sort – that workers eventually made their corporate organizations and their projects of collective regulation consonant with the revolutionary tradition. The idiom of association was elaborated in two distinct directions in the early 1830s. One of these was actually pioneered by *L'Artisan*. As early as October 17, 1830, *L'Artisan* proposed a novel kind of organization to the Parisian printing workers who were struggling against the introduction of mechanical presses in the printing shops. It was useless, *L'Artisan* argued, to constitute "a sort of association to maintain prices and inhibit the formation of apprentices." Instead,

> since you have been expelled from your shops by machines, cease being workers and become masters in your own right . . . Acting individually, no doubt, the worker finds it impossible to exercise the industry which he professes. But who is to prevent us from uniting a hundred workers, and, taking from our daily earnings a small sum incapable of affecting our real needs, why do we not form a capital sufficient to exploit our industry ourselves?

If a large number of workers would associate and contribute a few francs a week, they could quickly amass enough capital to become co-owners of their own printing shop.[15] By utilizing the principle of association, workers could thus overcome the tyranny of private property and themselves become associated owners of industrial enterprises.

It is not clear exactly how the editors of *L'Artisan* came upon this idea of producers' associations, nor how widely their statement was known. But it is clear that a variety of schemes for associated production were propounded in the early 1830s. One source of this idea of association was the writings of Saint-Simon and Fourier and of their disciples. Saint-Simon and especially Fourier advocated "association" as an antidote to the great scourge of the age – competition. But for both, associative organization of production was merely one aspect of a vast utopian project for a total reorganization of human society. For Saint-Simon, the organization of production could not be separated from a restructuring of scientific and artistic activity nor, in his later works, from the creation of a new religious basis for the social order. And for Fourier, the "phalanstery," which would introduce a new organization of production, was also to be a totally restructured and comprehensive community whose governing purpose was to harmonize and enhance the passions.[16]

The disciples of these brilliant but protean thinkers tended to turn their schemes in a more practical direction, and some of them placed particular emphasis on the need to reorganize production so as to overcome the anarchic effects of competition. But even then, their propaganda had a grandiose and utopian air, and it invariably contained a taste for hierarchy that was not calculated to attract working-class readers. Thus the Saint-Simonian newspaper, *Le Globe,* declared in October 1830:

> Let all the instruments of labor, land and capital, which today form the parceled funds of particular properties, be united in a social fund, and let this fund be exploited by association and hierarchically, in such a manner that the task of each will be the expression of his capacity, and his wealth the measure of his work.[17]

Propaganda of this sort may have attracted workers' attention to the idea of producers' associations. But the Saint-Simonian or Fourierist form of association was both too impractical and too hierarchial to be adopted without important modifications.

The elaboration of a more practical and egalitarian conception of association was accomplished above all by Philippe Buchez. A former Saint-Simonian himself, Buchez offered a series of public lectures in the fall of 1830 that drew a sizable audience of workers. Subsequent discussions with some of these workers seem to have had a major influence on Buchez's thought, and by the fall of 1831 his schemes for workers' associations had been radically transformed – from an initial plan for mutual insurance societies to a plan for producers' cooperatives.[18] When he published his first tract on associations in his newspaper, *L'Européan,* in December 1831, he paid tribute to his working-class collaborators. "This mode of association has been presented to workers," he noted, and many of them "have welcomed this project with enthusiasm."

> We have conversed with these men in their aprons and heavy shoes, with their rude speech, their simple language, about things which would certainly have been unintelligible to many men of the salons. Better than that, we have received memoirs from several of them, written in bad French, to be sure, but filled with ideas that would make the fortune of an economist.[19]

The essential feature of Buchez's doctrine was the notion of a "common social capital." This capital was to be formed out of dues paid by the associated workers and it was to be "inalienable and indissoluble." It was to belong not to the persons who made up the association but to the association itself; members who resigned would have no right to a share of its capital, and those who died could not pass on shares to their heirs. The association's internal organization was to be strictly democratic, and all associates were to be remunerated equally. These associations, in short, would be collective and democratic in spirit and of unlimited duration. Continually admitting new members and accumulating capital out of profits and by means of regular dues, they would eventually replace the competitive individualist system of production. Associations of this sort, Buchez argued, were practical above all in trades "that need few instruments" and in which skill was the principal capital – in other words, the skilled trades of the cities. It could not, however, be applied easily to factory workers; for the present, the best solution for them was an obligatory tarif and a better organization of production.[20] Initially developed in contact with Parisian workers, Buchez's proposals for associated production can be seen as a more formal, elaborate, and fully thought out version of the scheme proposed by *L'Artisan* a year earlier. In Buchez, the idea of producers' associations found a publicist of talent, and his articles on association in *L'Européan* did much to spread its popularity, both among workers and among the republican opposition to the July Monarchy.

The idea of associated production was predicated on an ambiguity of liberal discourse. If citizens possessed the right to associate freely, then they could use that right to create voluntary organizations intended to overcome the egoistic individualism and anarchy of the current liberal system. Just as the commercial code allowed for the pooling of capital in *sociétés anonymes* (joint stock companies), it could not stop workers from pooling their modest capital in producers' associations. As a typographer put it in a letter to the *Tribune,* defending a producers' cooperative founded by the tailors in 1833: "The legal codes . . . and the common law offer the field of association to all citizens. We associate, we wish to use the power given by the law to all citizens to ensure themselves mutually against disasters and to found industrial enterprises."[21] By purely peaceful and legal means, workers could supplant private production with associative production and thereby transform society.

Workers also exploited this ambiguity of liberal discourse by elaborating the idiom of association in another, more immediately practical, direction. Beginning around 1831, workers in various trades began to recast their corporation as "associations," thereby basing them rhetorically on the principles of liberty so often proclaimed as the foundation of the new regime. In June 1831, for example, the Parisian tailors formed a Société philanthropique des ouvriers tailleurs (Philanthropic Society of Tailor Workers). This society, which had the standard death and sickness benefits, was similar in many respects to dozens of mutual-aid societies formed under the Restoration. But there were also some significant differences. In the first place, it was not dedicated to a patron saint. As the term "philanthropic society" indicated, its bonds of solidarity were secular rather than religious. Second, it made no attempt to seek authorization by state officials. Under liberty of association as understood by the tailor workers, state tutelage was neither required nor desirable. Third, whereas many mutual-aid societies pursued goals reaching far beyond their official functions, they usually did so secretly; the Philanthropic Society of Tailor Workers, by contrast, openly declared its intention to provide aid for unemployed workers and for "other unforeseen cases," and it publicly established a "committee of surveillance" to watch over job placement and to judge in cases of disputes between masters and workers.[22]

Nor was the Parisian tailors' association an isolated example. Workers in dozens of trades formed societies on this philanthropic model both in Paris and in the provinces in 1832 and 1833.[23] Some also called themselves philanthropic societies, and others adopted a variety of analogous names: Society of Perfect Accord, Society of Fraternal and Philanthropic Union, United Brothers, Society of Fraternal Amity, Association of Brothers of Concord, and so on.[24] The philanthropic model was particularly popular in the tailoring and shoemaking trades, where societies were formed in several different cities and established a network of correspondence.[25] As noted in Chapter 7, tailors and shoemakers were suffering acutely in these years from the onslaught of the system of confection – with all the attendant problems of overcrowding, declining skills, and the decay of traditional relations of production. Their early and intense experience of deteriorating craft standards was surely a major factor in their eagerness to adopt new forms of labor organization in the early 1830s.

One distinctive characteristic of the "philanthropic" style of workers' corporations was their constant use of the term "fraternity" and its cognates "fraternal" and "brother." As part of the famous revolutionary motto "Liberty, Equality, Fraternity," the word fraternity had obvious revolutionary overtones. But it was also a part of the traditional corporate vocabulary. It therefore served perfectly to unite corporate and revolutionary idioms. It gave a revolutionary respectability to the corporate trades' traditional sense of moral solidarity, and at the same time it gave a more specific content to the abstract revolutionary term "Fraternity." "Fraternity," always the unaccented term of the revolutionary trinity in the liberal version of the revolutionary idiom, became dominant in the workers' version. It was largely by means of the vocabulary of fraternity that the moral solidarity of the corporate idiom was carried over into the workers' new revolutionary idiom of association.

If these workers' associations of the early 1830s differed significantly from the mutual-aid societies of the Restoration, they bore an almost uncanny resemblance to the workers' societies established in Paris in the years following 1789, such as the Typographic and Philanthropic Club of the printers and the Fraternal Union of Workers in the Art of Carpentry, which were discussed in Chapter 5. These societies, of course, were suppressed after the passage of the Le Chapelier law in 1791. The sudden appearance in the 1830s of workers' associations so similar in nomenclature and in practices to those of the early 1790s might seem to suggest the existence of an underground tradition of working-class "philanthropic" or "associationist" ideas that was somehow kept alive over the intervening years. But the reappearance of such organizations would by no means require a continuous underground tradition. After all, the idiom of philanthropic association and fraternal union was implicit in the language of the French Revolution as a whole. If the state itself is conceived of as a *society,* an association formed by the free and equal citizens of the nation and united by bonds of fraternity, then it is only to be expected that citizens will attempt to construct smaller, more limited associations along the same lines. Thus, if workers formed the same kind of organizations in 1832 or 1833 as they did in 1790 or 1791, it is because the Revolution of 1830 brought back a semblance of the moral, political, constitutional, and rhetorical climate of 1789. In 1830, as in 1789, workers were already organized into solidary corporations, struggling to impose order on their trades; with the return of the climate of 1789, workers once again attempted to reconstitute their corporations in a form consonant with a liberal revolution. Hence, the corporation became an association freely formed by those who labored in a trade, and the rules it proposed became not an assault on freedom of industry but an expression of the associated free wills of the producers, much as laws of a nation were an expression of the general will. In this way, claims for collective regulations became compatible with a certain interpretation of liberty.

THE WORKERS' MOVEMENT

In the months following the July Revolution, then, the revolutionary idiom was expanded and reshaped so as to overcome its individualist bias. By the end of 1831, the crucial linguistic and conceptual innovations had already been made. But it was only when these new ways of thinking and talking about association became a common framework for working-class action that the idiom of association was solidified, unified, and definitively fixed in the workers' language and consciousness. The history of the idiom of association, thus, is inseparable from the history of the struggles of workers' corporations.

As noted above, the intense agitation of the Parisian working class in the weeks following the July Revolution was very brief. The workers' newspapers that were founded so confidently in September 1830 ceased publication before the end of the year, and the extensive unemployment that followed the revolution discouraged workers from attempting strikes against the masters. The year 1831 was a low point of the Parisian workers' movement, and although there was some increase in 1832, it was not until 1833 that an economic upswing brought a major revival of strike activity.[26] Workers' actions in the rest of France generally followed this same rhythm.[27] The major exception to the lull of 1831 and 1832 was Lyons, where a long-simmering dispute in the silk industry led to a full-scale revolt in November 1831, and the silk weavers – or *canuts,* as they were called –

won full control of the city for a few days.[28] Although the victorious canuts had no political program and soon relinquished power to the authorities peacefully, their revolt shocked and astonished all of Europe and served as an inspiration to discontented workers. Their slogan, *"Vivre en travaillant ou mourir en combattant!"* (Live Working or Die Fighting!), seemed to announce a new era of terrible social conflict. As Louis Blanc put it, "Never was a more rending and more terrifying motto written on a standard on the eve of a combat; it showed the isurrection of the unfortunate workers . . . to be a genuine slave rebellion." For Blanc, the cause of this insurrection was evident.

> It was the bloody demonstration of the economic vices of the industrial regime inaugurated in 1789; it was the revelation of all the cowardice and hypocrisy contained in that so-called liberty of transactions which leaves the poor at the mercy of the rich, and promises an easy victory to cupidity.[29]

The prime minister, Guizot, hardly shared Louis Blanc's assessment of the causes of the Lyons uprising, but he concurred about its ominous significance.

> The Revolution of July only raised political questions, only questions of government. Society was by no means menaced by those questions. What has happened since? Social questions have been raised. The troubles of Lyon have raised them . . . Discussions of society have joined political questions, and today we have the difficulty of constructing a government and defending a society.[30]

On the French and European political stage, the Lyons uprising of 1831 came to symbolize and typify the increasingly distressing and puzzling problem of labor in modern society.

From the uprising of 1831 to the April 1834 insurrections that marked the end of this period of workers' agitation, the canuts of Lyons were the best-organized, the most self-confident, and – in the eyes of the government – the most dangerous workers in France. The canuts were organized into a number of associations, of which by far the most important was the Society of Surveillance and Mutual Indication, usually known simply as Mutualism.[31] They remained active throughout the generally depressed years of 1831 and 1832, working ceaselessly to maintain the vigor of their organizations and pressing the merchants to accept a general tarif. One sign of this intense activity was a flourishing working-class press. Whereas the Parisian workers' newspapers founded in the fall of 1830 ceased publication in a few weeks' time, *L'Echo de la fabrique,* founded by the Mutualists on the eve of the 1831 uprising, continued publishing weekly until it was suppressed after the insurrection of April 1834. And in 1833 it was joined by a second paper, *L'Echo des travailleurs.*[32]

But if Lyons was the unquestioned center of workers' agitation in 1831 and 1832, the general economic upturn of 1833 brought with it a great wave of strikes and an increase in working-class organizational activity throughout the country. Jean-Pierre Aguet's detailed study of strikes under the July Monarchy has identified a total of seventy-two in 1833, more than four times as many as he found in 1831 and 1832 combined. No fewer than fifty-four strikes occurred from September to December alone. All but a handful were in the urban skilled trades, and although Paris and Lyons accounted for more than half the total, there were also strikes in most major cities – Marseille, Rouen, Nantes, Le Havre, Toulon, Dijon, Montpellier, Metz, Orléans, Le Mans, and so on. The range of trades affected was also very wide – from silk weavers to carpenters to scissors makers to saddlers.[33] Many of these strikes were carried out by organizations that predated the July Revolution, although the new-style Philanthropic Societies were also active, particularly in shoemaking and tailoring. In these two trades, the workers' societies had established a tightly knit intercity network. Their organizations, usually called Philanthropic Societies in the case of the tailors and the Union of Perfect Accord in the case of the shoemakers, had virtually identical statutes in different cities and also presented the same sorts of demands to their masters. The strikes in these industries, at least, seem to have been planned and coordinated.[34] The appearance of intercity links between strikers magnified the authorities' consternation about this strike wave, and the government frequently intervened to break strikes by arresting their leaders for coalition.[35]

In addition to this great surge of labor unrest, the government had another reason for anxiety in the fall of 1833: Republicanism was making important headway among workers, particularly in Paris. The main agent of this republican advance was the Society of the Rights of Man. Originally a small but militant republican sect, the society began to recruit working-class members in 1832; by the fall of 1833, workers probably made up a majority of its total membership, at least in Paris.[36] This influx of workers into the society indicates both a growing political awareness on the part of workers and a change in the thinking and propaganda of certain republicans, who moved from purely political concerns in the first months after the July Revolution to a growing awareness of social and economic issues. The republicans also found a common ground with workers on the question of association. After all, the continued existence of republican societies depended on the government's willingness to accept the right of association. The result was a confluence of interests, ideas, and activities that joined the most radical of the Parisian republicans to the most militant of the Parisian workingmen, creating what Alain Faure has called "the workers' republic of 1833."[37]

As the Parisian Society of the Rights of Man came to be constituted mainly by workers, its activities began to reflect workers' concerns more and more clearly. During the fall of 1833, several of the "sections" that made up the Parisian group became nothing less than republicanized workers' corporations. Workers formed distinct sections organized by trade, instituted mutual aid for sick and unemployed *sectionnaires,* and discussed such questions as job placement and the establishment of tarifs in their trades. Workers from the society are known to have played leadership roles in several strikes in the fall of 1833 – those of the Parisian tailors, cabinetmakers, shoemakers, glovers, bakers, and typographers – and may have been involved in still others. The central committee of the society, far from opposing these developments, officially endorsed the principle of occupationally homogeneous sections in January 1834 and even attempted to establish them in trades where they had not been formed spontaneously. The society also published two pamphlets written by working-class militants that urged the need for both workers' associations and political reform: *Of the Association of Workers of All Trades,* by the shoemaker Efrahem, and *Reflections of a Tailor Worker on the Level of Wages, the Relations Now Established between Workers and Masters, and the Necessity of Workers' Associations as a Means to Ameliorate Their Condition,* by Grignon.[38] Although the central committee was still dominated by radical bourgeois, the Parisian Society of the Rights of Man had, by the fall of 1833, become almost as much a workers' association as a republican association.[39]

It was in this confluence of corporate and republican agitation in the fall of 1833 that the Parisian workers developed the idiom of association into a coherent framework of collective action. The importance of the Society of the Rights of Man for this development must not be underestimated. The organizational support and the intellectual cooperation of the young radicals who led the society was a great benefit not only to such prominent working-class militants as Efrahem and Grignon but to dozens of others who worked more anonymously to organize their trades, to bring pressure on the masters, and to disseminate the combined gospel of association and the republic. This does not mean, however, that workers' discourse was derived from or "trickled down" from the discourse of bourgeois republicans. On the contrary, the major themes of workers' discourse in the fall of 1833 had been set long before a significant recruitment of workers into the society began. It would be at least as accurate to say that the key ideas and themes of workers' discourse – the evil of competition, the workers' right to property in their labor, the identification of the bourgeoisie as aristocratic exploiters, the need for association – seeped upward to certain radical bourgeois whose contacts with workers caused them to rethink and modify their earlier, purely political, republicanism. This autonomy of workers' discourse is especially clear in the case of Lyons. There the republicans were weak and divided, and the Society of the Rights of Man, established only in

October 1833, never recruited a large working-class following.[40] Yet workers' discourse in Lyons, in their newspapers and in the manifestos of their associations, emphasized the same themes as did that of the frankly republican workers in the Parisian Society of the Rights of Man – and generally did so in advance of the Parisians.

The central term in the discourse – and in the practice – of workers in 1833 was "association." As used by workers in 1833, it could refer to three quite different things. First, and most fundamentally, it referred to workers' corporations: associations formed to overcome isolation and competition by instituting practices of solidarity and by establishing controls over the trade. To construct an "association," the republican shoemaker Efrahem tells us: "The workers of an *état* must form a corps among themselves; they must choose, from the midst of that society, a commission charged with representing it in debates with the masters, to fix wages according to tarifs discussed and decreed by its members."[41] As this brief quotation indicates, the goals of such associations had much in common with the goals of workers' corporations of the Empire or the Restoration, but they were now spoken about and justified in a language that merged corporate and associational terms. The "association" described by Efrahem in this quotation is designated as a "corps," formed by the workers of an "état," and is subsequently referred to as a "society." Nor is Efrahem's usage in any way unusual. "Corporation" was used regularly to refer to organizations known as the Philanthropic Society, the Society of Fraternal Amity, and the like.[42] "Corporation," "society," and "association" had become equivalent terms, or, to put it otherwise, corporations came to be thought of as free associations bound together by fraternal and philanthropic amity. When thousands of workers began to speak in this way in 1833, the corporate tradition was definitively assimilated into republican rhetoric, and the republican tradition was given a new corporate twist. Only in 1833 could a worker intelligibly be spoken of as a "citizen of the corporation."[43]

The second meaning of "association" in workers' discourse in 1833 was "producers' cooperatives." In several strikes in the fall of 1833, workers established cooperative workshops that provided employment for idled workers and increased the pressure on masters to come to a settlement. Such producers' associations were adopted, for example, by the tailors, casemakers, shoemakers, and cabinetmakers of Paris, by the shoemakers and tailors of Marseille, and by the shoemakers of Lyons.[44] Most of these associations were not envisaged as continuing beyond the end of the strike. Even the most ambitious – such as the "national workshop" that was formed by Parisian tailors during their long strike of October and November, which they saw as becoming a permanent part of the tailors' corporation – were conceived of strictly as a subordinate arm of the overall workers' corporation.[45] This subordination can be seen, for example, in Efrahem's pamphlet,

On the Association of Workers of All Trades. Efrahem does not designate workers' cooperatives as a separate kind of association but as one aspect of the general association or corps to be established in each trade. "Each trade," he says, should name a commission

> which discusses the interests of the trade with the masters or which receives work to be done from the hands of consumers and distributes it to the associates. In this way, when the workers complain of the inadequacy of their wages . . . their commission will undertake the defense of their rights and their interests; one day, at a given hour, at a signal given by it, all the workers will abandon their workshops and will cease working in order to obtain the price they demand from the masters.[46]

The construction of this passage implies that the association's activities as a producers' cooperative – receiving work from consumers and distributing it to associates – are directed toward a specific goal – toward strikes in which workers will "obtain the price they demand from the masters." There can be little doubt that Buchez's ideas about associations were an important model for the workers who established cooperative workshops in 1833: The "national workshop" formed by the tailors indicates that Buchez's utopian project of replacing private production by associated production was not totally absent from the workers' intentions. But for the time being, at least, producers' associations were subordinated to the more immediate practical goal of winning strikes.[47]

"THE CONFRATERNITY OF PROLETARIANS"

The use of the term "association" to designate workers' corporations and producers' cooperatives antedated the workers' movement of 1833; what the agitation of that autumn did was to bring them together in unified action. But the third meaning of "association" seems to have been invented only in 1833. Associations in the form of corporations or producers' cooperatives were normally thought of as encompassing only a single trade. In 1833 workers began to speak about a larger association that would unite all these single-trade societies into an association of all workers. Only the development of this third meaning of association authorizes us to speak of "class consciousness" in the 1830s, for it was as an "association" of workers in different trades that French workers first conceived of themselves as a united class. This new conception of association arose in part out of practical contacts and the exchange of moral and material assistance between workers in different trades who were engaged in parallel struggles with their masters. As usual, the workers of Lyons seem to have been the pioneers in this effort. As early as April 1833, for example, the stonecutters of

Lyons sent an address "to the silk workers," which appeared in *L'Echo de la fabrique*. Asking for assistance in a dispute with their masters, they declared: "We are no longer in a time where our industries engage in mutual insults and violence; we have at last recognized that our interests are the same, that, far from hating one another, we must aid one another." A response by silk workers noted that *L'Echo* had been founded "to bring into being the bonds of the confraternity of proletarians" and concluded, "the holy alliance of peoples will be born from the no less holy alliance of laborers."[48] The same theme was repeated in November 1833 in a letter to *L'Echo de la fabrique* by the Lyonnais silk braid and trimmings workers: "We think that if all the fraternities would extend themselves and join hands to sustain each other against oppression, they would be strong enough to stop the devastating torrent that opposes the progress of the century."[49]

It was the Parisian shoemaker Efrahem, however, who developed this theme most systematically. In his pamphlet, *On the Association of Workers of All Trades*, he likened the situation of individual workers' corporations to that of unassociated individual workers. Without association, "corporations" will "dissipate and dissolve . . . annihilate themselves in the individualism and the egoism of isolation." Instead of living in isolation, the different corporations should "create bonds of amity" by electing delegates who would constitute a central committee representing all the trades. By "agreeing among themselves" and "living in good understanding," these delegates would form "relations of fraternity" between trades. The delegates, in Efrahem's eyes, would stand for or represent the trade as a whole and, by fraternizing with one another, would symbolically bring their entire trades into relations of fraternal solidarity. In Efrahem's words, the delegates would be "the symbol of the amity which should unite us." The central committee formed by the delegates would also act as a common government for the united trades: "a head that thinks, an intelligent and firm will that informs our actions and directs our movements." One of the chief functions of the central committee would be to keep the funds of all its constituent corporations, which would then be distributed by the central committee "in order to sustain workers who are on strike."[50] By this means the corporations that composed the grand association of all trades would be bound together by "mutual aid and fraternal assistance"[51] – just as the individual workers in a trade were bound together by mutual aid in their philanthropic corporations. Efrahem, in other words, saw the association of all trades as a higher-level recapitulation of the corporate associations of which it was composed. Or to put it differently, feelings of class solidarity, when they first emerged in the early 1830s, were a generalization, a projection to a higher level, of feelings of corporate solidarity. To recur to the marvelously appropriate imagery of the workers of Lyons, "if all the fraternities would

. . . join hands to sustain each other" they could "bring into being the bonds of the confraternity of proletarians."[52]

In retrospect, the idea of a fraternal association of all trades seems obvious, but this is just a sign of the distance of today's world from that of the 1830s. For workers who developed it at the time, the idea was a revelation. The corporate idiom, as it existed under the old regime or under the Empire and Restoration, was capable of creating durable bonds between workers of a given trade or between members of a sect of compagnonnage. But far from emphasizing the commonality of all workers, it emphasized the internal cohesion of the corporation or sect by differentiating it from other trades or other sects. Sometimes this led to open rivalries or hatreds, such as between neighboring masters' corporations under the old regime or between rival sects of compagnonnage or between trades within compagnonnage. For other corporations, such as the numerous mutual-aid societies of the Restoration, it usually led workers simply to build their own organizations without any special concern for workers in other trades. It was only in the early 1830s, and above all in 1833, that an active sense of the brotherhood of all workers developed. As has been noted, this sense grew in part out of the great strike wave of the fall of 1833. But the mere simultaneity of a large number of strikes was not in itself a sufficient condition; strike waves, after all, had occurred even before the French Revolution without having this result. It was not until workers' corporations were themselves seen as free associations of productive laboring citizens, rather than as distinct corps, devoted to the perfection of a particular art, that the wider fraternity of all workers became thinkable. In other words, this essential feature of "class consciousness" was based on the development, during the years following the July Revolution, of revolutionary language and rhetoric that reformulated corporate notions of solidarity into a new idiom of association. Once this had occurred, the wave of simultaneous strikes in 1833 could lead not only to practical cooperation between workers in different trades but to a profound sense of moral fraternity and common identity on the part of "the confraternity of proletarians."

The workers' conviction of the necessity and the benefit of association was based on their analysis of the wrongs of society. This analysis still retained most of the themes and categories found in the 1830 prospectus of *L'Artisan:* the labor/idleness and worker/aristocrat dichotomies and the interrelated ideas of servitude, exploitation, property in labor, and emancipation. But all of these themes were much more fully and explicitly elaborated in the fall of 1833 than they had been in the fall of 1830. Moreover, where *L'Artisan*'s analysis of the wrongs of society led to no clear program of action, workers in 1833 saw their analysis as pointing unambiguously to association as the sole and necessary means of overcoming their oppression.

It was by forging this strong link between analysis and action that the workers created a unified and class-conscious workers' movement in 1833. As in the prospectus of *L'Artisan*, workers' discourse in 1833 was predicated on the workers' performance of the useful labor of society. As the Lyonnais Mutualists had put it at the beginning of their regulations of 1831, "Labor is a treasure; labor, which in appearance is only affliction [*peine*], is on the contrary an inexhaustible source of prosperity and happiness."[53] The useful labor of workers was ceaselessly contrasted to the idleness of the rich. Workers, in the words of the tailor Grignon, were "the laborious majority" who were "the prey of an idle and greedy minority" or, alternatively, "the most numerous and most useful class of society."[54] This latter formula is of course borrowed, but with a characteristic transformation, from Saint-Simon's famous "the most numerous and the poorest class." In Saint-Simon's version, the workers' claims are based on their suffering and depend on the philanthropic pity of their superiors; in Grignon's they are based on the workers' usefulness. By changing a single word, Grignon transforms the workers' claims from a matter of charity to a matter of rights and transforms the working class from a passively suffering mass to the active sovereign people. The same theme is well stated in "La prolétarienne," a song written in 1833 by the tapistry worker Mathon.

> Aux armes, Prolétaire.
> Prends pour ton cri de guerre:
> Moralité pour tous, pour tous égalité,
> La victoire au travail! Mort à l'oisiveté!
> . . . Faible est le bras de l'hereux de la terre
> Qui s'énerva dans un lâche repos.
> Mais il est fort le bras du prolétaire,
> Qui s'endurcit dans les travaux.
>
> (To arms, Proletarian.
> Take as your battle cry:
> Morality for all, for all equality,
> Victory to labor! Death to idleness!
> . . . Weak is the arm of the happy of the earth
> Which is enervated by a cowardly repose.
> But strong is the arm of the proletarian,
> Which is hardened by labor.)[55]

But if the "fecund sweat"[56] of the worker is the source of all prosperity, the present organization of society does not recognize this fact. Workers, rather than taking their rightful place as the "sovereign people," are held in servitude by "these new feudal lords," as the typographer Bannet termed them.[57] Or as *L'Echo de la fabrique* put it, workers are "subjected to the humiliations of a Helot or a Muscovy serf."[58] Their form of servitude is different, of course, from that of serfs or slaves. Exploitation, not the deprivation of legal freedom, was the servitude of the nineteenth century. But like all forms of servitude, it deprived men of their fundamental rights. The government, Grignon laments, "considers us only as an instrument of the pleasures of the rich idler." By allowing and perpetuating the exploitation of workers, by turning them over to the rich to be used as factors of production rather than guaranteeing their rights as men, the government in effect deprives them of their humanity. The government, Grignon says, "claims that we are not men like the others."[59] From the point of view of workers, their struggle against exploitation was a struggle for emancipation: "It is our dignity as men, it is our lives that we demand from the rich."[60]

This new servitude of exploitation arose in large part out of the vicious and egoistic system of property. Labor, the source of all riches, was also the source of all property. Yet labor itself was not recognized as property. As the typographer Jules Leroux put it: "Wages are our patrimony, our property . . . How does it happen that this property is not recognized? How does it happen that it is not protected against the forcible encroachments . . . of the class of masters? Isn't depriving a worker of his work just like expropriating a proprietor?"[61] Labor, in the words of *L'Echo de la fabrique,* was "the CAPITAL of the proletarian."[62] But far from recognizing the laborer's property in his labor and his salary, the present system gave all powers to the rich, the "exclusive and privileged possessors . . . of the instruments of labor."[63] This privileged form of possession allowed them to "claim a property right over us,"[64] to treat men and their labor as if they were simply machines or raw materials that could be bought and exploited. The property system, exploitation, and servitude were thus intimately linked in workers' discourse. The property system established by the French Revolution had created a new form of privilege that empowered the rich to exploit laborers and thus to place them in servitude. This meant that the bourgeoisie had become a new aristocracy, and that the sovereign people, who supported all of society by their labor, must destroy the privileges of the rich and emancipate themselves by a new revolution.

In the present organization of society, the path to emancipation was blocked by egoism, unbridled competition, cupidity, and isolation. These features of society were a product of privilege and exploitation and also ensured their reproduction. Only association could overcome isolation and bring emancipation within the workers' reach. The prospectus of the Industrial Circle, a Lyonnais workingmen's association centered around a mutual savings bank, stated the problem eloquently:

> In the present state of civilization, where Egotism . . . conducts men little by little to the point of isolation and cruelty . . . approaching the state of savages and menacing the dissolution of society, those who suffer most . . . are . . . the men who earn their subsistence through daily work with their hands and are called "proletarians."[65]

The vaunted "liberty" of the bourgeoisie and the July Monarchy was in fact a destructive anarchy: "Do not so profane this word. It is not liberty, it is isolation, complete isolation. The best organized human nature deteriorates under its influence; absolute solitude corrupts man; it turns all the generous passions sour, and changes them into poison."[66] The reign of egoism inevitably leads to misery, savagery, immorality, and crime. Yet the rich, blinded by their cupidity and egoism, strive to keep the workers in isolation from one another in order to maximize their profits and their pleasures. "They wish . . . in order to make our exploitation eternal, that we should remain disunited, isolated. That way . . . they may have us cheaply."[67]

The solution lay "in the spirit of association, which permits men to unite for the defense of rights and common interests."[68] Workers had to overcome their own egoism and create "bonds that make me suffer when my neighbor suffers."[69]

> If we remain isolated, scattered, we are feeble, we will be easily defeated and will submit to the law of the masters; if we remain divided, cut off from one another, if we do not agree among ourselves, we will be obliged to surrender ourselves to the discretion of our bourgeois. There must hence be a bond that unites us, an intelligence that governs us, there must be an *association*.[70]

By joining forces in associations – first in corporate trade associations and then in an association of all trades – workers could gain their rights, and society could be lifted from disorder, poverty, immorality, and anarchy to harmony, well-being, justice, and true freedom. In the words of *L'Echo de la fabrique,* "poverty gives birth to crimes, association kills poverty. Let us push on toward association; the people will become moral, the people will be happy."[71]

Given the workers' view of the function and significance of association, the exalted religious, almost messianic, tone of their discourse is understandable. In the world described by the militant workers of 1833, association was the source of all social order. Without it, industry was defeated by idleness, riches gave birth to poverty, selfishness was rewarded and sacrifice was punished. Only association could save society from annihilation in the egoism of isolation, from regression to the state of savagery, from corruption and deterioration of human nature itself. The establishment of workers' corporations, hence, became not only permissible but a supreme moral duty. And these corporations, now based on workers' utility and brotherhood as laborer-citizens, were duty-bound to form a larger association of the corporations of all trades, one that would actualize the brotherhood of all laborers, giving them the strength to arrest the "devastating torrent" of competition and make fruitful the labor that was now perverted into crime, poverty, and despair.

The workers' enthusiasm for association also explains the events that brought this period of intense discourse and action to an end. Alarmed by the great strike wave of the fall of 1833, by a long and menacing general strike of the canuts of Lyons in February 1834, and by the continuing vigor of the Society of the Rights of Man, the government launched a policy of outright repression. In March 1834 it introduced in the Chamber of Deputies a new law restricting the right of association so severely that all the major workers' associations and political associations formed since the July Revolution would be outlawed. On April 9, when the law on associations had passed the Chamber of Deputies and was being discussed in the Chamber of Peers, the workers of Lyons rose in revolt. On the thirteenth, just as the uprising in Lyons was finally being crushed, a smaller revolt also took place in Paris. The Parisian revolt was put down easily the following day.[72] The insurrectionaries' motives were clearly stated in a manifesto of the Mutualists of Lyons a few days before the insurrection.

> Considering as a general thesis that association is a natural right for all men, that it is the source of all progress . . .
> Considering, in particular, that the association of laborers is a necessity of our age, that it is a condition of existence . . .
> In consequence, the Mutualists protest the liberticidal law on associations and declare that they will never bow their heads under this arbitrary yoke and that their meetings will never be suspended. Relying on the most inviolable right, that is to say to live working [*vivre en travaillant*], they will resist with all the energy which characterizes free men.[73]

The government's new law on associations was a violation of natural rights, an act of liberticide, an assault on the fundamental principle of social order, a dissolution of the social contract. From the point of view of the workers of Lyons and Paris, insurrection was the only legitimate response.

The new law on associations and the unsuccessful insurrections of April 1834 terminated the era of contestation that the July Revolution had opened in 1830. The crushing defeat of the Lyonnais and Parisian insurgents demonstrated the superior force of the government, and the repression of the following months destroyed the Society of the Rights of Man and many of the workers' associations. Moreover, numerous opposition newspapers were closed down or hounded out of existence – not only *L'Echo de la fabrique* and *L'Echo des travailleurs* but a number of republican journals as well. The vigorous workers' movement of 1833 and 1834 was hobbled and driven underground, not to emerge with such force until 1840 and above all 1848. But if many of the workers' organizations were either destroyed or driven into clandestinity, their new idiom of association survived intact. If anything, the repression of 1834 made the need for association more evident than ever and made the practical achievement of association appear impossible without the coming of a republic. After 1834, most workers' corporations returned to the outward forms and to the level of activity of the Restoration years. But despite appearances, their world had been definitively transformed by the discourse and the actions of the early 1830s.

10 The paradoxes of labor

THE YEARS IMMEDIATELY FOLLOWING 1834 were outwardly quiet. It was not until 1839 and 1840 that the agitations of the early 1830s re-emerged in French public life. During the intervening period, the repressive policies of the government fostered underground forms of labor organization and political activity. Workers' corporations certainly continued to exist, and some of them even retained the "philanthropic" forms they had assumed in 1832 or 1833; strikes, however, were rare.[1] The flurry of working-class intellectual and organizational innovation of the early 1830s was also halted by the repression. Nevertheless, the ideas of exploitation, of association, and of the fecundity of labor were quietly ruminated by workers all over the country in the later 1830s, and they emerged in public with renewed force in 1839 and 1840, when several simultaneous events brought the problem of labor to the center of public attention. The year 1839 witnessed the first serious attempt at a workers' insurrection since 1834, an abortive rising in Paris led by Auguste Blanqui and the Society of the Seasons.[2] In the following year a wave of strikes occurred in the skilled trades of Paris, the first major strike wave since 1833.[3] These events were part of a more general reawakening, one that spawned and was intensified by the rebirth of a Parisian working-class press. La Ruche populaire (The People's Beehive), founded by a group of Saint-Simonian workers, published its first number in 1839; in 1840 it was joined by L'Atelier, organe des intérêts moraux et matériels des ouvriers (The Workshop, Organ of the Moral and Material Interests of the Workers). Both journals proved unusually hardy, La Ruche populaire lasting to the middle of the 1840s and L'Atelier until 1850.[4] From 1840 down to the Revolution of 1848, Parisian workers had their own journalistic forum for political expression.

The years 1839 and 1840 were also crucial in the development of socialism, for it was then that the three most important socialist tracts of the era were published: Etienne Cabet's Voyage en Icarie and Louis Blanc's Organisation du travail in 1839 and Pierre Joseph Proudhon's Qu'est-ce que la propriété? in 1840. From 1840 on, socialist ideas were discussed regularly and openly, in workshops and working-class cabarets, in the bourgeois and working-class press, and in journalistic and literary writings of all kinds. From the beginning, manual workers played a significant role in this discourse, writing articles for workers' newspapers, publishing tracts and manifestos, and intervening by means of letters in the bourgeois press.[5] Some workers actually became disciples of one or another socialist school, with the followers of Cabet by far the most numerous and most tightly organized.[6] But most were far more eclectic, regarding the speculations of various theorists as open-ended explorations rather than as received doctrine. In the course of the 1840s, ideas about cooperation, about the reorganization of labor, about joint ownership of the means of production, were discussed, debated, and assimilated by thousands of French workers. Invented in the struggles of the 1830s, these ideas became a familiar part of the workers' world in the 1840s and were immediately available as frameworks for action when a new revolutionary crisis occurred in 1848.

This great reawakening of the 1840s was experienced most intensely by an elite of literate militants, especially in Paris. But in less intense forms, it was also experienced by vast masses of ordinary workers in cities all over France. This can be nicely illustrated by the case of compagnonnage, surely the most obdurate and culturally archaic segment of the French working class. The early 1830s had been a period of agitation for compagnons as well as for other workers. During these years there were a number of schisms between established compagnons and more liberally minded dissidents – the latter usually including a large number of as yet uninitiated aspirants. In 1832 these schismatic groups joined to constitute a reformed version of compagnonnage, which they called the Société de l'union des travailleurs du tour de France (Society of Union of Laborers of the Tour of France). This new society, which was steeped in the associative language of the era, retained the federated multi-trade and multi-city structure of compagnonnage but eliminated the traditional myths and rituals, drastically shortened the period of novitiate, and abolished all ranks and distinctions between workers and between trades. The Société de l'union was intended to absorb and transcend compagnonnage and become a free and equal association of workers in all trades, but it suffered from implacable hostility on the part of the old compagnonnages. In practice it became only a new, more liberal, and very small sect of compagnonnage; the main body of compagnons continued more or less unchanged.[7] Many workers seem to have shared some of the Société de l'union's feelings about compagnonnage, but this was manifested more in a general decline in membership of compagnonnage and an increasing turn toward mutual-aid societies rather than in growth of the Société de l'union.

In the 1840s, however, compagnonnage itself became much less resistant to reform. In 1839 Agricol Perdiguier published his *Livre du compagnon-*

nage. In this work, which revealed the myths and customs of the compagnons to the public for the first time, Perdiguier argued passionately for an end to hostility between sects. Unlike the founders of the Société de l'union, Perdiguier felt that the traditional institutions of compagnonnage were both useful and morally uplifting and that its myths, traditions, and rituals, properly understood, were ennobling and inspiring. Rather than restructuring institutions, Perdiguier aimed to convince the mass of individual compagnons that they were all brothers regardless of sect or trade and that they should unite their efforts for the benefit of all instead of engaging in mutually destructive combat. The literary success of Perdiguier's book was enormous and quite unexpected: It was widely reviewed in the contemporary press and praised by such figures as Chateaubriand, Béranger, Lamennais, George Sand, Louis Blanc, and Lamartine.[8] The first edition quickly sold out, and a second edition was issued in 1841.

The reception of Perdiguier's ideas among compagnons was more mixed. Although some attacked him for publishing the secrets of compagnonnage, others praised his efforts to promote peace and unity between rival sects and were encouraged to publish their own ideas for reform. In any case, it is clear that the publication of the *Livre du compagnonnage* stimulated much discussion and some conflict about the state and future of the brotherhood.[9] These discussions produced no immediate reforms, but the tenor of life in compagnonnage changed significantly in the 1840s. The incidence of violent battles between sects declined sharply and outright cooperation became more prominent – culminating in the widely publicized carpenters' strike in Paris in 1845, which united the Enfants de Père Soubise and the Enfants de Salomon in a long struggle against the masters.[10] How much of this softening of rivalries was due to the efforts of reformers and how much to the broader cultural changes that they would have called "the progress of our century" is impossible to say. But by 1848 compagnonnage seemed on the verge of a historical reconciliation, one that would make the ancient brotherhood into an equal and fraternal association of all trades. Thus, even in compagnonnage, where resistance to the new idiom of association was continuous and obdurate, the new ideas made enormous progress between the early 1830s and 1848.

If the 1840s were a period of changing values and heightened awareness among workers, they were also a period of extraordinary interest in the problem of labor on the part of the bourgeoisie. Working-class unrest of the early 1830s had disturbed the bourgeoisie no less than it had engaged workers, and the two great risings of Lyonnais silk workers continued to haunt the public conscience. The silk workers' famous slogan, "Live Working or Die Fighting!" challenged the moral foundations of the social order and posed a threat of civil war. How could men be expected to accept a regime that boasted of prosperity and industrial progress if they could not live decently by their labor? The existence of widespread poverty was not only an evil in itself; it also threatened to produce workers' uprisings that could destroy the very bases of civilized life. These fears and anxieties drove thinkers of all persuasions to probe the problem of labor – not only socialists like Blanc, Cabet, and Proudhon but bourgeois moralists like Villermé, Buret, and Frégier, who wrote long tomes describing the appalling poverty and moral degradation of the laboring classes,[11] social novelists like George Sand and Eugène Sue,[12] and legions of worker-poets, who sprang up in cities all across the nation, publishing their verses both in the new working-class press and in dozens of books and pamphlets.[13] It was this general fascination with labor – a fascination that arose out of fear as much as sympathy – that explains the unexpected literary success of a book like Perdiguier's *Livre du compagnonnage*. Nor is it an accident that Marx's 1844 manuscripts, which present his most far-reaching statement of the creativity and moral power of labor, were written precisely in these years and in Paris.

One indication of the new public fascination with labor was an important change in the meaning of the word "social." As noted earlier, the eighteenth-century meaning – referring to a voluntary act of association between independent individuals, as in "social contract" or "social intercourse" – was overlaid in the first years of the nineteenth century by a new meaning – referring to an interrelated set of supra-personal institutions beyond the control of the individuals who composed them, as in "social laws," "social forces," and "social science." In the 1830s and 1840s, "social" underwent yet another transformation and began to have specific reference to problems of labor and poverty. Following the Revolution of 1830, the supra-personal institutions and forces that could be investigated by "social science" came to be seen as particularly bound up with the problem of labor and its organization; the terms "social question" and "socialism" came into common usage, and the adjective "social" came to imply sympathy for the poor. The change in the meaning of this term – one of the crucial words in the public vocabulary of the nineteenth century – is a sign of the centrality of the problem of labor in the thought and the public life of the 1830s and 1840s.

By the 1840s the enigma of labor was being attacked from all angles at once. Labor was praised as never before, hailed as the source of all order in the human world; yet at the same time, men who lived by labor were increasingly portrayed as morally and physically debilitated, as threatened by complete bestiality and degradation. The meaning and organization of labor were scrutinized, analyzed, meditated upon, and argued about in the most minute detail and from various points of view. Although an examination of this discourse on labor reveals a convergence on certain themes, it also reveals vast chasms along political and class lines. The views developed in the 1840s prefigure the class warfare that followed the Revolution of 1848.

The outlines of this discordant discussion will be traced by examining writings of three authors with sharply differing points of view: the bourgeois moralist Louis Villermé, the socialist theorist Louis Blanc, and the worker-poet Charles Poncy.

LOUIS VILLERMÉ AND THE PROBLEM OF DEMORALIZATION

Louis Villermé was a medical doctor and a member of the Academy of Moral and Political Sciences. In 1835 he was charged by the academy to carry out a detailed investigation in order to "state, as exactly as possible, the physical and moral conditions of the working classes."[14] Villermé was a man of order, who stood firmly behind the monarchical regime and the principles of contemporary society, and this made his shocking disclosures about the poverty and moral degradation of the working class all the more compelling. Like the handful of other intrepid observers who launched similar investigations in these years, Villermé concentrated especially on workers in the textile industry. The imposing and widely read two-volume report of Villermé's investigations deals with such issues as wages, working conditions, the impact of machinery, health, infant mortality, housing, child and female labor, family life, and the characteristic vices and virtues of workers in textile districts stretching from Lille in the north to Lodève in the Midi. Textiles constituted the most important factory industry in France, and factories were increasing rapidly in number and size in the early 1830s. Although workers in textile factories were far less numerous than workers in urban crafts, they were the object of a special fascination because of the novelty of factory industry and because of their low standards of living – they generally lived in a poverty that was matched only by particularly depressed urban crafts like tailoring and shoemaking. Indeed, Villermé paid particular attention in his investigations to the poorest of the poor, to the inhabitants of the dirtiest and most crowded slums of the most impoverished textile towns. Factory workers and destitute slum dwellers, in Villermé's eyes and in those of most of his readers, revealed "the physical and moral conditions of the working classes" more starkly, and therefore more exactly, than more prosperous workers employed in traditional urban crafts. He singled them out because they seemed to epitomize the new labor problem of the nineteenth century and because, he feared, they might represent the future of the working class as a whole.

Many of Villermé's pages depicted workers in miserable conditions, but the residents of the "hideous quarter" of the rue d'Etaques – the most notorious slum neighborhood in the northern cotton town of Lille – captured his horrified fascination most fully. Here poverty approached its human limits.

The poorest live in the cellars and attics. These cellars . . . open onto the streets or courtyards, and one enters them by a stairway which is very often at once the door and the window . . . Commonly the height of the ceiling is six or six and half feet at the highest point, and they are only ten to fourteen or fifteen feet wide.

It is in these somber and sad dwellings that a large number of workers eat, sleep and even work. The light of day comes an hour later for them than for others, and the night an hour earlier.

Their furnishings normally consist, along with the tools of their profession, of a sort of cupboard or a plank on which to deposit food, a stove . . . a few pots, a little table, two or three poor chairs, and a dirty pallet of which the only pieces are a straw mattress and scraps of a blanket.[15]

To demonstrate that his account was not exaggerated but "all too faithful," he also quoted another, yet more appalling, description contained in a report made to the municipal government of Lille in 1832.

In their obscure cellars, in their rooms, which one would take for cellars, the air is never renewed, it is infected; the walls are plastered with garbage . . . If a bed exists, it is a few dirty, greasy planks; it is damp and putrescent straw; it is a coarse cloth whose color and fabric are hidden by a layer of grime; it is a blanket that resembles a sieve . . . The furniture is dislocated, worm-eaten, covered with filth. Utensils are thrown in disorder all over the dwelling. The windows, always closed, are covered by paper and glass, but so black, so smoke-encrusted, that the light is unable to penetrate . . . everywhere are piles of garbage, of ashes, of debris from vegetables picked up from the streets, of rotten straw; of animal nests of all sorts: thus, the air is unbreathable. One is exhausted, in these hovels, by a stale, nauseating, somewhat piquante odor, odor of filth, odor of garbage . . .

And the poor themselves, what are they like in the middle of such a slum? Their clothing is in shreds, without substance, consumed, covered, no less than their hair, which knows no comb, with dust from the workshops. And their skin? . . . It is painted, it is hidden, if you wish, by indistinguishable deposits of diverse exudations.[16]

Yet more shocking than this material degradation was the moral degradation with which it was inevitably associated. Thus Villermé concluded his description of the cellars of the rue d'Etaques:

I would rather add nothing to this description of hideous things which reveal, at a glance, the profound misery of these unhappy inhabitants; but I must say that in several of the beds of which I have just spoken I have seen individuals of both sexes and of very different ages lying together, most of them without nightshirts and repulsively dirty. Father, mother, the aged, children, adults, all pressed, stacked together. I stop. The reader will complete the picture, but I warn him that if he wishes it to be accurate, his imagination must not recoil before any of the disgusting mysteries performed on these impure beds, in the midst of obscurity and drunkenness.[17]

To judge from Villermé, the life of the poorest workers in the slums of Lille was scarcely recognizable as human. In these dark, damp, fetid, filthy cellars, all the restraints of civilization had been corroded by poverty – a corrosion summed up by Villermé's image of promiscuous incest performed on "impure beds," drowned in "obscurity and drunkenness." But precisely at this point Villermé's account reveals itself as open to serious doubt. His leap from the poverty, darkness, and disarray of the working-class dwelling to an imputation of incest – "disgusting mysteries," as he delicately put it – is hardly an objective description. Incest seemed to Villermé a logical culmination of the disorder he had seen in poor people's lives – something that *must* have been true, given what he had actually observed. This unwarranted inference, presented with such an air of self-assurance, makes us keenly aware that Villermé's account is as much an interpretation of poverty as a description, an interpretation that must itself be subjected to interpretation and criticism.

It is clear from a variety of evidence that extreme poverty was common in the textile towns visited by Villermé and was particularly widespread in Lille.[18] Villermé was certainly describing what he had seen. Yet the similarity between his description of the cellars of Lille and the description contained in the 1832 report to the municipality – which he cites as evidence that he has faithfully described these dwellings as they actually were – can also be seen as evidence that his very observations of the slums of Lille were structured by preexisting descriptive conventions, conventions that made him see the living conditions of the poor in terms of brutishness and moral disorder.[19] Thus both accounts – and many others in their flourishing genre – emphasize darkness, airlessness, and disarray of the furnishings, with a special fixation on beds. And although both descriptions begin by making it clear that only some of the very poor lived in cellars, both end by focusing on cellars – dwellings sunk into the earth, whose darkness, humidity, and similarity to burrows made them compelling symbols of the degradation of humans to the level of animals. Attics, however cold, drafty, and objectively unhealthy, were too far above the earth and too close to the heavens to serve this rhetorical purpose.

Villermé's interpretation of poverty was a moral interpretation. The crucial problem, for him, was not that workers received inadequate material remuneration but that they had an inadequate moral constitution. Villermé points out cases of very badly paid workers who nevertheless lived decently and of well-paid workers who spent all their money on "costly pleasures" rather than on improving their real conditions.[20] At one point he even states that "those who gain the best wages are ordinarily the most dissolute. Bringing an equal ardor to pleasure and to labor, they often pass half their lives engaged in an extremely difficult labor, and the other half in disgusting orgies."[21] Material deprivation, in short, was more the product of moral degradation than its cause.

The nature of the workers' moral degradation is analyzed above all in a chapter entitled "Morals and Moral Principles" (Moeurs et principes moraux). Given its title, one might expect a discussion of the moral principles that guide – or perhaps of the principles that ought to guide – workers' lives. But instead of treating any recognizable "moral principles," this chapter is a catalogue of the workers' vices, taken up one after another under the headings "Drunkenness of the Workers," "Improvidence," "Lack of Economy," "Libertinage," "Bad Examples," and so on.[22] The key concept in Villermé's discussion of morality turns out to be not moral principles but "demoralization" – failure of workers to live up to civilized, bourgeois standards – and the main purpose of his chapter was to analyze the corrosive influences that caused workers to fall into depravity. Villermé's moral theory was thoroughly environmentalist.

> Like the qualities and the defects, like the virtues and the vices of other men, the qualities and the defects, the virtues and vices of workers are principally, I would almost say uniquely, the results of their environment, in a word, of the circumstances in which they live, and above all of those in which they are raised.[23]

Thus the children of the poor in Lille

> see nothing but disorders, hear nothing but obscene statements, are impregnated with nothing but vices: raised in an atmosphere of impurities, fashioned by bad examples, and unable to know anything else, they imitate what they see being done, and they necessarily become, like their parents, drunken, debauched, brutalized.
>
> Thus bad inclinations, deprivation and misery are transmitted from generation to generation by the force or the contagion of example and perpetuated by the force of habit, just as good morals and good qualities are perpetuated and transmitted in other classes, or among other workers, or even among workers of the same classes who live in different places.[24]

Workers, hence, were not really responsible for their immorality.

> Is it permissible, I ask, when one looks at things from this point of view, to reproach all the workers in the factories for their misconduct and

their indigence? Has everything possible always been done in these establishments . . . in order to uproot it? To those who would answer me yes, I must say no.

The responsibility for vice lies not with the workers, who are constitutionally incapable of resisting temptations, but with factory owners who do not always keep temptations from them. As an example, Villermé takes up the question of mixing male and female workers in the factories.

> What! You mix the sexes in your workshops when . . . you could so easily separate them? Are you then ignorant of the licentious discourses which this mixture provokes, of the lessons of bad morals which result . . . and of the driving passions which you encourage as soon as their voice begins to make itself heard? . . . In the workshops where there are girls, do you impose decency? The cynicism of language, the jealousy that innocence inspires in those who have already lost it, are these not causes of corruption which you see and which you do not prevent? Even among children, doesn't the mixture of sexes lead to a license in relations, and, even in the most vulgar acts of life, a scorn for decency, which must later bear its fruits? Whatever efforts you undertake afterwards to correct the evil, you would have done better to prevent it. You will never be able to escape the reproach of having allowed girls to be lost whose morals you could have saved by wise and honest precautions.[25]

As the quotation reveals, Villermé viewed workers as tragically susceptible to the temptations of evil. Good workers will be corrupted by association with evil ones; the mixing of sexes inevitably leads to sexual debauchery; bad examples in youth are more powerful than good examples later in life, and so on. In part, Villermé seems to be embracing a traditional Christian conception of the depravity of man, of man's innate propensity to sin. But only in part. In the first place, he never uses the word "sin." Demoralization, debauchery, licentiousness, unreason, disorder, misconduct, depravity, prodigality, indecency, but never sin. Nor is Villermé's argument developed within a religious framework. The only mention of religion is purely utilitarian.

> It must be avowed that the greatest consolation for the people, its most important restraint, is the belief in a life to come, with its penalties and its rewards. The mere suspicion that there is nothing after death renders them immoral, excuses in their eyes the most egoistic, the most materialistic passions, if I may put it this way, and those most prejudicial to the social order.[26]

Religion, in Villermé's moral world, figured only as a useful restraint on dangerous passions.

Moreover, whereas Villermé clearly saw *workers* as predisposed to immorality – often using such phrases as "dangerous, almost inevitable fall" or "he cedes almost inevitably to"[27] – he does not seem to view this predisposition as inherent in the condition of all humans. The workers' sad predisposition to misconduct resulted from the conditions in which they were brought up, conditions that inflamed their passions, encouraged improvidence, and taught them no restraints. But humans who were not brought up in such conditions did not share this predisposition to vice. Factory owners, for example, seem to have been predisposed to virtue. Villermé sometimes criticized them for not setting up their workshops in such a way as to maximize the encouragement of virtue, but he did not accuse them of actually embracing evil. Villermé seems to have assumed that the bourgeoisie was virtuous almost by definition – not an absurd notion, perhaps, given his equation of moral virtue with restraint of appetite, rather than, say, with such "aristocratic" qualities as generosity or elevation of spirit. The fault of the bourgeoisie was only a failure to impose its own virtuous restraint on the workers.

In many ways, Villermé's discussion of workers is reminiscent of the old-regime view that labor was inherently disorderly and a moral nullity. Villermé seems to be restating in a nineteenth-century vocabulary the judgment of the Parlement of Paris that manual workers are "beings born for the trouble of societies, whose passions, less tamed by education, join to the brute energy of nature that activity which they acquire in the midst of the license of cities."[28] Villermé also shares the old-regime view that labor must be made subject to moral discipline if social disorder is to be averted. Under the old regime, disorderly workers were tamed and disciplined by corporations, which raised labor to art by enforcing detailed rules and regulations. Although the battle of order against disorder or good against evil is the central theme of Villermé's book, he sees this battle in a nineteenth-century deterministic and "scientific" framework rather than in the Christian framework of the old regime. The traditional Christian opposition between the demands of man's immortal soul and the demands of his bodily appetites, an opposition resolved by the corporations' union of art and labor, is transformed in Villermé's account into a sociological opposition between the sort of people who are capable of moral action – that is, those who have been raised so that their appetites are restrained – and the sort who must be saved from demoralization. The battle of good and evil is fought out not so much in the soul of every man as in the relations between environmentally determined moral classes. Repression of sin and disorder, for Villermé, becomes the discipline of the bourgeoisie over the poor. Thus, in order to suppress vice and uphold virtue, the owners of factories must see to it that their workers are surrounded by good examples and preserved from the temptations of evil. This has already been done by a few factory owners, and it should be done by all. Are there not factories, Villermé asks,

> where the sexes are rigorously separated, and where care is taken to let the women off work a little earlier than the men? [This latter to assure that they will not walk home together!] Where in each workshop surveillants continually keep their eyes and ears open for everything said or done that might affect morals? Where one never suffers offenses against [morals]? Where drunkenness is proscribed without pity? Where workers are required to make deposits in a saving account? Where the master maintains a school at his expense, which he requires children to attend successively each day? Where he informs himself about the fate of the workers, has them cared for when they are sick . . . makes advances of money, even imposes sacrifices on himself in order to prevent their unemployment, and attempts on all occasions to come to their aid?[29]

If the moral degradation of workers is to be overcome, factories must be made into reformatories, into beneficial industrial prisons where the design of the work process, the paternal presence of the manufacturer, and the untiring eye of the overlooker banish disorder and immorality from the worker's long day.[30] And even outside the factory, the workers must be given moral guidance and be protected from temptations, above all from the temptation of alcohol, which Villermé calls "the greatest scourge of the laboring classes."[31] Although Villermé felt that the working day was too long in most textile factories, he did not feel that leisure should be greatly extended. It was important that the Sunday day of rest "not be extended into the following day by the workers, and not be passed at the cabaret."[32] It would be useful to occupy workers "on Sundays by entertainments useful to their health and by attractive studies directed in a way that would perfect them in their trades, that would give them, with ideas of order and economy, and with religious sentiment, moral and intellectual instruction." But Villermé was not convinced that offering such useful entertainments would be sufficient; too many workers would prefer to pass their Sundays in less serious pursuits. But even here, the benevolent bourgeoisie played an indispensable role.

> Reputable persons known by the workers, above all esteemed and respected by them, who would attend their games, their entertainments, who would preside over them, direct them with skill, would do much more good and be much more useful to them. Unfortunately, this is something one never or almost never sees.[33]

Even during their day of leisure, in their games and their entertainments, workers should be directed and protected from vice by ever-watchful moral guardians from the bourgeoisie.

These moralizing efforts by the bourgeoisie were urgently demanded by the condition of contemporary society and above all by powerful social trends that promised to increase demoralization by removing people from traditional sources of moral restraint. There were already thousands of workers whose lives had been literally brutalized, reduced to the level of animals, by poverty, debauchery, and addiction to alcohol – such men and women were particularly common in the slums of Lille. Unless the bourgeoisie took up the great work of moralization, conditions would inevitably get worse as modern industry grew. "With respect to morality," Villermé affirmed, "workers of the cities are less worthy than those of the country-side, and those of factories less worthy than those who work in their families."[34] Because industrial progress caused cities to grow at the expense of the countryside, and because factory labor was continually displacing work in small shops and in households, the number, as well as the proportion, of workers subjected to demoralizing conditions was growing constantly.[35] Hence, unless factory owners made their workshops into schools of moral-ity and restraint, the progress of industry would inevitably cast more and more workers into a state of physical and moral depravity.

Some factory owners had already adopted reforms of the sort advocated by Villermé, and with very encouraging results; but the universal adoption of these reforms would not be easy to achieve. Many factory owners did not see efforts to moralize their workers as being in their interests, and the system of free competition discouraged any innovations that might increase costs and thereby threaten the existence of the reforming firms. Although Villermé was optimistic about the possibilities of moral reform, the even-tual outcome was unclear. If the factory owners would cooperate with each other in works of moralization, the condition of the workers might be greatly improved, but if their efforts were too rare and scattered, the result could be massive moral deterioration. For all of Villermé's optimism about the possibilities of improvement, his book is haunted by the terrifying vision of an unregulated growth of factory industry that would drag workers in city after city into the dark underworld of bestial poverty and disorder that he had seen in the slums of Lille. It was this threat that industrial progress could usher in a future of subhuman poverty and vice for an ever-growing proportion of the population – and the even more terrifying thought that these human beasts might eventually rise in revolt – that made Villermé's work so startling and so compelling to his readers.

To the modern reader, this picture of a brutalized proletariat, wallowing in filth, stupefied by alcohol, utterly lacking the restraints of civilization, is bound to seem less an accurate assessment of working-class life than a night-mare of the bourgeois conscience, a negative projection onto the workers of the bourgeoisie's own preoccupation with cleanliness, sexual restraint, providence, and temperance. In fact, a close reading of Villermé's own text allows a glimpse of a human, morally structured working-class world, one whose signs of humanity were often obscured from Villermé by his own interpretive scheme. In discussing the impoverished cotton workers of Alsace, for example, he criticized them for wearing luxurious clothes on Sundays and allowing their clothes for the other days to be "as bad, as insufficient, as their dwellings."[36] From the workers' point of view, one suspects, this "luxury" served to maintain respectability and honor in spite of poverty, to ennoble the one day they could call their own. But for Villermé, always alert for signs of "demoralization," the workers' actions were only another indication of their unreason and prodigality.

A similar example is Villermé's discussion of drunkenness in Lille, which he believed to be the most important source of the workers' unspeakable miseries in that city. His remarks, intended to indicate how all of life was polluted by alcohol, unwittingly reveal a vital world of working-class sociability in the cabaret. Thus, he observes that Lille's mutual-aid societies, although "instituted for an entirely moral purpose," were ruined by alcohol. "The place where they assemble once a month to discuss their affairs is always a cabaret." Worse, they celebrated the end of the year by spending some of their accumulated dues "in debauchery" – that is, drinking in the cabaret. For Villermé, this was not only immoral but a perfect inversion of all morality. To convert accumulated savings into alcohol was to turn restraint into its opposite, to turn providence into prodigality, to make mutual-aid societies engines of debauchery rather than schools of virtue. Thus, although Lille had more mutual-aid societies per capita than any other city in France, their "bad organization . . . does not permit them to do any good."[37]

As noted in Chapter 8, workers instituted mutual-aid societies not solely as means of providing for savings in case of sickness but as encompassing communities of friendship, solidarity, and good fellowship, in which sharing a pot of beer or a few glasses of wine in the society's cabaret was as important as mutual aid to relieve illness or distress. For workers, the cabaret was a major center of social and even of moral life. In spite of himself, Villermé actually bore witness to this aspect of the cabaret when he remarked with horror: "It is in the cabaret that he makes his debts, that he pays them when he can, that he concludes his bargains, that he contracts his friendships, etc., and that he even accords his daughter in marriage."[38] The cabaret, in the lives of most workers, was a node of community, of social obligations, and of human solidarity; but Villermé could see it only as a destroyer of the bonds of civilization, a bottomless abyss of squalor and brutality. His own moral preoccupations blinded him to the palpable existence of an alternative working-class morality.

These inadvertent revelations of human community, these suppressed flickerings of an alternative morality, were lost in Villermé's vast and somber tableau of misery and vice, visible, perhaps, to the discerning eye of the modern reader but unnoticed by Villermé's contemporaries. The message of this book, and of others in its flourishing genre, was clear and distressing: that industrial progress threatened to intensify the suffering and the debauchery of the working class. This, in an era of repeated mass revolutionary outbreaks, meant that the continued existence of bourgeois liberty and bourgeois comfort were far from secure. This threat hung over all discussions of the problem of labor in mid-nineteenth-century France, clouding the horizons but also intensifying the search for solutions.

LOUIS BLANC AND THE ORGANIZATION OF LABOR

Much of Villermé's terrible vision of the physical and moral deterioration of the working class was shared by Louis Blanc, even though Blanc's analysis of the problem and his conclusions were utterly different. Blanc was a radical journalist, an avid republican, and an admirer of the Jacobins; his tract *Organisation du travail* was one of the most popular and influential early statements of socialist ideas.[39] *Organisation du travail* originally appeared as a series of articles in Louis Blanc's monthly magazine, *Revue du progrès,* in 1839 and was issued as a pamphlet in the following year. It was reissued, considerably expanded and revised, in 1841, 1845, 1847, 1848, and 1850.[40] In this tract, Blanc's moral indictment of contemporary society rested above all on his portrayal of the appalling poverty of the working class, which he claimed was the inevitable result of the current competitive social and economic system. To document this poverty, he quoted at length from a study of the poor in Nantes by Dr. Guépin.[41] The passage could easily have been written by Villermé.

> Enter into one of those streets where [the worker] lives penned in by misery . . . Stoop down as you enter one of these sewers which open onto the street and are below its level: the air is cold and damp as in a cellar; your feet slip on the dirty floor, and you fear to fall into the mud. On either side of the sloping hall . . . there is a large, dark, icy room, whose walls drip with dirty water, receiving air only by a window too small to let the light pass and too badly made to close properly. Push open the door and step in, if the fetid air does not make you recoil; but be careful, for the uneven floor is neither paved nor tiled, or else the tiles are covered by such a thickness of filth that they cannot be seen. Here are two or three beds, worm-eaten and shaky and held together by pieces of string; a straw mattress, a blanket made of frayed rags . . . As for cupboards, none are needed in these houses.
> . . . The children of this class spend their lives in the mud of the gutters, until the moment when they can increase the wealth of their families by a few pennies by means of painful and brutalizing labor.

They are pale, swollen, wilted, their eyes so runny and red with scrofulous infections that they can scarcely see; one would say they were of an entirely different nature from the children of the rich.[42]

Such was the "excess of misery" to which "the cowardly and brutal principle of competition has brought the people."[43]

One inevitable result of this gruesome poverty was moral disorder – especially crime and the dissolution of family life. In conditions of poverty, "the family gives away to illegitimate union," and thence to infanticide, which was three times more common in industrial districts than in the country as a whole.[44] Poverty also leads to crime. Manufacturing districts, Blanc points out, have crime rates twice as high as agricultural districts: "The galleys are recruited from the workshops." In later editions of *Organisation du travail*, Blanc cited Frégier's study of the "dangerous classes," which had appeared in 1840, as evidence of the moral perversion that resulted from poverty.[45] According to Blanc, Frégier had shown how, in certain quarters of Paris,

> the lepers of the moral world pile up in an abominable pell-mell and, lost in their hideous throng, certain poor creatures moved more by poverty than by vice! Here scenes occur to make one shiver! The faces one meets are full of ferocity and bestiality. The tongue they speak is a fatal tongue, invented to cover thought. Their excesses reach the point of orgies, and it happens every day that the habitués mingle the blood of their quarrels with the alcohol that revives and consumes their brutalization.[46]

Here poverty, abetted as usual by alcohol, created a world of crime that was a negation of bourgeois morality, a world where orgies, violence, ferocity, deception, and brutality reigned. Even their language was an inversion of bourgeois speech, a "fatal tongue" that "covered thought" rather than expressing it. Thus, the ultimate result of a competitive organization of labor was a negation and inversion of all morality in crime.

But if Louis Blanc agreed with Villermé in his assessment of the condition of the working class, his diagnosis of its causes was quite different. For Blanc, the crucial cause of moral degradation was the competitive and individualistic organization of labor. Blanc began with the system of private property, which deprived the poor of any place in society.

> Is the poor man a member of society or its enemy? . . . He finds the soil everywhere about him occupied.
>
> Can he cultivate the land for himself? No, because the right of the first occupier has become the right of property.
>
> Can he gather the fruits that the hand of God has caused to ripen along man's way? No, for as the soil has been appropriated, so have the fruits.

... What then shall this unfortunate one do? He will tell you "I have arms, I have intelligence, I have strength, I have youth; take all that, and, in exchange, give me a bit of bread." This is what the proletarians say and do today. But even here you may respond to the poor man: "I have no work to give you."[47]

The propertyless worker is thus at the mercy of proprietors. Under the individualistic system of contemporary society, labor, the poor's only source of livelihood, is distributed by competition to the lowest bidders. Hence wages, instead of being fixed at a level adequate to keep the proletarian from want, are driven ever lower. "Under the empire of unlimited competition, the continual decline of wages is a necessarily general fact, and not at all exceptional."[48] As long as society is ruled by competition, poverty will be the inevitable result, and "labor will bequeath to the future a generation decrepit, deformed, gangrenous, rotten."[49]

Thus, in spite of the similarity of Blanc's and Villermé's assessments of the moral and physical condition of the working class, their proposals for action differed radically. Although Villermé recognized that the competitive economic system made factory reform more difficult to attain, he did not challenge the basic framework of the social and economic order. The crucial thing for Villermé was not to increase workers' material remuneration – because without moral improvement such increases would merely result in greater drunkenness and prodigality – but to provide an environment that would encourage virtue and banish disorder. This reform was inconceivable without the enlightened capitalist, who could make his factory a school of morality and restraint. Although Blanc concurred with Villermé about the pernicious effect of bad moral examples, he saw the ultimate cause of the workers' physical and moral degradation in "a corrupted social order,"[50] especially in competition. For Villermé, moral degradation led to and perpetuated poverty; for Blanc, poverty, which resulted from competition, was the cause of moral degradation. Blanc therefore believed that the problem could be solved only by radically suppressing competition and by transforming the system of property that gave rise to wealthy capitalists and to impoverished proletarians alike.

What was required was a new "organization of labor." Blanc's scheme for organizing labor was similar in many respects to those worked out in the early 1830s by radical workers or by Buchez. Production would take place in democratically organized associations, which would compete against and eventually overwhelm private firms. These associations, which Blanc dubbed "social workshops" *(ateliers sociaux)*, would cooperate among themselves and would become the fundamental units of society when the competitive system was finally suppressed. The main innovation in Blanc's plan was the important role he assigned the state. The state itself was to establish the "social workshops," both providing them with credit and enacting statutes to govern their operations. It would then watch over and coordinate their activities and aid them in their righteous competition against private firms. The government, in Blanc's view, should become "the supreme regulator of production," charged with the task of "making competition disappear."[51]

Blanc's emphasis on state action fit his pessimistic assessment of the condition of the working class. If the competitive system had reduced workers to poverty and moral decay, then workers themselves could hardly be counted on to take the initiative in creating a new organization of labor. Under the contemporary regime of competition, according to Blanc, laborers were not free men but "slaves of ignorance, slaves of chance."[52] Only intervention by the state could give them the power to be genuinely free. "We want a strong government because, in the regime of inequality in which we are still vegetating, there are feeble men who need a social force to protect them."[53] As portrayed by Blanc, workers were essentially passive; although the final goal was to establish a society in which the worker would be the equal of any man, the working class in the present was more an object of solicitude than an active agent in social transformation. Thus Blanc's appeal in *Organisation du travail* was addressed to the educated and literate public and even to the rich, rather than to workingmen. The introduction to the 1845 edition begins: "It is to you, the rich, that this book is addressed, because it is a question of the poor. For their cause is yours."[54]

This feature of Blanc's theory attracted the wrath of some politically advanced workers. The editors of the newspaper *L'Atelier*, for example, were indignant when he spoke about workers "being emancipated," rather than calling for them to "emancipate themselves": "They wait to be emancipated! This is a sentiment that originates in a lack of courage; it is a sentiment almost analogous to that of the slave who has not the energy to break his chain and who waits with resignation for a superior force to raise him."[55] Yet, on the whole, Blanc got a far more enthusiastic response from workers than from the rich. According to a brief note at the beginning of the 1841 edition, it was "workers" who had pressed Blanc to issue a new edition,[56] and many of Blanc's ideas and the terms "organisation du travail" and "ateliers sociaux" were adopted widely by working-class radicals. It is a characteristic paradox of the 1840s that many active and articulate workers, most of them drawn from respectable skilled trades, were enthusiastic supporters of a book that portrayed laborers as ignorant, destitute, morally degraded, and passive. What counted for these workers was not the literal accuracy of Blanc's claims but their moral force and the practical conclusions he drew from them. Blanc's writings, after all, shared their own animus against individualism and competition, and his portrayal of the moral degradation and passivity of the workers could be read as reinforcing their own claims that workers had been reduced to slavery by exploitative capitalists. Moreover, Blanc's plans for the organization of labor, which were largely borrowed from the associationist schemes developed by workers in the early 1830s, foresaw a radical moral and practical revaluation of labor, which would eventually become the foundation of a just social order. In spite of the obvious differences between their perceptions of society, Blanc and radical workers found plenty of common ground in their struggles against the individualistic system.

CHARLES PONCY AND THE POETRY OF LABOR

At the same time that Louis Villermé, Louis Blanc, and others were discovering and anatomizing the moral and physical degradation resulting from modern conditions of labor, labor was also being praised as the height of human creativity and the source of all social order. This elevated conception of labor was already implicit in the writings of working-class militants in the 1830s, and it was elaborated and extended as a part of the general exploration of labor in the 1840s. A vision of the creativity of labor underlay all the socialist writings of this era, even when – as in the case of Louis Blanc – they emphasized the crippling effects of the present organization of labor more than the plenty and the moral perfection that would result when labor was correctly organized.[57]

A fascinating manifestation of this vision of the creativity of labor was the worker-poet movement. Worker-poets first began to appear in significant numbers in the late 1830s, and they multiplied in the favorable climate of the 1840s. They wrote poetry in various genres, with lyric poems and songs as the dominant types. Judgment on the worker-poets has generally been rather harsh – they are commonly dismissed as mediocre poets, as writing inferior imitations of Lamartine, in high romantic style and filled with lofty sentiments, rather than concentrating on their authentic experience as workers. Alternatively, they are criticized for having been naïve and politically ineffective.[58] But these criticisms of the worker-poets miss the most important point about the movement. The very existence of worker-poets, the coupling of the terms *poète* and *ouvrier*, was itself a novel and potent statement about labor. That manual laborers were capable of poetry, the most esteemed of the arts in this age of high romanticism, that mechanical art and poetic art could be mastered by the same person, signified that the long-presumed opposition between vile labor and lofty creativity was false, that labor and poetry were not opposite but basically the same. The worker-poets, whatever the subjects of their poetry, revealed the exalted mission of labor by their very existence. They were living representations of a great new truth: that labor was synonymous with creativity and an emanation of the sublime.

Sometimes, although not always, this equation of poetry and labor was made in the poems themselves. One of the most successful examples was a collection entitled *La Chanson de chaque métier* (The Song of Each Trade), by Charles Poncy, a stonemason from Toulon. Like many other worker-poets, Poncy was actively patronized by George Sand. In 1846 he had completed his second volume of poems, entitled *Le Chantier* (The Building Yard), which, in spite of its title, featured mainly romantic verses such as "Aurora Borealis," "The Nightingale," "Two Souls in Heaven," "A Bouquet of Violets," "Byron at Albano," and "The Angel and the Poet."[59] Finding himself "momentarily dry of inspiration" after completing this volume, he wrote to George Sand for advice.[60] It was she who suggested that he write *La Chanson de chaque métier,* "a collection of popular songs at once playful, naïve, serious and grand, above all simple," that would "poetize and ennoble each type of labor; pleading at the same time the bad social direction of this labor as it is understood today."[61] This suggestion filled Poncy with "a new ardor," and he set to work immediately.[62] He had nearly completed the volume when the February Revolution "was carried out in the name of the ideas that had inspired these couplets," making his book seem "like a hammer in the hands of a worker who no longer has anything left to destroy." But with the failure of the social revolution, he finally decided to publish his book in 1850, "because it will serve at a later date to make known, better than many others, the spirit and the situation of the workers during this time."[63]

Poncy portrayed a world of labor utterly different from that of either Villermé or Louis Blanc. It was, in the first place, a world composed primarily of the traditional skilled trades, of joiners, watchmakers, tailors, blacksmiths, bakers, rope makers, stonecutters, shoemakers, and the like; and although there is a "Song of the Miners," there is nothing about the textile factory operatives who so monopolized the attention of Villermé. As noted in Chapter 7, skilled trades of the sort portrayed by Poncy continued to dominate most French cities, particularly the capital, where textiles were virtually nonexistent. It was also these trades whose workers were most active in revolutionary movements, whether in the early 1830s, in 1848, or in 1871. In this sense, Poncy's book certainly does "make known, better than many others, the spirit and the situation of the workers" in the Revolution of 1848.

Second, although some of Poncy's songs complain at length about poverty and suffering, his understanding of poverty was utterly different from either Villermé's or Louis Blanc's. As noted earlier, real wages in the skilled trades declined slightly in the 1830s and 1840s, and the decline in living standards could be catastrophic in "sweated" trades such as shoemaking and tailoring. Poncy was fully aware of these problems, and the songs of the tailors and shoemakers emphasized their poverty. The tailor is so poor that he cannot even afford to wear the clothes he makes, and the shoemaker, who lives in constant hunger, actually harks back to one of Villermé's themes, complaining:

> Mes fils, sur un lit usé,
> Couchés pêle-mêle,
> De leur mère ont epuisé
> La maigre mamelle . . .
>
> (My sons, lying pell-mell
> On a worn-out bed,
> Have exhausted the emaciated breast
> Of their mother . . .) [64]

As in Villermé, poverty is represented by a worn-out bed where children and adults of both sexes sleep together pell-mell. Poncy, one suspects, may have read Villermé and at the very least must have been aware of the literary convention of symbolizing poverty in this way. Yet the moral implications of Poncy's account are precisley the opposite of Villermé's: The mysteries performed on the shoemaker's bed are not incest but the suckling of babies; Villerme's "impure bed" is transformed in Poncy's image into a scene of the purest of moral action. Instead of degrading the poor, poverty provides an arena for moral heroism, as the shoemaker and his wife preserve the bonds of family even under the most trying of conditions.

Poverty, for Poncy, was not an all-consuming affliction but a cross that workers must bear in their pursuit of higher goals. Labor, in Poncy's songs, brings joy as well as sorrow; far from being a moral nullity, labor was a sublime act of creation, one that gave form and value to brute nature. As the machinists (*mécaniciens*) sang,

> Armons nos bras des sonores marteaux,
> Et, pour la gloire et le bonheur du monde,
> Donnons la vie aux rebelles métaux.
>
> (Arm ourselves with sonorous hammers,
> And, for the glory and the happiness of the world,
> Give life to rebellious metals.) [65]

Similarly, the stonecutter's labor was a kind of poetry that "gives soul to the rough slab." Thus, the young stonecutter who travels through the country,

> Le coeur plein d'avenir,
> Partout, sur son passage,
> Salue un souvenir.

Il lève la paupière,
Et lit, d'un oil joyeux,
Ces poèms de pierre,
Ou'ont écrits ses aieux.

(His heart filled with the future
At each step of the way,
He greets a souvenir.
He raises his eyelids,
And reads with joyous eye,
Those poems of stone,
That his elders have written.)[66]

Indeed, labor was the source of all order in the world. As Poncy says in the opening poem of the volume, "To the Proletarians," if workers were to cease their labor and to worry instead about its troubles and dangers,

Nous n'aurions ni maisons, ni moisons, ni navires;
Le monde échapperait à la céleste loi,
Et couvert des débris de ses riches empires,
L'homme s'abdiquérait: le néant serait roi!

(We would have neither houses, nor harvests, nor ships;
The world would escape from celestial law,
And covered with the ruins of rich empires,
Man would abdicate, and nothingness be king!)[67]

Labor, in this vision of things, was not a curse of sinful man but a "celestial law." It is no accident that Christ himself was a laborer – the "divine proletarian"[68] – and it is by perfecting God's gift of labor that "man becomes dearer to God each day."[69] Hence the refrain of the "Song of the Ironsmith,"

Que ta voix de fer, mon marteau, résonne
Pour glorifier le Travail et Dieu,
Le Travail et Dieu.

(Let your voice of iron resound, my hammer,
To glorify Labor and God,
Labor and God.)[70]

As in the mechanical arts of the old regime, work as portrayed by Poncy was infused with spiritual meaning. But the romantic and humanistic Christianity of Poncy – and of most other worker-poets of this era[71] – gave work a spiritual meaning very different from that assigned to it by the hierarchical Christianity of the old regime. Work in the mechanical arts of the old regime was seen as an intersection of sharply opposed material and spiritual worlds, a combination of humiliating labor with ennobling art. It was the imposition of the spiritual rules and discipline of art over the disorderly domain of base labor that gave the mechanical arts a distinct, if lowly, standing in the hierarchical society of the old regime. In Poncy's vision, by contrast, labor and art, work and poetry, were not opposed categories but one and the same. Poncy understood art in a nineteenth-century romantic sense, not as the disciplined application of rules but as creativity, as the discovery and revelation of the sublimity immanent in all of God's works. All labor, whether manual or nonmanual, whether refined or painful, was equally a realization of the divine plan. Thus Poncy's spirituality implied not hierarchy but complete equality, an equality aptly symbolized by the "divine proletarian" with his message of universal brotherhood.

Equality, however, did not mean uniformity. As every mechanical art of the old regime had its own distinct rules and discipline, so different nineteenth-century trades undertook their holy labors in their own way. The world of work, as George Sand had remarked, had "an infinite variety."[72] Each trade had not only its particular skills and conditions of labor but its own personality. The shoemaker is always ready to join insurrections, the baker drinks too much wine and chases women, the stonecutter is footloose, the waggoner is light-hearted and loves his freedom, the fisherman is pious, the tapestry weaver is refined and generous, the printer is enlightened, the barber and the silk weaver are politicians.[73] Each trade lives and labors in its own fashion, each creating order in its own domain. But these distinct types of labor are also joined in an interdependent and egalitarian whole. As Poncy puts it in his preface:

> I have tried above all to demonstrate the solidarity that exists between all the trades, from those that industry and success have elevated to the level of an art, down to the lowliest and most obscure. I have tried to prove that no artisan has the right to believe himself more noble or useful than another: the printer, for example, no more than the plowman whom he instructs, but who renders him daily bread in exchange; the blacksmith, no more than the mason to whom he furnishes tools, but who builds him a forge for his nourishment and a roof for his shelter; the watchmaker, so wise and distinguished in appearance, no more than the poor miner who goes, among thousands of dangers, to dig from the flanks of the earth the metals indispensable to the fabrication of watches and clocks, and so on. It is a chain so admirably forged that no link can be detached without breaking it at every point.[74]

Labor, in other words, generates a harmonious and complete social order, composed of distinct but interdependent trades. Or rather, it would do so were its efforts not distorted and debased by the vicious social organization of the day. Miners, shoemakers, tailors, joiners, knife grinders, and others suffered from crushing poverty;[75] domestics were humiliated by subjection to the master of the house;[76] soldiers were forced to put down the revolts of their fellow workers;[77] and the gifted tapestry weaver regrets his "charming trade" because he must "sell his treasures to the vanity of the rich."[78] Labor must be properly organized for the true harmony of mankind to be realized. Thus the "Song of the Tailors," which bewails their poverty and oppression, ends on a positive note:

> Mais pour l'oeuvre des temps maudits
> S'ouvre la tombe noire.
> Frondon d'un gai *De produndis*
> Sa cendre et sa mémoire;
> Car des jours heureux
> L'éclat généreux,
> Déjà sur nos fronts brille.
> Courage, garcons,
> Au bruit des chansons,
> Enfilez votre aiguille.

> Oui, que pour le bonheur de tous
> Le travail s'organise,
> Et que du Seigneur, parmi nous
> Le regne s'éternise.
> Enfants, pour bénir
> Ce bel avenir,
> Qu'on chante et s'égosille.
> Courage, etc.

> (But for the works of these evil times
> The black tomb now opens.
> Cast off with a gay *De profundis*
> Their ashes and their memory;
> For the generous flame
> Of happy days
> Shines already on our brows.
> Courage, boys,
> To the sound of songs
> Thread your needles.

> Yes, for the happiness of all
> Let labor be organized,
> And let the Lord's reign
> Be eternal among us.
> Children, to bless
> This beautiful future,
> Let us sing and shout,
> Courage, etc.)[79]

God's justice, Poncy implies, is immanent in labor, but in order to move from conditions of poverty and sorrow to the eternal joy of "the Lord's reign," labor must be organized. The organization of labor was the great task of the century, the essential program of the revolution to come. Its achievement awaited only a unanimity of will among the people. Thus Poncy concluded his call "To the Proletarians!"

> Et le regne de Dieu descendra sur la terre
> Lorsque toutes vos voix l'appelleront en choeur.
>
> (And the reign of God will descend to the earth
> When all your voices call out in chorus.)[80]

It was to harmonize the voices of this working-class choir that Poncy wrote his songs.

In the complex and variegated discourse of the 1840s, labor was both lowered to the subhuman and raised to the sublime. Haunted by a chorus of lugubrious "scientific" observers like Villermé, the public could not dismiss the possibility that modern conditions of labor would reduce the working class to the condition of brutes, living in dark and airless urban burrows and enslaved to their basest and most disordered passions. Yet at the same time, worker-poets like Charles Poncy soared to lyrical heights, singing the praise of labor's spiritual mission and its order-giving powers. Where Villermé and even Louis Blanc saw only a drab and uniform drudgery, Poncy saw infinite variety and endless charm. These differences of perception were harbingers of the political conflict and class warfare that were to follow the Revolution of 1848. The workers, in 1848, believed that the state was henceforward based on the creativity of labor, and that the various corporately organized trades should work together to reconstitute society as a harmonious choir of fraternal laborers. Louis Blanc, elevated to the presidency of the Luxembourg Commission, which was established to elaborate plans for the organization of labor, made common cause with the workers but saw the new social order as the imposition of a benevolent state rather than as an emanation of the order already implicitly present in the corporate trades. But to the men of order who had heretofore controlled the political destinies of the nation, the clamor for the organization of labor looked very different: It was the criminal delusion of a degenerate working class, an emanation not of an order inherent in labor but of the disorder that resulted from alcohol, bestiality, resentment, and demoralization. In these circumstances, it is quite understandable that the Parisian insurrection of February 1848 touched off the most intense and explosive discussion and experimentation about the organization of labor that the world had ever seen, and that the workers' attempt to establish universal fraternity ended in a bloody civil war.

11 The Revolution of 1848

> The nation constitutes itself from this moment as a republic;
>
> All citizens must remain armed and defend their barricades until they
> have obtained the enjoyment of their rights as citizens and as laborers;
>
> Every adult citizen is a national guard;
>
> Every citizen is an elector;
>
> Absolute liberty of thought and of the press;
>
> Right of political and industrial associaiton for all . . .
>
> Brothers, let us be calm and dignified like the law, like force, in the
> name of human liberty, equality and fraternity.[1]

POSTED IN THE STREETS OF PARIS as a declaration of "The Sovereign People" on February 24, a few hours before the Provisional Government officially proclaimed the Second Republic, this placard declared the continuity of the Revolution of 1848 with the French revolutionary tradition. The "Sovereign People" began by proclaiming the republic and closed with an invocation of liberty, equality, and fraternity; in between they demanded their "rights as citizens." The rights demanded were all commonplaces of republicanism – universal suffrage, universal participation in the National Guard, and freedom of thought, press, and association. How commonplace they were was soon demonstrated by the Provisional Government. Although it was totally unaware of this ephemeral placard, it nevertheless proclaimed within the first day of its existence every one of the rights the placard specified. When the sovereign people demanded their rights as citizens, whether by explicit statements or simply by taking control of the streets of the capital, everyone knew what they meant.

But to the inevitable demand for rights as citizens, this placard appended a more novel and less well-defined demand: rights as laborers. Unlike citizens' rights, laborers' rights were not spelled out on the placard, except for a

243

passing reference to the "right of political and industrial association." The rights of labor were also recognized more haltingly by the Provisional Government. Improvised on the spot and granted only under pressure, the new rights of labor soon became the central issue of the Revolution. As early as February 25, the day after the proclamation of the republic, an immense throng of workers demonstrated before the Hôtel de Ville, forcing the Provisional Government to recognize formally "the right to labor" (*le droit au travail*). This demonstration and the favorable response of the government began a process of working-class demands and governmental responses that added up to the launching of a genuine social revolution. It was a social revolution that remained more a promise and a project than an effective transfer of state power. But to the Parisian workers, the message was clear: Labor had finally won the day and taken its rightful place as the essential basis of the state. From the decree on the right to labor of February 25 to the grim days before the bloody workers' insurrection of June 22–26, there was a monumental outpouring of energy and frenetic action. In these four months the workers of Paris did their best to construct an entire, new social order based on labor – from constituting new workers' corporations to electing workers to the National Assembly, from negotiating tarifs to elaborating general schemes for the organization of labor, from setting up producers' associations to establishing workers' power in the National Guard – the confusing, exhausting, exhilarating, contradictory, generous, desperate, and spontaneous action that is the unmistakable sign of a real revolution.

The workers' revolution of 1848 took place above all in Paris in the four months between late February and late June. By concentrating on this short and intense Parisian revolutionary spring, I will be swimming against the main currents of recent historiography. The best recent histories of the French Revolution of 1848 have tried to correct what their authors have seen – with good reason – as an undue emphasis on Paris and on the dramatic political events of the spring of 1848. These studies have demonstrated that far from being an essentially Parisian phenomenon that was effectively terminated by repression of the June workers' insurrection, the Revolution of 1848 created a vast nationwide political movement for a "Democratic and Social Republic" – a movement that, in spite of continuous repressive efforts by conservative authorities, was only eliminated in the violent aftermath of Louis Napoleon's coup d' état in 1851.[2] I accept all this revisionist historiography: Indeed, I began my own scholarly life with a study of the Revolution of 1848 in the provincial city of Marseille, a study that emphasized the crucial importance of developments in the post-June era.[3] But if the effects of the Revolution were played out on a nationwide scale and over the course of several years, the most important transformations of workers' consciousness took place in the streets, the meeting halls, and the workshops of Paris between February and June 1848. Although Paris was not all of France, Paris remains the key to the workers' Revolution of 1848.

THE FEBRUARY REVOLUTION

The insurrection of February 1848 began when officials of the July Monarchy outlawed a reform banquet planned for February 22. Popular protest against the cancellation soon led to scattered violence, and on February 23 and 24 barricades were raised in the popular quarters of Paris. After desultory attempts to put down the insurrection by force, Louis Philippe abdicated and fled to England on the twenty-fourth; later that afternoon a republic was proclaimed and a Provisional Government installed itself at the Hôtel de Ville. The Provisional Government was made up of a moderate republican majority and a radical republican minority, which included the socialist Louis Blanc and a militant worker named Albert.[4] During its first days, the Provisional Government labored under continuous pressure from an immense crowd of workers that gathered around the Hôtel de Ville. Indeed, it was the pressure of the crowd that convinced the Provisional Government to proclaim a republic immediately rather than waiting for an elected Constituent Assembly to decide on the form of the government.

On the morning of February 25, the Provisional Government began to organize the administration and to issue a flurry of decrees, proclaiming freedom of the press, assembly, and association, announcing the imminent convocation of a National Assembly to be elected by universal adult male suffrage, adopting the tricolor flag, opening the National Guard to all adult male citizens, abolishing the death penalty for political offenses, and the like. But the crowd outside the Hôtel de Ville also wanted the Provisional Government to take specific actions on behalf of workers. At one point a group of demonstrators forced their way into the room occupied by the government and demanded "the organization of labor" and a guarantee of "the right to labor." The Provisional Government was at first uncertain, but in the end Louis Blanc was charged with writing up a decree guaranteeing the *droit au travail* (right to labor).[5] The wording Blanc chose had far-reaching implications.

> The Government of the French Republic commits itself to guarantee the existence of the worker by labor.
>
> It commits itself to guarantee labor to all citizens.
>
> It recognizes that workers should associate with one another in order to enjoy the legitimate benefits of their labor.[6]

By issuing this decree, the government took on the responsibility of providing work for the unemployed. A few days later the government announced that National Workshops would soon be opened to provide jobs for the unemployed, and similar establishments were opened in the provinces in the following weeks. Unemployment was already high before the February Revolution, and it was pushed even higher by the economic crisis that inevitably succeeded the political crisis. Throughout the spring of 1848, the National Workshops were an essential resource for tens of thousands of workers who were left jobless by the economic slump. Most of the employment provided by the workshops was rudimentary digging and leveling on public works of dubious value; in this respect, the National Workshops were little different from the *ateliers de charité* (charity workshops) that were the traditional resort of French governments in times of massive unemployment.[7]

It seems likely that the majority of the Provisional Government intended the National Workshops as nothing but rechristened "charity workshops," as a temporary expedient to rescue workers from destitution in a time of particularly severe distress. But the decree that established the workshops did not base them on charity; it based them on a solemnly proclaimed right of all citizens, the right to labor. Consequently, the workers tended to regard the National Workshops as a potentially permanent feature of the new republic. This sense of permanence and importance was reinforced by the title National Workshops. To designate workshops as "National" implied that they were a fundamental institution of the republic, like the National Assembly or the National Guard. The term "National Workshops" also had another significance. It had first been employed by striking tailors in 1833 to designate their producers' association,[8] and it was reminiscent of Louis Blanc's "Social Workshops." Hence, the National Workshops were widely viewed, both by their supporters and by their detractors, as a first step in the direction of a state-aided system of producers' associations.

The implications of the decree proclaiming the right to labor thus went far beyond the provision of unemployment relief. As interpreted by the workers of Paris and of the other cities of France, it established the right to labor as a fundamental right of man. Furthermore, the recognition of this right seemed to imply the need for a radical restructuring of the entire social order. The statement that "workers should associate with one another in order to enjoy the legitimate benefits of their labor" implied both that they were presently being deprived of the legitimate benefits of their labor and that association – in other words, some form of collective control over production – was required to set things right. By its decree, the Provisional Government seemed to espouse the view that the proper organization of labor was a fundamental task facing the nation. The *Journal des travailleurs* spoke for revolutionary workers generally when, three and a half months later, it reminded the government of the republic of "the decree of 25 February which states: *labor is guaranteed to the worker,* this decree is the program of the Revolution of 1848. Yes governors, there is the revolution!"[9] When labor was recognized as a fundamental right, as a foundation of the republic, it implied a vast and radical revolutionary program.[10]

The decree on the right to labor led, both logically and historically, to the organization of labor. On February 28, another immense workers' demonstration converged on the Hôtel de Ville, now demanding a ministry that would undertake the organization of labor. After serious disagreements within the Provisional Government, a compromise was worked out; rather than a ministry, the government would establish a *Commission de gouvernement pour les travailleurs* (Commission of Government for the Laborers) to discuss the problem of labor and to propose solutions to the forthcoming National Assembly. From the point of view of the reluctant majority of the Provisional Government, a study commission, which implied no immediate action, was a way of buying time. But from the point of view of the Parisian workers, the establishment of the commission was another solemn engagement on the part of the government. This interpretation was certainly encouraged by the wording of the decree announcing the commission.

> Considering that the Revolution, made by the people should be made for it;
>
> That it is time to put an end to the long and iniquitous sufferings of the laborers;
>
> That the question of labor is of a supreme importance;
>
> That there are no more lofty, more dignified preoccupations of a republican government;
>
> That it is particularly suitable to France to study ardently and to resolve a problem posed today in all the industrial nations of Europe;
>
> That the ways of guaranteeing to the people the legitimate fruits of their labor must be considered without delay;
>
> The Provisional Government of the Republic decrees:
>
> A permanent commission, which will be entitled: Commission of Government for the Laborers, will be named, with the express and special mission of considering their destiny.[11]

This commission, which was to include representatives of all the trades of Paris, was to be headed by two members of the Provisional Government, Louis Blanc and the worker Albert. Furthermore, it was to hold its meetings in the Palais de Luxembourg, the former seat of the Chamber of Peers. Here, indeed, was a profound symbolic reversal; in the new regime labor replaced the peers as the noblest element in the state!

As early as March 1, then, the Revolution of 1848 had already become what was called a "social" revolution – that is, a revolution dedicated to solving the problem of labor. Against the wishes of its majority, the Provisional Government had been forced to declare the "right to labor," to open National Workshops, and to set up the Luxembourg Commission. It had also, for good measure, made another symbolic gesture – turning the Tuileries Palace, the former residence of the king, into a "home for disabled workers" *(Asile aux invalides du travail)*.[12] The Provisional Government, indulging in the romantic style that so characterized the spring of 1848, avoided concrete engagements whenever possible, but it counterbalanced this substantive conservatism with grandiose gestures and effusive language. Workers, hearing that they would henceforth occupy both the king's palace and the Chamber of Peers and told that they would henceforth be guaranteed "the legitimate fruits of their labor," not unreasonably concluded that they had won the revolution and had been recognized as the sovereign people. With all restrictions on freedom of press, speech, and association lifted, they enthusiastically set out to solidify their victory by forming political clubs, by revitalizing their corporations, by founding newspapers, and by engaging in all forms of spoken and written propaganda. Thus the experience of the workers in 1848 forms the sharpest possible contrast with their experience in 1830. In 1830 the workers discovered their unity and their political voice only in response to a closing off of revolutionary opportunity. In 1848 workers employed the political voice they had acquired in the early 1830s to force open the problem of labor at the very outset of the revolution.

The great outpouring of workers' speech and writing in the spring of 1848 was based on the conceptual and rhetorical innovations of the early 1830s. The idea that workers were the sovereign people because they do all the useful labor of society; that workers are exploited and thereby held in servitude by a new bourgeois aristocracy; that private ownership of the means of production constitutes a new form of privilege; that the only means of emancipating the workers and of overcoming egoism is association: This complex of ideas, originally formulated by workers and republicans between 1830 and 1834, became the standard justification for working-class revolutionary action in 1848. The ideas discovered in the early 1830s and elaborated in the course of the 1840s were spread to the working class as a whole in 1848; they became the possession of masses of workers, who built them into the foundations of their projected workers' republic. But whereas workers' discourse in 1848 generally followed the same themes as in the 1830s, there were some important differences in emphasis. One of these was the different weight assigned to the ideas of "labor" and "association." Association, which was the key term in workers' discourse in the 1830s, remained a fundamental principle in 1848. But the agitations of the 1830s had made the right of association a standard feature of the republican program, and all restrictions on the right of association were lifted immediately after the February Revolution. Although association remained a central value in the Revolution of 1848, it was no longer the central term of political controversy.

That place was assumed, in the spring of 1848, by "labor." If discourse about "association" had been codified and assimilated into the standard republican program between 1834 and 1848, discourse on labor had yielded no stable and agreed-upon republican solution. Although the new republic proclaimed the "right to labor," this right was proclaimed only reluctantly under strong popular pressure, and its meaning and implications remained in dispute. At one extreme was the view adopted by the minister of public works who was in charge of the National Workshops that the right to work meant only a right to work relief for the unemployed. A more common interpretation by workers was that all citizens should be guaranteed regular employment in the trade for which they had been trained.[13] The *Journal des travailleurs* had a more radical interpretation still. In order for the "RIGHT TO LABOR inscribed on proclamations to become a reality," the *Journal* claimed, it was necessary that "nothing which we produce be taken from us."[14] Here the right to labor was understood to include the right to appropriate the *product* of labor; it implied an entirely new regime of property. Although the right of association was an accomplished fact in the new republic of 1848, the right to labor was the very center of political controversy. It is therefore hardly surprising that labor assumed such a preponderant role in workers' discourse.

The fundamental premise of workers' discourse in 1848 was that labor was the source of all wealth and happiness, the essential human activity that fructified nature and made it useful to man. This was the foundation of the "right to labor." "Unemployment," the *Journal des travailleurs* declared, "is the most hideous sore of the current [social] organization."[15] This was not simply because unemployment caused hardship and suffering. It went much deeper: If labor was the essential human activity, then to deny a man the right to labor was to deny him his very humanity. The same premise, that labor was the source of all wealth and happiness, also underlay the workers' theory of popular sovereignty. This idea was, of course, already an important part of workers' revolutionary rhetoric in the 1830s. But in 1848 it was stated much more fully, elaborately, and forcefully. Perhaps the best example is a "Manifesto of the Delegates of the Corporations (Who Sat at Luxembourg)," written only two weeks before the June insurrection.

> The people, that multitude of producers whose appanage is misery, the people has only existed until today in order to procure for its exploiters, the enjoyments which it, the pariah of society, has never known.

Yes, it is by its labor that the people makes the bourgeois, the proprietors, the capitalists; yes, it is the people that makes all the happy ones of the earth.

The State, that is to say the men who govern the people, exists only at the expense of the taxes paid by all, taxes whose source is evidently the producer.

Suppress the producer, and you will annihilate in a single blow the bourgeois, the proprietors, the capitalists, and you will drive the State to bankruptcy.

Hence, the State is the people, the producer . . . is it not sovereign, the producer of all riches?[16]

Following a form of argument familiar since the Abbé Sieyès, the manifesto builds steadily to its ineluctable conclusion: *"L'etat c'est . . . le producteur."* From the fundamental premise that labor is the source of all wealth, the workers derived the twin supports of the republic they projected in the spring of 1848: the right to labor and the sovereignty of labor.

In order to put the sovereignty of labor into practice and to make the right to labor secure, it was necessary to establish a proper organization of labor. This was, of course, the special mission of the Luxembourg Commission. But workers also elaborated their own theoretical schemes for the organization of labor. These theoretical writings took various forms, from manifestos sent to the Provisional Government, to articles in newspapers, to brief treatises, to speeches given before political clubs and then published as brochures or pamphlets, to electoral manifestos, to petitions presented to the Luxembourg Commission. Sometimes they stayed very close to the issues affecting a particular trade.[17] Occasionally they could be marvelously incoherent. One brief manifesto on the organization of labor sent to the Provisional Government by a Parisian machinist urged it to print up eight million francs in paper money; to build one hundred warships; to establish "national workshops everywhere, even in the forests, today, tomorrow if possible"; to call up the class of conscripts for 1848 ("by this means we will soon have England in our hands"); and, finally, to legalize piracy ("if piracy were allowed we would find fifty and one hundred associations which would arm and outfit ships at their expense, and would give great profits to the nation").[18]

But most workers' tracts were sober and reasoned attempts to find principles for the organizaton of labor that would apply to all trades. Few were genuinely original – they usually recapitulated or recombined the arguments and proposals already put forward by dozens of writers in the 1840s. Almost without exception they proposed the establishment of producers' associations of one description or another. Thus, one proposed "the constitution of property for all by means of associated labor"; another concluded that "we must, under the title of Fraternal Association of Well-Being, found workshops in all the most common professions." Yet another proclaimed, "Henceforth in all industrial enterprises, all LABORERS OF BOTH SEXES, Day-laborers, Workers, Foremen, Engineers, Employees, Directors, will be ASSOCIATED." Still another stated as its goal "the abolition of the exploitation of man by man by the immediate association of producers, by the creation of workshops of associated workers."[19] Thinking, speaking, and writing within the general framework established in the early 1830s, the workers concentrated particularly on the theme of labor as it had been elaborated in the 1840s. Workers' ideology in 1848, in other words, was distinctly socialist in character.

The workers' movement of the spring of 1848 took many forms. Together with bourgeois democrats, workers participated in the hundreds of political clubs that sprang up in Paris and in the provinces in the aftermath of the February Revolution – clubs representing every conceivable nuance of republican opinion.[20] Workers founded newspapers of their own, or, more often, collaborated actively with a wide variety of other radical papers.[21] Above all, they reformed and revitalized their own trade organizations. Members of rival sects of compagnonnage, for example, established a *Club des compagnons,* which drew up a constitution unifying compagnons in a single organization. On March 20 it sponsored a massive demonstration at the Place de la République, where some ten thousand compagnons of all sects gathered, fraternized, and marched without regard for rank, sect, or trade to the Hôtel de Ville to offer their support to the Provisional Government. There the compagnons declared that should the republic be endangered, "all our little Republics will form but one to serve as a shield for our common Mother, and Tyranny will never touch her until it has crushed our bloodied bodies."[22] The February Revolution seemed capable of accomplishing what the indefatigable efforts of Agricol Perdiguier and other reformers had been unable to do: unite the hostile sects into a single brotherhood. In fact, the efforts at unity were eventually stalled by the hesitations of traditionalist compagnons, and once the political situation turned against the workers in May and June, the sects of compagnonnage returned to their traditional divisions. But by then the compagnons had been relegated to the margins by the growth of a much vaster and more comprehensive movement of organized workers' corporations.

THE LUXEMBOURG COMMISSION

The most impressive achievement of the workers in the spring of 1848, the movement of organized workers' corporations, was closely tied to the Luxembourg Commission. Establishment of the Luxembourg Commission was important not only because it committed the republic to seeking a solution for the problem of labor but because it invited the workers of Paris to join in the effort. From the very beginning of the February Revolution, trade communities had acted as units in revolutionary politics. The workers who demonstrated around the Hôtel de Ville on February 25 were generally grouped behind the banners of their trades, and through the rest of February and the first days of March, one trade after another marched in massive processions to the Hôtel de Ville to pledge their loyalty to the republic and to make their demands and wishes known to the Provisional Government. By formally recognizing trades as electoral constituencies of the Luxembourg Commission, the government powerfully reinforced the corporations' sense of themselves as legitimate public actors. This, together with the abrogation of all restrictions on freedom of association, encouraged workers to organize their corporations on a larger and more ambitious scale than ever before. In trades that had not been organized before February, the election of delegates to Luxembourg was often the occasion for forming a corporation for the first time. Where some sort of trade organization already existed – as in most skilled trades – only a minority of the total work force was likely to have been encompassed by the prerevolutionary corporation; hence, the general assembly that chose delegates to Luxembourg usually went on to elect a commission charged with reconstituting the corporation on a more inclusive and democratic basis.[23] Thus the new republican government not only tolerated workers' corporations; by forming the Luxembourg Commission it virtually required corporations to constitute themselves democratically and officially. Their elected delegates became public officials, and when they assembled at Luxembourg they were not only a government-sponsored study commission but a body that represented and was capable of mobilizing and coordinating the revolutionary working class of Paris. Luxembourg, in effect, constituted the working class as a public force.

The revolutionary significance of the Luxembourg Commission was demonstrated most dramatically on March 17, in the first of a series of massive processions that punctuated the political life of the capital in the spring of 1848. The demonstration of that day had originally been called by a coalition of clubs and workers' corporations to request a postponement of elections for the National Assembly and for officers of the newly enlarged Parisian National Guard – a postponement that democrats felt they needed in order to organize the electoral campaign effectively. The planned march took on an added significance when members of elite companies of the National Guard held a demonstration of their own on March 16, protesting against their forthcoming assimilation into democratically constituted companies. Hoping to overwhelm the reactionary demonstrators of the sixteenth by a massive turnout on the seventeenth, the Luxembourg delegates labored furiously to mobilize the workshops of the city. The result was the largest demonstration of a year of mammoth popular processions. According to contemporary estimates, some 150,000 to 200,000 marchers filed past the Hôtel de Ville, expressing their support for the Provisional Government against the reactionary demonstrators of the previous day and demanding a postponement of elections. Nearly all the demonstrators marched by trade, preceded by the banner of their corporation.[24]

The *journée* of March 17 was a great triumph for Parisian workers. The Provisional Government itself bowed to their power; on the nineteenth it called a special session of the Luxembourg Commission, which several of its members attended in person, in order to thank the "representatives of these powerful corporations" for "the magnificent, the imposing demonstration" of the seventeenth. At this same session, the government announced postponement of the National Guard elections until April 5, which also implied postponement of elections to the National Assembly.[25] The government's visit and its announcement amounted to an official recognition of Luxembourg's victory and to an acceptance of the organized working class as a major force in the republic. March 17 raised the prestige and the power of Luxembourg to their zenith, and in the following weeks the commission, the delegates, and the corporations they represented labored euphorically in the belief that they could create a genuine workers' republic.

In the workers' eyes, the Luxembourg Commission became something much grander than an advisory study commission; it became a kind of prototype of the future republic. Until the elections to the National Assembly on April 23, the workers' delegates at Luxembourg were the only elected representatives of the people in the French Republic. In these circumstances, the workers regarded the commission as nothing less than the grand republican spectacle of the people governing itself, as the "Estates General of Labor."[26] One radical newspaper put it this way: "The Revolution is social, it is there in its entirety in that session held on March first at Luxembourg, where 150 to 200 workers came in order to resolve with the Government the great problem of their destiny."[27] Nor was Louis Blanc ready to discourage such interpretations. As he said in a discourse to the commission on March 28:

> It is an admirable thing that we have succeeded in establishing the Etats Généraux du Peuple. You are here an assembly of deputies, an assembly of Deputies of the People. Whether the National Assembly is installed or not, I have confidence that this one shall not perish![28]

Luxembourg, in short, was seen as a kind of parallel National Assembly, composed of representatives of national labor, whose task was to legislate the organization of labor, or, as the delegates of the cabinetmakers put it, to elaborate "the constitution of labor."[29]

This view of Luxembourg was, of course, exaggerated. The authority of the commission was ambiguous at best, and although Louis Blanc stressed the grandeur and implied the sovereign character of Luxembourg in his speeches, in practice he did his best to limit it to a study commission. His speeches had a consistently patriarchal tone; he stressed the great intellectual difficulty of resolving the problem of labor, and he warned against "precipitousness" and implied that the workers' delegates should trust him to act wisely on their behalf.[30] True to his prerevolutionary writings, Blanc construed the role of the workers as essentially passive. Of the three delegates sent by each corporation, only one was to participate in the "interior work" of the commission; the others were merely to attend periodic general assemblies. Moreover, the day-to-day deliberations of the commission were carried out by a permanent committee composed of only ten workers together with Louis Blanc, Albert, and an assorted group of "experts" on the problem of labor, including the economists Pecqueur, Vidal, Dupont-White, Wolowski, and others.[31] To judge from minutes of this committee's proceedings, workers' delegates played a very minor part in its discussions.[32] Initiative was to come from the state and its enlightened experts; the assembly of workers' delegates at Luxembourg was merely to give advice and information when asked and to ratify the plans once they were worked out.

The Luxembourg Commission, then, was hardly the Estates General of Labor that the Parisian workers imagined. Yet in spite of its failings, Luxembourg became the most important locus, in 1848, of what Trotsky has called "dual power."[33] Trotsky argues that for revolutions to move beyond their opening phase, a revolutionary class must find autonomous institutions within which it can elaborate an alternative to the existing structures of government. In the radical phase of the French Revolution, from 1792 to 1794, dual power was embodied in the Parisian Commune and sections; in the Russian Revolution it was embodied in the soviets. The Revolution of 1848 was far less successful and far less radical than the French or the Russian revolutions, so it is hardly surprising that its institutions of dual power were far less developed. But the brief revolutionary spring of 1848 saw the birth of two complexes of revolutionary institutions that attempted to push the revolution beyond the accomplishments of February: the clubs and the workers' movement surrounding the Luxembourg Commission.

The clubs were a major political force in the frenetic spring of 1848, encompassing, at their peak, perhaps one hundred thousand Parisians.[34] Moreover, their vocation for dual power was quite explicit. In the words of the Republican Club of Free Laborers: "The clubs are the living barricades of Democracy . . . . it is by means of the clubs, it is by means of this second National Assembly, in permanent session, always active, that the new social order must be erected."[35] Yet, as their most recent historian has remarked, their record of ideological and institutional creativity was relatively barren.

Active in organizing demonstrations and in the democratic electoral campaign, incessantly discussing the political issues of the day, they actually did very little to erect a "new social order," either in practice or in theory.[36] The record of the workers' movement that grew up around Luxembourg was far more impressive. Where the activities of the clubs were chaotic and uncoordinated, the activities of the workers' movement were far more unified, adding up, in the end, to a surprisingly coherent project for revolutionary transformation. The revolutionary initiative in the workers' movement came not from the Luxembourg Commission, which was limited in its official capacity to discussing proposed legislation for the organization of labor, but from the democratic corporations that were its electoral constituencies. It was the commission, however, that gave the workers' movement a common focus and a center of coordination that were lacking in the clubs. As a meeting place of the delegates of the Parisian trades, Luxembourg was a kind of a government-sponsored fulfillment of the plan for an "association of all trades" sketched out by the shoemaker Efrahem as long ago as 1833.[37] What Luxembourg provided to the workers' movement in the spring of 1848 was not revolutionary leadership but an aura of high public purpose and an institutional framework – democratic corporations, delegates, and a central deliberative body – that enabled the workers to construct an embryonic alternative social and political order.

In addition to the coordination of effort made possible by the Luxembourg Commission, the workers' movement also differed from the club movement in the nature and purpose of its fundamental units. Although the clubs were purely voluntary organizations with no definite constituency and no power of governance over the daily lives of their members, the corporations saw themselves as the institutional embodiment of trade communities and considered the democratic governance of their trades as their primary duty. This meant both that their energies were consistently focused on the central problem of the Revolution of 1848 – the organization of labor – and that the workers' larger political visions and ideologies could be put directly into practice in the governance of their trades. Where the clubs tended to dissipate their energies by debating all manner of issues in the abstract, the corporations' actions and speculations were disciplined by the constraints inherent in the creation and animation of institutions. This gave their projects a solidity, a coherence, and a staying power that contrasts sharply with the ephemeral sound and fury of the clubs. Although they were organized on an occupational rather than a territorial basis, workers' corporations were the closest equivalent, in 1848, to the sections of 1792–4. They were at once centers of initiative in the larger battles of the revolution and units of government in their own right. Hence, in order to see what the Democratic and Social Republic meant to the workers in 1848 we must look closely at the corporations that were its institutional embodiment.

CORPORATIONS REPUBLICAINES

The corporations constituted by workers in the spring of 1848 were democratic and republican in structure. They embraced all workers in the trade and were governed by democratic procedures. All officers or delegates were chosen by universal suffrage of the trade,[38] and important matters were often debated and voted on by assemblies of the entire corporation. The Parisian tinsmiths, for example, held no fewer than twelve general assemblies between February and June 1848.[39] In trades that were too large to hold frequent general assemblies – the joiners, painters, locksmiths, and machinists, for example – corporations were sometimes organized by districts of the city, and each district sent elected delegates to compose a central committee of the trade.[40] Units of a republican social order, the workers' corporations were cast in the form of little republics with universal suffrage and representative government as their mode of action.

They were, nevertheless, still recognizable as corporations and were so termed in contemporary discourse. Their continuity with earlier forms of corporations was particularly evident in their practices of mutual aid, practices that marked them as moral communities. This is what the workers meant when they called their societies "philanthropic" or "fraternal." The statutes of the General Political and Philanthropic Society of Machinists and Locksmiths explained that the association

> is philanthropic because the Society creates itself as the mother of all its members, and because it must at all times and in every circumstance, labor for its children, by assuring them in all cases of lack of work, of sickness or old age, a well-being sufficient to enable them to resist the oppression of those who are their enemies.[41]

The employment of family imagery leaves no doubt: Practices of mutual aid were to be seen as establishing a moral community among the workers or, in the words of the tinsmiths' corporation, of "propagating the good spirit of cordiality that ought to exist among men of the same profession."[42]

Workers' corporations of 1848 included all the standard types of aid provided by the authorized mutual-aid societies of the Restoration and July Monarchy or by the confraternities of the old regime: aid for sick and injured workers and pensions for those too old to work and for widows and orphans. Many of the societies formed in 1848 also included payments for members who were unemployed.[43] Such payments had been provided by a few of the authorized mutual-aid societies of the Restoration and July Monarchy, but usually they were disallowed by the authorities on the ground that they could be used to support strikers as well as ordinary unemployed workers. Finally, although these societies had dropped the practice of naming themselves for patron saints, they usually maintained the ritual of corporate funerals. The funeral procession seems to have remained as potent a statement of solidarity for the Industrious Commercial, Laboring and Fraternal Association of Shoemakers or the Philanthropic Society of Tailor Workers or the General Society of Wall Paper Workers of the French Republic[44] as for the Societies of Saint Crispin or of Saint Honoré or of the Ascension of the Virgin Mary during the Restoration and July Monarchy. As the machinists and locksmiths declared, the corporation was to "come in aid to all its members by all means in our power from their admission up to and including their burial."[45] The corporate funeral signified that the corporation was still perceived as an enduring moral body that concerned itself with the whole life of its members.

Continuity with earlier forms of workers' corporations was also evident in the workers' attempts to regulate their trades. Here the favorable conditions created by the February Revolution enabled workers to accomplish in a few weeks what they had been unable to accomplish in three decades of struggle under the Restoration and July Monarchy. As soon as the workers' new corporations were formed, they began to press the masters for public agreements guaranteeing shorter hours, control over job placement, assorted regulations of working conditions, and above all higher and more uniform wages – sometimes in the form of a fixed daily wage but more often in the form of tarifs.[46] The special emphasis workers placed on tarifs in 1848 was consistent with their demands in the labor conflicts of the previous two decades and especially in the great strike waves of 1833 and 1840. Workers wanted fixed, uniform tarifs, as noted earlier, not only because they guaranteed a decent wage but because they imposed order on the trade by specifying and setting prices for all the operations that workers could legitimately perform. Tarifs were meant as a remedy to the disunifying forces of the competitive economic system: to sweating, skill dilution, subcontracting, increased division of labor, production of ready-to-wear items, and other practices that tended to fracture the trade into a congeries of separate workshops. Tarifs, one might say, were the indigenous working-class solution to the problem of "the organization of labor." As one Parisian carpenter put it: "The difficulty of the organization of labor is great, without doubt. However, there is a means of escaping from the labyrinth; it is known and so are its results. I am speaking of a tarif." This opinion was widely shared. "The only means of rendering workers happy," one contemporary tract claimed, was "a single tarif in each profession . . . established with the agreement of employers and workers." Another declared that "all work must be *tarifié* [subjected to a tarif] by the entrepreneur and the laborer, in order to abolish the exploitation of man by man." By establishing a tarif, workers could "prevent a disloyal competition which debases the trade, ruins the manufacturer and reduces the laborers to misery."[47]

Especially in the days and weeks following March 17, workers in dozens of trades drew up regulations and presented them to their employers. The widespread unemployment of the spring of 1848 of course limited the economic pressures workers could bring to bear on the masters. But this was more than counterbalanced by their political strength. Only rarely did w⁻ kers actually have to go on strike, and when they did, they called in the Luxembourg Commission to enforce conciliation. Usually, the workers' initiatives led directly to negotiations, often carried out by the trade's official delegates to the Luxembourg Commission – the workers' delegates who had been chosen in the week following March 1 and delegates of the employers, who were invited to join the commission in an advisory capacity and who held their first session on March 17, the very day of the workers' great demonstration.[48] The atmosphere of these negotiations was generally cordial, and the agreements worked out were usually very favorable to the workers. Drawn up as formal "conventions," many of these agreements were then signed in a public ceremony before officers of the Luxembourg Commission, thereby giving them the symbolic backing of state authority.[49]

This procedure was so effective that many workers envisaged it as a permanent feature of the new French Republic. Such, for example, was the proposal of one working-class candidate for the National Assembly.

> How can wages be guaranteed? By establishing chambres syndicales . . . for each corps de métier . . . composed of masters and workers . . . The wage for every task being established between them by convention . . . a general tarif will be drawn up, and this tarif will have to be applied to all the localities where it is accepted, because the State will set itself up as guarantor of its execution.[50]

But if the Luxembourg Commission was the guarantor of the conventions negotiated between workers and employers, day-to-day enforcement was left to the trades. "Each corps d'état," as one contemporary pamphlet put it, should become "a sort of truly fraternal disciplinary tribunal."[51] Thus the plumbers' convention with the masters specified that all infractions or complaints by either masters or workers were to be reported at the wineshop where the job-placement register was kept – to be adjudicated, presumably, by some kind of bipartite commission.[52] Under the publicly ratified conventions of March and April 1848, the trades of Paris were transformed into self-governing and self-adjudicating units, operating under the aegis of a benevolent state.

It was the militant actions of the workers' corporations that forced Luxembourg to intervene in labor disputes and act as a guarantor of conventions between workers and employers. As the commission itself declared:

> Such is the essentially social character of the Revolution of 1848, such is the imminent necessity of economic reforms, that a Commission instituted to elaborate legislative proposals, to search for the solution to

the problem of the organization of labor, is transformed incontinently, by the force of things, into a high court of arbitration and exercises a sort of moral government by the free will and the express call of laborers and heads of establishments.

The Commission thus finds itself required to pursue both theory and practice. This double role . . . it accepts as a duty.[53]

Conceived as an instrument to pursue the organization of labor in the style of Louis Blanc – formulating proposals to be imposed on industry by a benevolent state – the commission also found itself impelled to pursue the organization of labor in the style of the Parisian workers – imposing detailed regulations and a large measure of workers' control on the city's trades. "The force of things" made Luxembourg the guarantor of a new corporate organization of Parisian industry. In the months of March and April, in other words, the commission was not only a study commission but a de facto Ministry of Labor, a ministry controlled by the workers rather than by the government.

Although the initiative for this system of corporate regulation came almost exclusively from the workers, it is notable that they met little resistance from employers. In part this was because both sides believed that the workers had won the revolution. But the masters' willingness to come to terms also reveals at least a partial acceptance of a corporate organization of production. Masters, after all, were fully familiar with the workers' corporate notions, and many of the regulations formally imposed in the conventions of 1848 were already observed informally in the majority of workshops. Many masters sympathized with the goals of reducing competition and imposing more uniform conditions in the trade. As the plumbers said about their employers in March 1848: "Several of them have promptly signed the tarifs we have prepared. They have found them reasonable, we have understood one another: it will soon be recognized that we wish only what is just, that we too desire to heal that social wound called competition."[54] In extreme cases, such as the tailoring trade, small masters actually united with workers in a common struggle against *confectionneurs* (manufacturers of ready-made clothing), whom both the workers and masters regarded as "strangers to our trade [état]."[55] But even in trades where confection was not so widespread, masters accepted the workers' proposals for corporate regulation with surprisingly little resistance. There were, of course, differences between workers and masters. The conventions governing labor in the workshops were less consensual statutes than treaties between two opposing parties. Both workers and masters were willing for the time being to accept a framework of corporate regulation within a regime of private property. But neither side was unalterably committed to the new corporative industrial organization that took shape in March and April 1848. Some masters continued to prefer the "industrial liberty" of the pre-

1848 era, and once the political balance swung away from the workers in May and June, many simply ignored the solemn conventions of March and April and returned to their previous practices.

Nor were the workers permanently committed to the system that grew up in March and April 1848. In many trades the attempt to win conventions from the masters was supplemented by attempts to establish producers' associations. The best-known case was the Parisian tailors, who set up a huge corporative "national workshop" that obtained a concession from the state to manufacture uniforms for the National Guard.[56] Even in trades that made no attempt to actually found producers' associations in the spring of 1848, the statutes of workers' societies often included "the organization of labor in national workshops of the corporation" – or some equivalent statement – as one of their goals.[57] The idea of establishing producers' associations was ubiquitous in the workers' movement of 1848; it was embraced in the statutes and manifestos of workers' corporations, in tracts written by hundreds of working-class authors, and by the Luxembourg Commission itself. But rather than seeing associative production as a hoped-for gift of a benevolent state, the workers saw it as an extension of practical control over their trades. By inducing the Luxembourg Commission to ratify conventions that enabled their corporations to regulate labor in the workshops, the workers were ensuring that the commission's theoretical plans would rest on a solid foundation of workers' power. Winning conventions from the masters and governing the trade jointly with them was a crucial first step in the organization of labor. But the final goal remained the establishment of associations that would abolish the distinction between worker and master and make all who worked in the trade collective owners of the means of production.

Thus, although the corporations organized by workers in 1848 had evident continuities with workers' corporations of the Restoration and July Monarchy, or even with masters' corporations of the old regime, they were also novel in important respects. One crucial novelty was the prominent role they assumed in the political life of the republic. Workers saw their corporations not only as moral communities and as a means of regulating the trade but as actors in revolutionary politics. The statutes of the Fraternal and Democratic Association of Joiner Workers, for example, stated that the association had been formed not only "to discuss and accelerate the organization of labor" and "to guard their material and moral interests" but "to enlighten and instruct themselves about their political and social rights." The statutes then listed as one of the association's primary goals the maintenance of a "popular and democratic government" that would "make a counterrevolution impossible."[58] The statutes of the General, Political and Philanthropic Society of Machinists and Locksmiths made the same point more elaborately.

The great principle of Fraternity for all, is union; the equality of rights for everyone without distinction, and the liberty to think and to say what one thinks.

We have conquered these rights, citizens! We must make use of them ... We wish to form the most perfect fraternal union ... by that union we shall overthrow everything which tends to deceive us or to violate our rights ... this union, finally, is as much political as philanthropic.

It is political, because each of us must know and follow the steps of the Government which we have created, in order to be able to discuss its actions and protest against those which might tend to annihilate our rights ...

Citizens! we have abolished royalty; with time, with perseverance and with our good constitution, we will make all despots shout with us with all their hearts:

VIVE LA REPUBLIQUE![59]

The corporations, thus, doubled as political clubs; they maintained close scrutiny over the actions of the government; and they were ready to act when necessary.

The corporations' political vocation was tellingly revealed in the electoral campaign of April 1848. As elections for the Constituent Assembly neared, each corporation constituted itself as an electoral committee, and like the political clubs, they listened to a series of candidates who went about from club to club and from corporation to corporation to solicit votes. But the corporations were particularly eager to elect representatives from their own trade. Indeed, the tendency of each corporation to propose one of its own members as a candidate soon became alarming to the Luxembourg delegates and to Louis Blanc, who warned that establishing a single, agreed-upon list was imperative. Otherwise, Blanc counseled,

each corporation will cling to the candidate it will have named, each candidate will desire to become a definitive candidate. As a result, dispersion of votes, disunity in choices, and if it goes this way the people will be sacrificed once again ... You must start from the principle that you are not here as blacksmiths, joiners, machinists, you are here as men of the people, who are brothers, and who wish to carry out the liberation of the people.[60]

The Luxembourg delegates thus formed a Central Committee of the Workers of the Department of the Seine that would review candidates nominated by each trade and then establish a single definitive list. After long deliberation, the Central Committee finally published its list on the day before the election and charged each delegate with publicizing the names in his own trade.[61]

In the few hours that remained, the delegates organized the distribution of a million copies of their list in the workshops and summoned workers to the Champs-Elysées for an assembly on the morning of April 23. From there, in the words of the typographers' delegates, "each corporation, banner at its head, will parade with order and everyone will go to his respective voting place to cast his ballot."[62] But in spite of the delegates' efforts, the results were disappointing. Only one of Luxembourg's worker candidates was elected, Agricol Perdiguier, whose renown as an author and a reformer of compagnonnage had won him the endorsement of many other clubs and electoral committees as well. The campaign to elect workers to the Assembly was a failure. But one of the causes of this failure was the desire of each corporation to have a deputy of its own in the Assembly and to act as an autonomous political unit during the campaign. "The workers," as Gossez puts it, "conceived their political representation by professional category."[63]

The public role that workers assigned to their trades can also be seen in the great succession of parades and demonstrations in the spring of 1848. In these events, trades invariably participated as units, each marching behind its own banner. From the demonstrations of February 25 and 28 around the Hôtel de Ville, through the triumphant parade of March 17, through the tense and discouraging confrontation of April 16 and the disastrous would-be insurrection of May 15, Paris was presented with the periodic spectacle of great popular processions in which the sovereign people presented itself as an aggregation of workers' corporations. In addition, there were countless other parades and demonstrations of single corporations, in which workers marched to present petitions to the Luxembourg Commission, to pledge their loyalty to the Provisional Government, or simply to display their solidarity and republican enthusiasm after exiting from one of the innumerable trade assemblies that punctuated the spring of 1848.[64] In 1848 the workers' corporations took symbolic possession of the streets of the capital, seizing the revolution's traditional public space, and thereby solemnly announced themselves as public revolutionary actors.

This prominence of corporate groupings in street processions reveals the originality of the Revolution of 1848 in comparison with both the old regime and the French Revolution of 1789–94. Trade corporations, carrying their distinctive banners and insignia, had participated in many public ceremonies of the old regime – for example, royal entries, coronations, and religious festivals. As in 1848, they were displaying themselves as distinct components or units of the social order. But there was one enormous difference. Processions of the old regime included many other types of corps in addition to trade corporations: ecclesiastics, nobles, diverse bodies of magistrates and officers, learned professions, and so on. These various corps were always arranged in the strictest of ranked hierarchies, with churchmen at one extreme and trade corporations, inevitably, at the other. Thus, when the gens de métier participated in a procession under the old regime, they were recognizing their subordinate position in a spiritual and political hierarchy that culminated in the church and the king. In 1848 the trade corporations, together with democratically constructed political clubs, were the only constituted bodies that marched in processions, and they observed no particular order of march. Far from recognizing any social or political hierarchy or the authority of the church or the king, the trade corporations were displaying themselves as equal constituents of the sovereign people, the ultimate source of all political authority.

They were, in this respect, squarely in the tradition of the great processions, festivals, and insurrections of the French Revolution. But here, too, there was a marked contrast. During the Revolution, and especially under the radical republic of 1792 to 1794, the sovereign people occupied the streets not as an aggregation of distinct trades but as the undifferentiated "people." To gather behind the banner of a corporation would have been to declare oneself an enemy of the "One and Indivisible Republic," as a counterrevolutionary "federalist." This had all changed by 1848. For the revolutionary workers of 1848, labor was the source of sovereignty, and the organization of labor by association was the principle of social order. They therefore seized the streets as associated laborers, grouped into societies according to trade, but also sharing equally with all other trades in the grand association of the nation. For them, trade communities were the necessary constituent units of the sovereign people and of the republic. Thus, the form of their processions dramatically reveals the difference between the One and Indivisible Republic of the sans-culottes and the Democratic and Social Republic of the revolutionary workers in 1848.

The public vocation of corporations, then, went beyond the notion that they should act politically to support the revolution. Corporations, in the spring of 1848, were seen by workers as fundamental units of the republic. Labor, in this view, was not only the essential support of the entire society and the source of popular sovereignty, it was also an intrinsically public activity. This idea can be seen, for example, in the tendency of workers' societies to call their officers *fonctionnaires* (civil servants), a term normally used only for employees of the state who are deemed to perform what the French call a "public function."[65] This designation could even be extended to all workers exercising a trade. An example is an electoral manifesto, written in verse by a Parisian worker. This would-be candidate for the National Assembly had begun his career as a schoolteacher but became a cutler when his sight began to fail. He recounted that when he became a cutler:

> Un instant ce métier fit blessure à mon coeur;
> Mais qu'importe aujourd'hui dans notre République,
> Si le plus humble état est fonction publique.
>
> (For a moment this trade wounded my heart;
> but it no longer matters today under our Republic,
> when the humblest of trades is a public function.)[66]

From a penitence and a badge of vileness under the old regime to a useful activity and the source of private property in the French Revolution, labor here became a noble public service, not only the foundation of private wealth, but the very stuff of public life. In the eyes of the workers, the republican corporations that organized and performed the nation's labor became public institutions, both constituent units and units of government of the future Democratic and Social Republic.

The corporate workers' movement that grew up around the Luxembourg Commission thus developed a consistent and distinctive, if fragmentary and incomplete, version of the French Republic. This workers' republic was not merely or even mainly a theoretical creation, although it of course had a theoretical side. It was, rather, embodied in the corporations the workers created, just as the sans-culottes' "One and Indivisible Republic" was embodied in their sections. If the sections – with their incessant public activism, their continuous surveillance of public officials, and their unflagging pursuit of equality – were microcosms of the republic the sans-culottes envisaged, the workers' corporations of 1848 were microcosms of the Democratic and Social Republic. Take, for example, the General Society of Wallpaper Workers of the French Republic. Not only was it organized on democratic and republican principles, with all decisions reached by means of universal suffrage of the trade, but its statutes included a miniature declaration of the rights of man and citizen.

> The principle of association is a natural right made sacred since the foundation of our glorious Republic . . .
> For the laborer, his only property is his wage and his time . . .
> Idle persons [are] bad citizens and not worthy of the name of comrades. The Society considers man's labor as the most beautiful result of his intelligence; it wants, it asks for nothing but labor. Also it regards as sacred the right to fix tarifs in accord with the manufacturers.

The society's goals were the provision of mutual aid; the maintenance of a tarif, to be enforced by elected "commissioners of the industry . . . advanced sentinels to safeguard the interests of their brothers"; and the "organization of labor," which it defined as "the workers participating in the profits of the manufacturer or carrying on production on their own."[67] Such corporations were themselves little republics, governed by universal suffrage and founded on the sovereignty of labor and the right of association, republics that would organize labor in productive harmony and maintain brotherly solidarity among their citizens by mutual aid and protection. Or to put it the other way around, workers saw the future Democratic and Social Republic as a macrocosmic version of the microcosmic republics they had created in their trades. Composed of democratic workers' societies that incorporated and organized all the productive labor of the nation, bound together by the same sentiments of fraternity and the same norms of republican government that united workers in their particular corporations, capped by a deliberative assembly that was made up of representatives of all the trades and that was charged with organizing the labor of the nation as a whole – such was the republic that the organized workers of Paris projected and attempted to bring into being in and around the Luxembourg Commission in the spring of 1848.

This projected workers' republic was an embodiment of the socialism of 1848. This is true in the obvious sense that it assumed labor would eventually be organized in collectively owned producers' associations. But is also true in another, less obvious, sense. Socialism is more than the doctrine that the means of production should be collectively owned; socialism also assumes that labor, as the foundation of all social life, should be the foundation of the political order. Hence the workers' movement of the spring of 1848 was socialist in the sense that it envisaged a state built systematically upon the institutions of labor. Socialism, as developed by the workers in 1848, meant the belief that labor was a public function, that corporations were therefore public institutions with legitimate authority to organize labor associatively, and that the state itself should be constituted out of democratically organized trade corporations. These notions, which were to be characteristic of working-class socialism in France for the next few decades, derived directly from the practice of the workers' movement centered on the Luxembourg Commission in the spring of 1848.[68] In other words, the socialism that was first espoused by masses of French workers in 1848 was formed as much by the concrete political practice of revolutionary workers' corporations as by the abstract and "utopian" schemes of socialist theorists.

TOWARD CLASS WAR

In spite of the workers' untiring efforts in the spring of 1848, their version of the republic was never more than an incomplete project. For all their rhetorical dominance of Paris, the workers were too weak to establish their political hegemony over France as a whole. In part this was because their ideology was focused so sharply on their own specific concerns. But even in the cities, where the ideology of the democratic and social republic found widespread acceptance, provincial and Parisian workers' movements were badly coordinated. Workers in virtually all cities of France took advantage of the Revolution of 1848 to assert the power and legality of their corporations, and corporations frequently took an active part in political life. In Marseille, for example, the Republican Central Committee, which met to choose a slate of republican candiates for the elections, included representatives of workers' corporations as well as of republican political clubs.[69] There were, moreover, scaled-down versions of the Luxembourg Commission in a number of provincial cities: Lyons, Marseille, Lille, Reims, Nantes, Saint-Quentin, Valenciennes, and others.[70] But these provincial commissions had no direct links with Luxembourg and rarely had anything approaching its autonomy and authority. In Marseille, for example, the Commission of the Corps de Métier was formed by the commissioner of the republic to consult with him on labor questions, and it remained more or less under his control; it certainly never became an important locus of autonomous political activity. Parisian and provincial workers thus shared a common ideological outlook and had similar corporate organizations. But the provincial workers' movements lacked the institutional autonomy that Luxembourg made possible in Paris, and without any formal links to each other, they never coalesced into a unified, coordinated movement.

But even if all the urban workers' movements had been perfectly coordinated, it is hard to see how they could have imposed their version of the republic on the country. As has been noted, some three-quarters of the citizens of France still lived in rural areas, and agriculture, not industry, was the nation's dominant economic activity. In these circumstances, at least in a regime based on universal suffrage, workers could not hope to gain control of the state without significant support from peasants. An alliance between workers and rural people was by no means impossible in mid-nineteenth-century France; the powerful nationwide *démoc-soc* movement, whose successes have been chronicled so ably by recent historians of the Second Republic, was based on precisely such an alliance.[71] But the systematic attempt to extend the democratic movement to the countryside began in earnest only *after* the defeat of the Parisian workers. One of the most powerful legacies of the great French Revolution of 1789–94 was the myth that Paris was synonymous with the nation. Until this myth was decisively disproven – in the electoral defeat of late April 1848, the abortive insurrection of May, and the bloodbath of June – Parisian workers imagined that they could build a *French* Democratic and Social Republic in the limited arena of Paris. Assuming that peasants and provincial workers would automatically follow their lead, they scarcely gave them a second thought.

In principle, the workers regarded peasants as workers like themselves, and occasionally they even suggested specific plans for "the organization of agricultural labor."[72] But they did not attempt to inform themselves seriously about conditions of labor in agriculture or to form real contacts with agriculturalists. They tacitly assumed that schemes of associative production

266

and of corporate organization and representation growing out of the specific experience of urban skilled trades were applicable to labor in general. This attitude is perfectly reflected in a contemporary lithograph celebrating Louis Blanc and the Luxembourg Commission, which is reproduced here as Figure 2. Entitled *Etats Généraux du Travail* (Estates General of Labor), the lithograph is a portrait of Louis Blanc, encircled by an elaborate allegorical border. The border is composed of representations of the arts, sciences, commerce, and industry at the corners; of Blanc addressing the assembled workers at Luxembourg at the bottom; of a worker in his blouse, symbolizing labor, and Mercury, symbolizing commerce, joining hands before a feminine allegory of fraternity at the top; and representations of assorted trades along the two sides. Among these trades, agriculture, symbolized by a spade, a scythe, and a sheath of grain, is treated as exactly parallel to some twenty other trades – tailors with a bolt of cloth and scissors, printers with a press, masons with a trough and trowel, locksmiths with a key, lock, and file, and so on. Agriculturalists, in the mental world of the Parisian workers of 1848, were just another fraternal workers' corporation. Accepted as fellow laborers in the abstract, they were ignored in fact.

This tendency of the Parisian workers to assimilate all types of labor and the entire citizenry of France to themselves was enhanced by the abstract generality of revolutionary rhetoric. At one level, of course, the workers understood labor concretely as the kind of work performed by skilled artisans. But they also used the term abstractly, in a manner consistent with the revolutionary tradition, to refer to the whole variety of useful activities carried out by the sovereign people: unskilled labor, agriculture, domestic service, commerce, and even purely intellectual pursuits. In 1848 such terms as "workers of thought" (*ouvriers de la pensée*) and "laborers of the head" (*travailleurs de la tête*) were in common usage.[73] This abstract, universal definition of labor enabled workers to project onto the whole of society – and claim as authoritative – schemes that were elaborated from their own specific class perspective. Justice, they could insist, demanded that all the productive activities of the nation should henceforth be performed by egalitarian corporate associations in which the means of production were collectively owned. Thus all inequalities of remuneration and power and all egoistic individualism would be abolished in a harmonious egalitarian producers' republic. In this way workers could put forth an ideology of their own class as a gospel of universal social conciliation and harmony, one that would benefit "workers of the head" as much as "workers of the arms" and agriculturalists as much as artisans. The abstract universality of the workers' idiom helped to endow them with the essential revolutionary conviction that their actions were undertaken for the good of mankind as well as for the good of their class. But it also helped to blind them to the substantive narrowness of their appeals.

Figure 2. The Estates General of Labor. Source: Bibliothèque Nationale.

The universality of the workers' idiom was, of course, inherent in the revolutionary tradition. But this universality was compounded by a romantic style specific to 1848, by a taste for grandiose gesture and lofty sentiment and a belief in the all-conquering power of love. In part this was an expression of the contemporary romantic sensibility, but it was also a reaction against the bloodthirsty cruelty of the First French Republic. One of the Provisional Government's first acts was to dissociate itself from the Terror by abolishing the death penalty for all political offenses. As against the cruelty of Robespierre and the sans-culottes, the revolutionaries of 1848 found an alternative model of revolutionary change in Christ and the primitive Christians. A true and lasting social revolution, they believed, would result from inspiring examples of patient suffering and martyrdom, not from violence and hatred. According to the "Profession of Faith of the Organized People," written by a tapestry weaver shortly after the February Revolution, the republic would eventually bring harmony, peace, and affluence.

> But while awaiting that happy moment, it is necessary that everyone suffer, in order to suffer less long, and that they aid one another, above all the shopkeeper and the laborer . . . Then the act of regeneration of the human race will begin, the gospel of the people, as pure as the first, will come to illuminate the universe; like that of Christ, it has given, and will give again, if it must, its martyrs, and then erect its grandeur by gentleness on the ruins of despotism.[74]

The worker, the martyr of the nineteenth century, was the central figure of this religious and revolutionary drama; his role was nothing less than sacerdotal. Thus the electoral statement of one typographer included an apostrophe to the worker's blouse: "Blouse! noble chasuble of the worker, this indefatigable priest of industry." The worker, invested with his blouse, would conquer the world not by force but by the word: "You possess the word, the power of speech, miraculous tool that reforged the world eighteen centuries ago, in the gleaming fire of celestial charity: never let it rust."[75] The revolution, in this view, was a religious as much as a political phenomenon and would be carried out as much by preaching, moral example, and spiritual conversion as by struggle and force.

When the Parisian workers set out to construct a Democratic and Social Republic around the Luxembourg Commission, their actions were enveloped in an aura of abnegation, generosity, and fraternity. Their efforts, however – regardless of their belief that their actions were motivated by a desire for universal social harmony and that their projects were universally applicable – soon gave rise to implacable class conflicts that left them isolated and embattled in defense of their would-be workers' republic. The workers' rhetoric of harmony and conciliation may have convinced *them* that their projects would be accepted by all sincere and patriotic citizens, but the old governing classes of France – not just monarchists and ex-monarchists but many sincere bourgeois republicans as well – saw them as an attack on society itself. The workers, after all, wished to reform virtually all basic institutions. Most alarmingly, they intended to redefine drastically the nature and the rights of property. However generous the language in which such intentions were expressed, they were an assault on not only the political but the social and economic power of the bourgeoisie. "Property," as Tocqueville put it in his recollections on the Revolution of 1848, was "the foundation of our social order"; to abolish private property, hence, was to overthrow society itself.[76] Here conservatives saw the revolutionary consequences of the workers' projects more clearly than the workers themselves. Workers, who stood to gain from the transformation of property rights, could see such a measure as benefiting all classes simultaneously; the propertied classes, whose hegemony was threatened, knew better.

In addition to this recognition that workers intended to destroy society as it was then constituted, conservatives were also motivated by a deep fear and repugnance of workers – a fear and repugnance already encountered in the writings of Villermé. The bourgeoisie regarded workers as incapable of discipline and reason, as necessarily disorderly except when under the domination of their betters. Tocqueville, in most respects an unusually clearheaded observer, was here typical of his class. He spoke of an "unheard of disorder in the people's ideas"[77] brought about by the February Revolution: "This natural restlessness in the minds of the people, with the inevitable ferment in the desires, thoughts, needs and instincts of the crowd, formed the fabric on which the innovators drew such monstrous and grotesque patterns."[78] But Tocqueville's cavalier disregard for the actual content of the ideas of these "innovators" makes it clear that his judgments were entirely a priori. Thus at one point he characterized their doctrines as offering remedies "against that disease called work which has afflicted man since the beginning of this existence" – a remarkably distorted statement about a movement whose raison d'être was the "right to labor."[79] In Tocqueville's mind, "the people" were naturally disorderly; it therefore followed that the ideas they developed or adopted would be monstrous. Given this perception of the working class, the entry of workers into the political arena took on the color of a barbarian invasion. In the wake of the February Revolution, Tocqueville noted, Paris was

> in the sole hands of those who owned nothing . . . Consequently the terror felt by all the other classes was extreme; . . . the only comparison would be with the feelings of the civilized cities of the Roman world when they suddenly found themselves in the power of Vandals or Goths.[80]

The same image was repeated in the wake of the great workers' demonstration of March 17. As the *Courrier français* put it: "The capital trembled seeing these determined, silent hordes who needed nothing but their own impulsion to overturn without combat the very bases of society."[81] The bourgeoisie, in this metaphor, became defenders of civilization itself, morally obliged to act against the working-class barbarian hordes who threatened to impose a new dark age.

Given the Parisian workers' narrow base of support and the hostility of the most powerful classes of French society, the workers' victory in the spring of 1848 was bound to be ephemeral. While workers, during March and April, were using their new prestige and apparent power to impose a new industrial regime on their trades and to sketch out the ideological and institutional basis of a Democratic and Social Republic, conservatives both inside and outside the Provisional Government gathered their forces and awaited the opportunity to right the political balance. The workers' political reversals began with a massive demonstration on April 16, which they hoped would re-create the effect of March 17. But this time the Provisional Government lined the route of march with armed and hostile National Guardsmen, who hedged in the workers and heckled them with shouts of "down with Louis Blanc!" and "down with the Communists!" Intended as a display of the workers' dominance in the capital, the procession of April 16 revealed their weakness instead.[82] This weakness was demonstrated much more decisively in the elections of April 23. Not only did Luxembourg's candidates fail to carry Paris, but moderates and conservatives won massively in the provinces. From April 23 on, it was clear that the Parisian workers' movement represented only a small minority of the sovereign people. Its political and social projects, therefore, became terribly vulnerable.

If April 16 and April 23 put the workers' movement on the defensive, the events of May 15 put it to rout. The abortive insurrection of May 15 began as a demonstration in favor of Polish independence and was organized primarily by the clubs; when it degenerated into a feeble revolutionary coup, the National Assembly took advantage of the debacle to dissolve the Luxembourg Commission and to initiate charges against Louis Blanc.[83] From then until the workers' insurrection of the "June Days," the workers labored vainly to save some remnants of the social republic. The Luxembourg delegates attempted to maintain the central direction of the workers' movement by founding a Society of United Corporations and a newspaper, the *Journal des travailleurs.*[84] But these never attained anything approaching the Luxembourg Commission's authority. With the government hostile to the workers, the solemn conventions established in so many Parisian trades could no longer be enforced, and they were violated regularly by the masters. Not surprisingly, the mood of the workers' movement turned grim and sullen as the apparent achievements of February and March evaporated in May and June.

The workers' sense of betrayal was pushed to the limit on June 21, when the government issued a decree abolishing the National Workshops. The National Workshops, for all their practical defects, were the symbolic embodiment of the "right to labor" that had been declared by the Provisional Government on the morrow of the February Revolution. Their dissolution therefore signified the National Assembly's definitive abandonment of the social republic. To dissolve the National Workshops was to nullify the "right to labor," the fundamental right on which the workers' version of the republic was constructed. To the workers, the government's decree of June 21 was a violation of the solemn contract forged between the government and the people on February 25. With the contract violated, the people had no course but insurrection. Thus, just as the great workers' agitation of the early 1830s ended in an armed rising when the government restricted the sacred right of association, so the workers' agitation of the spring of 1848 flared up in insurrection when the government annulled the sacred right to labor. But where the workers' rebellion of 1834 was brief and easily put down, the uprising of June 1848 was long and bloody. It lasted for four days, at its maximum gaining control of virtually all of the eastern half of Paris, and it was put down only by a massive application of armed force. Some fifteen hundred insurgents were killed, and another twelve thousand were arrested and imprisoned.[85] Nothing could demonstrate more forcefully the power and depth of the workers' movement of the spring of 1848 than the terrible sacrifice of life and liberty that brought it to a close.

AFTER JUNE

The June Days and their repression reduced the Parisian workers' movement to a shambles. Thousands of militants were killed or arrested, Paris was put under a state of siege, the political clubs were closed, many radical newspapers ceased publication, the workers' corporations were in headlong retreat, and the National Assembly acquiesced in the dictatorship of Eugène de Cavaignac, the general who had put down the June rebellion. For several months, everything gained in the spring of 1848 seemed to be lost. But when some semblance of normal political life returned to the capital in the fall of 1848, the workers' movement gradually reemerged. Although it regained neither the scale nor the rapturous enthusiasm of the spring of 1848, the workers' movement again became a force to be reckoned with. In the new political circumstances, its forms and activities were inevitably changed. Although the corporations founded in the spring of 1848 lost something of their public aura and their mass participation, most of them continued to function right down to Louis Napoleon's coup d'état in December 1851, providing mutual aid, trying to enforce tarifs and uniform conditions in the workshops, and carrying out negotiations with the masters or organizing strikes and boycotts. But much of the effort that had gone into politics and into gaining support from the Luxembourg Commission and the state in the spring of 1848 now went into the establishment of producers' associations. No longer able to count on assistance from the state in realizing their aims, and without proximate hopes of victory by armed force, workers attempted to build a Democratic and Social Republic by organizing "the republic in the workshop."[86] As one tailor put it: "The armed struggle is adjourned, even impossible, well then! let us not be discouraged; let us employ other means . . . Let us swear by the dead to avenge them by applying all of our forces to the profit of *practical socialism.*"[87]

Far from abandoning the struggle, then, workers attempted to erect their republic independently, outside the institutions of the bourgeois state. They continued to think of their corporations as public institutions and of the labor performed by their associations as a public function. Thus the term "functionary" continued to crop up in their writings. The *Almanac of New Corporations,* written in 1851, stated:

> To the idea of pure resistance to the lowering of wages [the workers] have added the idea of association with a view to possession of the instruments of labor, associations which tend to raise them to the condition of functionaries of the corporations.[88]

Or, in the words of another worker, members of associations "make of themselves, as laborers, the functionaries of all."[89] Although the dissolution of the Luxembourg Commission broke all institutional ties between workers' corporations and the state, workers still regarded their associations as public bodies. The workers' corporations and the producers' associations they sponsored also continued to maintain fraternal links with one another. This will to solidarity between trades was manifested in a whole series of institutions set up to unify and coordinate the activities of the various corporations: the Bank of the People, the General Syndicate of Associations, the Chamber of Labor, the Mutuality of the Workers, the Solidarity, and the Union of Fraternal Associations.[90] As may be judged from the rapid succession of these organizations, none of them ever achieved the authority of the Luxembourg Commission as the center of the workers' movement. But their very proliferation also indicates how ubiquitous was the desire for unified action.

Hence, although the means and the tone of the workers' movement changed after June 1848, the essential vision remained remarkably constant. Workers continued to struggle for a society and state composed of democratically organized fraternal workers' corporations, working harmoniously at the great national task of productive labor. The schemes launched by workers in the later years of the Second Republic have an altogether familiar aspect. Thus the Bank of the People, a cooperative financial scheme founded in 1849 to unify the efforts of producers' associations, was to include a "General Syndicate of Production, composed of delegates elected in every industry," which would "constitute the free and democratic corporation as an absolute and definitive regime for all laborers."[91] In the same year a "Practical Essay on the Organization of Labor Applicable to the Bronze Industry" declared that each trade must meet

> to regulate its interests, defend its rights, give itself a power based on elections, rising hierarchically all the way to the central power which will be the organizer and the director of labor . . . [this power] will depend on a commission of delegates of different industries.[92]

In 1850 the newspaper *Le Socialiste* expressed a similar vision of a government of labor.

> Let the National Assembly be converted by organized universal suffrage and by vote according to specialities into a vast congress of laborers of all specialities, into a direct and universal representation of national labor always responsible and revocable, whose mandates would be imperative, then ministries and administrations would be only ministries and administrations of the diverse functions of labor, freely centralized.[93]

And in September 1851, the socialist Pierre Leroux addressed a massive banquet of the corporation of typographers. He was struck, he said, by

> the progress of the idea of the corporation . . . of corporations organized in view of the Republic on a republican model . . . Haven't you heard the delegates of typographers from Brussels, Geneva, Turin say to you that they adopt your goal and hope one day to form a single body with you? . . . Soon it will be known in all of Europe that it is in ASSOCIATION around the instruments of labor according to the diverse functions of science, of art and of industry that the true human society is found, that which makes all men solidary while rendering them free. You are, citizens, the germ of the corporation of typographers, you announce to the world the formation of this social function . . . The profession, thus understood, is a religion . . . Yes, you have made a great invention that will count for as much in centuries to come as Gutenberg's invention itself . . . you wish to proclaim the TYPOGRAPHICAL REPUBLIC! [thunder of applause]. Then, collective masters of the instruments of labor, there will no longer be a monarch among you and you will be associates.[94]

The future republic of labor, then, would be founded on democratic and republican corporations, organized as producers' associations and linked through elected representatives into a solidary workers' state. In the vision of Pierre Leroux, at least, the republic of labor would even transcend national boundaries, turning all the laborers of the world into one harmonious and productive family. The idea of a corporate workers' republic, which initially arose in the movement surrounding the Luxembourg Commission, remained the leitmotif of working-class socialism to the very end of the Second Republic.

The continuity of the workers' movement was definitively ruptured, however, by Louis Napoleon's coup d'état in December 1851. The repression following the coup d'état was far more disastrous for the workers than that which followed the June Days. The conservative governments that ruled France after June 1848 had been hampered in their attempts to repress the workers' movement by requirements of republican legality. But Louis Napoleon ignored all such bounds. He dissolved the National Assembly, purged all public officials who would not serve him loyally, shut down clubs and radical journals, outlawed all workers' corporations except for authorized mutual-aid societies, and jailed, exiled, or put under surveillance thousands of republican and socialist militants. The repressive apparatus of the Second Empire was far more efficient and harsher than that of the Restoration or the July Monarchy, and for a full decade after the coup d'état, workers' corporations had to observe the strictest clandestinity in order to survive at all. The institutional achievements of the workers' movement of the Second Republic were hardly lasting. The democratic workers' corporations founded in 1848 were shattered in 1851, and although a few producers' associations survived the shock, they were henceforth isolated, embattled, and dwindling.

But if few of the workers' institutional creations could survive the repression of the 1850s, the patterns established and the ideas elaborated from 1848 to 1851 had a lasting effect. It was between 1848 and 1851 that socialism first took shape as a mass movement, and French labor and socialist movements of subsequent years continued to bear the mark of their origins. As Bernard Moss has shown, a vision of the future socialist society as a federation of democratic self-governing trades that collectively owned the means of production dominated the French socialist and labor movement right down to World War I.[95] This "federalist trade socialism," as Moss calls it, passed through a number of transformations in the nineteenth century, from the moderate and pacific Proudhonism of the French section of the International in the 1860s, to the ephemeral socialist schemes of the Paris Commune, to the revolutionary collectivism of the years following 1880. This vision was particularly evident in the anarcho-syndicalism of the

Confédération Génerale du Travail, but it also underlay the programs of all the other factions of French socialism of the late nineteenth and early twentieth centuries – the Broussists, Guesdists and Allemanists, the Bourses du Travail, and the Parti Ouvrier. It was only with the outbreak of the World War, the Bolshevik Revolution, and the foundation of the Communist Party that French socialism definitively abandoned the corporate socialist vision it had assumed in 1848.

12 Conclusion: the dialectic of revolution

LET US POSE two final questions. Was there an underlying logic by which socialism and class consciousness developed? And what was the form of the class conflict and class consciousness that had emerged in France by 1848?

A DIALECTICAL LOGIC

The socialist vision of labor as the constituent activity of the social and political order can be seen as a logical development of certain fundamental Enlightenment concepts, concepts that are summed up in Diderot's vision of man as a sentient natural being who brings greater order and utility into the world by combining or transforming the substances available to him in nature. This vision, one could argue, was subsequently applied to political life by the Abbé Sieyès, who made the performance of useful labor a criterion of membership in the polity and redefined the nation as an association of productive citizens living under a common body of laws. The French revolutionaries also wrote it into their constitutions when they established ownership of property, which they saw as the legitimate fruit of labor, as a requirement for the full exercise of citizenship. Socialism, from this point of view, was a logical extension of what the French Revolution had already established; rather than representing human labor indirectly, through property, socialism insisted on direct representation of labor itself.

This account of socialism as a development of Enlightenment ideas contains an important element of truth, but it also conceals far more than it reveals. Socialism is a logical development of Diderot's vision only in a very loose sense. It cannot, that is, be derived from Diderot's assumptions and propositions by the application of formal logic. Rather, socialism is, or can be seen as, an *elaboration* or *extension* of certain ideas that were present in Diderot's article "Art," and were held in common by many of his contemporaries. It is by no means the only such elaboration and extension of these ideas that was possible, nor was it even the only one that was made: The capitalist vision of the progressive application of scientific technology

277

through private enterprise is a logical development from Diderot in the same sense that socialism is. To understand why socialism came into existence, it is necessary to know why certain extensions and elaborations were made rather than others and why they occurred in the order they did. The emergence of socialism out of Enlightenment ideas was a social and political development as much as a logical one. The intellectual innovations that culminated in socialism were formulated in response to changing social experiences in general and to the struggles and vicissitudes of political life in particular. The establishment of a new regime or a major shift in policy meant changes in public discourse, both on the part of the dominant elite who had to justify the new regime or policy and on the part of dominated or opposing groups who had to modify their own discourse in response – either to accommodate themselves to the new order of things or to oppose it more effectively. The elaboration of new ideas out of the Enlightenment notions brought to power by the French Revolution therefore proceeded not by a slow and linear progression but dialectically and in concentrated bursts. The equation Citizenship equals Useful Labor equals Property, for example, was developed between 1788 and 1791, and the emergence of the socialist vision of an identity between labor and public life took place mainly in three bursts: 1830–34, 1839–40, and 1848–51. This timing, it hardly need be said, was governed not by an even cadence of logical development but by the syncopated rhythms of political struggle.

The logic connecting socialism to the Enlightenment was dialectical; it proceeded by a movement of oppositions rather than by a process of deduction. Diderot's own views originated in a self-conscious movement of opposition; they were part of a broader attempt to give a purely natural account of the world that was elaborated in opposition to the traditional metaphysics of the French monarchy – an account that would serve as a rational basis for criticizing contemporary institutions. As long as Enlightenment discourse remained a discourse of opposition, its own internal ambiguities and contradictions were muted; what mattered was its contrast to traditional ideas and institutions. But when, in the French Revolution, Enlightenment discourse became constitutive of the social and political order, its ambiguities and contradictions became much more salient. Contradictions that seemed insignificant before the Revolution began to be pursued intensively once the Revolution took place, and some of them quickly became important nodes of social and political conflict.

The dialectical logic by which socialism grew out of Enlightenment ideas may, then, be characterized in the first instance as a development of contradictions inherent in Enlightenment ideas. This process is particularly clear for the Enlightenment conception of property, which initially emerged as a means of criticizing old-regime institutions – the tyranny of kings, the oppressiveness and inequity of taxation. It called up the figure of the sturdy agriculturalist whose property was the fruit of his personal labor, an appealing figure who neatly exemplified the moral and political point of the argument. But when the same notion of property became the basis of legal and political rights, important questions began to arise. If labor was the source of all property, why did some have to labor without accumulating property, whereas others possessed vast amounts of property but did not engage in labor? Why should the full rights of citizenship be limited to that category of men who possessed significant amounts of property rather than to the quite different category who engaged in productive labor? The French Revolution's conception was not necessarily self-contradictory; whether it was or not depended on how this conception was applied and interpreted. But by making this concept of property a foundation of the society and the state, the French Revolution ensured that the nature and the relationships of property and labor would be the subject of extensive speculation, a speculation that, although carried out within the terms inherited from the Enlightenment and the Revolution, challenged the assumptions of the new liberal social order.

A similar process can be seen with the ideals of Liberty, Equality, and Fraternity. This motto of the French Revolution served to distinguish the new order of things from the old. As against a corporate social order in which persons were distinguished from each other by their rank and privilege, with inferiors subject to the discipline of superiors and all subject to the discipline of the monarch, the revolutionary motto designated a social order composed of individual citizens free to order their lives as they saw fit (Liberty), living under laws that applied equally to all (Equality), and bound together by their common membership in the nation (Fraternity) rather than by ties of subordination or by a congeries of exclusive loyalties. As long as they were set against the old regime, Liberty, Equality, and Fraternity seemed in perfect harmony with each other. But under the new regime these ideals often seemed mutually contradictory. Liberty of the individual, as interpreted by postrevolutionary regimes, included the liberty to pursue one's own interests freely. This pursuit could easily be seen as selfishness or "egoism," which was the opposite of fraternity. Moreover, the unhindered accumulation of wealth by some implied a growing disparity in material conditions of life, and hence growing substantive inequality. These ambiguities were already the subject of bitter controversies in the 1790s. By the 1830s or 1840s, dissertations on the meaning of Liberty, Equality, and Fraternity had become a standard topos of French political rhetoric, and the claim that Equality and Fraternity had been sacrificed to an unregulated and misunderstood pursuit of Liberty had become a common argument of the more radical republicans. Here again, dissident ideas were worked out within the vocabulary and intellectual framework of the French Revolution. On the question of Liberty, Equality, and Fraternity, as on questions of property, one can easily discern a more or less consistent strand of radical republican opposition that stretched from the Jacobins and the sans-culottes through Babeuf, Buonarroti, and the Carbonari to the republican opposition under the Restoration and the July Monarchy. This dissenting strand grew in part out of logical contradictions in the ideas that were institutionalized in the French Revolution. But opposition was not only a response to purely formal inconsistencies; it was also a response to the practical effects of applying Enlightenment ideas to the details of social and political life. The dialectic of internal contradictions was compounded, in other words, by a dialectic of practical consequences. The effects of the new property rights and of the "liberty of industry" were particularly striking in the urban skilled trades. The new regime cast relations between workers and employers in terms of individual liberty and equality under the law. Workers and employers were to encounter each other as free individuals in the marketplace, where they would reach a mutually agreed-on arrangement; the employer was free to define the workers' duties as he saw fit, and the worker was free to accept or reject these terms. Although the two parties were legally equal, however, the owner of the means of production was actually at an immense advantage in these encounters, and the law forbade workers to form an association that might give them collectively the strength to right the balance. The employers, moreover, were free to dispose of their property as they saw fit, and this meant that each employer could organize production in his own way, limited only by the constraints of the market. Given the expansion of the national, European, and world economies in the first half of the nineteenth century, the opportunities available to innovative or unscrupulous entrepreneurs were particularly enticing. Standardizing products, intensifying the division of labor, diluting skills, introducing new techniques, reorganizing production by means of increased scale or various subcontracting arrangements; all of these were easy avenues to greater profitability in the urban artisan trades in these years. One important result of such petty capitalist commercial and organizational practices was a tendency for trades to become increasingly disunified over time, as different workshops were subjected to different regimes of production. Once again, workers were not allowed to unite to impose uniform standards. The absolute right of property and the principle of the liberty of industry impinged palpably on the organization of production in the craft workshop. In the eyes of the workers, and in those of their sympathizers in the bourgeois intelligentsia, the result was a chaos of egoism and oppression. These practical consequences of the new system stimulated both the practical efforts of organized resistance and the development of arguments opposing unlimited individual property rights and fostering equality and fraternity.

The way workers responded to these problems was not determined solely

280

by the characteristics of the new system. Their responses were also shaped by preexisting values, assumptions, practices, expectations, and sentiments. And given that the urban trades had been organized corporately for a half millennium prior to the French Revolution, most of these preexisting values, assumptions, practices, expectations, and sentiments were somehow corporate. The workers' sense that the new regime was resulting in egoism and chaos, for example, only makes sense given the traditional corporate feeling that each trade should be a unified community. Enlightenment individualism had originally been developed in opposition to the corporate social order of the old regime; after the Revolution, when Enlightenment concepts became dominant, corporate and individualist idioms remained fundamentally opposed. Workers therefore found the corporate idiom, which was already a familiar part of the everyday life of their trades, entirely appropriate as a framework for organizing practical resistance to the atomistic tendencies of the new system. In addition to a republican opposition that was formulated within the terms of the revolutionary idiom, then, the early decades of the nineteenth century also saw the growth of a widespread corporate workers' opposition that was based on a prerevolutionary idiom. Unlike the republican opposition, which was theoretically self-conscious and intellectually explicit, the corporate opposition was un-self-conscious and pragmatic. Workers' corporations were not necessarily opposed to the current political regime – whether Republic, Empire, or Constitutional Monarchy – and until 1830 they had no particular affinity with the radical republicans. Workers' corporations originated in a politically un-self-conscious attempt to counter the individualistic legal and economic tendencies of the new order.

CLASS CONSCIOUSNESS

Class consciousness first emerged in France during the agitation that followed the Revolution of 1830. In order to make their essentially corporate demands comprehensible in the liberal climate established by the July Revolution, workers took up the language of the Revolution and reshaped it to fit their own goals. The two crucial innovations were the identification of manual workers as "the people" by casting them as industrial serfs who must be emancipated from their exploitation at the hands of privileged proprietors and the elaboration of an idiom of fraternal association. This idiom of association redefined workers' corporations as free and voluntary societies based on the common will of the producers in the trade, and it projected the development of associative ownership of the means of production. Many workers actually formed fraternal trade associations structured along these lines, and in 1833 many of them joined a great wave of strikes that attempted to restore some measure of collective control over their trades.

By combining the corporate and revolutionary idioms in this way and by engaging in collective action based on these newly constructed premises, the workers created a new type of opposition to the dominant state and society, an opposition that proclaimed the workers' specific identity as laborers, opposed individualism with an ideal of fraternal solidarity, promised an end to the tyranny of private property, and implied the legitimacy of a revolution to achieve these ends. They created, in other words, what would today be called a class-conscious workers' movement. The agitations and conceptual innovations that took place between 1830 and 1834 constituted the first stage in the making of the French working class.

The unprecedented workers' agitation of the early 1830s and especially the dramatic uprisings of the workers of Lyons in 1831 and 1834 inaugurated a new political dialectic of class struggle. In the later 1830s and the 1840s, and especially in 1848, all the oppositions outlined here tended to coalesce around an overriding opposition between the working class and the bourgeoisie, an opposition between an individualistic, proprietary, liberal vision of the social order identified with a well-to-do class of property holders and a solidary, collectivist, socialist vision identified with a class of propertyless "proletarians." This opposition reached its peak in the Revolution of 1848, when the workers' attempt to create a new political order based on socialist corporations was crushed in the bloody insurrection of the June Days. Although the June Days marked the defeat of the working class, they also confirmed the depth of the opposition between the classes, making the class struggle and class consciousness inaugurated in the early 1830s into an irreversible fact of French political and social life.

The form that class consciousness and class struggle took in 1848, however, was still quite different from that embodied in the class-conscious proletarian parties of the late nineteenth and twentieth centuries. One obvious difference was in the significance of the term "class" itself. It was noted earlier how the Abbé Sieyès used the term in *What Is the Third Estate?* to designate his four categories of useful labor – agriculture, industry, commerce, and services. He did so because of its overtones of objectivity and scientific precision; "class" in 1789 meant nothing more than "category," in contrast to "order" and "estate," which were redolent with implications of hierarchy and solidarity. During the nineteenth century, class was increasingly used to designate groups in relations of superiority and inferiority, as in "dominant class," "bourgeois class," or "working class." But it also continued to be used for social categories of any kind, and workers frequently employed it as a synonym for "trade" or "profession." Thus, in 1833 a revolutionary typographer writing in favor of establishing a producers' cooperative spoke of "our class, the class of typographers and printers,"[1] and in 1848 a workers' tract on "The Organization of Laborers" said "the most numerous, strongest and most intelligent working class is that which works on iron."[2]

As late as 1848 the term "class," and even the term "working class," remained simply a descriptive designation; "proletarian" or "aristocrat" or "association" carried powerful political and emotional charges, but "class" did not. It was not until later in the nineteenth century, especially after the spread of Marxism, that "class" came to refer mainly to social categories in a relationship of superordination and subordination – and of struggle – and that class began to take on connotations of moral solidarity. "Class loyalty" would have sounded reprehensible to workers in 1848; it would have implied a loyalty to some selfish interest as against the common interest. By 1900, "class loyalty" had come to imply a selfless devotion to the cause of all workers. By then, "class" had become a word to conjure with, as "order" and "estate" had been under the old regime.

It was no accident that workers' consciousness in 1848 was more attuned to words that emphasized unity – like "association" – than to words that emphasized distinctions – like "class." Working-class consciousness in 1848 was universalist and inclusive in moral tone, and class conflict was not a matter of bald confrontation between workers and employers. In fact, the workers' main adversaries in 1848 were not the owners of the means of production in their trades. Employers in the artisan trades still shared some of the workers' corporate sensibilities, and relations between workers and employers in 1848 were often far from hostile. During March and April 1848, masters and workers in many trades joined to establish "conventions" that would govern their trades and cooperated in overseeing their application. During the period of increasing bitterness in May and June, outright cooperation between workers and employers was much rarer, but even then the workers' anger was not directed mainly at their employers. This same ambivalent pattern of relations can be seen in the workers' socialist schemes, which foresaw not an expropriation of the masters but the creation of fraternal associations that would absorb the employers and abolish the distinction between masters and workers by making all of them associated owners of the means of production. The masters, in other words, were seen as potential members of these perfected trade communities of the future.

This lack of sharp hostility to the masters does not indicate utopian delusion on the workers' part. Their hostility was directed not at their immediate employers, who were at worst nothing more than small-time exploiters, but at the larger social, political, and legal system that guaranteed the continuation of exploitation. "Class conflict," in 1848, was not so much a confrontation between two sharply divided classes of property owners and wage earners as it was an attempt by the workers to erect a complete countersystem, one in which labor rather than property would be the dominant and encompassing feature of the social order; in which all useful work, whether manual or mental, would be organized and rewarded in the same fashion; in which fraternal association would everywhere replace egoistic competition as the ordering principle of social life; and in which units of production would also be units of political organization. The revolutionary workers of 1848 inevitably defined themselves within the tradition of the French Revolution. Although their ideology was elaborated from their particular class perspective, it was stated, like the ideologies of the Revolution of 1789–94, in universal terms. As they understood it, theirs was the consciousness of enlightened humanity, not the consciousness of a class. And their socialism was not a revenge on their exploiters but a means of transcending exploitation and creating a just society.

Notes

1. Introduction

1 For France, see Bernard H. Moss, *The Origins of the French Labor Movement: The Socialism of Skilled Workers, 1830–1914* (Berkeley and Los Angeles, 1976); Georges Duveau, *1848* (Paris, 1965), or the English version, *1848: The Making of a Revolution* (New York, 1967); Rémi Gossez, *Les Ouvriers de Paris,* Book One, *L'Organisation, 1848–1851,* vol. 24, *Bibliothèque de la Révolution de 1848* (La Roche-sur-Yon, 1967); Alain Faure, "Mouvements populaires et mouvement ouvrier à Paris," *Le Mouvement social* 88 (July-September 1974): 51–92; Jacques Rougerie, "Composition d'une population insurgée: l'example de la Commune," *Le Mouvement social* 48 (July-September 1964):31–48, and *Procès des Communards* (Paris, 1964); Charles Tilly and Lynn Lees, "Le Peuple de juin 1848," *Annales: économies, sociétés, civilisations* 29 (September-October 1974):1061–91; Robert J. Bezucha, *The Lyon Uprising of 1834: Social and Political Conflict in a Nineteenth-Century City* (Cambridge, Mass., 1974); Yves Lequin, *Les Ouvriers de la région lyonnaise (1848–1914),* 2 vols. (Lyons, 1977); J.-P. Aguet, *Les Grèves sous la monarchie de juillet (1830–1847): Contribution à l'étude du mouvement ouvrier français* (Geneva, 1954); Peter N. Stearns, "Patterns of Industrial Strike Activity in France during the July Monarchy," *American Historical Review* 70 (January 1965):371–94; Edward Shorter and Charles Tilly, *Strikes in France, 1830–1968* (London, 1974); Christopher H. Johnson, *Utopian Communism in France: Cabet and the Icarians, 1839–1851* (Ithaca, N.Y., 1974); Joan Wallach Scott, *The Glassworkers of Carmaux: French Craftsmen and Political Action in a Nineteenth-Century City* (Cambridge, Mass., 1974). The leading role of artisans in England may be seen in E. P. Thompson, *The Making of the English Working Class* (London, 1963). For the United States, see Herbert Gutman, *Work, Culture and Society in Industrializing America* (New York, 1976). For Germany, see Theodore S. Hamerow, *Restoration, Revolution, Reaction: Economics and Politics in Germany 1815–1871* (Princeton, N.J., 1958), and R. Stadelmann, "Sociale Ursachen der Revolution von 1848," in H. U. Wehler, ed., *Moderne deutsche Sozialgeschichte* (Berlin, 1970).

2 See, e.g., Edouard Dolléans, *Histoire du mouvement ouvrier,* 3 vols. (Paris, 1936–53); Edouard Dolléans and Gérard Dehove, *Histoire du travail en France: mouvement ouvrier et législation sociale,* 2 vols. (Paris, 1953–5); Georges Lefranc, *Histoire du mouvement ouvrier en France des origines à nos jours* (Paris, 1947); Paul Louis, *Histoire du mouvement syndical en France,* 2 vols. (Paris, 1947); Georges Weill, *Histoire du mouvement social en France, 1852–1902* (Paris, 1904).

3 Agulhon's studies of popular sociability and political life in the Var from the old regime to 1851 are published in four volumes: *Pénitents et Francs-Maçons de l'ancienne Provence* (Paris, 1968); *La Vie sociale en Provence intérieure au lendemain de la Révolution* (Paris, 1970); *Une ville ouvrière au temps du socialisme utopique: Toulon de 1815 à 1851* (Paris and The Hague, 1970); and *La République au village* (Paris, 1970).

4 The fruitfulness of studying the period stretching from the late eighteenth to the nineteenth century has been demonstrated brilliantly for English labor history by Thompson, *Making of the English Working Class*.

5 Evidence for these assertions can be found in William H. Sewell, Jr., "The Structure of the Working Class of Marseille in the Middle of the Nineteenth Century" (Ph.D. diss., University of California, Berkeley, 1971); "La Classe ouvrière de Marseille sous la Seconde République: structure sociale et comportement politique," *Le Mouvement social* 76 (July-September 1971):27–65, reprinted in English as "The Working Class of Marseille under the Second Republic: Social Structure and Political Behavior," in Peter N. Stearns and Daniel J. Walkowitz, eds., *Workers in the Industrial Revolution* (New Brusnwick, N.J., 1974), pp. 75–116; and William H. Sewell, Jr., "Social Change and the Rise of Working-Class Politics in Nineteenth-Century Marseille," *Past and Present* 65 (November 1974):75–109. For a fascinating description of a thoroughly corporative trade, see Victor Nguyen, "Les Portefaix marseillais: Crise et déclin, survivance," *Provence historique* 12 (1962):363–97.

6 Gossez, *Les Ouvriers.*

7 Two particularly prominent recent examples are the controversies over whether old-regime France was a class society or a society of orders, and whether the French Revolution was a "bourgeois revolution." For excellent summaries and commentaries on these debates, see J. H. M. Salmon, "Venality of Office and Popular Sedition in Seventeenth-Century France: A Review of a Controversy," *Past and Present* 37 (July 1967):21–43; and Colin Lucas, "Nobles, Bourgeois and the Origins of the French Revolution," *Past and Present* 60 (August 1973):84–126.

8 The quotation is from the English translation, *French Rural History: An Essay on Its Basic Characteristics,* trans. Janet Sondheimer, foreword Bryce Lyon (Berkeley and Los Angeles, 1970), p. xxiii. The original French title is *Les Caractères originaux de l'historie rurale française* (Oslo, 1931). It was published in Paris in 1952, and a second volume, *Supplément établi d'après les travaux de l'auteur (1931–1944),* ed. Robert Dauvergne, appeared in 1956. Bloch's book remains the model of an essai de synthèse.

9 Albert Soboul, *Les Sans-culottes parisiens en l'an II: Mouvement populaire et gouvernement révolutionnaire, 2 juin 1793–9 thermidor an II* (Paris, 1958). An abridged version is available in English, *The Parisian Sans-Culottes and the French Revolution, 1793–4* (London, 1964). George Rudé, *The Crowd in the French Revolution* (London, 1959); Richard Cobb, *Les Armées révolutionnaires: Instrument de la Terreur dans les départements,* 2 vols. (Paris, 1961–3); Thompson, *Making of the English Working Class.*

10 Two extremely influential examples of the use of sociological methods and questions in historical research were Stephan Thernstrom, *Poverty and Progress: Social Mobility in a Nineteenth Century City* (Cambridge, Mass., 1964), and Charles Tilly, *The Vendée* (Cambridge, Mass., 1964). The influence of the great quantitative histories of the Annales school was also felt by the middle of the 1960s. Particularly important were Pierre Goubert, *Beauvais et le Beauvaisis de*

1600 à 1730, contribution à l'historie social de la France du XVIIe siècle (Paris, 1960), and Emmanuel Le Roy Ladurie, *Les Paysans de Languedoc* (Paris, 1966).

11 Some representative examples are Gareth Stedman Jones, *Outcast London: A Study in the Relationship Between Classes in Victorian Society* (Oxford, 1971); Michael Anderson, *Family Structure in Nineteenth-Century Lancashire* (Cambridge, 1971); John Foster, *Class Struggle and the Industrial Revolution: Early Industrial Capitalism in Three English Towns* (New York, 1975); David Levine, *Family Formation in an Age of Nascent Capitalism* (New York, 1977); Stephan Thernstrom, *Poverty and Progress* and *The Other Bostonians: Poverty and Progress in the American Metropolis, 1880–1970* (Cambridge, Mass., 1973); Gutman, *Work, Culture and Society;* Michael B. Katz, *The People of Hamilton, Canada West: Family and Class in a Mid-Nineteenth-Century City* (Cambridge, Mass., 1975); Alan Dawley, *Class and Community: The Industrial Revolution in Lynn* (Cambridge, Mass., 1976); Daniel J. Walkowitz, *Worker City, Company Town: Iron and Cotton Worker Protest in Troy and Cohoes, New York, 1855–84* (Urbana, Ill., 1978); Rolande Trempé, *Les Mineurs de Carmaux, 1848–1914,* 2 vols. (Paris, 1971); Agulhon, *Une ville ouvrière;* Michelle Perrot, *Les Ouvriers en grève: France, 1871–1890,* 2 vols (Paris, 1974); Scott, *Glassworkers of Carmaux;* Bezucha, *Lyon Uprising of 1834;* Lequin, *Les Ouvriers de la région lyonnaise;* Louise A. Tilly and Joan W. Scott, *Women, Work and the Family* (New York, 1978).

12 Elizabeth Fox-Genovese and Eugene D. Genovese have argued, in a recent and blisteringly polemical article, that a failure to deal adequately with political struggles is characteristic of contemporary social history in general. I tend to agree with this assessment, although I am far from sure that they would approve of my attempts to remedy the problem. "The Political Crisis of Social History: A Marxian Perspective," *Journal of Social History* 10 (Winter 1976):205–20.

13 For my efforts, see the works cited in note 5. Local social histories with similar problems include Scott, *Glassworkers of Carmaux;* Agulhon, *Une ville ouvrière;* and Lequin, *Les Ouvriers de la région lyonnaise,* vol. 2. A partial exception is Bezucha, *Lyon Uprising of 1834.* Lyons, in the early 1830s, was the most important center of labor struggles in France and consequently usurped something of the role usually played by Paris in the development of new ideologies. However, Bezucha's account of the ideology of the Lyonnais workers is also limited by the purely local perspective of the study; the importance of what happened in Lyons could have been made much clearer had he considered the relationship between the ideology of Lyons's workers and the similar but not identical ideology that grew up among Parisian workers in the same years.

14 G. D. H. Cole, *A History of Socialist Thought,* vol. 1, *The Forerunners, 1789–1850* (London, 1955); Geroge Lichtheim, *The Origins of Socialism* (New York, 1969); Frank E. Manuel, *The Prophets of Paris: Turgot, Condorcet, Saint-Simon, Fourier and Compte* (Cambridge, Mass., 1962) and *The New Moral World of Henri de Saint-Simon* (Cambridge, Mass., 1956); C. Bouglé, *Socialismes français* (Paris, 1932); Sébastien Charléty, *Histoire du Saint-Simonisme* (Paris, 1931); Hubert Bourgin, *Fourier* (Paris, 1905); Maurice Dommanget, *Babeuf et la conjuration des Egaux* (Paris, 1922), *Victor Considérant, sa vie et son oeuvre* (Paris, 1929), and *Les Idées politiques et sociales d'Auguste Blanqui* (New York, 1957); Alan B. Spitzer, *The Revolutionary Theories of Louis Auguste Blanqui* (New York, 1957); Edouard Dolléans, *Proudhon* (Paris, 1941); Leo A. Loubère, *Louis Blanc: His Life and His Contribution to the Rise of French Jacobin Socialism* (Evanston, Ill., 1961); J. L. Peuch, *La Vie et l'oeuvre de Flora Tristan* (Paris, 1925); Armand Cuvillier,

Hommes et idéologies de 1840 (Paris, 1956) and *P.-J.-B. Buchez et les origines du socialisme chrétien* (Paris, 1948).

15 In one of his most provocative essays, Michel Foucault suggests that the study of "authors" and their "works" should in any case be abandoned in favor of the study of "discourse." What Foucault advocates for the study of thought in general is inescapable in the study of certain moments of ideological development. Michel Foucault, "What Is an Author?" in *Language, Counter-Memory, Practice: Selected Essays and Interviews,* trans. Donald F. Bouchard and Sherry Simon (Ithaca, N.Y., 1977), pp. 113–38.

16 Souboul, *Les Sans-culottes;* Christopher Hill, *The World Turned Upside Down: Radical Ideas During the English Revolution* (New York, 1972); and Thompson, *Making of the English Working Class.*

17 Particularly prominent examples are Keith Thomas, *Religion and the Decline of Magic* (New York, 1971); Natalie Zemon Davis, *Society and Culture in Early Modern France* (Stanford, Calif., 1975); and Emmanuel Le Roi Ladurie, *Montaillou: Village occitan de 1294 à 1324* (Paris, 1975).

18 Clifford Geertz, *The Interpretation of Cultures* (New York, 1973), p. 405. Here I am consciously espousing the approach of a particular school of anthropology, one that is by no means accepted by all anthropologists. Important examples of this general approach, in addition to the works of Geertz, are Marshall Sahlins, *Culture and Practical Reason* (Chicago, 1978); David M. Schneider, *American Kinship: A Cultural Account* (Englewood Cliffs, N.J., 1968), and Victor W. Turner, *The Forest of Symbols: Aspects of Ndembu Ritual* (Ithaca, N.Y., 1967).

19 Clifford Geertz, "On the Nature of Anthropological Understanding," *American Scientist* 63 (January–February 1975):48.

20 *Making of the English Working Class,* p. 12.

21 See, e.g., Max Gluckman, *Rituals of Rebellion in South-east Africa* (Manchester, 1954).

22 Some attempts to write more historically aware ethnographies are Clifford Geertz, *The Social History of an Indonesian Town* (Cambridge, Mass., 1965); William A. Christian, Jr., *Person and God in a Spanish Valley* (New York, 1972); John W. Cole and Eric R. Wolf, *The Hidden Frontier: Ecology and Ethnicity in an Alpine Valley* (New York, 1974); Jane Schneider and Peter Schneider, *Culture and Political Economy in Western Sicily* (New York, 1976); James A. Boon, *The Anthropological Romance of Bali, 1597–1972* (Cambridge, 1977); Stephen Gudeman, *The Demise of a Rural Economy: From Subsistence to Capitalism in a Latin American Village* (London, 1978); Renato I. Rosaldo, Jr., *Ilongot Headhunting, 1883–1974: A Study in History and Society* (Stanford, Calif., 1979). Two works by historians that are barely distinguishable from such historical ethnographies are Steven Feierman, *The Shambaa Kingdom: A History* (Madison, Wis., 1974) and Ronald B. Inden, *Marriage and Rank in Bengali Culture: A History of Caste and Clan in Middle Period Bengal* (Berkeley, Calif., 1976).

23 Here my thinking has been much influenced by E. P. Thompson, "Eighteenth-Century English Society: Class Struggle Without Class?" *Social History* 3 (May 1978):133–65, and Ronald B. Inden, "Cultural-Symbolic Constitutions in Ancient India," paper presented at the Social Science Seminar at the Institute for Advanced Study, 1978.

24 This fact has recently been emphasized by Alain Faure and Jacques Rancière in *La Parole ouvrière, 1830–1851* (Paris, 1976). In their introductions to texts written by working-class authors, they point out that workers' discourse was elabo-

rated in systematic linguistic opposition to the dominant discourse of the bourgeoisie; "workers' speech" was "a struggle for the appropriation of words" (p. 18) in which "words from above were one after another challenged and reappropriated" (pp. 16–17).

2. Mechanical arts and the corporate idiom

1 Pierre Goubert, *The Ancien Régime, French Society 1600–1750*, trans. Steve Cox (New York, London, 1973), p. 53; Ernest Labrousse, Pierre Léon, Pierre Goubert, Jean Bouvier, Charles Carrière, and Paul Harsin, *Histoire économique et sociale de la France*, vol. 2, *Des derniers temps de l'âge seigneurial aux préludes de l'âge industriel (1660–1789)* (Paris, 1970), p. 85.

2 Labrousse, et al., *Historie économique et sociale de la France*, 2:74. On eighteenth-century industrial growth, see J. Marczewski, "The Take-off and French Experience," in W. W. Rostow, ed., *The Economics of Take-off into Sustained Growth* (New York, 1963), pp. 119–38.

3 Marcel Reinhard, "La Population des villes: sa mesure sous la Révolution et l'Empire," *Population* 9 (1954):279–88.

4 Bad harvests resulted in high grain prices, and given the extraordinary importance of bread in the diet and the budget of the majority of the population, high grain prices necessarily led to a fall in demand for manufactured goods of all kinds, and thus to high unemployment, a contraction of credit, bankruptcies, and a general business slump. It was only when grain prices fell again that the accumulated demand for manufactured goods could spur a recovery in the industrial and commercial sectors of the economy. Ernest Labrousse, *Esquisse du mouvement des prix et des revenus en France au XVIIIe siècle*, 2 vols. (Paris, 1932), and *La Crise de l'économie française à la fin de l'Ancien Régime et au début de la Révolution* (Paris, 1944). Labrousse et al., *Histoire économique et sociale de la France*, 2:529–66.

5 The classic study of rural textile workers is Goubert, *Beauvais et le Beauvaisis*. See also Franklin F. Mendels, "Proto-industrialization: The First Phase of the Process of Industrialization," *Journal of Economic History* 32 (1972):241–61, and *Aux origines de la révolution industrielle: Industrie rurale et fabriques* special issue *Revue du Nord* 61 (January-March 1979).

6 F. Braesch, "Essai de statistique de la population ouvrière de Paris vers 1791," *La Révolution française* 63 (1912–13):289–321.

7 Thus, although the négociants of Rouen deliberated as a body and drew up their own cahier de doléances (list of grievances) in preparation for the Estates General of 1789, they were classified by the municipal authorities as a "body assimilated to judicial bodies or colleges" – that is, to government officials, lawyers, physicians, notaries, and architects – rather than to the humbler "communities of arts and trades." Marc Bouloiseau, *Cahiers de doléances du tiers état du baillage de Rouen pour les Etats Généraux de 1789*, 2 vols. (Paris, 1957), 1:60.

8 Lists of the corps de métiers of Paris dating from the fourteenth through the eighteenth centuries can be found in Alfred Franklin, *Dictionnaire historique des arts, métiers et professions exercés dans Paris depuis le treizième siècle* (Paris, 1906), pp. 63–5, 211–13, 291–6, 520–2. For Rouen, see Ch. Ouin-Lacroix, *Histoire des anciennes corporations d'arts et métiers et des confréries religieuses de la capitale de la Normandie* (Rouen, 1850). For Beauvais, see Goubert, *Beauvais et le Beauvaisis*, pp. 302–4. On the "six corps," see Franklin, pp. 645–7.

9 Steven Kaplan, "Réflexions sur la police du monde du travail, 1700–1815," *Revue historique* 261 (January-March 1979):20–1.

10 It is a mark of the influence of corporate forms of organization that even these "marginal" categories sometimes formed their own secret corporate bodies with ranks, regulations, and internal discipline. An example is the "kingdom" of the beggars of Paris in the fifteenth and sixteenth centuries. See Christian Paultre, *De la répression de la mendicité et du vagabondage en France sous l'ancien régime* (Paris, 1906; reprint ed., Geneva, 1975), pp. 42–54; and Roger Chartier, "La 'Monarchie d'argot' entre le mythe et l'histoire," in Bernard Vincent, ed., *Les Marginaux et les exclus dans l'histoire, Cahiers Jussieu,* no. 5, Université Paris 7 (Paris, 1979), pp. 275–311.

11 Charles Loyseau, *Traité des ordres et simples dignitz,* in *Les Oeuvres* (Paris, 1666), p. 80. The *Traité* was originally published in 1610.

12 *Le Dictionnaire de l'Académie françoise,* 2 vols. (Paris, 1694), 2:591–2.

13 Labor was also capable of being inverted in a typically Christian fashion. Because labor signified humility, and humility was a sign of submission to God, labor could, in special circumstances, be a mark of the highest, rather than the lowest, status. Thus, a requirement of manual labor was originally built into the daily round of the Benedictine monks. It is also significant, however, that this requirement soon ceased to be honored in practice.

14 *Le Grand Vocabulaire françois,* 2nd ed., 30 vols. (Paris, 1762–74), 3:115, entry under "Art."

15 Ibid.

16 Ibid., entries "Arts liberaux" and "Arts méchaniques."

17 *Traité des ordres,* p. 80.

18 *Encyclopédie, ou dictionnaire raisonné des sciences, des arts et des métiers,* 17 vols. (Paris, 1751–65), 1:745, entries "Artiste" and "Artisan."

19 The best recent work on compagnonnage is Cynthia Truant, "Compagnonnage: Symbolic Action and the Defense of Workers' Rights in France, 1700–1848," (Ph.D. diss., University of Chicago, 1978). See also Emile Coornaert, *Les Compagnonnages en France du moyen age à nos jours* (Paris, 1966), and Etienne Martin Saint-Léon, *Le Compagnonnage* (Paris, 1901).

20 *Traité des ordres,* p. 80.

21 At the same time, corporations were seen by the authorities as a means of maintaining order in a segment of the population that would otherwise be of doubtful orderliness. See Kaplan, "La Police du monde du travail," pp. 26–7.

22 For a fuller discussion of "état," see William H. Sewell, Jr., "Etat, Corps, and Ordre: Some Notes on the Social Vocabulary of the French Old Regime," in Hans-Ulrich Wehler, ed., *Sozialgeschichte Heute, Festschrift für Hans Rosenberg zum 70. Geburtstag* (Göttingen, 1974), pp. 52–4.

23 *L'Organisation corporative de la France d'ancien régime* (Paris, 1938).

24 Emile Coornaert, *Les Corporations en France avant 1789* (Paris, 1941), pp. 83, 121.

25 Etienne Martin Saint-Léon, *Histoire des corporations de métiers, depuis leurs origines jusqu'à leur suppression en 1791* (Paris, 1909); Henri Hauser, *Ouvriers du temps passé (XVe-XVIe siècles)* (Paris, 1899); Olivier-Martin, *L'Organisation corporative;* and Coornaert, *Les Corporations en France.* See also the older work by E. Levasseur, *Histoire des classes ouvrières en France depuis la conquête de Jules César jusqu'à la Révolution,* 2 vols. (Paris, 1859), republished as *Histoire des classes ouvrières et de l'industrie en France avant 1789,* 2 vols. (Paris, 1900).

26 The Annales school refers to the historians who have published regularly in the French journal *Annales d'histoire économique et sociale,* founded in 1929 by Marc Bloch and Lucien Febvre, and its postwar successor, *Annales: économies, sociétés, civilisations.* Works representing the range of the school are Goubert, *Beauvais et le Beauvaisis;* Le Roy Ladurie, *Les Paysans de Langeudoc;* Michel Vovelle, *Piété baroque et déchristianisation: Les Attitudes devant la mort au XVIIIe siècle d'après les clauses des testaments* (Paris, 1973); Yves Castan, *Honnêté et relations sociales en Languedoc (1715–80)* (Paris, 1974).

27 Particularly useful are Goubert, *Beauvais et le Beauvaisis;* Pierre Deyon, *Amiens, capitale provinciale: Etude sur la société urbaine au XVIIe siècle* (Paris, The Hague, 1967); Jean-Claude Perrot, *Genèse d'une ville moderne: Caen au XVIIIe siècle,* 2 vols (Paris, 1975), and Maurice Garden, *Lyon et les lyonnais.* See also Agulhon, *Pénitents et Francs-Maçons,* Chap. 3. An excellent recent article touching on the problem of corporations is Kaplan, "La Police du monde du travail."

28 Olivier-Martin, *L'Organisation corporative,* pp. 205–10.

29 Ibid., p. 206.

30 Quoted in Coornaert, *Les Corporations en France,* p. 207.

31 Quoted in Olivier-Martin, *L'Organisation corporative,* p. 207.

32 *Le Grand Vocabularie françois.*

33 Ouin-Lacroix, *Anciennes corporations,* p. 642.

34 Perrot, *Genèse d'une ville moderne,* 1:327–35.

35 Deyon, *Amiens, capitale provinciale,* p. 203; Goubert, *Beauvais et le Beauvaisis,* p. 307; Garden, *Lyon et les lyonnais,* p. 312.

36 Ouin-Lacroix, *Anciennes corporations,* p. 705.

37 Ibid., pp. 608–9.

38 Coornaert, *Les Corporations en France,* pp. 213–17.

39 Ibid., pp. 217–20.

40 Ouin-Lacroix, *Anciennes corporations,* p. 610.

41 Ibid., pp. 609, 644.

42 Coornaert, *Les Corporations en France,* p. 275.

43 Ibid., pp. 194–200.

44 Seventeenth-century Amiens and eighteenth-century Lyons and Caen experienced shrinking access to masterships. The proportion of new masters who were sons of masters rose between the early and late seventeenth century in Amiens but fell in eighteenth-century Caen. Deyon, *Amiens, capitale provinciale,* pp. 218, 344; Garden, *Lyon et les lyonnais,* p. 314; Perrot, *Genèse d'une ville moderne,* 1:336–40.

45 Coornaert, *Les Corporations en France,* p. 275.

46 Ibid., p. 64.

47 Ibid., p. 204.

48 For a fascinating discussion of the problem, see Natalie Zemon Davis, "Les Femmes dans les arts méchaniques à Lyon au XVIe siècle," in Jean-Pierre Gutton, ed., *Mélanges en hommage de Richard Gascon* (Lyons, 1979).

49 Coornaert, *Les Corporations en France,* pp. 203–4.

50 Ibid., p. 233.

51 See note 17.

52 Olivier-Martin, *L'Organisation corporative,* p. 206.

53 Coornaert, *Les Corporations en France,* p. 235; Olivier-Martin, *L'Organisation corporative,* p. 93.

54 See, for example, Ouin-Lacroix, *Anciennes corporations,* pp. 685, 688, 695.

55 As Coornaert puts it, "Leur organisation saisit l'homme entier," p. 230. Trade confraternities were only one of a wide variety of types of confraternities, some purely devotional, others engaging in any number of communal activities. See Agulhon, *Pénitents et Francs-Maçons;* Ouin-Lacroix, *Anciennes corporations.*

56 Coornaert, *Les Corporations en France,* pp. 231–6; Hauser, *Ouvriers du temps passé,* pp. 161–74. As Garden puts it, "In each trade, the confraternity . . . was the symbol of unity. When various rules were multiplying restrictions, cleavages, fetters on the liberty of work by all sorts of conditions for access to mastership, the confraternity remained in principle a common property." *Lyon et les lyonnais,* p. 313.

57 On oaths of métiers jurés, see Olivier-Martin, *L'Organisation corporative,* p. 139, and Coornaert, *Les Corporations en France,* p. 64. On other oath-swearing ceremonies see Loyseau, *Traité des ordres,* pp. 53, 75.

58 See. e.g., the statutes appended in Ouin-Lacroix, *Anciennes corporations,* pp. 555–749.

59 Loyseau, *Traité des ordres,* p. 3.

60 Coornaert, *Les Corporations en France,* pp. 150, 207, 256.

61 See the article "Enterrements" in Franklin, *Dictionnaire historique des arts, métiers et professions,* p. 306; Coornaert, *Les Corporations en France,* p. 59; Hauser, *Ouvriers du temps passé,* p. 164.

62 Coornaert, *Les Corporations en France,* p. 150.

63 For a fuller discussion of the word "corps" and of the general cultural and moral forms of the old regime, see Sewell, "Etat, Corps and Ordre." See also Roland Mousnier, "Les Concepts d'ordres, d'états, de fidelité et de monarchie absolue en France de la fin du XVe siècle à la fin du XVIIIe siècle," *Revue historique* 502 (April-June 1972):289–312.

64 On the militia, see Franklin, *Dictionnaire historique des arts, métiers et professions,* article on "Bannières, ordonnance dite des," pp. 63–5. For Rouen, see Ouin-Lacroix, *Anciennes corporations,* pp. 517–22. See also Coornaert, *Les Corporations en France,* pp. 71, 229–30.

65 Pierre Deyon makes a similar point in his discussion of the corporations of seventeenth-century Amiens. "The trade community, the fundamental cell of urban life, served as the framework for their professional defense and constituted at the same time a cultural and religious milieu. In a society that ignored the individual and recognized only orders, that knew no juridical equality and respected only privileges, it was the chivalry of the artisan and the symbol of his organic participation in the providential order of society." *Amiens, capitale provinciale,* p. 344.

66 Etienne Boileau, *Réglemens sur les arts et métiers de Paris régiés au XIIIe siècle, et connus sous le nom de livre des métiers d'Etienne Boileau,* notes and introduction by G.-B. Depping (Paris, 1837).

67 Olivier-Martin, *L'Organisation corporative,* pp. 92–104. On Provençal trade confraternities, see Agulhon, *Pénitents et Francs-Maçons,* chap. 3.

68 Olivier-Martin, *L'Organisation corporative,* p. 206.

69 Ibid., pp. 208–9.

3. Journeymen's brotherhoods

1 See, e.g., Germain Martin, *Les Associations ouvrières au XVIIIe siècle (1700–1792)* (Paris, 1900); Hauser, *Ouvriers du temps passé;* and Kaplan, "La Police du monde du travail," pp. 30–54.

2 Martin, *Les Associations ouvrières*, pp. 53–60.
3 On confraternities, see Hauser, *Ouvriers du temps passé*, pp. 169–74, and Kaplan, "La Police du monde du travail," pp. 60–5.
4 On compagnonnages, see Martin Saint-Léon, *Le Compagnonnage;* Coornaert, *Les Compagnonnages;* Martin, *Les Associations ouvrières;* Luc Benoist, *Le Compagnonnage et les métiers* (Paris, 1966); Henri Hauser, *Les Compagnonnages d'arts et métiers à Dijon aux XVIIe et XVIIIe siècles* (Paris, 1907); and Truant, "Compagnonnage."
5 Natalie Zemon Davis, "A Trade Union in Sixteenth-Century France," *Economic History Review*, 2nd ser., 19 (April 1966):48–69, and "Strikes and Salvation at Lyon," in her *Society and Culture in Early Modern France* (Stanford, 1975), pp. 1–16. This latter article originally appeared in *Archiv für Reformationsgeschichte*, 56 (1965):48–64.
6 Davis, "A Trade Union," p. 59.
7 Ibid., pp. 56–7. On recreational associations, or "youth abbeys," see Natalie Zemon Davis, "The Reasons of Misrule: Youth Groups and Charivaris in Sixteenth-Century France," *Past and Present* 50 (February 1971):41–75, reprinted in *Society and Culture in Early Modern France*, pp. 97–123. See also Agulhon, *Pénitents et Francs-Maçons*, Chap. 2.
8 On the strike of 1539, see Hauser, *Ouvriers du temps passé*, pp. 176–234.
9 Davis, "A Trade Union," pp. 58–60.
10 See the article "Past" in Franklin, *Dictionnaire historique des arts, métiers et professions*, pp. 549–50.
11 Olivier-Martin, *L'Organisation corporative*, p. 139.
12 Loyseau, *Traité des ordres*, pp. 53, 75.
13 Davis, "A Trade Union," p. 60.
14 On godparents, see John Bossy, "Blood and Baptism: Kinship, Community and Christianity in Western Europe from the Fourteenth to the Seventeenth Centuries," in Derek Baker, ed., *Sanctity and Secularity: The Church and the World*, vol. 10, *Studies in Church History* (Oxford, 1973), pp. 129–43.
15 See Davis, "Strikes and Salvation," passim.
16 Ibid., p. 6.
17 Davis, "A Trade Union," pp. 61–5; Hauser, *Ouvriers du temps passé*, pp. 177–96.
18 Davis, "Strikes and Salvation," p. 5.
19 Davis, "A Trade Union," p. 61.
20 Ibid., p. 53.
21 *Les Compagnonnages*, pp. 30–1.
22 Paul Labal, "Notes sur les compagnons migrateurs et les sociétés de compagnons à Dijon à la fin du XVe et au début du XVIe siècles," *Annales de Bourgogne* 22 (1950):189, 191.
23 The general practices and institutional structure of compagnonnage are described in many places, for example Coornaert, *Les Compagnonnages* and Martin, *Les Associations ouvrières*, pp. 92–164.
24 See, e.g., the "Livre de règles des jolis compagnons tourneurs," dating from 1731 in Bordeaux, reproduced in Coornaert, *Les Compagnonnages*, pp. 368–9.
25 Martin, *Les Associations ouvrières*, pp. 161–2.
26 Ibid.
27 "Livre de règles," in Coornaert, *Les Compagnonnages*, p. 373.
28 Ibid., pp. 356–81.
29 Martin, *Les Associations ouvrières*, pp. 149–52.
30 "Livre de règles," in Coornaert, *Les Compagnonnages*, pp. 257–60.

31 For an excellent analysis of the reception, see Cynthia M. Truant, "Solidarity and Symbolism among Journeymen Artisans: The Case of Compagnonnage," *Comparative Studies in Society and History* 21 (April 1979):217–20, and "Compagnonnage," pp. 116–58. For various accounts of reception ceremonies, see Coornaert, *Les Compagnonnages,* pp. 349–93.

32 Truant, "Compagnonnage," pp. 69–70.

33 "Livre de règles," in Coornaert, *Les Compagnonnages,* pp. 359, 367, 379.

34 Davis, "A Trade Union," pp. 58–9.

35 Truant, "Compagnonnage," pp. 144–52.

36 Ibid.

37 Ibid., pp. 80–115. See also Truant, "Solidarity and Symbolism," pp. 220–4, and Martin Saint-Léon, *Le Compagnonnage,* pp. 2–10. An alternative set of myths traced the origins of compagnonnage back to construction of the cathedrals in the Middle Ages.

38 For Perdiguier, see Jean Briquet, *Agricol Perdiguier, Compagnon du tour de France et représentant du peuple 1805–1875* (Paris, 1955); Agricol Perdiguier, *Le Livre du compagnonnage* (Paris, 1839) and *Mémoires d'un compagnon* (Geneva, 1854–5; reissued, Paris, 1964).

39 George Sand, *Le Compagnon du tour de France* (Paris, 1841); Agricol Perdiguier, *Correspondance inédite avec George Sand et ses amis, lettres choisies et commentées avec une introduction par Jean Briquet* (Paris, 1966). In his 1848 edition of *L'Organisation du travail* (Paris, 1848), Louis Blanc published a scheme for reorganizing work in France that was authored by Perdiguier.

40 Davis, "A Trade Union," pp. 63–4.

41 Perrot, *Genèse d'une ville moderne,* 1:332.

42 Truant, "Compagnonnage," pp. 299–307.

43 For only one example among many of this type of conflict, in this case concerning confraternities of penitents, see Agulhon, *Pénitents et Francs-Maçons,* pp. 112–6.

44 "Livre de règles," in Coornaert, *Les Compagnonnages,* p. 381.

45 To judge from their wording, the authorities' decrees forbidding job placement by compagnons were often directed as much against the masters as against the compagnons. Martin, *Les Associations ouvrières,* pp. 157, 174–5.

46 Truant, "Compagnonnage," pp. 75–7.

4. The abolition of privilege

1 Thus the carpet weavers of Bourges demanded in their cahier de doléances in 1789 "that the corps de métiers may enjoy their privileges and that they may be enabled to prevent chambrelans." Alfred Gandillhon, ed., *Cahiers de doléances du baillage de Bourges et des baillages secondaires de Vierzon et d'Henrichemont pour les Etats Généraux de 1789* (Bourges, 1910), p. 575.

2 See note 5, Chap. 2.

3 See, e.g., Gandillhon, *Cahiers . . . de Bourges;* Bouloiseau, *Cahiers . . . de Rouen;* Joseph Fournier, *Cahiers de doléances de la sénéchaussée de Marseille pour les Etats Généraux* (Marseille, 1908).

4 On Turgot and his ministry, see Douglas Dakin, *Turgot and the Ancien Régime in France* (London, 1939); Edgar Faure, *La Disgrâce de Turgot* (Paris, 1961); and Keith Michael Baker, *Condorcet: From Natural Philosophy to Social Mathematics* (Chicago, 1975), pp. 55–72.

5 Loyseau, *Traité des ordres*, p. 2.
6 17 vols. (Paris, 1751–65).
7 The standard biographical study of Diderot in English is Arthur M. Wilson, *Diderot* (New York, 1972). Part I was originally published separately as *Diderot: The Testing Years* (New York, 1957). On the *Encyclopédie*, see Jacques Proust, *Diderot et l'Encyclopédie* (Paris, 1963) and *L'Encyclopédie* (Paris, 1965).
8 "Art," in *Encyclopédie*, 1:714.
9 Ibid., p. 717.
10 Ibid., p. 714.
11 Ibid., p. 717.
12 Ibid., p. 714.
13 Ibid.
14 Ibid.
15 Ibid.
16 "Encyclopédie," in *Encyclopédie*, 5:647.
17 "Art," in *Encyclopédie*, 1:715.
18 "Encyclopédie," in *Encyclopédie*, 5:647.
19 "Métier," in *Encyclopédie*, 10:483.
20 "Art," in *Encyclopédie*, 1:715.
21 Ibid.
22 Ibid., p. 714.
23 On the Physiocrats, see Georges Weulersse, *Le Mouvement physiocratique en France (de 1756 à 1770)*, 2 vols. (Paris, 1910), and Elizabeth Fox-Genovese, *The Origins of Physiocracy: Economic Revolution and Social Order in Eighteenth-Century France* (Ithaca, N.Y., 1976).
24 See, e.g., Simon Clicquot de Blervache, *Mémoire sur les corps de métiers* (The Hague, 1758).
25 See note 4.
26 For the grain riots, see George Rudé,"La Taxation populaire de mai 1775 à Paris et dans la région parisienne," *Annales historiques de la Révolution française* 143 (April-June 1956):139–79; "La Taxation populaire de mai 1775 en Picardie, en Normandie et dans le Beauvaisis," *Annales historiques de la Révolution française* 165 (July-September 1961):305–26; and *The Crowd in History: A Study of Popular Disturbances in France and England, 1730–1848* (New York, 1964), pp. 19–32.
27 F.-A. Isambert, A.-J.-L. Jourdan, and Decrusy, eds., *Recueil général des anciennes lois françaises depus l'an 420 jusqu'à la Révolution de 1789*, 29 vols. (Paris, 1822–33), 23:379.
28 Ibid., pp. 371–6.
29 Ibid., p. 380.
30 Ibid., p. 382.
31 For an excellent discussion of the political and intellectual crisis of the monarchy, see Keith Michael Baker, "French Political Thought at the Accession of Louis XVI," *Journal of Modern History* 50 (June 1978):279–303.
32 Jules Flammermont, ed., *Remontrances du Parlement de Paris au XVIIIe siècle*, 3 vols. (Paris, 1888–98), 3:344.
33 Ibid., pp. 344–5.
34 Ibid., p. 345.
35 For a good statement of this view, see Steven Kaplan, *Bread, Politics and Political Economy in the Reign of Louis XV*, 2 vols. (The Hague, 1976), 1:62–3.

36 Flammermont, *Remontrances,* 3:310.
37 Ibid., p. 354.
38 Ibid., p. 347.
39 Ibid., p. 348.
40 Ibid., p. 315.
41 Ibid., pp. 356–7.
42 Ibid., p. 312.
43 Ibid., pp. 309–10.
44 Ibid., p. 310.
45 Ibid., p. 309.
46 Ibid., pp. 345–6.
47 Martin Saint-Léon, *Histoire des corporations,* pp. 585–99.
48 See Jean Egret, *La Pré-révolution française, 1787–1788* (Paris, 1962). The classical account of the first phase of the French Revolution is Georges Lefebvre, *1789* (Paris, 1939). It is available in English, trans. R. R. Palmer, *The Coming of the French Revolution* (Princeton, N.J., 1947). See also Georges Lefebvre, *The French Revolution,* 2 vols. (New York, 1964–5); F. Furet and D. Richet, *La Révolution française,* 2 vols. (Paris, 1965); Albert Soboul, *Précis d'histoire de la Révolution française* (Paris, 1963); Michel Vovelle, *La Chute de la monarchie, 1787–1792* (Paris, 1972); M. J. Sydenham, *The French Revolution* (New York, 1965).
49 An excellent recent critical edition is Emmanuel Sieyès, *Qu'est-ce que le Tiers Etat?* introd. and notes by Roberto Zapperi (Geneva, 1970). The best edition in English is Emmanuel Joseph Sieyès, *What Is the Third Estate?* trans. M. Blondel, ed. with notes by S. E. Finer, introd. by Peter Campbell (London, 1963). My citations are all to the Zapperi edition.
50 Sieyès, *Qu'est-ce que le Tiers Etat?* p. 119.
51 Ibid., p. 121.
52 Ibid., p. 122.
53 Ibid.
54 Ibid.
55 Ibid., p. 123.
56 Ibid., p. 124.
57 Ibid., p. 125.
58 Ibid., p. 124.
59 Ibid., p. 126.
60 Ibid., p. 193.
61 Ibid., p. 194.
62 Ibid., p. 140.
63 Ibid., p. 144.
64 Ibid., p. 189.
65 Ibid., p. 202.
66 The classic study of the peasant revolts is Georges Lefebvre, *La Grande Peur de 1789* (Paris, 1932). It is available in English as *The Great Fear of 1789: Rural Panic in Revolutionary France* (New York, 1973).
67 The proclamations decided upon in principle on August 4 were debated and amended over the next few days and definitively decreed on August 11. The text is available in many places, e.g., M. J. Mavidal and M. E. Laurent, eds., *Archives parlementaires de 1787 à 1860,* 1st ser. (1787–9), 82 vols. (Paris, 1879–1913), 8:397–8.

68 Ibid., p. 398.
69 The text of the declaration is available in many places, e.g., Lefebvre, *The Com-*
70 Mavidal and Laurent, *Archives parlementaires,* 8:349.
71 Ibid., 23:199.
72 Ibid.
73 Ibid., p. 202.
74 Ibid., p. 203.
75 Martin, *Les Associations ouvrières,* pp. 223–41.
76 Ibid., p. 233.
77 P.-J.-B. Buchez and P.-C. Roux, *Histoire parlementaire de la Révolution française,* 40 vols. (Paris, 1834–8), 10:193.
78 Ibid.
79 Ibid., p. 194.
80 Ibid.
81 Ibid., p. 195.
82 Ibid.
83 Ibid.
84 Ibid., p. 196.
85 Ibid., p. 193.
86 Lefebvre, *The French Revolution,* 1:165–6.
87 Vovelle, *La Chute de la monarchie,* p. 174.
88 Le Chapelier proposed a law for this purpose at the end of February 1791, a law that met with considerable opposition in the Assembly and was finally passed only after considerable amendment. Mavidal and Laurent, *Archives parlementaires,* 23:558–66.
89 Ibid., and 25:678–87.

5. From gens de métier to sans-culottes

1 Rudé, *The Crowd in the French Revolution,* pp. 246–8.
2 Ibid., and Soboul, *Les Sans-culottes.*
3 Bouloiseau, *Cahiers . . . de Rouen,* pp. 159–60.
4 Gandilhon, *Cahiers . . . de Bourges,* pp. 534–5.
5 Bouloiseau, *Cahiers . . . de Rouen,* pp. 85–9.
6 Ibid., p. 85.
7 Ibid., p. 88.
8 Ibid.
9 Ibid., p. 85.
10 Grace M. Jaffé, *Le Mouvement ouvrier à Paris pendant la Révolution française (1789–1791)* (Paris, 1924), pp. 65–73, 101–58; Paul Chauvet, *Les Ouvriers du livre en France de 1789 à la constitution de la Fédération du livre* (Paris, 1964), pp. 7–27; Martin, *Les Associations ouvrières,* pp. 224–39.
11 Martin, *Les Associations ouvrières,* pp. 227–9.
12 This document is reprinted in Chauvet, *Les Ouvriers du livre,* pp. 637–44.
13 Ibid., p. 637.
14 Ibid., p. 643–4.
15 Jaffé, *Le Mouvement ouvrier,* pp. 123, 154.
16 Rudé, *The Crowd in the French Revolution,* p. 85.
17 Martin, *Les Associations ouvrières,* pp. 232–6.
18 Ibid., pp. 235–6.

19 Ibid., p. 236.
20 Ibid., p. 234.
21 The classic interpretation of this phase of the Revolution is Albert Mathiez, *La Révolution française* (Paris, 1922), available in English as *The French Revolution*, trans. Catherine Allison Phillips (New York, 1964). See also Lefebvre, *The French Revolution;* Sydenham, *The French Revolution;* Soboul, *Précis* and *Les Sans-culottes;* and Rudé, *The Crowd in the French Revolution.*
22 Soboul, *Les Sans-culottes*, esp. pp. 439–51; Rudé, *The Crowd in the French Revolution*, passim.
23 On revolutionary celebrations, see Mona Ozouf, *La Fête révolutionnaire, 1789–1799* (Paris, 1976).
24 Walter Markov and Albert Soboul, eds., *Die Sansculotten von Paris, Dokumente zur Geschichte der Volksbewegung, 1793–1794* (Berlin, 1957). The documents are published in the original French and in German translation. See also Albert Soboul, "Problèmes du travail en l'an II," *Annales historiques de la Révolution française* 28 (July-September 1956):236–54.
25 On Condorcet's conception of the republic, see Baker, *Condorcet*, esp. pp. 303–16.
26 Soboul, *Les Sans-culottes*, pp. 599–614.
27 Ibid., pp. 549–58.
28 Ibid., p. 559.
29 Ibid., pp. 413–21.
30 Ibid., p. 409.
31 Markov and Soboul, *Die Sansculotten*, p. 4.
32 Soboul, *Les Sans-culottes*, pp. 570–6. See also Markov and Soboul, *Die Sansculotten*, pp. 140–54, for a particularly detailed account of fraternization between the section du Pont Neuf (rebaptized "section Revolutionnaire" as a result of the fraternization) and the section de la Cité.
33 Markov and Soboul, *Die Sansculotten*, p. 4.
34 Quoted in Soboul, *Les Sans-culottes*, p. 458.
35 Ibid., p. 470.
36 Ibid., p. 458; Markov and Soboul, *Die Sansculotten*, pp. 176, 218.
37 Markov and Soboul, *Die Sansculotten*, p. 425.
38 Soboul, *Les Sans-culottes*, p. 425.
39 Ibid., p. 454.
40 Ibid.
41 Real wages were only 9 percent higher in the 1840s than in the 1790s, and bread remained the staple of the diet. See Jürgen Kuczynski, *A Short History of Labour Conditions in France, 1700 to the Present Day* (London, 1946), p. 86.
42 Soboul, *Les Sans-culottes*, p. 427.
43 Ibid., p. 473.
44 Ibid., p. 453.
45 Ibid., p. 452.
46 Ibid., p. 453.
47 Ibid., p. 429.
48 Markov and Soboul, *Die Sansculotten*, p. 2.
49 Soboul, *Les Sans-culottes*, pp. 411–3.
50 Ibid., p. 413.
51 *Qu'est-ce que le Tiers Etat?* p. 121.
52 Markov and Soboul, *Die Sansculotten*, p. 176.
53 Soboul, *Les Sans-culottes*, pp. 413–4.

54 See the address from the section of the sans-culottes to the National Convention in Markov and Soboul, *Die Sansculotten*, pp. 136–40.
55 Soboul, *Les Sans-culottes*, pp. 464–7.

6. A revolution in property

1 On the right of property in the Civil Code, see André-Jean Arnaud, *Les Origines doctrinales du Code civil français* (Paris, 1969), pp. 179–95.
2 Antoine Furetière, *Dictionnaire universel*, 2 vols. (The Hague, 1691), 2:476.
3 The classic account is Marc Bloch, *Les Caractères originaux*, esp. chaps. 2 and 6.
4 See the brief but illuminating discussion in Ralph E. Giesey, "Rules of Inheritance and Strategies of Mobility in Prerevolutionary France," *American Historical Review* 82 (April 1977): esp. 281–5. The standard work on venal offices is Roland Mousnier, *La Vénalité des offices sous Henri IV et Louis XIII*, 2nd ed. (Paris, 1971).
5 Once again, the classic account is Bloch, *Les Caractères originaux*, esp. chaps. 3 and 4.
6 Flammermont, *Remontrances*, 3:278.
7 Ibid., p. 320.
8 The figures for Parisian entry fees are from Martin Saint-Léon, *Histoire des corporations*, pp. 590–3. Seamstresses, it should be pointed out, were the only women's corporations in Paris. The lowest fee for a men's corporation prior to 1776 was 350 livres for shoemakers. The reformed corporations reestablished after the revocation of Turgot's decree in 1776 had considerably lower fees, ranging between 100 and 1,000 livres, with the majority between 300 and 800. These fees still corresponded to considerably more than half of most journeymen's annual earnings. Wage figures for Parisian journeymen in this period can be found in Levasseur, *Histoire des classes ouvrières*, 2:836–43.
9 Flammermont, *Remontrances*, 3:309–10.
10 For the attack on collective obligations, see Marc Bloch, "La Lutte pour l' individualisme agraire dans la France du XVIIIe siècle," *Annales d'histoire économique et sociale* 2 (1930):329–83, 511–56.
11 John Locke, *Two Treatises of Government*, with a supplement, *Patriarcha*, by Robert Filmer, ed. Thomas I. Cook (New York, 1947), p. 134. The most up-to-date critical edition is edited by Peter Laslett, *Two Treatises of Government*, 2nd ed. (Cambridge, 1967). I have quoted the Cook edition, which modernizes Locke's spelling.
12 Locke, *Two Treaties*, ed. Cook, 134.
13 Ibid., pp. 136–7.
14 Ibid., p. 136.
15 Ibid., p. 184.
16 Ibid.
17 Ibid.
18 Ibid., p. 186.
19 The quote is from Filmer's *Observations on Hobbes, Milton, etc.*, as cited in Locke *Two Treatises*, ed. Cook, p. 56. Filmer's *Patriarcha* is printed in full in ibid., pp. 251–308.
20 *Encyclopédie*, 13:491, entry under "Propriété."
21 Loyseau, *Traité des ordres*, pp. 79–80.
22 As Locke put it, "Every one who enjoys his share of the protection should pay out of his estate his proportion for the maintenance of it. But still it must be with

his own consent – i.e., the consent of the majority, giving it either by themselves or their representatives chosen by them. For if any one shall claim a power to lay and levy taxes on the people, by his own authority and without such consent of the people, he thereby invades the fundamental law of property and subverts the end of government; for what property have I in that which another may by right take, when he pleases, to himself?" *Two Treatises*, p. 193.

23 The *Mémoire* is printed in full in Ann-Robert-Jacques Turgot, baron de l'Aulne, *Oeuvres de Turgot et documents le concernant*, 4 vols., Gustave Schelle, ed. (Paris, 1913–23), 4:568–628. For an illuminating discussion of the *Mémoire*, see Baker, *Condorcet*, pp. 202–14.

24 Turgot, *Oeuvres*, 4:619.

25 Ibid., p. 583.

26 Ibid., pp. 584–5.

27 Ibid., pp. 587–8.

28 Ibid.

29 Ibid., p. 588.

30 Ibid.

31 Ibid., p. 589.

32 Ibid., p. 576.

33 Ibid., p. 584.

34 Ibid., p. 600.

35 Ibid., p. 601.

36 Ibid.

37 Ibid., pp. 600, 603.

38 Ibid., p. 603.

39 Isambert et al., *Recueil général des anciennes lois*, 23:371.

40 Ibid., p. 375.

41 Ibid.

42 Ibid., p. 376.

43 Ibid.

44 Charles Vellay, ed., *Oeuvres complètes de Saint-Just*, 2 vols. (Paris, 1908), 2:513.

45 Mavidal and Laurent, *Archives parlementaires*, 8:344.

46 On these matters, see Ph. Sagnac and P. Caron, *Les Comités des droits féodaux et de législation et l'abolition du régime seigneurial (1789–1793)* (Paris, 1907), and Ph. Sagnac, *La Législation civile de la Révolution française (1789–1804)* (Paris, 1898).

47 Robespierre's address, which was delivered in January 1790, may be found in Mavidal and Laurent, *Archives parlementaires*, 11:319–25.

48 Ibid., 22:119.

49 Adult male domestics were relatively rare in cities but quite common in the countryside. To my knowledge, the only detailed study of the practical effects of the active/passive citizen distinction is in Paul Bois, *Paysans de l'Ouest: Des structures économiques et sociales aux options politiques depuis l'époque révolutionnaire dans la Sarthe* (Le Mans, 1960), pp. 222–45.

50 Women were denied suffrage even in those cases when they were property owners and heads of households in their own right.

51 Bois, *Paysans de l'Ouest*, pp. 224–6; and Jacques Godechot, *Les Institutions de la France sous la Révolution et l'Empire* (Paris, 1951), p. 74.

52 Godechot, *Les Institutions de la France*, p. 74. The Assembly decided upon this high property requirement for electors only a few days before the constitution was passed. Originally the requirement was to have been only the payment of a direct tax equal to ten days of labor, whereas eligibility to serve as a deputy was

to be restricted to those who possessed landed property and paid a marc d'argent (fifty francs) in taxes. The property requirements for deputies were dropped as a concession to the democrats, but this concession was counterbalanced by sharply increasing the property requirement for electors.

53 The constitution of 1793 not only abolished all property requirements but instituted the direct election of deputies and even abolished domesticity as a legal category, thereby assuring the vote to male servants. Females, however, were not given the vote even in the constitution of 1793. Although the constitution of 1799 had no property qualifications, it imposed a four-tiered system of indirect elections, with an appointed Senate making the final choice of legislators. The possibility of unpropertied men surviving this process was of course negligible. For the texts of these and other constitutions, see Jacques Godechot, ed., *Les Constitutions de la France depuis 1789* (Paris, 1970).

54 See Sagnac, *La Législation civile;* Sagnac and Caron, *Les Comités des droits féodaux;* Georges Lefebvre, *Questions agraires au temps de la Terreur,* 2nd ed. (La Roche-sur-Yon, 1954) and "La Révolution française et les paysans" and "La Vente des biens nationaux," both in *Etudes sur la Révolution française,* 2nd ed. (Paris, 1963), pp. 307–67.

55 Buchez and Roux, *Histoire parlementaire,* 10:195.

56 Ibid., p. 193.

7. Industrial society

1 The early usage of the term "social science" has been studied most closely by Keith M. Baker. See especially "The Early History of the Term 'Social Science,'" *Annals of Science* 20 (1964):211–26, and *Condorcet,* pp. 391–5. It was Condorcet and his successors – particularly the "Ideologues" Garat and Destutt de Tracy – who first used the term in public discourse in the 1790s. The works of Saint-Simon and Compte, of course, brought it into general usage. It is revealing that when Condorcet and his circle began to make a few rare and hesitant uses of the term "social science," they also commonly employed another analogous locution: "social art." (See Baker, *Condorcet,* pp. 272–85.) Because "social" implied *voluntary* action, action subject to changes of mind or will among the persons who enter into relations with one another, it was above all a matter of *art* – of executing something well – rather than a matter of *science.* The terms "moral sciences" and even "moral and political sciences" were in common usage in the eighteenth century. But "social science" sounded paradoxical until – in the early nineteenth century – the terms "social" and "society" began to be used in their current reified sense.

2 See Pierre Goubert, *Louis XIV and Twenty Million Frenchmen* (New York, 1970), p. 124. This book is an English translation of *Louis XIV et vingt millions de français* (Paris, 1966). As Goubert puts it, "The essential goal of what has been anachronistically called Colbert's 'economic policy' was to put the people in a position to finance the nation's glory."

3 Karl Marx, *The Class Struggles in France (1848–1850)* (New York, n.d.), p. 36.

4 Fourth ed. (London, 1936), p. 53. The first edition was published in 1921.

5 The classic account of the English industrial revolution is Paul Mantoux, *La Révolution industrielle au XVIIIe siècle: Essai sur les commencements de la grande industrie moderne en Angleterre* (Paris, 1906). Translated as *The Industrial Revolution in the Eighteenth Century: An Outline of the Beginnings of the Modern Factory*

System (London, 1928; rev. ed., 1961). See also J. L. and Barbara Hammond, *The Rise of Modern Industry* (London, 1925); and T. S. Ashton, *The Industrial Revolution, 1760–1830* (London, 1928). For a particularly lucid account of the technological changes of the industrial revolution, see David S. Landes, *The Unbound Prometheus: Technological Change and Industrial Development in Western Europe from 1750 to the Present* (London, 1969), esp. Chap. 1.

6 See, e.g., S. B. Clough, "Retardative Factors in French Economic Development in the Nineteenth and Twentieth Centuries," *Journal of Economic History* 6 (1946), Suppl., 91–210; and "Retardative Factors in French Economic Growth at the End of the Ancien Régime and during the French Revolutionary and Napoleonic Periods," in M. Kooy, ed., *Studies in Economics and Economic History: Essays in Honor of Harold F. Williamson* (Durham, N.C., 1972); David S. Landes, "French Entrepreneurship and Industrial Growth in the Nineteenth Century," *Journal of Economic History* 9 (1949):45–61; "French Business and the Businessman: A Social and Cultural Analysis," in E. M. Earle, ed., *Modern France: Problems of the Third and Fourth Republics* (Princeton, N.J., 1951), and "New Model Entrepreneurship in France and Problems of Historical Explanation," *Explorations in Entrepreneurial History* 1 (1963):56–75; R. E. Cameron, "Profit, croissance et stagnation en France au XIXe siècle," *Economie appliquée* 10 (1957):409–44; and "Economic Growth and Stagnation in Modern France, 1815–1914," *Journal of Modern History* 20 (1958):1–13; Tom Kemp, "Structural Factors in the Retardation of French Economic Growth," *Kyklos* 15 (1962):325–50; and C. P. Kindleberger, *The Economic Growth of France and Britain, 1851–1950* (Cambridge, Mass., 1964).

7 The results of this collaborative project have been published as volumes of the *Cahiers de l'Institut de Science Economique Appliquée,* series AF. See, e.g., J. Marczewski, "Le Produit physique de l'économie française de 1789 à 1913 (Comparison avec la Grande Bretagne)," 4 (1965); J.-C. Toutain, "Le Produit de l'agriculture française de 1700 à 1958," 2 (1961) and "La Population de la France de 1700 à 1959," 3 (1963); and T. J. Markovitch, "L'Industrie française de 1789 à 1964," 4, 6, and 7 (1965–6). The best summary statement is J. Marczewski, "The Take-off and French Experience," in W. W. Rostow, ed., *The Economics of Take-off into Sustained Growth* (New York, 1963). See also François Perroux, "Prise de vues sur la croissance de l'économie française, 1780–1950," in Simon Kuznets, ed., *Income and Wealth,* ser. 5 (London, 1955). Other calculations confirming this same general picture have been made by M. Lévy-Leboyer, "La Croissance économique en France au XIXe siècle: Résultats préliminaires," *Annales: économies, sociétés, civilisations* 23 (1968):788–807. The figures for physical product per capita are from Marczewski, "The Take-off and French Experience," p. 135. These and other figures are, of course, subject to considerable margins of error. They must be taken only as approximations.

8 The most thorough and impressive statements of this position are Patrick O'Brien and Caglar Keydar, *Economic Growth in Britain and France 1780–1914: Two Paths to the Twentieth Century* (London, 1978); Richard Roehl, "French Industrialization: A Reconsideration," *Explorations in Economic History* 13 (1976):233–81; and M. Lévy-Leboyer, "Le Processus d'industrialisation: le cas de l'Angleterre et de la France," *Revue historique* 239 (1968):281–98. See also, Don R. Leet and John A. Shaw, "French Economic Stagnation, 1700–1960: Old Economic History Revisited," *Journal of Interdisciplinary History* 8 (Winter 1978):530–44.

9 The population of France increased from about 23.8 million in 1801 to about 38.5 million in 1901, or an increase of only 36 percent. This rate was adversely affected by the loss of Alsace and Lorraine to Germany in 1871. But even without this loss, the French population increase in the nineteenth century would have been under 45 percent. For the population of various European countries, see B. R. Mitchel, *European Historical Statistics, 1750–1970* (New York, 1975), pp. 19–26. For France in 1801, I have used the corrected figures of J. Bourgeois-Pichat, "Evolution de la population française depuis le XVIIIe siècle," *Population* 6 (1951):661–2.

10 The estimates of J.-C. Toutain put the increase in rural population for this period at between 2.8 million and 5.4 million and the increase in urban population at between 2.7 million and 4.7 million. Calculated from Table 15 in "La Population de la France," pp. 54–5. Although the range of these estimates is very wide, the general point remains: A very substantial proportion of the total growth in French population in the first half of the century took place in the countryside.

11 Calculated from Toutain, "Le Produit de l'agriculture française," pp. 64, 207.

12 According to the figures collected by J.-C. Toutain ("La Population de la France," pp. 54–5), the number of rural people engaged in agriculture grew very slowly from 1801 to 1851, whereas the rural nonagricultural population more than doubled, from about 3 million to about 7 million. These figures cannot be taken very literally, however. The figure for 1801 is extrapolated from a single estimate, of doubtful validity; moreover, because many inhabitants of the countryside engaged in both agricultural and industrial pursuits, in widely varying proportions, any attempt to assign people definitively to one or the other is bound to be misleading. Finally, Toutain's estimate is inherently implausible, because it implies that the rural nonagricultural population actually increased more rapidly than the urban population. If, as I suspect, Toutain's figures overstate the rise in the rural nonagricultural population, this would mean that the agricultural population rose by more than his figures indicate. This, in turn, would imply that the estimate of a 38 percent increase in agricultural productivity from 1801 to 1851 is too high. An increase of perhaps 30 percent would be more likely.

13 Charles Pouthas, in *La Population française pendant la première moitié du XIXe siècle* (Paris, 1965), p. 79, concluded that there was no compelling evidence for more rapid growth in urban than in rural population until after 1831. Toutain, in "La Population de la France," p. 53, remains agnostic about the period from 1801 to 1831. Both, however, agree that urban population grew faster than rural population over the period from 1801 to 1851 as a whole.

14 The figure for 1806 is calculated from Reinhard, "La Population des villes," p. 287. The 1851 figure is derived from Toutain, "La Population de la France," pp. 54–5.

15 These figures – admittedly very rough for 1801 – are derived from Toutain, "La Population de la France," pp. 54–5.

16 There were, however, five additional cities – Versailles, Clermont-Ferrand, Troyes, Aix-en-Provence, and Grenoble – ranked twenty-first through twenty-fifth in 1801 that grew by less than 26 percent and had been displaced from the list by 1851. Pouthas, *La Population française,* p. 98.

17 The population figures for British cities are taken from B. R. Mitchell and Phyllis Deane, *Abstract of British Historical Statistics* (London, 1962), pp. 24–7.

18 The French figure is from Toutain, "La Population de la France," pp. 54–5. The

British figure is from Adna Ferrin Weber, *The Growth of Cities in the Nineteenth Century: A Study in Statistics* (New York, 1899; reprinted ed., Ithaca, N.Y., 1963), p. 43.

19 The figure for France is from Toutain, "La Population de la France," pp. 54–5. The British figure is from Mitchell and Deane, *British Historical Statistics,* p. 60.

20 The crucial importance of the home market in British industrialization is cogently argued in Phyllis Deane and W. A. Cole, *British Economic Growth, 1688–1959* (London, 1964), pp. 82–97.

21 David S. Landes makes much of the urban tendency toward "emulation" in stimulating demand for mass-produced objects. See *The Unbound Prometheus,* pp. 50–1.

22 For figures on enclosures, see Deane and Cole, *British Economic Growth,* p. 94.

23 This is not to say that enclosures actually forced a large number of people off the land, as was once widely held. On the effects of enclosures in England, see J. C. Chambers, "Enclosure and Labour Supply in the Industrial Revolution," *Economic History Review,* 2nd ser., 5 (1953):319–43.

24 Maurice Lévy-Leboyer makes a similar argument in "Le Processus d'industrialisation."

25 Flammermont, *Remontrances,* 3:347.

26 Lévy-Leboyer, "Les Processus d'industrialisation," pp. 290–1.

27 Thimor J. Markovitch, "Le Revenu industriel et artisanal sous la Monarchie de Juillet et le Second Empire," *Cahiers de l'Institut de Science Economique Appliquée,* series AF, 4 (1967):87.

28 For a lucid account of the transformation of an artisan labor force into semi-skilled factory operatives in the 1880s and 1890s, see Scott, *Glassworkers of Carmaux.*

29 For a more detailed description of workers in the machine construction industry of Marseille, see Sewell, "The Structure of the Working Class," pp. 205–9.

30 As E. P. Thompson has noted, the story of handloom weaving in Britain was far more complicated than the destruction of a traditional trade by the competition of factory technology. The first effect of the industrial revolution on handloom weavers was a vast multiplication of their numbers – a result of the rise in output and decline in cost of cotton yarns that followed the introduction of new spinning machinery. It was this greatly inflated number of handloom weavers who were then extinguished by the power loom. Moreover, the rapid expansion had the more vulnerable once the downturn came. The rise as well as the fall of handloom weaving was a consequence of the new industrial technology. Thompson, *Making of the English Working Class,* pp. 260–1, 269–77.

31 Bezucha, *Lyon Uprising of 1834,* p. 195.

32 William M. Reddy has found this to be true both in the Armentières linen industry and the Rouen cotton industry. See "Family and Factory: French Linen Weavers in the Belle Epoque," *Journal of Social History* 8 (Winter 1975):102–12, and "The Textile Trade and the Language of the Crowd at Rouen, 1752–1871," *Past and Present* 74 (February 1977):78–9.

33 See Reddy, "The Textile Trade," and "Skeins, Scales, Discounts, Steam and other Objects of Crowd Justice in Early French Textile Mills," *Comparative Studies in Society and History* 21 (April 1979):204–13.

34 See Christopher H. Johnson, "Economic Change and Artisan Discontent: The Tailors' History, 1800–48," in Roger Price, ed., *Revolution and Reaction: 1848*

and the Second French Republic (London, 1975), pp. 87–114; Johnson, *Utopian Communism in France,* esp. pp. 177–82, and "Communism and the Working Class before Marx: The Icarian Experience," *American Historical Review* 76 (June 1971):657–67; and Moss, *French Labor Movement* esp. Chap. 1. See also Thompson's discussion of the London artisans in *Making of the English Working Class,* Chap. 8.

35 The quotation is from the Provisional Government's decree of March 2, 1848, as reprinted in *Les Murailles révolutionnaires de 1848,* 17th ed., 2 vols., preface by Alfred Delvau (Paris, 1868), 1:241. As far as I know there exists no adequate study of marchandage. Our knowledge of the system derives almost exclusively from the attempts to abolish it in 1848. On this, see Duveau, *1848,* pp. 73–4 and Gossez, *Les Ouvriers,* pp. 24–6, 100–9.

36 The marchandeurs, against whom most of the complaints in 1848 were directed, had their own grievances against the capitalist contractors and sometimes made common cause against them with the workers. This was true of the Parisian joiners, where the Commission of Joiner Marchandeurs merged with the Fraternal and Democratic Association of Joiner Workers in March 1848 in opposition to the "general contractors" *(entrepreneurs généraux).* Gossez, *Les Ouvriers,* pp. 140–1.

37 Kuczynski, *A Short History of Labour Conditions,* p. 77; Jean Lhomme, *Economie et histoire* (Paris, 1967), pp. 147–67; Jacques Rougerie, "Remarques sur l'histoire des salaires à Paris au XIXe siècle," *Le Mouvement social* 63 (1968):71–108; Sewell, "The Rise of Working-Class Politics in Nineteenth-Century Marseille," pp. 85–8.

8. Workers' corporations

1 Emile Laurent, *Le Pauperisme de les associations de prévoyance: Nouvelles études sur les sociétés de secours mutuels, histoire – économie politique* – administration, 2nd ed., 2 vols. (Paris, 1865), 1:388. In 1819 the requirement of prior authorization was formalized in Article 291 of the Penal Code.

2 Laurent, *Les Associations de prévoyance,* 1:270–3.

3 These generalizations are based primarily on my own research on mutual-aid societies in Marseille. Statutes of many societies, together with registers of members, can be found in the *Archives départementales des Bouches-du-Rhône,* M6/1045–50.

4 For a description of the range of confraternities under the old regime, see Agulhon, *Pénitents et Francs-Maçons,* pp. 21–160.

5 Victor Gelu, *Marseille au XIXe siècle,* ed. Lucien Gaillard and Jorgi Reboul (Paris, 1971), pp. 156–8.

6 In Marseille, the only city where I have examined the question systematically, a majority of all mutual-aid societies in the first half of the nineteenth century had members from diverse occupations. This was also true in Paris in 1850 (Gossez, *Les Ouvriers,* p. 41). In other cities, however, single-trade societies may have been more common.

7 This was true, as will be discussed later in this chapter, of the society formed in Marseille by the tanners.

8 In fact this pattern – a small, tightly organized core acting on behalf of a much larger mass of only intermittently active workers – has been characteristic of French labor history down to the present. Typically, less than half the workers

have maintained formal membership in the labor organizations of their trades – whether these be compagnonnages, mutual-aid societies, or, more recently, *syndicats* or trade unions. Here it is significant that in the late 1860s, when workers were allowed to form trade unions legally, they called them *syndicats* or *chambres syndicales*. *Syndic* under the old regime meant (in the words of *Le Grand Vocabulaire françois*) "officer established to take care of a community, of a corps of which he is a member." A *syndicat* or *chambre syndicale*, then, meant "a body composed of such officers." The use of these terms probably implies that workers in the 1860s conceived of their organizations as bodies that acted *on behalf of* workers in the trade, not as bodies that encompassed the entire work force.

9 Georges Bourgin and Hubert Bourgin, eds., *Les Patrons, les ouvriers et l'état: Le régime de l'industrie en France de 1814 à 1830,* 3 vols. (Paris, 1912–41), 1:285–6.

10 Ibid., p. 286.

11 For a fascinating account of the life of a joiner compagnon on his tour de France in the 1820s, see Perdiguier, *Mémoires d'un compagnon.*

12 The list is reproduced in Agricol Perdiguier, *Le Livre du compagnonnage,* 3rd ed. (Paris, 1857), pp. 258–9.

13 For an excellent discussion of all these tendencies, see Truant, "Compagnonnage," pp. 218–52.

14 Ibid., pp. 31–2.

15 Perdiguier, *Mémoires d'un compagnon,* pp. 237–8.

16 One historian who has recognized this is Maurice Agulhon, "Aperçu sur le mouvement ouvrier à Toulon sous la Monarchie de Juillet," *Provence historique* 7 (1957):147.

17 Bourgin and Bourgin, *Le Régime de l'industrie,* 2:201 and 3:160–171; *Archives départementales des Bouches-du-Rhône,* M6/1049 and M6/1635.

18 The statutes of these societies can be found in the *Archives départementales des Bouches-du-Rhône,* M6/1049 and M6/1635.

19 Jean Vial, *La Coutume chapelière: histoire du mouvement ouvrier dans la chapellerie* (Paris, 1941), pp. 30–4.

20 Ibid., pp. 26, 70.

21 Gossez, *Les Ouvriers,* p. 177.

22 *Associations professionelles ouvrières,* published by the Office du Travail of the French Government, 4 vols. (Paris, 1894–1904), 2:177.

23 *Archives départementales des Bouches-du-Rhône,* M6/1049.

24 *Archives départementales des Bouches-du-Rhône,* M6/1635.

25 The National Assembly's *Enquête sur le travail industriel et agricol* of 1848–9 gives a figure of 650. *Archives nationales,* C947. My analysis of the manuscript census schedules from 1851 yields a similar figure of 630. The census schedules are in the *Archives de la ville de Marseille,* series 2F.

26 *Archives départementales des Bouches-du-Rhône,* XIV M 25/1.

27 Armand Audiganne, *Les Populations ouvrières et les industries de la France,* 2nd ed., 2 vols. (Paris, 1860), 2:270.

28 These figures are based on the occupations of grooms and of grooms' fathers taken from an analysis of the marriage registers of Marseille for 1821–2 and 1846–51. The registers of *actes de marriage* for Marseille are preserved in the *Archives départementales des Bouches-du-Rhône,* series 201E. The research on which these figures are based has been aided by a grant from the National Science Foundation, SOC 72-05249 A01.

29 Vial, *La Coutume chapelière.*
30 Ibid., pp. 40, 74.
31 Ibid., p. 61.
32 Ibid., p. 78.
33 Ibid., p. 61.
34 Ibid., pp. 41–2.
35 Ibid., p. 76.
36 Ibid., pp. 38, 42, 78.
37 Ibid., pp. 36–9.
38 In Bourgin and Bourgin, *Le Régime de l'industrie,* 1:263.
39 Vial, *La Coutume chapelière,* p. 46.
40 Bourgin and Bourgin, *Le Régime de l'industrie,* 1:270.
41 Ibid.
42 Ibid., p. 271.
43 Ibid., pp. 94–5.
44 Ibid., p. 95.
45 Ibid., pp. 99–110.
46 Ibid., pp. 265–6.
47 Ibid., p. 267.
48 Ibid., p. 272.
49 J.-P. Aguet, *Les Grèves sous la Monarchie de Juillet (1830–1847)* (Geneva, 1954), pp. 24–5.
50 These estimates may be found in the *Enquête sur le travail industriel et agricol* of 1848–9. *Archives nationales,* C947.
51 The shoemakers were prominent in the numerous battles between compagnons that took place in Marseille during the Restoration. See Bourgin and Bourgin, *Le Régime de l'industrie,* 1:292–3, 315; 2:95, 245–6; 3:223. On their mutual-aid society, see *Associations professionnelles ouvrières,* 2:56.
52 Octave Festy, *Le Mouvement ouvrier au début de la Monarchie de Juillet (1830–1834)* (Paris, 1908), p. 258.
53 *Archives départementales des Bouches-du-Rhône,* 403 U 53, *Judgment du tribunal correctionnel,* 19 December 1845.
54 *Archives départementales des Bouches-du-Rhône,* M6/1635.
55 Paul Masson, ed., *Les Bouches-du-Rhône: Encyclopédie départementale,* vol. 10, *Le Mouvement social* (Paris and Marseille, 1923), p. 92.
56 *Archives départementales des Bouches-du-Rhône,* XIV M 25/1.
57 Sewell, "The Working Class of Marseille," p. 84.
58 See, e.g., Martin Nadaud, *Mémoires de Léonard, ancien garçon maçon* (Paris, 1912).
59 Eighty percent of Marseille's masons who married in 1821–2 had been born in Marseille, and in spite of an increase of more than 100 percent in the number of masons in the city, this figure had only dropped to 68 percent by 1846–51. By this time, however, a third of the masons were sons of cultivators, mostly from the commune of Marseille. All of these figures are drawn from my analysis of the marriage registers of Marseille.
60 See, e.g., Gossez, *Les Ouvriers,* pp. 169, 176, 194, 213.
61 See, e.g., Aguet's *Les Grèves,* the Bourgin's three-volume *Le Régime de l'industrie,* and the four-volume collection entitled *Associations professionnelles ouvrières,* published by the Office du Travail of the French government.
62 The main exception seems to have been the building trades, where payment by

the day was common. Alain Faure, "Mouvements populaires et mouvement ouvrier à Paris," *Le Mouvement social* 88 (July–September 1974):59.

63 For an example of a tarif, see the ordinance of the mayor of Lyons, dating from 1817, regulating piece rates in the hat-making industry. This tarif, which was discussed briefly earlier in this chapter, specified sixty distinct rates for different types and sizes of hats. Bourgin and Bourgin, *Le Régime de l'industrie*, 1:96–9.

64 Perdiguier, *Mémoires d'un compagnon*, pp. 237–8.

65 Aguet, *Les Grèves*, p. 250.

66 *Mémoires d'un compagnon*, p. 237.

67 See, e.g., Martin, *Les Associations ouvrières*, pp. 149–62.

68 On the strikes of 1833, see Faure, "Mouvements populaires et mouvement ouvrier," pp. 53–71; Aguet, *Les Grèves*, pp. 66–125; and Shorter and Tilly, *Strikes in France*, pp. 107–8.

69 Alain Faure has shown that establishing a uniformity of pay rates in all workshops was one of the major goals of Parisian workers in the strikes of the early 1830s. "Mouvements populaires et mouvement ouvrier," p. 60.

70 *Encyclopédie*, 4:260–1.

71 Gossez, *Les Ouvriers*, p. 72. For a similar distinction see "Pensées d'un ouvrier," in *Les Murailles*, 1:153, where "hommes de peine" are distinguished from "ouvriers majeurs, travaillant comme ouvriers." The former, according to the author, should be guaranteed a minimum wage of three francs a day, the latter a wage of four francs.

72 See the discussion in Chapter 2, and Sewell, "Etat, Corps and Ordre," pp. 52–4.

73 Gossez, *Les Ouvriers*, p. 112. The different collective behavior of these two types of workers has become a commonplace of recent social history, although the difference has usually been attributed to divergent skill levels rather than to a difference in cultural traditions. See note 1, chap. 1.

74 "Les ouvriers menuisiers de la Ville de Paris ayant reconnu la nécessité de se réunir en un seul corps pour s'éclairer et s'instruire sur nos droits . . ." Statutes of a joiners' association formed in March 1848, quoted in Gossez, *Les Ouvriers*, p. 142.

75 "Formons une société de travailleurs pour tous les ouvriers du corp d'état." Declaration of the Société Nationale des Ouvriers Fondeurs Réunis in 1848, quoted in ibid., p. 205.

76 "Il faudrait que chaque corps d'état s'organisât par lui-même," and "que l'Etat encourage les corps d'état à s'organiser en entreprises." From a Manifesto of the delegates of the Corporations who Sat at Luxembourg, and a statement by Viez, a porcelain worker from Limoges, quoted in ibid., pp. 292–3 and 382.

77 "Que chaque corps d'état soit donc une sorte de tribunal disciplinaire vraiment fraternel," from a pamphlet by F. V. Coinze entitled *Question de l'organisation du travail, de la représentation industrielle et de la représentation ouvrière pour le travail*, quoted in ibid., p. 86.

78 Two typical examples are: "Il devait y avoir pour chaque corps de métier une caisse commune" (There should be a common fund for each corps de métier) and "en établissant des chambres syndicales . . . pour chaque corps de métier" (by establishing chambres syndicales . . . for each corps de métier). Both quotations come from ibid., pp. 9, 82.

79 "Aux ouvriers à établir une justice distributive . . . en constituant tout d'abord les corporations en chaque profession." Quoted in ibid., p. 129.

80 "Chaque corporation, bannière en tête, défilera avec ordre . . ." Statement by delegates of the typographers in April 1848, quoted in ibid., p. 257.

9. The July Revolution and the emergence of class consciousness

1 According to David H. Pinkney's figures on the nearly fifteen hundred men who died or were wounded during the insurrection, more than 80 percent were manual workers, and the majority of these worked in skilled trades. "The Crowd in the French Revolution of 1830," *American Historical Review* 70 (October 1964):3–4. Calculations by Edgar Leon Newman confirm this picture. "What the Crowd Wanted in the French Revolution of 1830," in John M. Merriman, ed., *1830 in France* (New York, 1975), pp. 33–4.

2 The best recent history of the July Revolution is David H. Pinkney, *The French Revolution of 1830* (Princeton, 1972). See also Louis Blanc, *Histoire de dix ans, 1830–1840*, 4th ed., 5 vols. (Brussels, 1845). For an excellent sampling of recent work on the revolution, see Merriman, *1830 in France*.

3 Newman, "What the Crowd Wanted," pp. 23–71; Festy, *Le Mouvement ouvrier*, pp. 27–46.

4 Quoted in Festy, *Le Mouvement ouvrier*, p. 61.

5 Ordinance of August 25, 1830, quoted in ibid., p. 44.

6 Newman, "What the Crowd Wanted," p. 20.

7 On the economic crisis of 1830, see Ernest Labrousse, "1848, 1830, 1789: Comment naissent les révolutions?" in *Actes du congrès historique du centenaire de la révolution de 1848* (Paris, 1948). On the timing of workers' agitation and its relation to unemployment, see Faure, "Mouvements populaire et mouvement ouvrier," pp. 52–7.

8 These papers were founded on September 22, September 19, and September 30, respectively. See Festy, *Le Mouvement ouvrier*, p. 65.

9 *L'Artisan*, September 22, 1830. The larger part of the prospectus is reprinted in Faure and Rancière, *La Parole ouvrière*, pp. 214–8.

10 *L'Artisan*, September 22, 1830.

11 Ibid.

12 *L'Artisan*, September 26, 1830.

13 See, e.g., the selections in Faure and Rancière, *La Parole ouvrière*, pp. 48–104, 155–67.

14 *L'Artisan*, September 26, 1830.

15 Ibid., October 14, 1830.

16 Writings on Saint-Simon and Fourier are, of course, endless. For a discerning guide to the literature and a fine discussion of their thought, see Manuel, *The Prophets of Paris*. Convenient English-language selections of their work are Henri de Saint-Simon, *Social Organization, the Science of Man and Other Writings*, ed. and trans. Felix Markham (Oxford, 1952), and Mark Poster, ed., *Harmonian Man, Selected Writings of Charles Fourier*, trans. Susan Hanson (Garden City, N.Y., 1971).

17 Quoted in Festy, *Le Mouvement ouvrier*, p. 85.

18 For an excellent discussion of the changes in Buchez's ideas during this period, see Cuvillier, *Buchez et les origines du socialisme*, pp. 41–2.

19 Ibid., pp. 42–3.

20 Ibid., pp. 43–5.

21 Faure and Rancière, *La Parole ouvrière*, p. 89.

22 Festy, *Le Mouvement ouvrier*, p. 78.

23 Ibid., pp. 263–4.

24 Ibid., pp. 138, 254–6, 294.

25 Ibid., pp. 237, 248, 252–8, 399.
26 Faure, "Mouvements populaires et mouvement ouvrier," pp. 52–8.
27 Shorter and Tilly, *Strikes in France*, p. 360.
28 The story of the insurrection has been told many times. The definitive work is Fernand Rude, *Le Mouvement ouvrier à Lyon de 1827 à 1832* (Paris, 1944; new ed., Paris, 1969). For an excellent brief account in English, see Bezucha, *Lyon Uprising of 1834*, pp. 60–6.
29 Blanc, *Histoire de dix ans*, 3:60.
30 From the *Moniteur universel*, December 22, 1831, quoted in Bezucha, *Lyon Uprising of 1834*, p. 66.
31 Mutualism, which was founded in 1827, was an organization not of journeymen but of the small dependent masters who were the most important part of the labor force of the Lyonnais silk industry, and who, by the early 1830s, identified themselves as *travailleurs,* or workers. For a description of the structure of the silk industry, see Bezucha, *Lyon Uprising of 1834*, pp. 13–47. The journeymen's association, the *Société des Ferrandiniers,* was formed in 1831. It generally cooperated with Mutualism as a sort of junior partner in the common struggle against the great capitalist silk merchants. The masters' society could be characterized as an unusually large and complex – and unauthorized – mutual-aid society, with masonic overtones. At its peak in early 1834, it had some three thousand members. The society was divided into lodges of twenty members, with names like "Perseverance" or "Unyielding," each of which sent representatives to a central governing body. As in most mutual-aid societies, there was a particular concern for funerals of departed brothers. Members who failed to attend burial services were assessed a fine for committing "an act of ingratitude." The society concerned itself with all aspects of the silk industry; it not only attempted to impose a uniform tarif on the merchants but set up an annual competition awarding a ribbon to the brother who made the best suggestion for improving the quality of work in the industry (pp. 101–4). Also see "Reglement du Mutuellisme," reprinted as a document in Blanc, *Histoire de dix ans,* 4:345–52.
32 For a fascinating account of the Lyonnais workers' movement in these years, see Bezucha, *Lyon Uprising of 1834.* On the working-class press, see esp. pp. 61, 112–8.
33 Aguet, *Les Grèves,* pp. 1–125. Official figures for prosecutions for coalition show a considerably less pronounced peak in 1833, although 1833 still stands out as by far the most active year of the entire decade of the 1830s (p. xxii). See also Shorter and Tilly, *Strikes in France,* p. 360.
34 Aguet, *Les Grèves,* pp. 123–5; Festy, *Le Mouvement ouvrier,* p. 237.
35 Festy, *Le Mouvement ouvrier,* p. 269.
36 Alain Faure has analyzed a list of some 685 members, representing between a fifth and two-fifths of the total Parisian membership. It was drawn up in January 1834 and subsequently seized by the police. Three-quarters of the members on this list were workers. Faure, "Mouvements populaires et mouvement ouvrier," pp. 79–81.
37 Ibid., p. 85.
38 Both are reprinted in Faure and Rancière, *La Parole ouvrière,* pp. 74–81, 159–68.
39 Faure, "Mouvements populaires et mouvement ouvrier," pp. 85–7.
40 For an excellent analysis of republicanism in Lyons, see Bezucha, *Lyon Uprising of 1834,* pp. 73–95.
41 In Faure and Rancière, *La Parole ouvrière,* p. 160.

42 See, e.g., Festy, *Le Mouvement ouvrier*, pp. 77, 254.
43 The quote is from a pronouncement by a Parisian shoemakers' association in the fall of 1833, ibid., p. 254.
44 Ibid., pp. 240–8, 256, 258; Faure, "Mouvements populaires et mouvement ouvrier," pp. 87–9.
45 On the tailors' association, see Faure, "Mouvements populaires et mouvement ouvrier," p. 88, and Aguet, *Les Grèves*, pp. 75–87.
46 Quoted in Faure and Rancière, *La Parole ouvrière*, p. 161.
47 Here my interpretation agrees with Faure, "Mouvements populaires et mouvement ouvrier," pp. 88–9.
48 Quoted in Festy, *Le Mouvement ouvrier*, p. 181.
49 Ibid., p. 294.
50 Quoted in Faure and Rancière, *La Parole ouvrière*, pp. 166–7.
51 Ibid., p. 163.
52 From *L'Echo de la fabrique*, quoted in Festy, *Le Mouvement ouvrier*, pp. 181, 294.
53 Reprinted in Blanc, *Histoire de dix ans*, 4:354.
54 The quotation is from "Réflexions d'un ouvrier tailleur" in Faure and Rancière, *La Parole ouvrière*, pp. 74, 81.
55 Quoted in Faure, "Mouvements populaires et mouvement ouvrier," p. 90.
56 The term is from a public letter by the Saint-Simonian typographer Jules Leroux to his fellow typographers, reprinted in Faure and Rancière, *La Parole ouvrière*, p. 92.
57 Ibid., p. 87.
58 Quoted in Bezucha, *Lyon Uprising of 1834*, p. 112.
59 Faure and Rancière, *La Parole ouvrière*, p. 74.
60 Ibid., p. 80.
61 Ibid., p. 96.
62 Quoted in Bezucha, *Lyon Uprising of 1834*, p. 112.
63 From a letter by the typographer Bannet, reprinted in ibid., p. 87.
64 From Grignon, "Réponse au manifeste des maîtres tailleurs," November 7, 1833, reprinted in ibid., p. 87.
65 Quoted in Bezucha, *Lyon Uprising of 1834*, p. 105.
66 Jules Leroux, in Faure and Rancière, *La Parole ouvrière*, p. 94.
67 Bannet, in ibid., p. 87.
68 Prospectus of the Industrial Circle, quoted in Bezucha, *Lyon Uprising of 1834*, p. 105.
69 Jules Leroux in Faure and Rancière, *La Parole ouvrière*, p. 94.
70 Efrahem, "De l'association des ouvriers de tous les corps d'état," reprinted in ibid., p. 160.
71 Quoted in Festy, *Le Mouvement ouvrier*, p. 298.
72 For accounts of these revolts, see Bezucha, *Lyon Uprising of 1834;* Dolléans, *Histoire du mouvement ouvrier*, 1:98–107; and Blanc, *Histoire de dix ans*, 4:172–202.
73 Quoted in Bezucha, *Lyon Uprising of 1834*, p. 143.

10. The paradoxes of labor

1 For a trade whose organization survived this period intact, see Octave Festy, "Dix années de l'histoire des ouvriers tailleurs d'habits (1830–1840)," *Revue d'histoire des doctrines économiques et sociales* 5 (1912):166–99. On strike activity, see Aguet, *Les Grèves*, pp. 125–65.

2 On the rising of 1839, see Dolléans, *Histoire du mouvement ouvrier,* 1:175–9, and Maurice Dommanget, "Blanqui et l'insurrection du 12 mai 1839," *La Critique sociale* (March 1934).

3 Aguet, *Les Grèves,* pp. 166–228.

4 On the working-class press, see Armand Cuvillier, "Les Journaux ouvriers en France avant 1840," in *Hommes et idéologies,* pp. 87–94, and *Un journal d'ouvriers: "L'Atelier,"* 1840–1850 (Paris, 1954).

5 Examples of such works are collected in Faure and Rancière, *La Parole ouvrière.*

6 See Johnson, *Utopian Communism in France.*

7 See the excellent analysis of the Société de l'union in Truant, "Compagnonnage," pp. 299–307, and Agulhon, *Une ville ouvrière,* pp. 131–6.

8 Briquet, *Agricol Perdiguier,* pp. 172–7.

9 In the second edition of *Le Livre du compagnonnage* (Paris, 1841), Perdiguier printed a large number of letters by compagnons, both praising and criticizing his work.

10 Aguet, *Les Grèves,* pp. 300–9.

11 Louis Réné Villermé, *Tableau de l'état physique et moral des ouvriers employés dans les manufactures de coton, de laine et de soie,* 2 vols. (Paris, 1840); Eugène Buret, *De la misère des classes laborieuses en Angleterre et en France avec l'indication des moyens propres à en franchir les sociétés,* 2 vols. (Paris, 1840); Honoré Antoine Frégier, *Des classes dangereuses dans la population des grandes villes et des moyens de les rendre meilleures,* 2 vols. (Paris, 1840). On the work of Villermé and Buret, see Hilde Rigaudias-Weiss, *Les Enquêtes ouvrières en France entre 1830 et 1848* (Paris, 1936; reprinted, New York, 1975), pp. 25–157. A fascinating study of the problem of moral degradation and crime in the period is Louis Chevalier, *Classes laborieuses et classes dangereuses à Paris pendant la première moitié du XIXe siècle* (Paris, 1958), available in English as *Laboring Classes and Dangerous Classes in Paris during the First Half of the Nineteenth Century,* trans. Frank Jellinek (New York, 1973). Chevalier, however, tends to take the writings of the era uncritically as evidence of what working-class life was actually like. For an excellent evaluation of Chevalier's argument, see Robert J. Bezucha's review of the English edition in *Journal of Social History* (Fall 1974), pp. 119–24.

12 Sand, *Le Compagnon du tour de France;* Eugène Sue, *Les Mystères de Paris* (Paris 1842–3) and *Le Juif errant* (Brussells, 1844–5).

13 On the worker-poets, see Edgar Leon Newman, "Sounds in the Desert: The Socialist Worker Poets of the Bourgeois Monarchy, 1830–1848," *Proceedings of the Third Annual Meeting of the Western Society for French History* 3 (1975):269–99.

14 Rigaudias-Weiss, *Les Enquêtes ouvrières,* p. 26.

15 Villermé, *Tableau,* 1:82–3.

16 Ibid., pp. 86–8.

17 Ibid., p. 83.

18 For an admirably detailed study of the workers of Lille, see Pierre Pierrard, *La Vie ouvrière à Lille sous le Second Empire* (Paris, 1965). Although this book concentrates on the 1850s and 1860s, the grim picture of working-class life it presents is surely essentially valid for the 1830s and 1840s as well.

19 My own awareness of the pervasiveness and durability of such conventions stems from a paper by William M. Reddy, "What Jaurès Saw" (Paper presented to the Seminar on Symbolic Anthropology at the Institute for Advanced Study Princeton, N.J., 1976). Reddy shows how various observers on the right and on

the left, ranging from Villermé to Victor Hugo to Engels to Emile Zola to Jean Jaurès, describe the conditions of the poor in remarkably similar terms, terms which imply that poverty reduces humans to the level of beasts. My interest in and interpretation of Villermé has also been influenced by another of Reddy's papers: "Carnival's Other Mask: Reformers' Images of Factory Laborers in Nineteenth-Century France" (Paper presented to the Social Science Seminar at the Institute for Advanced Study, Princeton, N.J., 1975).

20 Villermé, *Tableau,* 1:47, 90.

21 Ibid., 2:67.

22 Ibid., pp. 34ff.

23 Ibid., p. 50.

24 Ibid., p. 49.

25 Ibid., pp. 51–2.

26 Ibid., p. 69.

27 Ibid., pp. 52–67.

28 Flammermont, *Remontrances,* 3:310.

29 Ibid., p. 61.

30 For the parallels between Villermé's conception of a well-ordered factory and contemporary ideas about prisons, see Michel Foucault, *Surveiller et punir: naissance de la prison* (Paris, 1975). An English translation is available under the title *Discipline and Punish: The Birth of the Prison,* trans. Alan Sheridan (New York, 1977). Villermé actually began his career in moral sciences with a study of prisons: Louis Réné Villermé, *Des prisons telles qu'elles sont et telles qu'elles devraient être, ouvrage dans lequel on les considère par rapport à l'hygiène, à la morale et à l'économie politique* (Paris, 1820). See Rigaudias-Weiss, *Les Enquêtes ouvrières,* pp. 26–7.

31 Villermé, *Tableau,* 2:37.

32 Ibid., p. 67.

33 Ibid., p. 68.

34 Ibid., pp. 49–50.

35 Ibid., pp. 301–26.

36 Ibid., 1:130.

37 Ibid., pp. 103–5.

38 Ibid., 2:37.

39 On Louis Blanc, see Loubère, *Louis Blanc.*

40 New French-language editions appeared in Paris in each of these years, in Brussels in 1845 and in London in 1848. An English edition, entitled *The Organization of Labor,* was also published in London in 1848. A later English translation of the first edition is *Organization of Work* by Louis Blanc, trans. by Marie Paula Dickoré, *University of Cincinnati Studies,* series 2, 7 (1911).

41 Dr. Ange Guépin wrote various books on medicine as well as studies of the city of Nantes, including *Nantes au XIXe siècle: statistique topographique, industrielle et morale, faisant suite à l'histoire des progrès de Nantes* (Nantes, 1832).

42 Blanc, *Organisation du travail* (1841 ed.), pp. 19–21.

43 Ibid., p. 22.

44 Ibid., p. 25.

45 Frégier, *Des classes dangereuses.*

46 Blanc, *Organisation du travail,* 4th ed. (Paris, 1845), p. 25.

47 Blanc, *Organisation du travail* (1841 ed.), pp. 9–10.

48 Ibid., p. 12.

49 Ibid., p. 33.
50 Blanc, *Organisation du travail* (1845 ed.), p. 27. Blanc even agreed with Villermé about the nature of these "bad examples." Thus he remarked: "From the moral point of view, can we think of anything more disastrous than this mixing of the sexes in factories? It means to innoculate children with vice." *Organisation du travail* (1841 ed.), p. 31.
51 Ibid., p. 76.
52 Blanc, *Organisation du travail* (1845 ed.), p. xxiv.
53 Ibid., p. xxv.
54 Ibid., p. v.
55 Cuvillier, *Hommes et idéologies,* p. 120.
56 Blanc, *Organisation du travail* (1841 ed.), p. 1.
57 A socialist writer who took precisely the opposite tack from Blanc was Etienne Cabet, whose most famous work was his *Voyage en Icarie,* first published in 1839. In the classical utopian manner, this book described an imaginary land called Icaria in which Cabet's socialist principles had been fully enacted. On Cabet and his followers, see Johnson, *Utopian Communism in France.*
58 The best recent study of the worker-poets is Newman, "Sounds in the Desert."
59 Charles Poncy, *Le Chantier* (Paris, 1846).
60 Charles Poncy, *La Chanson de chaque métier* (Paris, 1850), p. v.
61 Poncy includes a copy of George Sand's letter in the preface to *La Chanson de chaque métier,* pp. vi–ix.
62 Ibid., p. ix.
63 Ibid., pp. xvi–xvii.
64 Ibid., pp. 80–5.
65 Ibid., p. 72.
66 Ibid., pp. 20–5.
67 Ibid., pp. 3–8.
68 Ibid., p. 148.
69 Ibid., p. 75.
70 Ibid., pp. 36–40.
71 See Newman, "Sounds in the Desert," pp. 272–4.
72 Ibid., p. vii.
73 Ibid., pp. 11–16, 20–30, 75–85, 115–20, 174–8, 227–30.
74 Ibid., pp. xi–xii.
75 Ibid., pp. 55–9, 62–9, 80–5, 98–102, 414–6.
76 Ibid., pp. 120–3.
77 Ibid., pp. 127–9.
78 Ibid., pp. 211–4.
79 Ibid., pp. 141–6.
80 Ibid., p. 8.

11. The Revolution of 1848

1 *Les Murailles,* 1:26.
2 See, esp. Agulhon, *1848 ou l'apprentissage de la république* (Paris, 1973), *La République au village,* and *Les Quarante-huitards* (Paris, 1975); Frederick De Luna, *The French Republic under Cavaignac, 1848* (Princeton, N.J., 1969); John M. Merriman, *The Agony of the Republic: The Repression of the Left in Revolutionary France, 1848–1851* (New Haven, 1978); Roger Price, *The French Second Republic: A Social History* (London, 1972); *Revolution and Reaction: 1848 and the*

Second French Republic (London, 1975); 1848 in France (Ithaca, N.Y., 1975); Philippe Vigier, La Seconde République dans la région alpine, 2 vols. (Paris, 1963); and Ted W. Margadant, French Peasants in Revolt: The Insurrection of 1851 (Princeton, N.J., 1979).

3 Sewell, "Structure of the Working Class," esp. pp. 368–91.
4 The best brief account of the February Revolution remains Duveau, 1848.
5 Gossez, Les Ouvriers, pp. 10–4.
6 Les Murailles, 1:36.
7 See Donald C. McKay, The National Workshops (Cambridge, Mass., 1933).
8 See Chap. 10.
9 From the issue of 4/8 June 1848, quoted in Gossez, Les Ouvriers, p. 286.
10 This interpretation of the decree on the right to labor is very close to that of Gossez in ibid., pp. 10–14.
11 Les Murailles, 1:26.
12 Decree of the Provisional Government, February 25, 1848, reprinted in Les Murailles, 1:31.
13 According to Corbon, a printer who was elected to the National Assembly in 1848, the right to labor "was generally given the interpretation . . . that the state owes labor in his profession to every worker who demands it." Quoted in Gossez, Les Ouvriers, p. 57.
14 Faure and Rancière, La Parole ouvrière, p. 299.
15 Quoted in Gossez, Les Ouvriers, p. 286.
16 Reprinted in Faure and Rancière, La Parole ouvrière, pp. 305–6.
17 This was true, for example, of a petition to the Luxembourg Commission drawn up by the cooks and pastry makers reproduced in Les Murailles, 2:410–2.
18 Ibid., 1:357.
19 Ibid., 2:8, 259; 1:462; and Faure and Rancière, La Parole ouvrière, p. 314.
20 On the clubs, see Peter H. Amann, Revolution and Mass Democracy: The Paris Club Movement in 1848 (Princeton, N.J., 1975).
21 Rémi Gossez, "Presse parisiènne à destination des ouvriers (1848–1851)," in Jacques Godechot, ed., La Presse ouvrière, 1819–1850, vol. 23, Bibliothèque de la Révolution de 1848 (La Roche-sur-Yon, 1966), pp. 123–90.
22 Quoted by Truant, "Compagnonnage," p. 37. See also pp. 38–41 and 307–10.
23 See Gossez, Les ouvriers, pp. 36–7.
24 The best account of the journée of March 17 is Amann, Revolution and Mass Democracy, pp. 78–110. For the role of the corporations and their delegates, see Gossez, Les ouvriers, pp. 244–7. See also Louis Blanc, Pages d'histoire de la révolution de février 1848 (Paris, 1850), pp. 89–94.
25 Louis Blanc, La Révolution de février au Luxembourg (Paris, 1849), pp. 37–42.
26 See Figure 2.
27 Le Semeur, March 17, quoted in Gossez, Les Ouvriers, p. 23.
28 Quoted in ibid., p. 225.
29 Les Murailles, 1:286.
30 Blanc, La Révolution de février, pp. 21–2, 38.
31 Ibid., pp. 4–5, 22–4; Gossez, Les Ouvriers, pp. 234–7.
32 Blanc, La Révolution de février, pp. 9–14, 43–59.
33 Leon Trotsky, History of the Russian Revolution, 3 vols., trans. Max Eastman (New York, 1932).
34 Amann, Revolution and Mass Democracy, p. 325.
35 Les Murailles, 1:281.
36 Amann, Revolution and Mass Democracy, pp. 24–31.

37 Faure and Rancière, *La Parole ouvrière*, pp. 159–67.
38 Gossez, *Les Ouvriers*, p. 370.
39 Ibid., p. 156.
40 Ibid., pp. 129, 141, 207.
41 Ibid., p. 209.
42 Ibid., p. 156.
43 See, e.g., ibid., pp. 176, 194, 199, 273–4.
44 Ibid., pp. 169, 176, 194.
45 Ibid., p. 213.
46 Ibid., pp. 61–76.
47 Ibid., pp. 74, 81, 194.
48 Blanc, *La Révolution de février*, pp. 26–37.
49 Sample conventions are reproduced in Louis Blanc, *Pages d'histoire*, pp. 325–52, and *Révélations historiques en réponse au livre de Lord Normanby*, 2 vols. (Brussels, 1859), 2:314–24. See also Gossez, *Les Ouvriers*, pp. 268–74.
50 Electoral statement by the foundry worker Hallier, quoted in Gossez, *Les Ouvriers*, p. 82.
51 F. V. Coinze, *Question de l'organisation du travail, de la représentation industrielle et de la représentation ouvrière pour le travail*, quoted in ibid., p. 86.
52 Blanc, *Révélations*, 2:322–3.
53 *Le Moniteur universel*, March 28, 1848.
54 Quoted in Gossez, *Les Ouvriers*, p. 156.
55 On the tailors, see ibid., pp. 160–6. The quotation is from a workers' delegate to a "mixed corporate assembly" on March 13, 1848, ibid., p. 164.
56 Ibid., pp. 164–6. For other attempts, see pp. 131–3, 146, 149, 185, 312–3.
57 The quotation is from the General Society of the Corporation of Boot- and Shoemakers, ibid., p. 174.
58 Ibid., p. 141.
59 The statutes are reproduced in facsimile in ibid., pp. 208–11.
60 Quoted in ibid., p. 254.
61 Blanc, *Pages d'histoire*, pp. 133–9.
62 Gossez, *Les Ouvriers*, p. 257.
63 Ibid., p. 253.
64 Ibid., pp. 19–20, 37–9, 174, 244–7, 265.
65 For an example of this usage, see the tract entitled *Organisation du travail* by Confais, a house painter, reprinted in Faure and Rancière, *La Parole ouvrière*, p 332.
66 *Les Murailles*, 2:111.
67 Gossez, *Les Ouvriers*, p. 194.
68 On the "federative trade socialism" of the French working class in the years following 1848, see Moss, *French Labor Movement*.
69 Sewell, "Structure of the Working Class," pp. 345–6.
70 Gossez, *Les Ouvriers*, pp. 62, 224.
71 See note 2.
72 See, e.g., *Les Murailles*, 2:276.
73 *Les Murailles*, 1:474; 2:291.
74 Ibid., 1:125.
75 Ibid., 2:26.
76 Alexis de Tocqueville, *Recollections*, trans. George Lawrence, ed. J. P. Mayer and A. P. Kerr (Garden City, N.Y., 1970), p. 95.
77 Ibid., p. 93.

78 Ibid., p. 95.
79 Ibid., p. 94.
80 Ibid., pp. 90–1.
81 Quoted in Gossez, *Les Ouvriers*, p. 247.
82 For accounts of April 16, see Duveau, *1848*, pp. 87–92, and Gossez, *Les Ouvriers*, pp. 260–4.
83 The charges against Blanc soon had to be dropped because of a lack of evidence. On May 15, see Peter Amann, "A *Journée* in the Making: May 15, 1848," *Journal of Modern History* 42 (March 1970):42–69, and *Revolution and Mass Democracy*, pp. 205–47; Duveau, *1848*, pp. 113–25; Gossez, *Les Ouvriers*, pp. 264–6.
84 A facsimile of the manifesto of the Society of United Corporations is reprinted in Gossez, *Les Ouvriers*, pp. 292–3. Several long excerpts from the *Journal des travailleurs* are reprinted in Faure and Rancière, *La Parole ouvrière*, pp. 298–323.
85 On the June Days, see Duveau, *1848*, pp. 132–56; Tilly and Lees, "Le peuple de Juin 1848"; Pierre Caspard, "Aspects de la lutte des classes en 1848: le recrutement de la Garde Nationale mobile," *Revue historique* 511 (July-September 1974):81–106.
86 Quoted in Gossez, *Les Ouvriers*, pp. 155–6. For the statutes of one such association, the Union of Stevedores and Unloaders of the Port of Le Havre, see Faure and Rancière, *La Parole ouvrière*, pp. 427–34.
87 Quoted in Gossez, *Les Ouvriers*, p. 316.
88 Quoted in ibid., p. 355.
89 "Des differentes formes de l'association ouvrière," by the tailor-worker Pierre Wahry, reprinted in Faure and Rancière, *La Parole ouvrière*, p. 441.
90 Gossez, *Les Ouvriers*, pp. 334–51.
91 Ibid., p. 336.
92 Ibid., p. 154.
93 Ibid., p. 370.
94 Ibid., pp. 360, 389.
95 Moss, *French Labor Movement*.

12. Conclusion: the dialectic of revolution

1 Faure and Rancière, *La Parole ouvrière*, p. 91.
2 Gossez, *Les Ouvriers*, p. 203.

Bibliography

Aguet, J. P. *Les Grèves sous la monarchie de juillet (1830–1847): Contribution à l'étude du mouvement ouvrier français.* Geneva, 1954.

Agulhon, Maurice, "Aperçus sur le mouvement ouvrier à Toulon sous la Monarchie de Juillet." *Provence historique* 7 (1957):131–54.

Pénitents et Francs-Maçons de l'ancienne Provence. Paris, 1968.

La République au village. Paris, 1970.

La Vie sociale en Provence intérieure au lendemain de la Révolution. Paris, 1970.

Une ville ouvrière au temps du socialisme utopique: Toulon de 1815 à 1851. Paris and The Hague, 1970.

1848 ou l'apprentissage de la république. Paris, 1973.

Les Quarante-huitards. Paris, 1975.

Amann, Peter, "A *Journée* in the Making: May 15, 1848," *Journal of Modern History* 42 (March 1970):42–69.

Revolution and Mass Democracy: The Paris Club Movement in 1848. Princeton, N.J., 1975.

Anderson, Michael. *Family Structure in Nineteenth-Century Lancashire.* Cambridge, 1971.

Arnaud, André-Jean. *Les Origines doctrinales du Code civil français.* Paris, 1969.

Ashton, T. S. *The Industrial Revolution, 1760–1830.* London, 1928.

Associations professionelles ouvrières. Published by the Office du travail of the French Government. 4 vols. Paris, 1894–1904.

Audiganne, Armand. *Les Populations ouvrières et les industries de la France.* 2nd ed. 2 vols. Paris, 1860.

Aux origines de la révolution industrielle: Industrie rurale et fabriques. Special issue. *Revue du Nord* 61 (January-March 1979).

Baker, Keith Michael. "The Early History of the Term 'Social Science.' " *Annals of Science* 20 (1964):211–26.

Condorcet: From Natural Philosophy to Social Mathematics. Chicago, 1975.

"French Political Thought at the Accession of Louis XVI." *Journal of Modern History* 50 (June 1978):279–303.

Benoist, Luc. *Le Compagnonnage et les métiers.* Paris, 1966.

Bezucha, Robert J. *The Lyon Uprising of 1834: Social and Political Conflict in a Nineteenth-Century City.* Cambridge, Mass., 1974.

Blanc, Louis. *Organisation du travail.* Paris, 1841; 4th ed., Paris, 1845.

Histoire de dix ans, 1830–1840. 4th ed. 5 vols. Brussels, 1845.

Organisation of Labor. London, 1848.

Bibliography

La Révolution de février au Luxembourg. Paris, 1849.

Pages d'histoire de la révolution de février 1848. Paris, 1850.

Révélations historiques en réponse au livre de Lord Normanby. 2 vols. Brussels, 1859.

Organization of Work. Translated by Marie Paula Dickoré. University of Cincinnati Studies, ser. 2. Vol. 7. 1911.

Bloch, Marc. "La Lutte pour l'individualisme agraire dans la France du XVIIIe siècle." *Annales d'histoire économique et sociale* 2 (1930):329–83, 511–56.

Les Caractères originaux de l'histoire rural française. Oslo, 1931.

French Rural History: An Essay on Its Basic Characteristics. Translated by Janet Sondheimer. Foreword by Bryce Lyon. Berkeley and Los Angeles, 1970.

Boileau, Etienne. *Réglemens sur les arts et métiers de Paris régiés au XIIIe siècle, et connus sous le nom de livre des métiers d'Etienne Boileau*. Notes and introduction by G.-B. Depping. Paris, 1837.

Bois, Paul. *Paysans de l'Ouest: Des structures économiques et sociales aux options politiques depuis l'époque révolutionnaire dans la Sarthe*. Le Mans, 1960.

Boon, James A. *The Anthropological Romance of Bali, 1597–1972*. Cambridge, 1977.

Bossy, John. "Blood and Baptism: Kinship, Community and Christianity in Western Europe from the Fourteenth to the Seventeenth Centuries." In *Sanctity and Secularity: The Church and the World*, edited by Derek Baker. *Studies in Church History*, vol. 10. Oxford, 1973.

Les Bouches-du-Rhône: Encyclopédie départmentale. Edited by Paul Masson. *Le Mouvement social*, vol. 10. Paris and Marseille, 1923.

Bouglé, C. *Socialismes français*. Paris, 1932.

Bouloiseau, Marc. *Cahiers de doléances du tiers état du baillage de Rouen pour les Etats Généraux de 1789*. 2 vols. Paris, 1957.

Bourgeois-Pichat, J. "Evolution le la population française depuis le XVIIIe siècle." *Population* 6 (1951):661–2.

Bourgin, Georges, and Bourgin, Hubert, eds. *Les Patrons, les ouvriers et l'état. Le Régime de l'industrie en France de 1814 à 1830*. 3 vols. Paris, 1912–41.

Bourgin, Hubert. *Fourier*. Paris, 1905.

Braesch, F. "Essai de statistique de la population ouvrière de Paris vers 1791." *La Révolution française* 63 (1912–13):289–321.

Briquet, Jean. *Agricol Perdiguier, compagnon du tour de France et représentant du peuple, 1805–1875*. Paris, 1955.

Buchez, P.-J.-B., and Roux, P.-C. *Histoire parlementaire de la Révolution française*. 40 vols. Paris, 1834–8.

Buret, Eugène. *De la misère des classes laborieuses en Angleterre et en France avec l'indication des moyens propres à en franchir les sociétés*. 2 vols. Paris, 1840.

Cabet, Etienne. *Voyage en Icarie*. Paris, 1839.

Cameron, R. E. "Profit, croissance et stagnation en France au XIXe siècle." *Economie appliquée* 10 (1957):409–44.

"Economic Growth and Stagnation in Modern France, 1815–1914." *Journal of Modern History* 20 (1958):1–13.

Caspard, Pierre. "Aspects de la lutte des classes en 1848: le recrutement de la Garde Nationale mobile." *Revue historique* 511 (July-September 1974):81–106.

Castan, Yves. *Honnêté et relations sociales en Languedoc (1715–80)*. Paris, 1974.

Chambers, J. D. "Enclosure and Labour Supply in the Industrial Revolution." *Economic History Review*, 2nd ser. 5 (1953):319–43.

Charléty, Sébastien. *Histoire du Saint-Simonisme*. Paris, 1931.

Chartier, Roger. "La 'Monarchie d'argot' entre le mythe et l'histoire." In *Les Margi-*

Bibliography

naux et les exclus dans l'histoire, edited by Bernard Vincent. *Cahiers Jussieu,* no. 5, Université Paris 7 (Paris, 1979).

Chauvet, Paul. *Les Ouvriers du livre en France de 1789 à la constitution de la Fédération du livre.* Paris, 1964.

Chevalier, Louis. *Classes laborieuses et classes dangereuses à Paris pendant la première moitié du XIXe siècle.* Paris, 1958.

Laboring Classes and Dangerous Classes in Paris during the First Half of the Nineteenth Century. Translated by Frank Jellinek. New York, 1973.

Christian, William A., Jr. *Person and God in a Spanish Valley.* New York, 1972.

Clapham, J. H. *The Economic Development of France and Germany, 1815–1914.* 4th ed. Cambridge, 1936.

Clicquot de Blervache, Simon. *Mémoire sur les corps de métiers.* The Hague, 1758.

Clough, S. B. "Retardative Factors in French Economic Development in the Nineteenth and Twentieth Centuries." *Journal of Economic History* 6 (1946): Supplement, 91–210.

"Retardative Factors in French Economic Growth at the End of the Ancien Régime and during the French Revolutionary and Napoleonic Periods." In *Studies in Economics and Economic History: Essays in Honor of Harold F. Williamson,* edited by M. Kooy. Durham, N.C., 1972.

Cobb, Richard. *Les Armées révolutionnaires: Instrument de la Terreur dans les départements.* 2 vols. Paris, 1961–3.

Cole, G. D. H. *A History of Socialist Thought.* Vol. I. *The Forerunners, 1789–1850.* London, 1955.

Cole, John W., and Wolf, Eric R. *The Hidden Frontier: Ecology and Ethnicity in an Alpine Valley.* New York, 1974.

Coonaert, Emile. *Les Corporations en France avant 1789.* Paris, 1941.

Les Compagnonnages en France du moyen age à nos jours. Paris, 1966.

Cuvillier, Armand. *P.-J.-B. Buchez et les origines du socialisme chrétien.* Paris, 1948.

Un journal d'ouvriers: "L'Atelier, 1840–1850." Paris, 1954.

Hommes et idéologies de 1840. Paris, 1956.

Dakin, Douglas. *Turgot and the Ancien Régime in France.* London, 1939.

Davis, Natalie Zemon. "Les Femmes dans les arts méchaniques à Lyon au XVIe siècle." In *Mélanges en hommage de Richard Gascon,* edited by Jean-Pierre Gutton. Lyons, 1979.

"Strikes and Salvation at Lyon." *Archiv für Reformationsgeschichte* 56 (1965):48–64.

"A Trade Union in Sixteenth-Century France." *Economic History Review,* 2nd ser., 19 (April 1966):48–69.

"The Reasons of Misrule: Youth Groups and Charivaris in Sixteenth-Century France." *Past and Present* 50 (February 1971):41–75.

Society and Culture in Early Modern France. Stanford, 1975.

Dawley, Alan. *Class and Community: The Industrial Revolution in Lynn.* Cambridge, Mass., 1976.

Deane, Phyllis, and Cole, W. A. *British Economic Growth, 1688–1959.* London, 1964.

De Luna, Fredrick. *The French Republic under Cavaignac, 1848.* Princeton, N.J., 1969.

Delvau, Alfred, ed. *Les Murailles revolutionnaire de 1848.* 17th ed. 2 vol. Paris, 1868.

Deyon, Pierre. *Amiens, capitale provinciale. Etude sur la société urbaine au XVIIe siècle.* Paris, The Hague, 1967.

Le Dictionnaire de l'Académie françoise. 2 vols. Paris, 1694.

Bibliography

Dolléans, Edouard. *Histoire du mouvement ouvrier.* 3 vols. Paris, 1936–53.
Proudhon. Paris, 1941.
Dolléans, Edouard, and Dehove, Gérard. *Histoire du travail en France: mouvement ouvrier et législation sociale.* 2 vols. Paris, 1953–5.
Dommanget, Maurice. *Babeuf et la conjuration des Egaux.* Paris, 1922.
Victor Considérant, sa vie et son oeuvre. Paris, 1929.
"Blanqui et l'insurrection du 12 mai 1839," *La critique sociale* (March 1934).
Les Idées politiques et sociales d'Auguste Blanqui. New York, 1957.
Duveau, Georges. *1848.* Paris, 1965.
1848: The Making of a Revolution. New York, 1967.
Egret, Jean. *La Pré-révolution française, 1787–1788.* Paris, 1962.
Encylopédie, ou dictionnaire raisonné des sciences, des arts et des métiers. 17 vols. Paris, 1751–65.
Faure, Alain. "Mouvements populaires et mouvement ouvrier à Paris." *Le Mouvement Social* 88 (July-September 1974):51–92.
Faure, Alain, and Rancière, Jacques. *La Parole ouvrière, 1830–1851.* Paris, 1976.
Faure, Edgar. *La Disgrâce de Turgot.* Paris, 1961.
Feierman, Steven. *The Shambaa Kingdom: A History.* Madison, Wis., 1974.
Festy, Octave. *Le Mouvement ouvrier au début de la Monarchie de Juillet (1830–1834).* Paris, 1908.
"Dix années de l'histoire des ouvriers tailleurs d'habits (1830–1840)." *Revue d'histoire des doctrines économiques et sociales* 5 (1912):166–99.
Flammermont, Jules, ed. *Remontrances du Parlement de Paris au XVIIIe siècle.* 3 vols. Paris, 1888–98.
Foster, John. *Class Struggle and the Industrial Revolution: Early Industrial Capitalism in Three English Towns.* New York, 1975.
Foucault, Michel. *Surveiller et punir: naissance de la prison.* Paris, 1975.
Discipline and Punish: The Birth of the Prison. Translated by Alan Sheridan. New York, 1977.
"What Is an Author?" In *Language, Counter-Memory, Practice: Selected Essays and Interviews.* Translated by Donald F. Bouchard and Sherry Simon. Ithaca, N.Y., 1977.
Fournier, Joseph. *Cahiers de doléances de la sénéchaussée de Marseille pour les Etats Généraux.* Marseille, 1908.
Fox-Genovese, Elizabeth. *The Origins of Physiocracy: Economic Revolution and Social Order in Eighteenth-century France.* Ithaca, N.Y., 1976.
Fox-Genovese, Elizabeth, and Genovese, Eugene D. "The Political Crisis of Social History: A Marxian Perspective." *Journal of Social History* 10 (Winter 1976):205–20.
Franklin, Alfred. *Dictionnaire historique des arts, métiers et professions exercés dans Paris depuis le treizième siècle.* Paris, 1906.
Frégier, Honoré Antoine. *Des classes dangereuses dans la population des grandes villes et des moyens de les rendre meilleures.* 2 vols. Paris, 1840.
Furet, François, and Richet, Dennis. *La Révolution française.* 2 vols. Paris, 1965.
Furetière, Antoine. *Dictionnaire universel.* 2 vols. The Hague, 1691.
Gandilhon, Alfred, ed. *Cahiers de doléances du bailliage de Bourges et des baillages secondaires de Vierzon et d'Henrichemont pour les Etats Généraux de 1789.* Bourges, 1910.
Geertz, Clifford. *The Social History of an Indonesian Town.* Cambridge, Mass., 1965.
The Interpretation of Cultures. New York, 1973.

Bibliography

"On the Nature of Anthropological Understanding." *American Scientist* 63 (January-February 1975):47–53.

Gelu, Victor. *Marseille au XIXe siècle.* Edited by Lucien Gaillard and Jorgi Reboul. Paris, 1971.

Giesey, Ralph E. "Rules of Inheritance and Strategies of Mobility in Prerevolutionary France." *American Historical Review* 82 (April 1977):271–89.

Gluckman, Max. *Rituals of Rebellion in South-east Africa.* Manchester, 1954.

Godechot, Jacques. *Les Institutions de la France sous la Révolution et l'Empire.* Paris, 1951.

ed. *Les Constitutions de la France depuis 1789.* Paris, 1970.

Gossez, Rémi. "Presse parisiènne à destination des ouvriers (1948–1851)." In *La Presse ouvrière, 1819–1850,* edited by Jacques Godechot, pp. 123–90. *Bibliothèque de la Révolution de 1848,* vol. 23. La Roche-sur-Yon, 1966.

Les Ouvriers de Paris. Book One. *L'Organisation, 1848–1851. Bibliothèque de la Révolution de 1848,* vol. 24. La Roche-sur-Yon, 1967.

Goubert, Pierre. *Beauvais et le Beauvaisis de 1600 à 1730, contribution à l'histoire sociale de la France du XVIIe siècle.* Paris, 1960.

Louis XIV et vingt millions de français. Paris, 1966.

Louis XIV and Twenty Million Frenchmen. Translated by Anne Carter. New York, 1970.

The Ancien Régime, French Society, 1600–1750. Translated by Steve Cox. New York, London, 1973.

Le Grand Vocabulaire françois. 2nd ed. 30 vols. Paris, 1762–74.

Gudeman, Stephen. *The Demise of a Rural Economy: From Subsistence to Capitalism in a Latin American Village.* London, 1978.

Guépin, Ange. *Nantes au XIXe siècle: statistique topographique, industrielle et morale, faisant suite à l'histoire des progrès de Nantes.* Nantes. 1832.

Gutman, Herbert. *Work, Culture and Society in Industrializing America.* New York, 1976.

Hamerow, Theodore S. *Restoration, Revolution, Reaction: Economics and Politics in Germany 1815–1871.* Princeton, N.J., 1958.

Hammond, J. L., and Hammond, Barbara. *The Rise of Modern Industry.* London, 1925.

Hauser, Henri. *Ouvriers du temps passé (XVe-XVIe siècles).* Paris, 1899.

Les Compagnonnages d'arts et métiers à Dijon aux XVIIe et XVIIIe siècles. Paris, 1907.

Hill, Christopher. *The World Turned Upside Down: Radical Ideas During The English Revolution.* New York, 1972.

Inden, Ronald B. *Marriage and Rank in Bengali Culture: A History of Caste and Clan in Middle Period Bengal.* Berkeley, Calif., 1976.

"Cultural-Symbolic Constitutions in Ancient India." Paper presented to the Social Science Seminar at the Institute for Advanced Study, Princeton, N.J., 1978.

Isambert, F.-A., Jourdan, A.-J.-L., and Decrusy, eds. *Recueil général des anciennes lois françaises depuis l'an 420 jusqu'à la Révolution de 1789.* 29 vols. Paris, 1822–33.

Jaffé, Grace M. *Le Mouvement ouvrier à Paris pendant la Révolution française (1789–1791).* Paris, 1924.

Johnson, Christopher H. "Communism and the Working Class before Marx: The Icarian Experience." *American Historical Review* 76 (June 1971):642–89.

Utopian Communism in France: Cabet and the Icarians, 1839–1851. Ithaca, N.Y., 1974.

Bibliography

Jones, Gareth Stedman. *Outcast London: A Study in the Relationship Between Classes in Victorian Society.* Oxford, 1971.

Kaplan, Steven. *Bread, Politics and Political Economy in the Reign of Louis XV.* 2 vols. The Hague, 1976.

"Réflexions sur la police du monde du travail, 1700–1815." *Revue historique* 261 (January-March 1979):17–77.

Katz, Michael B. *The People of Hamilton, Canada West: Family and Class in a Mid-Nineteenth-Century City.* Cambridge, Mass., 1975.

Kemp, Tom. "Structural Factors in the Retardation of French Economic Growth." *Kyklos* 15 (1962):325–50.

Kindleberger, C. P. *The Economic Growth of France and Britain, 1851–1950.* Cambridge, Mass., 1964.

Kuczynski, Jürgen. *A Short History of Labour Conditions in France, 1700 to the Present Day.* London, 1946.

Labal, Paul. "Notes sur les compagnons migrateurs et les sociétés de compagnons à Dijon à la fin du XVe au début du XVIe siècles." *Annales de Bourgogne* 22 (1950).

Labrousse, Ernest. *Esquisse du mouvement des prix et des revenus en France au XVIIIe siècle.* 2 vols. Paris, 1932.

La Crise de l'économie française à la fin de l'Ancien Régime et au début de la Révolution. Paris, 1944.

"1848, 1830, 1789: Comment naissent les révolutions?" *Actes du congrès historique du centenaire de la Révolution de 1848.* Paris, 1948.

Labrousse, Ernest; Léon, Pierre; Goubert, Pierre; Bouvier, Jean; Carrière, Charles; and Harsin, Paul. *Histoire économique et sociale de la France.* Vol. 2. *Des derniers temps de l'âge seigneurial aux préludes de l'âge industriel (1660–1789).* Paris, 1970.

Landes, David S. "French Entrepreneurship and Industrial Growth in the Nineteenth Century." *Journal of Economic History* 9 (1949):45–61.

"French Business and the Businessman: A Social and Cultural Analysis," In *Modern France: Problems of the Third and Fourth Republics,* edited by E. M. Earle. Princeton, N.J., 1951.

"New Model Entrepreneurship in France and Problems of Historical Explanation." *Explorations in Entrepreneurial History* 1 (1963):56–75.

The Unbound Prometheus: Technological Change and Industrial Development in Western Europe from 1750 to the Present. London, 1969.

Laurent, Emile. *Le Pauperisme de les associations de prévoyance: Nouvelles études sur les sociétés de secours mutuels, histoire – économie politique – administration,* 2nd ed. 2 vols. Paris, 1865.

Leet, Don R., and Shaw, John A. "French Economic Stagnation, 1700–1960: Old Economic History Revisited." *Journal of Interdisciplinary History* 8 (Winter 1978):530–44.

Lefebvre, Georges. *La Grande Peur de 1789.* Paris, 1932.

1789. Paris, 1939.

The Coming of the French Revolution. Translated by R. R. Palmer. Princeton, N.J., 1947.

Questions agraires au temps de la Terreur. 2nd ed. La Roche-sur-Yon, 1954.

Etudes sur la Révolution française. 2nd ed. Paris, 1963.

The French Revolution. 2 vols. New York, 1964–5.

The Great Fear of 1789: Rural Panic in Revolutionary France. New York, 1973.

Lefranc, Georges, *Histoire du mouvement ouvrier en France des origines à nos jours.* Paris, 1947.

Bibliography

Lequin, Yves. *Les Ouvriers de la région lyonnaise (1848–1914)*. 2 vols. Lyon, 1977.

Le Roi Ladurie, Emmanuel. *Les Paysans de Languedoc*. Paris, 1966.

Montaillou: Village occitan de 1294 à 1324. Paris, 1975.

Levasseur, E. *Histoire des classes ouvrières en France depuis la conquête de Jules César jusqu'à la Révolution*. 2 vols. Paris, 1859.

Histoire des classes ouvrières et de l'industrie en France avant 1789. 2 vols. Paris, 1900.

Levine, David. *Family Formation in an Age of Nascent Capitalism*. New York, 1977.

Levy-Leboyer, M. "La Croissance économique en France au XIXe siècle: Résultats préliminaries." *Annales: économies, sociétés, civilisations* 23 (1968):788–807.

"Le Processus d'industrialisation: le cas de l'Angleterre et de la France." *Revue historique* 239 (1968):281–98.

Lhomme, Jean. *Economie et histoire*. Paris, 1967.

Lichtheim, George. *The Origins of Socialism*. New York, 1969.

Locke, John. *Two Treatises of Government*. With a supplement, *Patriarcha*, by Robert Filmer. Edited by Thomas I. Cook. New York, 1947.

Two Treatises of Government. 2nd ed. Edited by Peter Laslett. Cambridge, 1967.

Loubère, Leo A. *Louis Blanc: His Life and His Contribution to the Rise of French Jacobin Socialism*. Evanston, Ill., 1961.

Louis, Paul. *Histoire du mouvement syndical en France*. 2 vols. Paris, 1947.

Loyseau, Charles. *Traité des ordres et simples dignitez*. In *Les Oeuvres*. Paris, 1666.

Lucas, Colin. "Nobles, Bourgeois and the Origins of the French Revolution." *Past and Present* 60 (August 1973):84–126.

Mantoux, Paul. *La Révolution industrielle au XVIIIe siècle: Essai sur les commencements de la grande industrie moderne en Angleterre*. Paris, 1906.

The Industrial Revolution in the Eighteenth Century: An Outline of the Beginnings of the Modern Factory System. London, 1928; rev. ed. 1961.

Manuel, Frank E. *The New Moral World of Henri de Saint-Simon*. Cambridge, Mass., 1956.

The Prophets of Paris: Turgot, Condorcet, Saint-Simon, Fourier and Compte. Cambridge, Mass., 1962.

Marczewski, J. "The Take-off and French Experience." In *The Economics of Take-off into Sustained Growth*, edited by W. W. Rostow. New York, 1963.

"Le Produit physique de l'économie française de 1789 à 1913 (Comparison avec la Grande Bretagne)." *Cahiers de l'Institut de Science Economique Appliquée*, series AF, 4 (1965).

Markov, Walter, and Soboul, Albert, eds. *Die Sansculotten von Paris, Dokumente zur Geschichte der Volksbewegung, 1793–1794*. Berlin, 1957.

Markovitch, T. J. "L'Industrie française de 1789 à 1964." *Cahiers de l'Institut de Science Economique Appliquée*, series AF, 4, 6 and 7 (1965–6).

"Le Revenu industriel et artisanal sous la Monarchie de Juillet et le Second Empire." *Cahiers de l'Institut de Science Economique Appliquée*, series AF, 4 (1967):87.

Martin, Germain. *Les Associations ouvrières au XVIIIe siècle (1700–1792)*. Paris, 1900.

Martin Saint-Léon, Etienne. *Le Compagnonnage*. Paris, 1901.

Histoire des corporations de métiers, depuis leurs origines jusqu'à leur suppression en 1791. Paris, 1909.

Marx, Karl. *The Class Struggles in France (1848–1850)*. New York, n.d.

Masson, Paul, ed. *Les Bouches-du-Rhône: Encyclopédie départmentale. Le Mouvement social*, vol. 10. Paris and Marseille, 1923.

Bibliography

Mathiez, Albert. *La Révolution française*. Paris, 1922.

The French Revolution. Translated by Catherine Allison Phillips. New York, 1964.

Mavidal, M. J., and Laurent, M. E., eds. *Archives parlementaires de 1787 à 1860*. First Series (1787–9). 82 vols. Paris, 1879–1913.

McKay, Donald C. *The National Workshops*. Cambridge, Mass., 1933.

Mendels, Franklin F. "Proto-industrialization: The First Phase of the Process of Industrialization." *Journal of Economic History* 32 (1972):241–61.

Merriman, John M. *The Agony of the Republic: The Repression of the Left in Revolutionary France, 1848–1851*. New Haven, 1978.

ed. *1830 in France*. New York, 1975.

Mitchell, B. R. *European Historical Statistics, 1750–1970*. New York, 1975.

Mitchell, B. R., and Deane, Phyllis. *Abstract of British Historical Statistics*. London, 1962.

Moss, Bernard H. *The Origins of the French Labor Movement: The Socialism of Skilled Workers, 1830–1914*. Berkeley and Los Angeles, 1976.

Mousnier, Roland. *La Vénalité des offices sous Henri IV et Louis XIII*. 2nd ed. Paris, 1971.

"Les Concepts d'ordres, d'états, de fidelité et de monarchie absolue en France de la fin du XVe siècle à la fin du XVIIIe siècle." *Revue historique* 502 (April-June 1972):289–312.

Nadaud, Martin. *Mémoires de Léonard, ancien garçon maçon*. Paris, 1912.

Newman, Edgar Leon. "Sounds in the Desert: The Socialist Worker Poets of the Bourgeois Monarchy, 1830–1848." *Proceedings of the Third Annual Meeting of the Western Society for French History* 3 (1975):269–99.

"What the Crowd Wanted in the French Revolution of 1830." In *1830 in France*, edited by John M. Merriman. New York, 1975.

Nguyen, Victor. "Les Portefaix marseillais. Crise et déclin, survivance." *Provence historique* 12 (1962):363–97.

O'Brien, Patrick, and Keydar, Caglar. *Economic Growth in Britain and France 1780–1914: Two Paths to the Twentieth Century*. London, 1978.

Olivier Martin, François. *L'Organisation corporative de la France d'ancien régime*. Paris, 1938.

Ouin-Lacroix, Ch. *Histoire des anciennes corporations d'arts et métiers et des confréries religieuses de la capitale de la Normandie*. Rouen, 1850.

Ozouf, Mona. *La Fête révolutionnaire, 1789–1799*. Paris, 1976.

Paultre, Christian. *De la répression de la mendicité et du vagabondage en France sous l'ancien régime*. Paris, 1906; reprint ed. Geneva, 1975.

Perdiguier, Agricol. *Le Livre du compagnonnage*. Paris, 1839.

Memoires d'un compagnon. Geneva, 1854–55; reissued, Paris, 1964.

Correspondance inédite avec George Sand et ses amis, Lettres choisies et commentées avec une introduction par Jean Briquet. Paris, 1966.

Perrot, Jean-Claude. *Genèse d'une ville moderne: Caen au XVIIIe siècle*. 2 vols. Paris, 1975.

Perrot, Michelle. *Les Ouvriers en grève: France, 1871–1890*. 2 vols. Paris, 1974.

Perroux, François. "Prise de vues sur la croissance de l'économie française, 1780–1950." In *Income and Wealth*, series 5, edited by Simon Kuznets. London, 1955.

Peuch, J. L. *La Vie et l'oeuvre de Flora Tristan*. Paris, 1925.

Pierrard, Pierre. *La Vie Ouvrière à Lille sous le Second Empire*. Paris, 1965.

Pinkney, David. "The Crowd in the French Revolution of 1830." *American Historical Review* 70 (October 1964):1–17.

The French Revolution of 1830. Princeton, 1972.

Bibliography

Poncy, Charles. *Le Chantier.* Paris, 1846.

La Chanson de chaque métier. Paris, 1850.

Poster, Mark, ed. *Harmonian Man, Selected Writings of Charles Fourier.* Translated by Susan Hanson. Garden City, N.Y., 1971.

Pouthas, Charles. *La Population française pendant la première moitié du XIXe siècle.* Paris, 1965.

Price, Roger. *The French Second Republic: A Social History.* London, 1972. *1848 in France.* Ithaca, N.Y., 1975.

Revolution and Reaction: 1848 and the Second French Republic. London, 1975.

Proust, Jacques. *Diderot et l'Encyclopédie.* Paris, 1963.

L'Encyclopédie. Paris, 1965.

Reddy, William M. "Carnival's Other Mask: Reformers' Images of Factory Laborers in Nineteenth-Century France." Paper presented to the Social Science Seminar at the Institute for Advanced Study, Princeton, N.J., 1975.

"Family and Factory: French Linen Weavers in the Belle Epoque." *The Journal of Social History* 8 (Winter 1975):102–12.

"What Jaurès Saw." Paper presented to the Seminar on Symbolic Anthropology at the Institute for Advanced Study, Princeton, N.J., 1976.

"The Textile Trade and the Language of the Crowd at Rouen, 1752–1871." *Past and Present* 74 (February 1977):62–89.

"Skeins, Scales, Discounts, Steam and Other Objects of Crowd Justice in Early French Textile Mills." *Comparative Studies in Society and History* 21 (April 1979):204–13.

Reinhard, Marcel. "La Population des villes: sa mesure sous la Révolution et l'Empire." *Population* 9 (1954):279–88.

Rigaudias-Weiss, Hilde. *Les Enquêtes ouvrières en France entre 1830 et 1848.* Paris, 1936; reprinted New York, 1975.

Roehl, Richard. "French Industrialization: A Reconsideration." *Explorations in Economic History* 13 (1976):233–81.

Rosaldo, Renato I., Jr. *Ilongot Headhunting, 1883–1974: A Study in History and Society.* Stanford, Calif., 1980.

Rougerie, Jacques. "Composition d'une population insurgée: l'exemple de la Commune." *Le Mouvement social* 48 (July-September 1964):31–48.

Procès des Communards. Paris, 1964.

"Remarques sur l'histoire des salaires à Paris au XIXe siècle." *Le Mouvement social* 63 (1968):71–108.

Rude, Fernand. *Le Mouvement ouvrier à Lyon de 1827 à 1832.* Paris, 1944; new ed., Paris, 1969.

Rudé, George. "La Taxation populaire de mai 1775 à Paris et dans la région parisienne." *Annales historiques de la Révolution française* 143 (April-June 1956):139–79.

The Crowd in the French Revolution. London, 1959.

The Crowd in History: A Study of Popular Disturbances in France and England, 1730–1848. New York, 1964.

"La Taxation populaire de mai 1775 en Picardie, en Normandie et dans le Beauvaisis." *Annales historiques de la Révolution française* 165 (July-September 1961):305–26.

Sagnac, Ph. *La Législation civile de la Révolution française (1789–1804).* Paris, 1898.

Sagnac, Ph., and Caron, P. *Les Comités des droits féodaux et de législation et l'abolition du régime seigneurial (1789–1793).* Paris, 1907.

Sahlins, Marshall. *Culture and Practical Reason.* Chicago, 1978.

Bibliography

Saint-Simon, Henri de. *Social Organization, the Science of Man and Other Writings.* Edited and translated by Felix Markham. Oxford, 1952.

Salmon, J. M. H. "Venality of Office and Popular Sedition in Seventeenth-Century France: A Review of a Controversy." *Past and Present* 37 (July 1967):21–43.

Sand, George. *Le Compagnon du tour de France.* Paris, 1841.

Schneider, David M. *American Kinship: A Cultural Account.* Englewood Cliffs, N.J., 1968.

Schneider, Jane, and Schneider, Peter. *Culture and Political Economy in Western Sicily.* New York, 1976.

Scott, Joan Wallach. *The Glassworkers of Carmaux: French Craftsmen and Political Action in a Nineteenth-Century City.* Cambridge, Mass., 1974.

Sewell, William H., Jr. "La Classe ouvrière de Marseille sous la Seconde République: structure sociale et comportement politique." *Le Mouvement social* 76 (July-September 1971):27–65.

"The Structure of the Working Class of Marseille in the Middle of the Nineteenth Century." Ph.D. dissertation, University of California, Berkeley, 1971.

"Etat, Corps, and Ordre: Some Notes on the Social Vocabulary of the French Old Regime." In *Sozialgeschichte Heute, Festchrift für Hans Rosenberg zum 70. Geburtstag,* edited by Hans-Ulrich Wehler. Göttingen, 1974.

"Social Change and the Rise of Working-Class Politics in Nineteenth-Century Marseille." *Past and Present* 65 (November 1974):75–109.

"The Working Class of Marseille under the Second Republic: Social Structure and Political Behavior." In *Workers in the Industrial Revolution,* edited by Peter N. Stearns and Daniel J. Walkowitz, pp. 75–116. New Brunswick, N.J., 1974.

Shorter, Edward, and Tilly, Charles. *Strikes in France, 1830–1968.* Cambridge, 1974.

Sieyès, Emmanuel Joseph. *What Is the Third Estate?* Translated by M. Blondel. Edited with notes by S. E. Finer. Introduction by Peter Campbell. London, 1963.

Qu'est-ce que le Tiers Etat? Introduction and notes by Roberto Zapperi. Geneva, 1970.

Soboul, Albert. "Probèmes du travail en l'an II." *Annales historiques de la Révolution française* 28 (July-September 1956):236–54.

Les Sans-culottes parisiens en l'an II: Mouvement populaire et gouvernement révolutionnnaire, 2 juin 1793 – 9 thermidor an II. Paris, 1958.

Précis d'histoire de la Révolution française. Paris, 1963.

The Parisian Sans-Culottes and the French Revolution, 1793–4. London, 1964.

Spitzer, Alan B. *The Revolutionary Theories of Louis Auguste Blanqui.* New York, 1957.

Stadelmann, R. "Soziale Ursachen der Revolution von 1848." In *Moderne deutsche Sozialgeschichte,* edited by H. U. Wehler. Berlin, 1970.

Stearns, Peter N. "Patterns of Industrial Strike Activity in France during the July Monarchy." *American Historical Review* 70 (January 1965):371–94.

Sue, Eugène. *Le Juif errant.* Brussells, 1844–5.

Les Mystères de Paris. Paris, 1842–3.

Sydenham, M. J. *The French Revolution.* New York, 1965.

Thernstrom, Stephan. *Poverty and Progress: Social Mobility in a Nineteenth-Century City.* Cambridge, Mass., 1964.

The Other Bostonians: Poverty and Progress in the American Metropolis, 1880–1970. Cambridge, Mass., 1973.

Thomas, Keith. *Religion and the Decline of Magic.* New York, 1971.

Bibliography

Thompson, E. P. *The Making of the English Working Class.* London, 1963.
"Eighteenth-Century English Society: Class Struggle Without Class?" *Social History* 3 (May 1978):133–65.
Tilly, Charles. *The Vendée.* Cambridge, Mass., 1964.
Tilly, Charles, and Lees, Lynn. "Le peuple de juin 1848." *Annales: économies, sociétés, civilisations* 29 (September-October 1974):1061–91.
Tilly, Louise A., and Scott, Joan W. *Women, Work and the Family.* New York, 1978.
Tocqueville, Alexis de. *Recollections.* Translated by George Lawrence. Edited by J. P. Mayer and A. P. Kerr. Garden City, N.Y., 1970.
Toutain, J. C. "Le Produit de l'agriculture française de 1700 à 1958." *Cahiers de l'Institut de Science Economique Appliquée,* series AF, 2 (1961).
"La Population de la France de 1700 à 1959." *Cahiers de l'Institut de Science Economique Appliqée,* series AF, 3 (1963).
Trempé, Rolande. *Les Mineurs de Carmaux, 1848–1914.* 2 vols. Paris, 1971.
Trotsky, Leon. *History of the Russian Revolution.* 3 vols. Translated by Max Eastman. New York, 1932.
Truant, Cynthia. "Compagnonnage: Symbolic Action and the Defense of Workers' Rights in France, 1700–1848." Ph.D. dissertation, University of Chicago, 1978.
"Solidarity and Symbolism among Journeymen Artisans: The Case of Compagnonnage." *Comparative Studies in Society and History* 21 (April 1979):214–26.
Turgot, Ann-Robert-Jacques, baron de l'Aulne. *Oeuvres de Turgot et documents le concernant.* 5 vols. Edited by Gustave Schelle. Paris, 1913–23.
Turner, Victor W. *The Forest of Symbols: Aspects of Ndembu Ritual.* Ithaca, N.Y., 1967.
Vial, Jean. *La Coutume chapelière: histoire du mouvement ouvrier dans la chapellerie.* Paris, 1941.
Vigier, Philippe. *La Seconde République dans la région alpine.* 2 vols. Paris, 1963.
Villermé, Louis Réné. *Des prisons telles qu'elles sont et telles qu'elles devraient être, ouvrage dans lequel on les considère par rapport à l'hygiène, à la morale et à l'économie politique.* Paris, 1820.
Tableau de l'état physique et moral des ouvriers employés dans les manufactures de coton, de laine et de soie. 2 vols. Paris, 1840.
Vovelle, Michel. *La Chute de la monarchie, 1787–1792.* Paris, 1972.
Piété baroque et déchristianisation. Les attitudes devant la mort au XVIIIe siècle d'après les clauses des testaments. Paris, 1973.
Walkowitz, Daniel J. *Worker City, Company Town: Iron and Cotton Worker Protest in Troy and Cohoes, New York, 1855–84.* Urbana, Ill., 1978.
Weber, Adna Ferrin. *The Growth of Cities in the Nineteenth Century: A Study in Statistics.* New York, 1899. Reprint ed: Ithaca, N.Y., 1963.
Weill, Georges. *Histoire du mouvement social en France, 1852–1902.* Paris, 1904.
Weulersse, Georges. *Le Mouvement physiocratique en France (de 1756 à 1770).* 2 vols. Paris, 1910.
Wilson, Arthur M. *Diderot: The Testing Years.* New York, 1957.
Diderot. New York, 1972.

Index

Index

Index

Index

Index

Index

Index

Index

Index

Index

Index